the
gap-year
guidebook
05/06

Consultant Editor: Alison Withers
Editor in Chief: Derek Bingham

Peridot Press

Consultant Editor	Alison Withers
Production	David Ahier
	Shaun Lay
Advertising Sales	Andrew Ducksbury
	Michael Ridley
Administration	Alison Collett
Accounts	Sarah Green
Distribution/Book Sales	Margaret Sadler
Business Development Manager	David Ahier
Sales & Marketing Manager	Nicola Gray
Information & Logistics Manager	Christine Evans
Editor in Chief	Derek Bingham
Managing Director	Jonathan Evans

Published in 2004 by Peridot Press, a division of John Catt Educational Ltd,
Great Glemham, Saxmundham, Suffolk IP17 2DH, UK
Tel: 01728 663668   Fax: 01728 663415
E–mail: info@gap-year.com   Website: www.gap-year.com

First published by Peridot Press in 1992; Thirteenth edition 2005
© 2005 John Catt Educational Ltd

The Sex Discrimination Act 1975.
The publishers have taken all reasonable steps to avoid a contravention of Section 38 of the Sex Discrimination Act 1975. However, it should be noted that (save where there is an express provision to the contrary) where words have been used which denote the masculine gender only, they shall, pursuant and subject to the said Act, for the purpose of this publication, be deemed to include the feminine gender and vice versa.

British Library Cataloguing in Publication Data.

ISBN: 1 904724 06 X

Designed and typeset by Peridot Press, a division of John Catt Educational Limited, Great Glemham, Saxmundham, Suffolk IP17 2DH.

Printed and bound in Great Britain by Unwin Brothers Limited, The Gresham Press, Old Woking, Surrey GU22 9LH

contents

contents...continued

With thanks to Grizelda for her cartoons throughout the book.

Not convinced a gap year is for you?

Here's what some returning gappers have to say...

"I reaped so much from my travels including the knowledge that I can rely on myself and not let fear hold me back. The confidence I brought away from the project encouraged me to apply for an access course so hopefully I can go on to teacher training at university" *Zara*

"My advice to anyone who is thinking of volunteering is to go for it. You may only be able to give one week, but you will come away with a different outlook on life. I can't wait to go again next year." *Sacha*

"This is amazing here!! I love it. Everything is so different, but it's actually become normal too.... there's so much crazy Peruvian stuff that I love. I especially love the relaxed timekeeping (saying you are meeting at 10 invariably turns into 11 or later!)." *Katherine*

"The experience was amazing; the sum of the work, the people, patients and the diverse culture was truly unforgettable." *Beatrice in Fiji*

"I had a fantastic time. I was teaching English in a little primary school with only 23 children. I lived with a local family who were extremely welcoming. Highlights included a sports day we organised and an event at the local police station where all the local schools put on a little show. We did a dance in which all the kids took part and thoroughly enjoyed. I have kept in touch with the school, my host family and the other volunteers in the area. It was a great experience and I made some very good friends." *Rose, 18*, went to South Africa with Teaching & Projects abroad.

"I had been searching for an experience like this for as long as I can remember. I craved something more than the normal safari experience. My dream was to be in the middle of it all, to travel to Africa and feel like I was making a contribution. I wanted to be more than a tourist.

I was assigned the privilege of raising a baby cheetah named Porsche. She had arrived at the centre at 6 weeks old due complications with her mother on a nearby reserve. By the time I arrived she was a 10-week-old energetic ball of fur that needed constant attention. Being with her was an experience that has probably changed the course of my life".

Tasha

Introduction

HUMAN beings have always had itchy feet, from the medieval pilgrims who trekked across the world to visit the holy places of the Middle East, to the 18th and 19th Century young aristocrats on their "Grand Tour" to the 1970s equivalent, the Hippie Trail to South Asia...

Changing Worlds

change your life forever

a year out with changing worlds
learning to make a difference

For details of our voluntary placements,
visit www.changingworlds.co.uk
or telephone 01892 770000

CHILE
INDIA
LATVIA
NEPAL
ROMANIA
TANZANIA

YEAR OUT
GROUP

8

Introduction

HUMAN beings have always had itchy feet, from the medieval pilgrims who trekked across the world to visit the holy places of the Middle East, to the 18th and 19th Century young aristocrats on their "Grand Tour" to the 1970s equivalent, the Hippie Trail to South Asia.

So it is no surprise that gap years are becoming more and more popular.

Companies and organisations have cottoned on to this and are responding by providing an ever-increasing variety of opportunities, from digging wells in remote African villages to drama courses.

Increasingly parents and universities are seeing gap years as an important step in personal development. A 'good' gap year will give you a chance to prove yourself and to stretch your personal boundaries. By discovering new people, places and circumstances it is an opportunity to learn self-reliance, to stand on your own two feet, make your own decisions, and to learn to deal with adults as an adult yourself.

So who goes on a gap year?

Anybody and everybody, people from all walks of life. A gap year doesn't have to cost a fortune, and there are ways to make your year out pay for itself.

In recent years there has been a growing trend for older people, often in their mid-30s, to take a year's career break to use their skills to contribute to what they see as worthwhile projects for disadvantaged people all over the world. *(See page 15)*

When should you go?

Traditionally gap years are taken after A levels, and provide a welcome and deserved rest from the hard slog of study and the anxiety of exams, exam results and applying for university places. Most universities (not necessarily all) think gap years are great because gappers come to them fresher, wiser, more mature, and able to cope with looking after themselves, not to mention being less jaded about more studying.

Some universities, especially if you're applying to a very popular course, don't welcome gap years. So some students opt to take their gap year after graduating before getting a 'proper' job. For these gappers they can take a year out secure in the knowlege that their studies are over, their degree is in the bag, and now they have a chance to cut free before a career and adult responsibilities take over.

9

visit: www.gap-year.com

What to do?

Whenever you take your year out, no one should think that taking a gap year is an easy option. Sitting around watching day-time TV and going to the pub for 12 months doesn't count as a gap year and would pretty quickly become very boring. If you're going to make the most of the opportunity then you need to make sure you do end up doing something that you find exciting, fun and challenging. This

may mean travelling to Thailand, helping with conservation work in Scotland or learning to snowboard. With a whole year ahead of you, you could even manage all three if you wanted. The point is to do what you think is right (don't just follow your friends to the nearest beach), do something that gives you a sense of achievement

The trick to having a good gap year is to get the organisation sorted. That doesn't mean you can't be spontaneous, but it would be a real let down if you got to the border of Nepal and found you hadn't got the right visa to get in! Or, while you're in Australia, you get the chance of a great job working with a local TV company but they can't take you on because you couldn't be bothered to get a work permit sorted before you left the UK. Organising your gap year doesn't have to be dull - it can be an opportunity to look forward to the exciting 12 months to come - and as you're making your plans you might find out about new things.

After 9/11 and Iraq is a gap year safe?

There is no denying that after recent events the world is a less safe place for travellers. Terrorists are targeting places known to be frequented by first world travellers and you should always check with the Foreign Office whether a country is safe to travel to and if there are any areas that you should avoid.

This shouldn't stop you from taking a gap year, but it may influence where to go. Don't dismiss Europe - you could end up teaching in Poland, studying art in Florence or inter-railing across the whole continent.

Personal safety should always be your number one priority. A real adult won't put themselves in danger rather than risk someone thinking that they're stupid or scared. If in doubt - don't. We highly recommend that you take a gappers safety

course before you go. It's not as dull as it sounds - the two companies that we know about *(See page 214)* have staff who are ex-SAS! How cool is that? They will teach you how to recognise danger (from people as well as natural disasters), and how to look after yourself in a bad situation - it could be the thing that saves your life.

11

A year off: the figures

The number of students accepted to university and college places by November 2003 was 374,307, according to UCAS figures.

By September 16 2004, the number of accepted applicants had reached 358,229, an increase of 2.1% on the same time in 2003.

For some, the decision to take a year off is made well in advance. Many students have already chosen to defer university entrance because there are things they would like to use the time to do. For 2004 entry, 26,261 accepted applicants have so far deferred places to 2005, though the final total will not be known until after the guide is published.

Some students choose not to apply at all until after they get their A level grades. Others find themselves taking a gap year on shorter notice. For example, they may take a year off because their A level grades are not what they had expected - either too low to win the university place they accepted, or high enough to win them a place at a better university than the ones they applied to. Whatever the reason, the result is a gap year.

How do you pay for it?

It depends on what you want to do, your interests, age, skills and qualifications.

For younger gappers the options range from voluntary work, maybe after working and saving money for part of their gap year, to paid work using existing skills, for example teaching English or working as an au pair, to adding to skills and qualifications by doing an internship or perhaps doing a sports or sailing course. There are many contacts and options listed throughout this guide.

For career break gappers who already have professional skills to offer the United Nations Volunteer Programme, UNV, is a good place to start looking at the options. UNV has links to local charities, NGOs (Non Governmental Organisations) and projects, in countries all over the world. Some will be looking for people willing to work with them for living expenses, others will be looking for volunteers.

For general information visit the website:

www.unv.org/volunteers

The Gap-Year Guidebook 2005/2006

Grown-up Gapping - taking a career break

In the last couple of years the popularity of taking a career break has soared, principally among people in their mid-thirties, but among older workers and early retirees as well. Whole families have even taken time out to go to projects together.

Some of you will have seen the diary by Julia Ransome on our website **www.gap-year.com**.

Julia decided in 2003 to leave her job when her friend Sam phoned to tell her he was taking the Rampant, a boat on which she had crewed across the Atlantic in 2000, back to the Caribbean and asked did she want to come along.

But you don't always have to quit your job to take a year out as many companies offer sabbaticals after a specified period of employment.

The surge of interest has been so huge that Anthony Lunch, Managing Director of Mondo Challenge, calculates it is now taking up more than half of all his placements:

He said: "More and more people are wanting to give their lives some balance; to do something 'real' that they will remember and which will change the normal working routine. The short term career break provides the perfect answer. One can leave work for a few weeks or months, organise a worthwhile activity and return refreshed for the fray.

"Sometimes the career break allows breathing space to consider new work options. Maybe it can provide a chance to think about going into teaching, for example, or changing tack within one's current career. In other cases, the existing

15

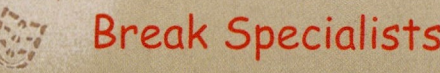

MONDO CHALLENGE

The Career ⧖ Break Specialists

"a small step to a fairer world"

Volunteer programmes:
 - teaching to HIV/Aids support
  - from the Himalayas to Tanzania
   - 2 - 6 months

Projects across Africa, Asia and South America.
Contact:
www.mondochallenge.org
Tel 01604 858225
Email info@mondochallenge.org

16

Is this all there is?

employer is particularly keen to have you back and the break can act as the catalyst for a new post or a promotion.

"Doing something useful during the break, and planning it carefully, is the key to a successful experience. For those seeking a challenge, a volunteer programme abroad is a perfect solution. The chance to travel, to see new places and share one's life with a small community in a developing country can be a life changing experience. And the feeling that one is making a small contribution to improve the lives of those less fortunate is a strong motivator.

"At Mondochallenge, 57% of our volunteers are over 25 and many are in the 40s and 50s. Often couples will come together. And occasionally a child comes too! Most will spend their time abroad working in small schools as teachers, although few have any formal teaching experience before hand. Good communication skills are the key and a desire to have fun will help the kids to learn! However, many volunteers are sharing their business skills in Tanzania, Gambia and India, so the

17

You choose where you go,
what you do and for how long.

This is your chance.

4, 7 & 10 week programmes available in 2005/06.

020 7371 8585

info@raleigh.org.uk

www.raleighinternational.org

Raleigh International Trust is a registered UK charity No. 1047653

CHILE   COSTA RICA & NICARAGUA   FIJI   GHANA   MALAYSIA   NAMIBIA

visit: www.gap-year.com

opportunities to do something really positive are enormous.

"Many employers will welcome this initiative but you will need to approach them well in advance to ensure the timing is right. Keep in mind the costs involved in a volunteer programme abroad. Your flights, visas and inoculations will probably cost around £700 and local board and lodging a fairly modest £20 per week. At MondoChallenge, we charge £900 for 3 months, which is the average length of time volunteers go for. This normally allows time for trekking, a safari or whatever tourist opportunities are available in the country chosen.

"You may never get this chance again - at least not for several years, so make the most of it, learn from it and above all enjoy it.

"So where do you start? Right here - this newly updated edition of The Gap-Year Guidebook is packed with ideas, advice, projects and hundreds of contacts."

Robert, a physiotherapist, and Alice, a speech and language therapist, both from Dorset settled on the Nightingales Children's Project, in S.E. Romania.

They said:

"We were both keen to take a step outside our current existence and experience something that would challenge us. The project, which is all funded by money and donations raised from the UK, fosters 30 children with HIV and offers an education in a loving environment.

Our experience was a wonderful yet harrowing one. We met some incredible people who worked with the children, and the children themselves demonstrated such happiness at such simple little things."

Robert and Alice spent most of their remaining time with children from the state-run orphanage adjacent to the 'Nightingales Children's project.' The volunteers have just 20 minutes to spend with each child. Unfortunately toys have to be removed from the room whilst collecting children, as they often 'go missing' if left unattended. Conditions within the orphanage are stark to say the least. Most of the children at the orphanage suffer from autism, or visual / hearing impairments of varying degrees.

Alice concluded:

One month is not enough to feel that we have made any lasting progress, but enough to feel we had had a 'life-changing' experience. We will undoubtedly continue to support both the charity and children. Romania itself is way behind the UK in so many ways. It is hard to believe that these conditions exist just 1000 miles away.

19

"Tell a lie and your nose will grow longer."

Gap Year Opportunities – Autumn 2005

Bristol, Cambridge, Cardiff, East Midlands, Gatwick, London, Milton Keynes, Plymouth, Reading, Southampton, St Albans and West London

A lot of things you're led to believe don't turn out to be entirely true. Some people, for instance, say that to succeed in life you need to go straight from school to university. At PricewaterhouseCoopers (PwC), however, we have a different option open to you.

If you like the idea of university but you want to get some life experience first, a gap year placement with PwC could be just what you're looking for. In your first week we'll give you everything you need to get started; from IT and business training, to your own laptop. Once you're in the office you'll continue to benefit from regular workshop and training days, as well as on-the-job training, and we'll give you the opportunity to make a real contribution to the work we do.

With opportunities in Assurance & Public Services, Tax, Actuarial or Forensic Services, the breadth of experience you'll gain will set you up for a career after university and, we hope, a long-term relationship with PwC. If you're successful we'll even give you a scholarship to help you with your studies. And don't think you need to have studied business or finance related subjects to apply. As long as you're good with numbers and have a strong academic record (and 300 UCAS points), we're more interested in your willingness to work hard and eagerness to learn.

To separate the facts from the fiction, and to find out how to apply, visit our website.

www.pwc.com/uk/careers/

PRICEWATERHOUSECOOPERS

visit: www.gap-year.com

Another option suitable for Career Break gappers wanting to work on special projects that they cannot find funding for elsewhere is the Winston Churchill Memorial Trust.

"The Winston Churchill Memorial Trust is an inclusive organisation that is looking to support people who want to travel overseas to better themselves and the community in which they live and work," explains Air Vice-Marshal Nigel Sudborough, the Trust's Director General.

"We have wide-ranging categories for Travelling Fellowships that are changed each year so even if this year's categories don't attract you please continue to look each year."

The Trust's contact details are:

15 Queen's Gate Terrace
London SW7 5PR, UK
Tel: +44(0)207 584 9315
Fax: +44 (0) 207 581 0410
E-mail: office@wcmt.org.uk
http://www.wcmt.org.uk

The Trust awards Travelling Fellowships to projects that are interesting and unusual. These are awarded to allow UK citizens of all ages and background to carry out innovative projects and acquire knowledge and experience abroad, which they will then use for the benefit of others in their home community.

Categories cover a huge range of topics over a three-year cycle, of which these are just a few examples: animal welfare, agriculture, health, public services, the citizen and society, science & technology, adventure and sports.

Fellowships usually provide funds for 4-8 weeks and roughly 100 are awarded each year. The closing date for applications is in October and applicants must be resident in the UK. Their proposed project must be their own individual plan - not part of a joint or group undertaking.

Air Vice-Marshal Sudborough stresses that the WCMT is delighted to consider applications complying with the trust's criteria but stresses that: **Fellowships are not granted to gappers looking to fund academic studies, attend courses or take part in volunteer placements arranged for them by other organisations.** His advice is to look at the website carefully.

He said: "The Trust is delighted to receive applications from people taking career breaks for their own projects. We feel that our Fellowships may be more appropriate to this group than to younger gappers."

21

Brenda, 52, left her family home in Essex in August, armed with only a rucksack, a passport and a few photos of family and friends.

She has been a science teacher for almost 30 years and says:

I love my job. I really enjoy being at the front of the classroom and teaching, but I'd reached a point in both my professional and personal life, where things were at a bit of a stalemate. I needed something new, an adventure to re-charge my batteries and get me fired up!

As a result, Brenda spent the next year working on a number of volunteering projects. She taught music and dance in Kathmandu, before moving on to environmental work in southern India, and then a project, working with the street children of Ho Chi Minh City.

There is so much information out there, finding the right project can be a bit of a minefield. It's almost impossible to piece everything together. The database took all the work out of it. By using the right search criteria, I was able to shortlist and finalise my projects really quickly, with no hassle

Brenda sourced all her projects through WorldWide Volunteering.

There is no hard statistical information yet on how many older people are taking gap years but many of the contributors to the Gap-Year Guidebook say that it's a trend they've all noticed.

One organisation told us it has even allocated one of its projects in Africa specifically for older gappers.

We hope by the next edition to have a separate chapter giving useful listings for older gappers, but we know several of our listings contributors have already started catering for them, so older gappers, too, can use this guidebook to help them decide where they want to go and what they want to do.

visit: www.gap-year.com

Sally and Paul: 2003-04

Sally and *Paul* are aged 34 and 37. A year after they got married, they decided to take a year break from their jobs:

"We wanted to do some travelling and adventuring in remote places but also wanted to live and work closely with the local people. We looked at a lot of different volunteer agencies and decided that Mondo Challenge offered the most interesting projects and the greatest flexibility.

"Our first volunteer placement was in Sri Lanka. The placement worked well because we lived together but taught in different temples. In the evenings we could chat about our day and share experiences and teaching ideas. It was a creative experience, inventing ways to make the classes really fun and stimulating. We had a good mix of daily classes, from children learning their first English phrases to adults with quite advanced English who were enthusiastic to debate. The debating provided a fascinating insight into the issues important to young people today, such as traditions, politics, dowries and job prospects.

"Our other volunteer placement was in Tanzania. We lived in a remote mountain village and taught in a secondary school. The setting was breathtaking - banana and maize fields on steep slopes, picturesque streams and each family with their small-holding of chickens and goats. Only saw 1 car in the village in 2 months! Going to the local weekly market involved a 45 minute walk. Overall it was a good lesson in simple living and recycling!

"It was eye opening, how basic the facilities were for the school. They were lacking a physics teacher, so Paul taught physics, making much use of locally found objects to demonstrate principles - sticks for levers, elastic for springs and our bicycles for gears."

Sally taught English grammar:

"It was a totally different experience, teaching from a syllabus. We also joined in with Friday afternoon sports: football and netball. There was one computer in the school - not used a great deal - and we tried to make more use of it in our lessons.

"On several weekends different teachers took us to visit their families - often several hours away. We felt really privileged to be welcomed into their mud houses and be introduced to various generations of the family."

The school had a 'clubs' period, so Paul ran a science club and Sally a drawing club and both say:

"It was very rewarding to introduce new skills and activities to the students."

The couple found their placements through MondoChallenge:

"We were very happy to have chosen Mondo Challenge to help with our placements. They were organised and professional but also very approachable, friendly and adaptable. They were always quick to respond to emails and phonecalls and provided useful information about the country and previous teachers' experiences. It was good knowing that there would be continuity: more teachers coming after us to continue the international relationship."

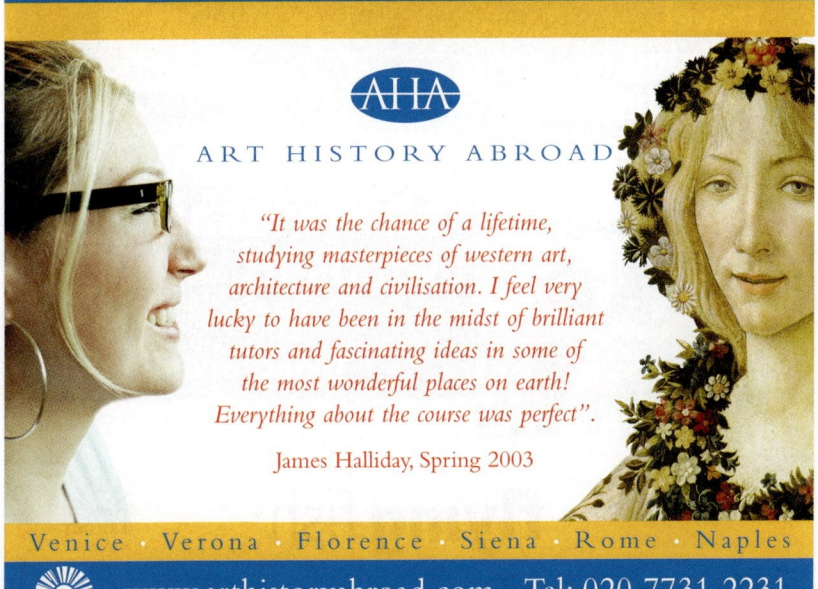
The Gap-Year Guidebook 2005/2006

Gap Year Fun - Worldwide

by Roger Potter, Director, WorldWide Volunteering

Getting behind the wheel of your own car and embarking on a gap year between school and university must be two of the most exciting rites of passage from schooldays to university and beyond. Both literally widen your horizons but the benefits of a gap year are likely to be much more far reaching and enduring.

The wealth of options for would-be gappers can be bewildering. Possibilities include: helping others in the United Kingdom or abroad; expeditions; travel; experiencing another lifestyle or culture; learning new skills or developing existing interests; taking time off from academic study; earning money to finance the rest of the year or university. Whatever you choose, a gap year provides the opportunity to break away from the inevitably tighter restraints of school and family.

Clearly, a gap year will not be the right choice for everyone and it's essential to consider the possible downsides before making up your mind. Will you lose academic motivation if you take so long away from study? How will you finance such a long period that is bound to involve considerable expense? Is it right to delay your working (and paid!) life for another year? Can you cope with the risk and discomfort associated with life in a completely new environment possibly thousands of miles from home?

30

The crucial thing is to make a well-considered decision. Think carefully about what you want to get out of or put into your gap year and begin your research and planning as soon as possible. An ideal gap year will probably consist of a well-structured combination of two, three or more of the range of options available. It's always a good idea to check the attitude of your chosen universities before committing yourself - particularly if you are embarking on longer courses such as medicine. You may end up deciding to take a gap year after university although it must be said that the decision is more difficult at that stage, and will become harder with every passing year.

An encouraging factor as you lay your plans is that universities and employers increasingly look favourably on a gap year, provided that it is well constructed and planned. You do not have to fill every moment with worthwhile and self-denying activity but simply wandering around the world courtesy of your father's American Express card cuts little ice.

With this proviso, the vast majority of universities look favourably on a gap year. They see it as a valuable maturing experience, which inevitably improves communication skills and develops a wider understanding of the world away from the ivory tower of school. Moreover, many gap year activities can have a direct relevance to one's chosen course - travel for languages, volunteering for medicine, expeditions for geography, and work experience for law all spring readily to mind. And the evidence suggests that those who have undertaken a worthwhile gap year are less likely to drop out of university.

31

32

An added bonus is that evidence of preparation for a well-structured year out will make a very favourable impression in section 10 of your UCAS application - another reason for planning a soon as possible, however difficult that may be at the same time as you are making university and course choices. You don't have to have everything signed and sealed but do need to show evidence that you have a good idea of what you want to do and have begun your planning.

Employers are likely to take a similar view. They like the initiative that a well planned year out shows and recognise that such time helps to develop non-academic skills that are vital in the work place - not least the ability to work with others in new circumstances. An applicant with a gap year under his or her belt is simply more experienced than one without and this is seen as every bit as valuable as an additional A level.

It's worth bearing in mind that parents may well have mixed feelings about waving goodbye to you for a year. The more considered your choice of activities and the better your planning the more likely they are to give the green light - and often end up wishing that they could go themselves!

Of all the options available, volunteering in this country or abroad can be one of the most personally rewarding as well as attracting all the advantages outlined above. For those who are contemplating a spell of volunteering there is no better organisation to contact than WorldWide Volunteering, a charity specialising in helping potential volunteers to identify placements that suit their background, circumstances and aspirations. WorldWide Volunteering has developed the UK's most comprehensive database of full-time volunteering opportunities around the

34

world with over 250,000 placements each year in more than 200 countries.

WorldWide Volunteering's search and match CD-Rom software enables volunteers to match in considerable detail their own wishes against the requirements of over 1,100 volunteer organisations. There is, literally, something for everyone and access will soon be available online for a small fee.

Placements range from those that cost nothing, and even provide a pocket money allowance, to those that cost many hundreds, even thousands of pounds. They last anything from a week to a year or more and are located in the next-door county and on the other side of the world. Many schools and colleges subscribe to the programme so that their students will be able to track down the database with little difficulty. For those without easy access, a growing number of public careers centres, libraries and other organisations have the database and details of these are posted on WorldWide Volunteering's website at **www.wwv.org.uk** Alternatively you can use the database online, also accessible from that website.

So if you like the idea of helping children with disabilities in the South of England, playing football and spreading AIDS awareness among children in Africa, working with wild animals in a rescue centre in Bolivia or trying your hand at working on an organic farm and residential centre in Somerset, WorldWide Volunteering is the place to start. Whether or not volunteering takes up all or part of your gap year you could be about to embark on the adventure of a lifetime. Why not give your rite of passage the extra zest that will come from knowing that you have given something of yourself to others as well as having a great experience?

For more details about volunteering options, please contact:

WorldWide Volunteering
7 North Street Workshops
Stoke Sub Hamdon
Somerset TA14 6QR
Tel: 01935 825588
Fax: 01935 825775
E-mail: worldvol@worldvol.co.uk
Web: www.wwv.org.uk

The Gap-Year Guidebook 2005/2006

How to use this book:

We've divided it into two: Your Gap Year Abroad and Your Gap Year in the UK. Even if you have a fairly good idea of where you want to go read the other sections to give you ideas. If you want to go somewhere sunny, but can't afford just to travel, you could spend some time in the UK working to save money first, or why not get a qualification that will help you get a job abroad - how about working as a scuba diving instructor.

The information under the travel section includes important information, even if you're going abroad with a company or charity, ultimately you're responsible for your own well being and safety.

37

Editor's note:

Thanks to all those contributors who gave us stories from their returned gappers, particularly WWV, Price Waterhouse Cooper, MondoChallenge, VentureCo and African Conservation Experience who responded magnificently to being given no time at all!

Chapter 1
Working Abroad

So you desperately want to go abroad but you really can't afford it and the bit you have managed to save won't cover much more than an airfare? A great way to experience a different culture is to live and work in it. You might think this could get a bit dull, but most jobs give you enough spare time in the evenings and at weekends to enjoy yourself and make friends. You'll be meeting locals and experiencing what the country is really like. You don't have to be tied to one place for your whole gap year - you can work for a bit and save up for your travels. That way you can learn more about the place and get the inside information from the locals about the best places to see before you set off.

There are loads of different jobs you can get abroad even if you don't speak any languages. From au pair and ski chalet jobs, waitressing and bar work to summer camp staff and teaching English. If you're lucky, you might even find an internship with pay - which would look good on your CV.

Planning ahead

Choosing your destination

Since the terrorist attacks around the world, international tourism has dropped off. But even in a globally disrupted economy there are still pockets of job stability: seasonal farm work still needs to be done and speaking English is always an advantage for jobs in tourism at ski resorts, beach bars and hotel receptions.

If you are a UK citizen or hold an EU (European Union) passport, you can work in any other EU member country without a visa or work permit and there are countless jobs available to students who can speak the right languages. Not all European countries are EU members - go to the European Union website **http://europa.eu.in** to check.

If you do want to be more adventurous and venture outside Europe, then check the Foreign Office website for the list of countries they consider simply too dangerous to even go to

Getting your paperwork sorted

Before you go, make sure you have all the paperwork you need, including **visas** and **work permits**, and that you understand all the regulations and restrictions. **You can get into serious trouble if you work without the necessary documents** - you probably don't want to be deported during your gap year! Some countries will only grant you a visa or work permit if you can prove you already have a job lined up for when you arrive. The best place to get information is the embassy in London for the country you're going to - there's a link on **www.gap-year.com** to the embassy websites, or look in the country info section at the back of this book for embassy phone numbers.

Take a couple of copies of all your paperwork, leave one copy at home with someone reliable and pack another copy separate from the papers themselves just in case they get stolen or lost. It's a good idea to take photocopies of your relevant qualifications with you, and some spare copies of your CV preferably in the local language. Even if you already have a job set up before you go over there, you might not like it and want to apply for another job.

When you're getting your **insurance**, remember to check that you'll be covered if you're working. We've heard of at least one person whose stuff was damaged, but his insurance wouldn't pay because he was working at the time. Read through the travel section in Tips for Travellers.

Finding a job

You'll need to be proactive: only the luckiest people (usually in a totally unrealistic Hollywood movie) walk down the street and get offered a job - and if it does happen to you, be careful, it may be a con! Finding a job may take time and effort. The more places you can get your CV the more likely you are to get a job. Register with all the international employment agencies that are free and make sure you know what the agency fee will be if you get employed. If you use an agency, always insist on talking to someone who has used them before - that way you'll really find out what the deal is.

If you want to go to a particular place, do a search to see if there's a website for that area and then send or **e-mail your CV** with a short covering note to any interesting local companies. Don't expect to be flooded with replies. Some companies are simply too busy to respond to every enquiry - but you may get lucky and have exactly the skills or qualifications they're looking for.

Some companies will also advertise vacant posts on specialist employment websites which often have an international section. You can register with the sites too, usually for free.

Tell everyone you know, including relatives and your parents' friends, that you are looking for a job abroad - someone may know someone who has a company abroad who can help you or let you stay with them.

It's always easier to find employment when you're living locally. Lots of jobs are advertised in the local papers, or by 'staff wanted' notices put up in windows. So if you get there and hate the job you've got, don't put up with it, or come running home - see if you can find something better.

Over the next few pages we've listed ideas on types of employment and any companies we know about that will find you work. Always ask a company to put you in contact with someone they have placed before - if they say no then don't use them: they may have something to hide.

Au Pairing

Being an au pair is a good way to immerse yourself in a different culture, learn a new language and hopefully save some extra cash. You should be given enough time out of work to take some language courses as well as have fun. If you want to get to grips with a foreign language and don't fancy forking out for food and a dismal flat, being an au pair can be a brilliant solution. It involves living with a foreign family, often in Europe, for several months.

Au pairing used to be considered similar to babysitting, but since the Louise Woodward case in 1998 (the conviction of an English nanny in the USA for the murder, later reduced to manslaughter, of a baby in her charge) people have become more cautious about taking on work abroad as a nanny, and nanny/au pair agencies found themselves having to give legal advice.

You don't need any qualifications to be an au pair, although obviously some experience with children is a bonus. Many au pair agencies now require written references, police checks and other proof of suitability. Also, you should seriously think about whether you can cope - au pairing is not like babysitting for a couple of hours - it is a hard job and a big responsibility.

Finding an au pair agency

The internet is now an excellent source of information on au pair work worldwide. You can usually register for free and your name will be matched to the families around the world that have registered on the site that meet your specifications (but make sure you make human contact at home and abroad before you make your final decision).

The safest bet, however, may be to look for a placement through a UK-based au pair agency. It's also better for the prospective family abroad, since they will be dealing with a UK agency (possibly working together with an agency in the family's own country) that has met you, interviewed you and taken up references. Remember they're going to be taking you into their family home and trusting you with their children.

Check that the au pair agency is a member of either the Recruitment and Employment Confederation (which has a website listing all its members and covering au pair employment in many countries), or of the International Au Pair Association. There are of course good agencies which do not belong to trade associations, either because they are too small to afford the membership fees, or because they are well-established and have a good independent reputation.

International
Au Pair Association

Bredgade 25 H
DK-1260 Copenhagen K,
Denmark
Tel: +45 3317 0066
Fax: +45 3393 9676
www.iapa.org

Agencies should ask for an interview and references, and maybe a medical certificate.

The Government has revised the Conduct of Employment Agencies and Employment Business Regulations. A DTI Spokeswoman confirmed that from April 6, 2004, the regulations governing the Employment Agencies Act (Charging Fees to Au Pairs) Regulations 1981 (d) have been revoked. Therefore au pair agencies operating in this country and sending au pairs abroad can no longer, under specified circumstances, charge the au pair up to £40 for finding them a placement.

If you have a complaint against a UK agency it's best to take it up with the Employment Agency Standards Helpline, Tel: +44 (0) 845 955 5105.

Make sure the agency has connections where you'll be working, get a list of other local au pairs so you have support when you're out there, and take time finding a suitable family. The fewer children the better, and you should expect your own room. It's also worth checking what there is to do in your free time - you don't want to spend every weekend in your bedroom because you're stuck in the middle of nowhere.

Before you go, check you have written confirmation of the hours, duties and pay agreed as well as copies of important documents such as passport, birth certificate, and translations of any academic certificates to prove your student status. Extra passport photos are a good idea, as is the number and address of the local British Consulate - just in case.

Au pairing in Europe

European law stipulates that au pairs should not be younger than 17 and should provide a current medical certificate for an au pair job (participating in normal family duties); that an employment agreement should be made in writing between the au pair and host family, with conditions of employment clearly defined; that the au pair should receive pocket money (exempt from tax) and have enough free time to study; and that the au pair should not be expected to work more than five hours a day and have at least one full free day a week.

The agreement also set up a 'model contract' for young people placed as au pairs. This is now the accepted definition for au pair jobs in the EU, but not necessarily in other countries. Some countries have different local rules.

Take a look at: http://conventions.coe.int/treaty/en/Treaties/Html/068.htm for this and the details of the European Agreement.

In return for board, lodgings and pocket money, you'll be expected to look after the children and do light domestic chores like ironing, cooking, tidying their bedrooms and doing their washing, for up to five hours a day (six hours in France or Germany), five days a week, as well as spending two or three evenings a week baby-sitting. If you are asked to work more than this then technically you are not doing the work of an au pair, but of a mother's help (which pays more). Or slave. Remember that an au pair is classified as 'non-experienced', and you should never be left in sole charge of a baby. If the family gives you more responsibility than you can handle say so; if they don't stop - quit.

It's important to complete all the necessary paperwork for living and working in another country. Most agencies will organise the paperwork side for you, and make sure the legal documents are in order before you leave. Most French agencies require a set of passport photos, a photocopy of your passport, two references (preferably translated into French), and your most recent academic qualifications, as well as a hand-written letter in French to your prospective family which tells them something about you, your reasons for becoming an au pair and any future aspirations. The agency may also ask for a medical certificate (showing you are free of deadly contagious diseases etc) dated less than three months before you leave, and translated into French. Au pairs also have to have a medical examination on arrival in France.

The French Consulate advises you to check that the family you stay with obtains a 'mother's help' work contract (accord de placement au pair d'un stagiaire aide-familiale). If you are a non-EU citizen you are expected to do this before you leave for France, but British au pairs do not need to.

Consulat Britannique	9 Avenue Hoch 75008 Paris, France . Tel: +33 1 44 513100
French Consulate	21 Cromwell Road London SW7 2EN, UK Tel: +44 (0) 20 7838 2000

Au Pair Agencies – Europe

Accueil Familial des Jeunes Etrangers
23 Rue du Cherche Midi, 75006, Paris, France   Tel: +33 1 4222 5034

This agency places young people with families in the suburbs of Paris as well as in the city itself and in other towns throughout France where recognised language schools are situated.

Accueil International
2a rue Ducastel, 7, 8100,
Saint-Germain-en-Laye, France   Tel: +33 1 3973 0498

Based outside the centre of Paris and run by Edith Drilhon, this agency places au pairs all over France but specialises in western Paris. Arranges 30-hour week au pair placements.

ACI (Alliance Culturelle Internationale)
4 Avenue Felix Fauré, 06000, Nice, France   Tel: +33 4 9313 4413

ACI places au pairs between 18 and 28 years old. Telephone interviews are possible. It can also accept a few au pairs for a month or two in the summer as paying guests in families (no charge if the stay is in July or August). ACI operates within a large catchment area in the South of France, from Menton to Marseille, Aix-en-Provence, Arles, Var, St Tropez and Corsica. In touristy areas of the Côte d'Azur au pair placements can last for two months in summer (July - August) or six months; and at other times of the year from six months to a year.

Consulat Britannique
18bis rue d'Anjou   Tel: +33 1 44 513100
75008, Paris, France   www.amb-grandebretange.fr

The British Consulate in France. Contact direct for info on living and working in France.

French Consulate
21 Cromwell Road   Tel: +44 (0) 20 7838 2000
London SW7 2EN, UK   www.ambafrance.org.uk

Contact direct for advice on finding work as an au pair or mother's help in France.

Global Au Pairs
Premier Global Aupairs & Nanny Services
14 Burleigh Close, Addlestone,   Tel: +44 (0)1932 855327
Surrey KT15 1PW, UK   Fax: +44 (0)7092 118043

Global Aupairs & Nanny Services is a British-based nanny and au pair agency. They pride themselves on using the latest technology together with their extensive contacts throughout the world, to find the right family for you. They pay close attention to your requirements and make every effort to find the right match as soon as possible.

Pebbles Unlimited
UK Office, 58 Northcourt Road,
Worthing, Sussex BN14 7DT, UK   Tel: 0870 0664743

Pebbles Unlimited is a friendly and professional agency run by sisters Antonia and Zoë. Both have worked as au pairs, so have first-hand knowledge of the job.

Solihull Au Pair & Nanny Agency
5 Parklands
Blossomfield Road, Solihull,   Tel: +44 (0) 7973 886 979
West Midlands B91 91NG, UK   Fax: +44 (0) 121 233 9731

This agency offers au pair and nanny positions in major European cities, mainly France, Italy and Spain.

Au pairing in North America

You must be 18 or over and it is considered to be a full-time position - the au pair is often in sole charge of the children. You will receive at least 8 hours of child safety and 24 hours of child development instruction before you take up your placement. Looking after children aged under two is more demanding and therefore most agencies ask that you have at least 200 hours of experience with that age group and are at least 19 years old.

All au pair programmes are legislated and regulated by US law, which means (at the time of going to press), that all au pairs receive $139.05 (about £96) pocket money in return for 45 hours work a week, regardless of the agency. You can expect a good standard of living, full-board, your own bedroom and use of a car. US government regulations stipulate that au pairs must attend education courses (because au pair work is seen primarily as a cultural exchange) 'putting in a minimum of three hours a week during term-time. This is financed by the host family up to a limit of $500.'

There are support networks for au pairs once you arrive in the US: agencies should provide assigned co-ordinators who will act as mediators between the au pair and the family if there are problems - and it is possible to be reassigned to a different family.

British and English-speaking Europeans can go to the USA on a 'cultural exchange' with a J1 visa which is valid for a year. Candidates must be between 18 and 26 years of age, have a secondary education, experience or training in childcare, hold a clean drivers' licence and be in good health. Be careful: the USA has a confusing bureaucratic system, and if you're not careful you risk earning money illegally and even being deported. That's why it is important to go with a good agency that will check you have the right paperwork.

Because of strict government regulations, most agencies that organise au pairs in the USA offer very similar services. However it's worth registering with a number of agencies if only to have a range of 'perfect match' host families to choose from.

EduCare

EduCare places au pairs with families who have school-aged children and need childcare before and after school hours. Au pairs on the EduCare scheme work no more than 30 hours per week in return for $124.29 and must complete a minimum of 12 hours of academic credit or its equivalent during the programme year (financed by the host family for up to $1,000. The US Department of State website has all the up-to-date legislation **http://exchanges.state.gov/education/jexchanges/private/aupair brochure.htm** and information about the necessary visas:

US Embassy (Visas)

5 Upper Grosvenor Street
London W1A 2JB
Tel: +44 (0) 90 6820 0290

49

Au Pair in America (APIA)

37 Queen's Gate
London SW7 5HR, UK

Tel: +44 (0) 20 7581 7311
www.aupairamerica.co.uk

in America, Au Pair Extraordinaire and EduCare in America. The APIA package includes free return flights to New York from London, medical insurance (candidates must contribute $100 toward medical insurance), a month travel period and a four-day orientation course near New York covering first aid, culture shock and general childcare. Au pairs receive a weekly payment of $139.05 and a $500 study allowance in exchange for up to 45 hours of childcare plus room and board. If you have a childcare qualification and are at least 20 years old with two years of recent childcare experience under your belt, you could earn $200 per week as an Au Pair Extraordinaire. EduCare has fewer childcare hours and is available for those interested in a taste of US college life.

Au Pair in America and Au Pair Extraordinaire require a $400 'good faith deposit' (about £277) that is payable when you are matched with a host family, and is reimbursed after completing the 12 months. To participate you must be aged 18 to 26 and have a driving licence. You will be invited to meet a local interviewer to complete the application process. APIA's US office will match you with a family based on your experience, interests and skills.

Childcare International

Trafalgar House, Grenville Place,
London NW7 3SA, UK

Tel: +44 (0) 20 8906 3116

Childcare International is the UK agent for APIA, and sends au pairs to Europe, the USA, Canada, Australia and South Africa.

EF Au Pair

EF Centre Boston
One Education Street,
Cambridge, MA 02141, USA

Tel: +1 800 333 6056
www.efaupair.org

Although EF Au Pair (an affiliate of EF International Language Schools) deals mostly with non-English speaking Europeans, people from Britain have a huge language advantage and are always well-received. EF Au Pair says it can place au pairs in every state of the USA except Hawaii.

Global Au Pairs

Premier Global Aupairs & Nanny Services
14 Burleigh Close, Addlestone,
Surrey KT15 1PW, UK

Tel: +44 (0)1932 855327
Fax: +44 (0)7092 118043

Global Aupairs & Nanny Services is a British-based nanny and au pair agency. They pride themselves on using the latest technology together with their extensive contacts throughout the world, to find the right family for you. They pay close attention to your requirements and make every effort to find the right match as soon as possible.

InterExchange

161 Sixth Avenue
New York NY 10013, USA

Tel: +1 (212) 924 0446
Fax: +1 (212) 924 0575

InterExchange runs an Au Pair USA programme in for 18- to 26-year-olds. You provide up to 45 hours of live-in childcare per week in exchange for room, board and about $140 per week, plus up to $500 toward 6 credits at an accredited educational institution.

The company takes its selection process seriously so you'll be screened in your home country - a process which includes an interview, a written application, photographs, an essay, two child care references, one character reference, proof of secondary education, police clearance report and a confidential medical history report. The host families are also interviewed. Au pairs and families are carefully matched according to needs and skills and you'll have at least two telephone interviews with your host family before the placement is confirmed. There's also an orientation programme in New York before you join your host family. Au pair placements last for a year, after which you may stay in the States on your visa for a month to travel, but not to work.

Solihull Au Pair & Nanny Agency

5 Parklands
Blossomfield Road, Solihull,
West Midlands B91 91NG, UK

Tel: +44 (0) 7973 886 979
Fax: +44 (0) 121 233 9731

The Solihull Au Pair & Nanny Agency will put you in touch with families who have been vetted by AuPairCare San Francisco in the States. You need to be aged between 18 and 26 and available for a full 12 months, (opportunity to travel for the 13th month). Childcare experience is essential, however, formal qualifications are not necessary. A driving licence is obligatory. You get your own bedroom and live as a member of the family. You're paid $138.00 per week, plus 2 week's paid holiday and possibly some holidays with the host family. Au Pairs are sent on a legal J1 visa and they are required to study a subject of their own choosing in the USA on a part-time basis. Your fares are paid to and from the States. There is a 4-day orientation in central New York Hotel and a 24-hour helpline telephone number.

Internships &
paid work placements

If you want to use your gap year to gain relevant work experience, then why not sign up for an internship? It'll give your CV a competitive edge and give you an insight into what that job is really like. Traditionally internships are one-year paid employment postings for undergraduate or graduate students, arranged from a university. These websites are useful:

www.cartercenter.org

www.internship-usa.com

www.internabroad.com

www.internships-usa.com

www.internshipprograms.com

www.summerjobs.com

Before you sign up make sure you're clear just what your placement will involve. An 'internship' should mean you are able to do interesting paid work related to your degree studies, current or future, for at least six months. Sitting behind a reception desk for very little money is not an internship, but a badly-paid job.

Intern programmes

Alliances Abroad
2423 Pennsylvania Avenue NW
Washington, DC 20037,
USA

Tel: +1 (202) 467 9467
Fax: +1 (202) 467 9460

Alliances Abroad is one of only a few educational travel companies in the world that offers international students paid internships and summer work programmes in the United States. With dozens of locations and numerous employers around the country for you to choose from, they'll help you find work that turns into the experience of a lifetime. All you do is choose the location, length of time you're willing to stay, and give them an idea of the type of position you'll consider. Their experienced staff in America will do the rest. Positions are available in many categories including import-export, communication, tourism, social work, information technology, secretarial work, economics, law, marketing, banking, finance, public relations and many more.

CCUSA
Unit 4CC
Green Dragon House
64-70 High Street, CR0 9XN Croydon, UK

Tel: +44 (0) 20 8688 9051
Fax: +44 (0) 20 8680 4539
www.ccusa.com

CUSA's Work Experience USA programme enables you to live and work in America for a summer on a J1 5-month work and travel visa (available to students only). You can choose a secure guaranteed job from their extensive job directory, for example: working on a ranch in Colorado, in the Grand Canyon National Park in California, at a resort on New York or even in a casino in Nevada! Or you can find your own placement if you prefer. Or, if you want to try somewhere a bit more unusual, you can spend either 3 or 6 months in the Brazilian sunshine. You'll live with a host family and work in a job of your choice.

All CCUSA programmes offer guaranteed placement before departure, return flights, the highest wages, visas, insurance, airport pickup, local orientation, and full-time support before, during and after the programme.

CCUSA offers many other programmes, please see their other listings in this chapter in the sections on Seasonal Work in North America, Seasonal Work in Australia and New Zealand and Seasonal Work in Europe for full details. Over the last 16 years, CCUSA have organised working holidays for over 100,000 students from all over the world.

CIEE (Council on International Educational Exchange)
52 Poland Street
London W1F 7AB
UK

Tel: +44 (0) 20 7478 2020
Fax: +44 (0) 20 7734 7322
www.councilexchanges.org.uk

CIEE's Internship USA programme offers more serious jobs aimed at providing valuable work experience. You have to be a current student (HND or above) or a recent graduate. The internship you apply for should be related to your degree subject. The fees start from £270 for the first two months and £30 for each additional month, up to 18 in total - this includes your legal sponsorship (necessary for the visa) as well as insurance and all CIEE's support services and e-mail advisory service on finding your ideal internship.

College Northside
CP480
916 14 Ëme Avenue, Val-Morin,
Québec JOT 2RO, Canada

Tel: +1 819 322 1133
Fax: +1 819 322 2111

Don Quijote
PO Box 218
Stoneleigh Epsom,
Surrey KT19 OYF, UK

Tel: +44 (0) 20 8786 8081
Fax: +44 (0) 20 8786 8086
www.donquijote.org

The Don Quijote internship programme has three phases: about 6 weeks intensive Spanish course (depending on your language ability), professional orientation and finally a three-month placement (which can sometimes be extended). Placements are in private sector companies.

Entrance requirements are high and each step is competitive with an expectation of high levels of performance.

Euro Academy
2nd Floor
67 -71 Lewisham High Street, Lewisham,
London SE13 5JX, UK

Tel: +44 (0) 20 8297 0505
Fax: +44 (0) 20 8297 0984

Though mainly a language school, Euro Academy also arranges unpaid work placements for up to six months in France, Germany, Spain and Italy. Contact Euro Academy for further details.

European Training Services
Suite 1, Langton House, Bird Street,
Lichfield, Staffordshire WS13 6PY, UK

ETS can help you find internships and paid jobs around Europe: Austria, France, Germany, Italy, Sweden and Gran Canaria. They also work with the French departments of Reunion Island and Martinique if you want to get your work experience somewhere a bit farther afield.

53

Futuresense Ltd
6 Forest Hill
Great Bedwyn
SN8 3LP Marlborough, UK

Tel: +44 (0) 1672 871 661
Fax: +44 (0) 1672 871 661
www.gapguru.com

Can't decide whether to work or travel in your Gap year? Combine both with exciting new programmes organised by Futuresense Limited.

The India experience gives a unique insight into India - whilst improving your CV. Opportunities are available to work with multi-national organisations, gaining a greater understanding of how businesses work and what career you would like in the future. Placements are available all over India, and the best bit? you get paid!

Also included is the chance to learn more about Indian culture with combined volunteer projects, living with an Indian family and working to improve the local community. Time is also taken out for tailor-made travel adventures, giving you a totally exclusive but comprehensive Indian experience.

Global Adventures Project
38 Queens Gate
SW11 5HR London
UK

Tel: +44 800 085 4197
Fax: +44 207 7590 7444
www.globaladventures.co.uk

Global Adventures Project is an exciting new Gap Year programme that allows you to design your own truly unique travel experience abroad. It is being organised as a new division of the American Institute for Foreign Study (AIFS) and will enjoy the benefit of the experience and resources of this worldwide organisation.

For a one-off fee, you get a round-the-world ticket with up to 6 or 10 stops and the opportunity to join up to four of our six core programmes in the USA, Brazil, Europe, South Africa, India and Australia/New Zealand with plenty of time for independent travel in between.

Gwendalyne

67-71 Lewisham High Street
SE13 5JX London, UK

Tel: +44 (0)20 8297 3251
Fax: +44 (0)20 8297 0984

Gwendalyne offers a wide range of internship and work placement across the world, from the US to EU countries, from Latin America to South Africa to Down Under. All the programmes include assistance throughout all the processing and in finding a job, emergency line, help in finding housing, insurance coverage (if requested) and orientation or information on life and work in your chosen country.

InterExchange

161 Sixth Avenue
New York NY 10013, USA

Tel: +1 (212) 924 0446
Fax: +1 (212) 924 0575

InterExchange run a four-month summer internship programme and an international practical training programme. The international practical training programme lasts six, 12 or 18 months and is aimed at students who have already spent at least two years in higher education. Placements are very career-orientated, and can be in the following fields: information media and communication; management, business, commerce and finance; the sciences, engineering, architecture, mathematics and industrial occupations; and public administration and law.

International Employment and Training (IET)

45 High Street, Tunbridge Wells,
Kent TN1 1XL, UK

Tel: +44 (0) 1892 516164

IET is a job agency specialising in placing international workers in US companies. Placements are available across the USA, but most jobs are in the major metropolitan areas. You are paid at the same rate as an American would be, so you should have enough money to enjoy life. Fields of employment include marketing, media, engineering, finance, web design, IT/hi tech, law, sales, HR, insurance and other specialist workers, such as arborist/tree climbers. At the end of your placement you can take a 30-day travel break to explore the country.

To apply you need to have graduated from a recognised UK university and work experience in your chosen field. Specialist workers with work-related certificates and work experience don't need to have a degree. A few entry-level jobs require less experience. The application process takes around 10 weeks. Registration and application are free; placements cost £250 (up to 6 months), £300 (6-12 months); £375 (13-18 months). You'll also have to pay a £32 visa fee to the American Embassy.

Interspeak

Stretton Lower Hall
Stretton, Nr. Malpas,
South Cheshire SY14 7HS, UK

Tel: +44 (0) 1829 250 641
Fax: +44 (0) 1829 250596

Interspeak organises unpaid work placements in France, Germany and Spain from between one and six months. You pay a registration fee of £80 up front, then a flat fee of £320 for arranging the placement. Interspeak will also organise a family for you to stay with, although you can make your own plans if you prefer. Placement jobs vary widely, but Interspeak says it can find placements in banking, law, marketing, media, hotels and restaurants - citing one student working in a fashion photography studio in France and another for a radio station in Spain.

i-to-i

Woodside House
261 Low Lane
Leeds LS18 5NY, UK

Tel: +44 (0) 870 333 2332
Fax: +44 (0) 113 205 4619
www.i-to-i.com

i-to-i provides internships in journalism, media, business and medicine. You can also combine this with another of i-to-i's projects (for details see i-to-i's listings in Work Abroad: TEFL and Volunteering Abroad).

Language Courses Abroad

67 Ashby Road
Loughborough
Leicestershire LE11 3AA, UK

Tel: +44 (0) 1509 211612
Fax: +44 (0) 1509 260037
www.languagesabroad.co.uk

Alongside its language courses, Language Courses Abroad offers internships and work experience programmes in Alicante, Cadiz, Madrid and San Rafael de Coronado (Costa Rica). Although the internships are not remunerated, the majority of the companies grant a bonus or monthly compensation.

Mountbatten Internship Programme

5th Floor
Abbey House 74-76 St John Street,
London EC1M 4DZ, UK

Tel: +44 (0) 20 7253 7759
Fax: +44 (0) 20 7831 7018
www.mountbatten.org

This organisation aims to promote educational and business links between the USA and the UK. It arranges 12-month internship programmes in New York with a variety of American companies which sponsor the programme. By the end of the course you should have gained the 'Certificate in International Business Practice', accredited by UCLES. To take part in this programme you need to be at least 21 and to have studied to higher education level. A typing speed of 50 wpm is also recommended.

Smallpeice Trust

Holly House, 74 Upper Holly Walk
Leamington Spa,
Warwickshire CV32 4JL, UK

Tel: +44 (0) 1926 333200
Fax: +44 (0) 1926 333202
www.smallpeicetrust.org.uk

The Smallpeice Trust runs the European Engineering Foundation Programme, a gap year for students who defer their entry to university on an engineering-related degree course.

This pinnacle of engineering gap years uniquely combines study, language, travel and work in Europe:

- 3 months academic study at a UK university
- 1 month language tuition at a language school in France, Germany or Spain
- 3 months work placement in one of 9 European countries

The entire programme is arranged and subsidised through The Trust, and starts in September, finishing the following May. The cost per student is £4950, which includes all tuition, accommodation, placements, return travel etc. No other opportunity offers such a firm grounding in engineering, together with personal development, to put students 'head and shoulders' above their peers at university.

Telepassport-Bulgaria
Str, Floor 1, Suite 1,
8000 Bourgas, Bulgaria   Tel: +359 56 816 277

Telepassport-Bulgaria is a crew manning agency, so if you're interested in spending your year out on a ship travelling the world then it could be worth your while getting in touch. A huge range of jobs are available.

Sport Instructors

Working as a sports instructor is a great way to use your skills to earn money during your gap year. It's also a good way to finance living in a foreign country and maybe some travel after the job ends.

Ski resorts are probably the biggest sports instructor employers, but for every sport that exists - from kayaking to cricket, from sailing to snowboarding - there will be people who want to learn more, and you might be the person to teach them. Snowboarding and all watersports are really popular at the moment. The great thing is that there are jobs for sport instructors all around the world - from Bermuda to Belgium; from Boston to Bavaria.

If you don't already have your instructor qualifications then you could spend the first part of your gap year getting qualified (take a look at Chapter 3 Learning abroad: Sport) - lots of the sports schools will help you get a job, although it's always worth asking before you sign up for the course. Also check that the qualification they are offering is what the resorts want.

You can contact resorts/sports schools direct (find them on the internet) or go through an agency, though some agencies have age restrictions and may want specific qualifications. As always, the internet is a good place to search for jobs. Take a look at: **www.skijobs.net**, **www.skiingthenet.com** or **www.jobmonkey.com**. These are just a few we found after doing a quick search - there are bound to be loads more. If you find a really helpful site you could share your luck by telling other gappers on the **www.gap-year.com** message board.

If you can't find what you're looking for in the list of companies below, try searching the internet for national and international sporting associations - explain to them that you're looking for work using your sports skills and ask for their help - they may be able to put you in touch with companies or local groups. Make sure you have an up-to-date and relevant CV ready to go which lists all your sporting achievements and qualifications and which highlights your leadership skills.

Sports instructor jobs

Acorn Adventure
22 Worcester Road,
Stourbridge, West Midlands
DY8 1AN, UK   Tel: +44 (0) 1384 446057

Acorn Adventure runs adventure holiday camps from April until September based in nine centres in France, Italy, Spain and the UK - their main customers are school groups.

Allan Dive

Borneo, Malaysia

Tel: +60 88 711 715
Fax: +60 88 711 715

The Allan Dive school on the island of Borneo in Malaysia offers both PADI and SSI (Scuba School International) Instructors training facilities doing basic training to instructor level, marine conservation projects etc. They also offer internship programmes taking beginners to instructor level in six months to a year. Course prices range from £1500 to £3000 depending on the course you choose. Cost includes training, accommodation & certification. There may be an opportunity for employment.

Base Camp Group
Unit 30
Baseline Business Studios,
Whitchurch Road, W11 4AT London, UK

Tel: +44 (0) 20 7243 6222
Fax: +44 (0) 20 7243 6222

Base Camp Group runs Ski & Snowboard Instructor Courses in the resorts of Meribel, Val d'Isere, Verbier and Whistler.

BUNAC (British Universities North America Club)
16 Bowling Green Lane
London EC1R 0QH, UK

Tel: +44 (0) 20 7251 3472
www.bunac.org

Spend a summer working as a counsellor on a children's summer camp. BUNAC arranges about 3500 placements a year. They also organise visa, flights, insurance, accommodation and food. Applicants need to be over 19 on June 1st 2005 and have experience of working with groups of children in a leadership role. Sporty students with experience of instructing activities such as soccer, tennis, swimming, horse-riding, golf and sailing are in demand. See BUNAC's listing later in this chapter under Work Abroad: Seasonal - North America

Camp America
37A Queen's Gate
London SW7 5HR, UK

Tel: +44 (0) 20 7581 7333
Fax: +44 (0) 20 7581 7377

Each year Camp America sends thousands of young people to work on summer camps and resorts in the States between June and August.

CCUSA
Unit 4CC
Green Dragon House
64-70 High Street, CR0 9XN Croydon, UK

Tel: +44 (0) 20 8688 9051
Fax: +44 (0) 20 8680 4539
www.ccusa.com

Over the last 16 years, CCUSA have organised safe and secure working holidays for over 100,000 students from all over the world. If you like working with kids and you have 9 weeks to spare this summer then the CCUSA programmes are perfect for you. CCUSA works with summer camps in Europe, America, and Australia. You don't need any experience or qualifications but you do need to be at least 18 years old. All CCUSA programmes offer guaranteed placement before departure, free return flights, highest wages, visas, insurance, airport pickup, local orientation, and full-time support before, during and after the programme.

CCUSA offers many other programmes, please see their other listings in the sections on Seasonal Work in Europe, Seasonal Work in Australia and New

Zealand and Internships for full details.

Crewseekers
Hawthorn House, Hawthorn Lane,
Sarisbury Green, Southampton,
Hampshire SO31 7BD, UK   Tel: +44 (0) 1489 578319

Work available as yachting crew cruising, racing, yacht delivering around the world.
Beginners welcome.

Goal-Line Soccer Clinics
PO Box 1642
Corvallis, OR 97339-1642,   Tel: 1 (541) 753-5833
USA   Fax: 1(541) 753-0811

Goal-Line offers paid soccer coaching vacations for qualified applicants. Their
programme operates in a number of communities in the Pacific Northwest
(Washington, Oregon) of the USA. Summer camp sessions begin in early July and
end mid-August. Remuneration for 1st year coaches is $300/week.

Marine Divers (British Sub-Aqua Club School 388) Hong Kong
3E, Block 18, Dynasty View, 11 Ma Wo Road,
Tai Po, New Territories, Hong Kong, China   Tel: +852 2656 9399

Become a BSAC Open Water Instructor. In 6-8 weeks train from beginner to
instructor. Training and fun in Hong Kong (The City of Life), with optional 5-day trip
to the Philippines. Various packages. Dive the World once qualified - and get paid!
Possible employment opportunities.

60

Mark Warner

George House
61-65 Kensington Church Street,
London W8 4BA, UK

Tel: +44 (0) 20 7761 7300
www.markwarner-recruitment.co.uk

Mark Warner is a leading tour operator with hotels located around the Mediterranean.
We employ windsurf, waterski, dinghy, kitesurf and canoe instructors for our waterfronts and also tennis and aerobic instructors.

Natives

39-43 Putney High Street
SW15 1SP London, UK

Tel: +44 (0)8700 463377
Fax: +44 (0) 8451 275 048

Natives run a 5-day chalet cookery course for those planning to work as a chalet host at a ski resort. On successful completion of the course, the company guarantees to find a job for those aged 21+. Staff from previous courses ended up working for companies such as Lotus Supertravel, Crystal Holidays, Thomson Holidays, Ski Morgins, Skiworld Ski Beat and various private chalets.

PGL

PGL Recruitment Team
Alton Court, Penyard Lane, Ross-on-Wye,
Herefordshire HR9 5GL, UK

Tel: 0870 401 4411
Fax: 0870 401 4444

PGL runs activity holidays and courses for children. Each year the company employs over 2000 young people to work as instructors, group leaders, catering and support staff at its centres in the UK, France and Spain.

PJ Scuba

Level 13
Country Tower B, 225/274 Sumpwut Road,
Bang Na, Bangkok 10260, Thailand

Tel: +166 864 4490
Fax: +166 720 7520

P J offers gap year students the chance to study scuba diving to instructor level (PADI) and then teach in Thailand, Vietnam or Cambodia upon graduation through their 'internship programme'. There is no entry qualification apart from good interpersonal skills and the ability to swim. On graduation you will be internationally recognized as a PADI dive professional allowing you to work worldwide in exotic places. P J Scuba also offers additional courses FREE of charge tailored to the individual needs of the applicant such as underwater photography, marine life studies or deep diving.

The programme costs US$5000 (less if you already have diving experience or your own equipment). Included in the price are accommodation, insurance and one meal per day, as well as a full set of scuba diving equipment (tools of the trade), all certification fees, manuals, training aids and full training. They have a pro-active job placement scheme at the end of the training programme to help you find work. The programme is ongoing and can be joined at any time convenient to you.

Teaching & Projects Abroad

Aldsworth Parade
Goring
Sussex BN12 4TX, UK

Tel: +44 (0) 1903 708300
Fax: +44 (0) 1903 501026
www.teaching-abroad.co.uk

Teaching & Projects Abroad is an agency which organises voluntary work placements abroad. As its name suggests, many of the work opportunities it offers are in teaching - in such far flung places as Bolivia, Chile, China, Ghana, India, Mexico, Mongolia, Nepal, Peru, Romania, Russia, Senegal, South Africa, Sri Lanka, Swaziland, Thailand and Togo. Placements in India, South Africa and Thailand can include teaching sports.

Placements start any time and last from as little as one month to as long as a year. Charges range from £995 for three months in Romania to around £1800, and include food, lodging, travel, insurance and local back-up. The organisation holds several open days which give you the opportunity to meet staff and people who have already participated in programmes arranged by Teaching & Projects Abroad. See Volunteering Abroad for more details.

Travellers Worldwide

7 Mulberry Close
Ferring, West Sussex
BN12 5HY, UK

Tel: +44 (0) 1903 502595
Fax: +44 (0) 1903 500364
www.travellersworldwide.com

Travellers provides voluntary placements overseas. Volunteers don't need any qualifications apart from enthusiasm, dedication and a sense of humour. The projects include Teaching, Conservation, Work Experience and Community Development, as well as Language and Cultural courses. Prices start at £895 (excluding airfare) for three months, though placements can last for any length of time from two weeks to one year. Placements are currently available in Argentina, Brazil, Brunei/Borneo, China, Cuba, Ghana, Guatemala, India, Kenya, Malaysia, Nepal, Russia, South Africa, Sri Lanka, Ukraine, Vietnam and Zimbabwe; the list of countries, length and projects is ever expanding.

Examples of programmes include:

Teaching projects: English, IT, Football, Music, Drama Workshops.

Conservation: working with Orang-utans, Elephants, Lions, Rhinos, Marine, Dolphins, Coral, Plants.

Work Experience: Law, Journalism, Medicine, Veterinary, Tourism, Radio.

Language course: Spanish, Russian, Mandarin, plus Tango, Photography, Music.

Most importantly, Travellers Worldwide can tailor placements to individual requirements - just let them know what you want and they will see if they can do it for you.

UKSA (United Kingdom Sailing Academy)

West Cowes,
Isle of Wight, UK

Tel: +44 (0) 1983 203014
Fax: +44 (0) 1983 295938

The United Kingdom Sailing Academy (UKSA), based in Cowes trains watersport instructors, professional skippers and crews for yachts. The Academy has modern facilities, including residential accommodation and a fleet of over 300 craft. Gap year students train with UKSA for six months, in Cowes and Barbados, to become multi-qualified water sport instructors. The comprehensive training is designed to finish just as the major water activity holiday companies are recruiting staff for their summer seasons. Six hundred companies worldwide recruit directly through the Academy. The UKSA careers department helps their 'gap graduates' find employment for the second six months of their year. If you have a yachting background you can complete the Professional Crew and Skipper Training (PCST) course in the first six months, before seeking employment for the rest of the year. These qualifications last from 2 to 4 years. You can use your qualifications to find further employment in the international holiday market in future university vacations.

Teaching English
as a Foreign Language

Teaching English as a Foreign Language - TEFL - is the ideal combination of doing something useful (if you're any good) and earning some money whilst enjoying life in another culture.

There are a lot of organisations happy to persuade you that a TEFL qualification is a very useful thing to have. Probably too many, in fact, because it's quite difficult for under-21s to get TEFL work abroad. Ask course organisers if they can help to find you TEFL jobs abroad as well as train you.

TEFL courses are available throughout the UK with many different certificates. CELTA is widely recognised by the industry and the Trinity College Certificate in TESOL (Teaching English to Speakers of Other Languages) is recognised by the British Council. Both are open to 18-year-olds.

Courses that do not lead to recognised qualifications are only worth doing if linked to a voluntary work placement, or if it has been recommended by an organisation you'll be working for. But you don't have to have any certificates to teach English informally (or as an au pair) abroad, and a short course will give you some idea of how to teach, increase your confidence and give you some lesson plans.

How to find TEFL work

Availability of work for people who can teach English varies, particularly outside the EU. In most countries it is possible to give private lessons. The best way to find out more about individual countries is to contact the relevant embassy in the UK, which will give you up-to-date details of visas, salaries, qualifications needed and a view about the availability of work. You can find links to embassy websites on **www.gap-year.com**. TEFL jobs are advertised in The Times Educational Supplement (on Fridays), the Guardian (on Tuesdays), in the education section of The Independent and in the EFL Gazette.

Teaching English in private lessons

Giving private tuition, either formally or in conversation classes, is a good way to earn extra cash. Advertisements can be placed in local schools, universities, newspapers and shops when you've been in a country long enough to know the local language and be streetwise. Be careful about

63

wording your advertisement, particularly if you are young and female. Do not give any indication of your gender, and never write: 'Young English girl gives English lessons' - you could get some heavy-breathing phone calls. Try to meet prospective students in a public place before inviting them to your home or going to theirs. Usually, you'll be inundated by friends of friends as word gets round there's an English person willing to give private lessons.

TEFL

Teaching & Projects Abroad
Aldsworth Parade
Goring
Sussex BN12 4TX, UK

Tel: +44 (0) 1903 708300
Fax: +44 (0) 1903 501026
www.teaching-abroad.co.uk

Teaching & Projects Abroad is as an agency which organises voluntary work placements abroad. As its name suggests, many of the work opportunities it offers are in teaching - in such far flung places as Bolivia, Chile, China, Ghana, India, Mexico, Mongolia, Nepal, Peru, Romania, Russia, Senegal, South Africa, Sri Lanka, Swaziland, Thailand and Togo. Placements in India, South Africa and Thailand can include teaching sports.

Placements start any time and last from as little as one month to as long as a year. Charges range from £995 for three months in Romania to around £1800, and include food, lodging, travel, insurance and local back-up. The organisation holds several open days which give you the opportunity to meet staff and people who have already participated in programmes arranged by Teaching & Projects Abroad. See Volunteering Abroad for more details.

Travellers Worldwide
7 Mulberry Close
Ferring
West Sussex BN12 5HY, UK

Tel: +44 (0) 1903 502595
Fax: +44 (0) 1903 500364
www.travellersworldwide.com

Travellers provides voluntary placements overseas. Volunteers don't need any qualifications apart from enthusiasm, dedication and a sense of humour. The projects include Teaching, Conservation, Work Experience and Community Development, as well as Language and Cultural courses. Prices start at £895 (excluding airfare) for three months, though placements can last for any length of time from two weeks to one year. Placements are currently available in Argentina, Brazil, Brunei/Borneo, China, Cuba, Ghana, Guatemala, India, Kenya, Malaysia, Nepal, Russia, South Africa, Sri Lanka, Ukraine, Vietnam and Zimbabwe; the list of coutries, length and projects is ever expanding.

Examples of programmes include:

Teaching projects: English, IT, Football, Music, Drama Workshops.

Conservation: working with Orang-utans, Elephants, Lions, Rhinos, Marine, Dolphins, Coral, Plants.

Work Experience: Law, Journalism, Medicine, Veterinary, Tourism, Radio.

Language course: Spanish, Russian, Mandarin, plus Tango, Photography, Music. Most importantly, Travellers Worldwide can tailor placements to individual requirements - just let them know what you want and they will see if they can do it for you.

UKSA (United Kingdom Sailing Academy)
West Cowes,   Tel: +44 (0) 1983 203014
Isle of Wight, UK   Fax: +44 (0) 1983 295938

The United Kingdom Sailing Academy (UKSA), based in Cowes trains watersport instructors, professional skippers and crews for yachts. The Academy has modern facilities, including residential accommodation and a fleet of over 300 craft. Gap year students train with UKSA for six months, in Cowes and Barbados, to become multi-qualified water sport instructors. The comprehensive training is designed to finish just as the major water activity holiday companies are recruiting staff for their summer seasons. Six hundred companies worldwide recruit directly through the Academy. The UKSA careers department helps their 'gap graduates' find employment for the second six months of their year. If you have a yachting background you can complete the Professional Crew and Skipper Training (PCST) course in the first six months, before seeking employment for the rest of the year. These qualifications last from 2 to 4 years. You can use your qualifications to find further employment in the international holiday market in future university vacations.

TEFL Jobs

Alliances Abroad
2423 Pennsylvania Avenue NW   Tel: +1 (202) 467 9467
Washington, DC 20037, USA   Fax: +1 (202) 467 9460

Alliances Abroad has an extensive range of teaching opportunities across the world. For example, in China you are placed in a school for 3 months to a year. All positions include free accommodation, and some include partial board, plus you will be paid a competitive salary. Positions tend to be with universities and trade schools.

In Spain you teach the family you're living with in exchange for accommodation and meals and getting to live the Spanish way of life. Whichever country you choose to teach in, the experienced Alliances Abroad staff will help you with all of your travel needs, including travel arrangements, recommendations on what to do while abroad, visa/work permit procurement, airport transfers and all that other organisational stuff.

Changing Worlds
11 Doctors Lane   Tel: +44 (0) 1883 340 960
Chaldon   Fax: +44 (0) 1883 330783
Surrey CR3 5AE, UK   welcome@changingworlds.co.uk

Changing Worlds offers opportunities to teach conversational English in a variety of countries around the world. Voluntary placements are offered in primary and secondary schools in Chile, India, Nepal and Tanzania for three to six months. Other subject areas are also taught.

EF English First
Arthur House
Chorlton Street,   Tel: +44 (0) 161 2361359
Manchester, M1 3EJ, UK   Fax: +44 (0) 161 2360949

EF English First, a world leader in language education with 160 schools worldwide, offers full or part-time TEFL courses leading to guaranteed teaching jobs in EF schools in China or Indonesia - with employment possibilities elsewhere. Candidates wishing to apply for courses in Brighton or Manchester do not need previous teaching experience or foreign language skills but must have qualifications enabling them to enter higher education. Course price £400

En Famille Overseas
4 St Helena Road
60b Maltravers Street, Colchester,   Tel: +44 (0) 1206 546 741
Essex CO3 3BA, UK   Fax: +44 (0) 1206 546 740

En Famille Overseas arranges for you to stay with a family in France or Spain as a paying guest. You can use your 'homestay' as a springboard for finding a local job and you can stay with a family for a week to a year, with the board and lodging costs negotiable if you stay more than a month.You can also attend a suitable language course nearby or have private coaching from your host. Prices start from £200 a week for full board accommodation in Spain, including excursion expenses. Apply about a month in advance.

Espero Language Centre
Szkola Jezykow Obcych 'Espero'
al. Jana Pawla II 17/1,   Tel: +48 77 4838325
47-220 Kedzierzyn-Kozle, Poland   Fax: +48 77 4838325

If you fancy a more unusual teaching experience, what about Poland? The Espero Language Centre, 50km from the Czech border in the small town of Kedzierzyn-Kozle, are keen for 'responsible and cheerful' gap year students to teach English. You would be teaching 15-20 classes a week, mainly conversational English, to Polish locals from 3.30pm to 7.30pm. Here's the crunch - you wouldn't be paid! The main cost to you will be your travel to Poland and a bus pass ($18/month). Accommodation and food are free - you stay with a local Polish 'host' family, so this would be a great way to experience the culture and learn about Polish traditions and customs as well as day-to-day life. Write to Barbara Piechocka, Director of Study, if you are interested. She is happy to put you in touch with one of the gappers teaching there last year.

Euro Academy
2nd Floor, 67 -71 Lewisham High Street,   Tel: +44 (0) 20 8297 0505
Lewisham, London SE13 5JX, UK   Fax: +44 (0) 20 8297 0984

Though mainly a language school, Euro Academy also arranges unpaid work placements for up to six months in France, Germany, Spain and Italy. Contact Euro Academy for further details.

i-to-i
Woodside House   Tel: +44 (0) 870 333 2332
261 Low Lane   Fax: +44 (0) 113 205 4619
Leeds LS18 5NY, UK   www.i-to-i.com

i-to-i, a highly respected gap year organisation, pioneered the weekend and online TEFL courses. The i-to-i TEFL course fully prepares participants to teach English abroad with maximum convenience - both of time and money. Fully qualified TEFL tutors conduct courses all over the UK and Ireland, and, whether you want to travel and teach or simply try something different, the i-to-i TEFL course is open to everyone. Also, with its innovative online course (at www.onlinetefl.com) i-to-i's TEFL training is available anywhere in the world, so you can even earn a certificate whilst travelling. The i-to-i TEFL course is both creative and dynamic, and enables you to plan, prepare and teach your own lessons with confidence. Employment information is also provided. The cost for the live or online course is £195, and will award you a TEFL certificate. i-to-i is an ODLQC-accredited TEFL provider.

JET - Japan Exchange and Teaching Programme

JET Desk
Embassy of Japan
101-104 Piccadilly, London W1J 7JT, UK

Tel: +44 (0) 20 7465 6668/6670
Fax: +44 (0) 20 7491 9347
www.jet-uk.org

You can apply to take part in the JET programme if you have a bachelors degree in any subject. JET recruits from 41 countries, and in 2004 the programme had over 6000 participants, over 400 of them from the UK.

Muyal Liang Trust

53 Blenheim Crescent,
London W11 2EG, UK

Tel: +44 (0) 20 7229 4774

The Muyal Liang Trust places teachers in the Denjong Pedma Cheoling Academy, a school for disadvantaged children and orphans, to teach English. The school is located in Sikkim, north of Darjeeling. The Indian government restricts foreign visitors to a two-month stay in Sikkim, a sensitive area due to its proximity to the Chinese border; permits can sometimes be extended for those interested in a longer-term commitment. Teachers will be provided with room and board at Pemayangtse, a 17th century Buddhist monastery in the Himalayan foothills, with magnificent views of Kangchendzonga, the world's third highest mountain.

Obninsk Humanities Centre

Dubravushka, 249020
Kaluga Oblast, Obninsk, Pionersky Proezd 29, Russia

The Obninsk Humanities Centre, an independent boarding school two hours from Moscow, employs two or three native English speakers a year to assist in teaching English. Knowledge of Russian isn't necessary, and TEFL qualifications are desirable but not essential. The school provides a moderate salary, food, accommodation, emergency medical insurance and free tuition in Russian. The school has excellent sports facilities including volleyball grounds, ping-pong tables, a football pitch which doubles as a skating-rink in winter, scenic cross-country skiing pistes in the surrounding forest and mountain-skiing slopes. The length of the teaching post can be negotiated, and there is help with air fares if you teach for the three summer months or longer.

Saxoncourt & English Worldwide

124 New Bond Street
London W15 1DX, UK

Tel: +44 (0) 20 7491 1911
Fax: +44 (0) 207 493 3657

Saxoncourt is an EFL recruitment consultancy placing over 600 English instructors with private language schools in up to 20 different countries worldwide each year. If you don't yet have your TEFL qualification, Saxoncourt also runs full-time four-week courses in London and Oxford, leading to either the Trinity TESOL diploma or the Cambridge CELTA qualification.

Syndicat Mixte Montaigu-RocheserviĒre
Hôtel de l'Intercommunalité
35 Avenue Villebois Mareuil,   Tel: +33 (0) 2 51 46 45 45
85607 Montaigu, Cedex, France   Fax: +33 (0) 2 51 46 45 40

This French organisation receives local government funding to teach English in primary schools, offering four posts annually - and it also employs a fifth person to work as a language assistant in a local college and lycée.

Teaching & Projects Abroad
Aldsworth Parade   Tel: +44 (0) 1903 708300
Goring   Fax: +44 (0) 1903 501026
Sussex BN12 4TX, UK   www.teaching-abroad.co.uk

Teaching & Projects Abroad organises teaching placements in such far-flung places as Bolivia, Chile, China, Ghana, India, Mexico, Mongolia, Nepal, Peru, Romania, Russia, Senegal, South Africa, Sri Lanka, Swaziland, Thailand and Togo. You pay them a deposit, tell them where you want to go and for how long, and if they can't find what you're looking for, your deposit is returned in full. Fees range from £995 for three months in Romania up to £1800 - this includes food, lodging, travel, insurance and local back-up. Though strictly speaking not a work placement as you don't get paid, this is ideal if you want some teaching experience in an unusual setting. The organisation holds several open days which give you the opportunity to meet staff and people who have already participated in programmes arranged by Teaching & Projects Abroad.

Xuzhou Normal College
20 Kuihe Xiyan   Tel: +86 5163 822 022
Xuzhou Normal College, Xuzhou, China   Fax: +86 5163 822 022

Xuzhou Normal College in China has two positions for teachers from English-speaking countries to teach oral English for one year, starting in September. No previous experience is required, and your salary would be the same as that of the local college teachers. On average you would be teaching 10-12 English lessons, five working days per week. Accommodation is free and you are entitled to three months' holiday - summer holiday starts in June, and other holidays include winter holiday and public holidays. In addition, the college also offers two or three touring holidays free of charge.

The College is maintained by local government and has roughly 1000 students and 130 staff. This year, the college intends to enrol 100 new students majoring in English Education who will work as English teachers in primary schools and middle schools once they have graduated.

The City: Xuzhou (population 6 million+), is in the north of Jiangsu, which is one of the most prosperous provinces in China. Xuzhou is famous for its long history and historical relics, and earned the title of 'Historical City of China'. Xuzhou has convenient train and air links. The school lies in the south of the city within easy reach of supermarkets, department stores, theatre, park, restaurants, university, library and museums. The Head Teacher, Mrs Xianghua Zhang, says "we are looking forward to hearing from you. If you want to know more, don't hesitate to contact us. Welcome to our school! Welcome to China!"

Please send your CV first to the UK contact, Dr Xiang Zhang (Tel: +44 (0) 1235 203758 evening only, email: Xiang.Zhang@ntlworld.com)

Spreading the word

My decision to take a TEFL gap-year was founded on a lack of ideas as to what else to do. I had done a degree that involved a lot of sitting in cafes, discussing the rights and wrongs of the world with attractive and interesting foreigners. Not surprisingly, when I discovered that it was possible to do essentially the same thing, only in Paris, and be paid a decent wage, I jumped at it. I became an English teacher.

It turned out to be the perfect way to look at different career options. I taught people who had jobs I barely knew existed – interactive media planners, in-house telecoms lawyers, headhunters, advertising creatives, political opinion pollsters... In particular, I gave classes to a group of magazine journalists in a publishing house – and decided I wanted their job. My lack of a career plan was solved, and I'm now back in England at journalism school. Similarly, one of my colleagues taught at Yahoo! France, and is now training as a web designer.

Finding work was surprisingly easy. With a TEFL course under my belt from the summer, I had lined up a couple of interviews through speculative letters sent to schools which I had found in a directory [try **www.schoolsearch.co.uk**]. I also looked in the FUSAC, a magazine for the Paris anglophone community, listing hundreds of jobs, courses, places to live and services.

My first job was with an independent training company on the Left Bank. I was on a vacataire contract. Vacataires earn a good hourly rate – up to 25/hour – but the work is often unstable and there is no fixed minimum monthly salary. Next I got a job with a school specialising in teaching English in the sexy world of advertising and media. The new contract was a CDI, meaning that it was permanent and with a fixed salary, free public transport and health insurance. What's more, we wrote our own teaching materials, which added a whole new dimension to the job. Most of all, I was utterly seduced by the glamour of the advertising agencies. I loved it, and stayed eighteen months.

I had no problems with the famously dire French bureaucracy – as an EU national, the processes for registration are very slow, but work. I needed my passport, and proof of having an address and a job in order to open a bank account.

So my French is now fluent and I know a lot about all sorts of different jobs. I've lived in Paris for two years and loved every minute of it. And most of all, teaching helped me find my career. All I have to do now is to make it happen.

Josh

Seasonal work in Europe

The following companies should be able to help you get casual work in Europe, or try doing a search on the internet or using gap-year message boards to find out if any other gappers know what's available.

Work opportunities - Europe

Acorn Adventure
22 Worcester Road, Stourbridge,
West Midlands DY8 1AN, UK   Tel: +44 (0) 1384 446057

Acorn Adventure runs adventure holiday camps from April until September based in nine centres in France, Italy, Spain and the UK - their main customers are school groups.

An experience to Remember!

Looking to gain <u>valuable work</u> and <u>life experience</u> in France?

Come to our <u>language and activity centre</u> for British School groups.

You will:-

• Discover how to <u>inspire and motivate young minds</u>, entertain and instruct children on exciting activities.

• Be a part of a <u>lively, enthusiastic</u> team working together in a communal atmosphere.

• Face challenges requiring you to use initiative and <u>test your strength of character</u>.

We offer a good employment package including full board.

Contact: Email: recruitment@chateau-beaumont.co.uk
   Chateau Beaumont,   Telephone: 0844 8000 125
   Les Courgés,
   53420 Chailland,
   France.

Camp Beaumont
The Old Rectory   Tel: +44 (0) 1263 823000
Beeston Regis, Norfolk NR27 9NG, UK   Fax: +44 (0) 1263 823002

Have the Summer of your life working at Camp Beaumont Summer Camps! We need vibrant and energetic people to work as Group Leaders, responsible for the round-the-clock welfare of a group of children.

visit: www.gap-year.com

CCUSA
Unit 4CC
Green Dragon House
64-70 High Street, CR0 9XN Croydon, UK

Tel: +44 (0) 20 8688 9051
Fax: +44 (0) 20 8680 4539
www.ccusa.com

Over the last 16 years, CCUSA have organised safe and secure working holidays for over 100,000 students from all over the world. CCUSA Camp Counselors Russia gives you the chance to work with children for 4 or 8 weeks at a Russian summer camp. All CCUSA programmes offer guaranteed placement before departure, free return flights, the highest wages, visas, insurance, airport pickup, local orientation, and full-time support before, during and after the programme. CCUSA offers many other programmes, please see their other listings in this chapter in the sections on Seasonal Work in North America, Seasonal Work in Australia and New Zealand and Internships for full details.

French Encounters
63 Fordhouse Road
Bromsgrove
Worcestershire B60 2LU, UK

Tel: +44 (0) 1527 873645
Fax: +44 (0) 1527 832794
www.frenchencounters.com

Every year French Encounters, a small, friendly, family run company, employs eight gap year students to act as animateurs/animatrices in their two ch,teaux centres in Seine Maritime for the season (mid-February to mid-June). The work includes tour guiding, functioning as couriers, entertainers, supervisors and role models to 10- to 13-year-old British children in school groups (all domestic chores such as cooking, meal service and general cleaning are done by other staff).

You're paid about £80 a week, with a £20 weekend allowance. Full board and lodging, travel costs to and from Normandy and reasonable incidental and miscellaneous expenses during the season are covered. All insurance requirements are included.

The two-week initial training programme for animateurs is extremely thorough and incorporates a French Red Cross first aid course and professional presentation skills coaching. You will get training to develop your courier skills, tour guide techniques and all that these entail, including: how to manage groups, organise itineraries, use your personal initiative, take responsibility for groups and even how to use a microphone. A week is made available for the preparation and assessment of an English Speaking Board Professional Presentation Skills Certificate: very useful to add to your CV. Although you might not consider this an exotic gap year project, most previous animateurs say they learned a great deal, had enormous fun and were sad when the season came to an end - in fact many have remained friends with the owners for years.

GALA
Woodcote House
8 Leigh Lane, Farnham,
Surrey GU9 8HP, UK

Tel: +44 (0) 1252 715 319
Fax: +44 (0) 1252 715 319

Gala organises work experience placements in Spanish hotels.

Gwendalyne
67-71 Lewisham High Street
SE13 5JX London, UK

Tel: +44 (0)20 8297 3251
Fax: +44 (0)20 8297 0984

Gwendalyne can offer you different seasonal work programmes in Europe: Work Experience in Ireland, Language Assistant in Spain, Internship in Germany, Work

Experience and Internship in France. Most of the programmes include a placement and accommodation, do not have specific requirements and can be taken throughout all year.

Holidaybreak
Overseas Recruitment Dept
Hartford Manor, Greenbank Lane,
Northwich, Cheshire CW8 1HW, UK

Tel: +44 (0) 1606 787522
Fax: +44 (0) 870 366 7640

Holiday Break (Eurocamp and Key Camp) organises camping holidays throughout Europe (excluding the UK) and employs people of 18 and over to help from April/May to July or September/October. Jobs last for at least two months. You can be a courier, (helping customers plus cleaning accommodation), provide activities for children, put up or take down tents or supervise. Minimum wage is £100 per week. Travel costs, uniform, accommodation and subsidised insurance are also provided.

Interspeak
Stretton Lower Hall
Stretton, Nr. Malpas,
South Cheshire SY14 7HS, UK

Tel: +44 (0) 1829 250 641
Fax: +44 (0) 1829 250596

Interspeak organises unpaid work placements in France, Germany and Spain from between one and six months. You pay a registration fee of £80 up front, then a flat fee of £320 for arranging the placement. Interspeak will also organise a family for you to stay with, although you can make your own plans if you prefer. Placement jobs vary widely, but Interspeak says it can find placements in banking, law, marketing, media, hotels and restaurants - citing one student working in a fashion photography studio in France and another for a radio station in Spain.

Jobs in the Alps
17 High Street
Gretton, Northamptonshire
NN17 3DE, UK

Tel: +44 (0) 7050 121648
Fax: + 44 (0) 1536 771914

Jobs in the Alps offers seasonal jobs in mountain resorts for gap year students who have good French or German, usually A-level or equivalent, and want to use or improve their language skills whilst enjoying winter skiing or summer sports. All jobs pay a good wage and usually include free board and accommodation. The winter ski season is from mid-December to April, and applications are best in by early September. The summer season varies but is about mid-June to mid-September - applications should be made by April.

Mark Warner
George House
61-65 Kensington Church Street,
London W8 4BA, UK

Tel: +44 (0) 20 7761 7300
www.markwarner-recruitment.co.uk

Mark Warner is a leading tour operator with hotels located around the Mediterranean and in top ski resorts in the Alps.

We employ chefs, restaurant staff, watersports, tennis and aerobic instructors, nannies, pool attendants and more.

Working Abroad | Seasonal work in Europe

Natives

| 39-43 Putney High Street | Tel: +44 (0)8700 463377 |
| SW15 1SP London, UK | Fax: +44 (0) 8451 275 048 |

One way to work a season in the Alps, or even to get into the industry in the UK, is to be a ski or snowboard technician - repairing and fitting ski and snowboard gear. Natives offer 3 different one-day courses to teach you the skills required - two on being a snow technician (beginner & advanced) and one on boot fitting. All are recognised by the main UK retailers and overseas employers. Amongst other things, you can learn the wonders of waxing theory and practice, gouge filling and patching, base and side edge sharpening and tuning, extruder guns and base planers, belt sanding/stone grinding theory and foot morphology. Once you have your qualification, Natives will help you find a job either in the Alps or in the UK. Courses are held in Kendal (Cumbria) and Basingstoke (Hampshire) from late May through to November. Prices range from £130 for a single course in Kendal to £380 for all three courses in Basingstoke. All tuition fees and workshop products are included in the price, but you must arrange and pay for your own accommodation, travel and food.

PGL

PGL Recruitment Team

| Alton Court, Penyard Lane, | Tel: 0870 401 4411 |
| Ross-on-Wye, Herefordshire HR9 5GL, UK | Fax: 0870 401 4444 |

Each year PGL employs over 2000 people to work at its children's activity centres in the UK, France and Spain. You'll receive full board and accommodation in addition to £60-£100 per week (depending on your role and location).

Solaire Holidays

1158 Stratford Road, Hall Green,

| Birmingham B28 8AF, UK | Tel: +44 (0) 121 7785061 |

Work available at their campsites in France and Spain - especially general couriers, children's couriers, bar staff and maintenance staff. Pay ranges from £84 to £140 a week plus bonuses with free accommodation and travel.

Telepassport-Bulgaria

| Str, Floor 1, Suite 1, 8000 Bourgas , Bulgaria | Tel: +359 56 816 277 |

Telepassport-Bulgaria is a crew manning agency, so if you're interested in spending your year out on a ship travelling the world then it could be worth your while getting in touch. A huge range of jobs are available.

Seasonal Work in North America

Since the terrorist attacks in September 2001 the US Government has set up The Department of Homeland Security, which has tightened up on visas and regulations for getting into the USA.

New visa regulations for British citizens were introduced in October 2004 and more are planned for 2005.

Although working for a summer in the USA shouldn't be a problem US bureaucracy is complicated and precise and you don't want to arrive thinking you have the right visa only to find yourself deported because you haven't.

So it is important to get the correct visa and work permit documents and there are many categories.

You can get more information on 09055 444 546 or visit **www.usembassy.org.uk**

Probably the most popular job for young gappers is working on a summer camp. There are about 10,000 camps and they come in all shapes, sizes and specialisms from single sex to religious to sport to music. Many of the organisations listed below can help you find both work and visas but check out the small print about pay, accommodation and other expenses. The blanket minimum wage in the USA at the time of going to press is $5.15, which doesn't buy you much.

If camp life doesn't appeal, there's a broad range of travel and work programmes. Take a look at the section on Internships as well.

Work Opportunities - North America

Alliances Abroad
2423 Pennsylvania Avenue NW
Washington, DC 20037, USA

Tel: +1 (202) 467 9467
Fax: +1 (202) 467 9460

Alliances Abroad is one of only a few educational travel companies in the world offering international students paid internships and summer work programmes in the United States. With dozens of locations and numerous employers around the country for you to choose from, they'll help you find work that turns into the experience of a lifetime. All you do is choose the location, length of time you're willing to stay, and give them an idea of the type of position you will consider. Their experienced staff in America will do the rest. Positions are available in many categories including import-export, communication, tourism, social work, information technology, secretarial work, economics, law, marketing, banking, finance, public relations and many more.

BUNAC (British Universities North America Club)
16 Bowling Green Lane
London EC1R 0QH, UK

Tel: +44 (0) 20 7251 3472
www.bunac.org

Spend a summer working as a counsellor on a children's summer camp in the USA. BUNAC arranges about 3500 placements a year. They also organise visa, flights, insurance, accommodation and food. Applicants need to be over 19 on June 1st 2005 and have experience of working with groups of children in a leadership role. Sporty students with experience of instructing activities such as soccer, tennis, swimming, horse-riding, golf and sailing are in demand as are applicants with experience of teaching arts and crafts, drama and music.

Summer Camp USA offers a low up-front cost chance to go on a working holiday. You pay £67 registration fee, about £120 for insurance and approximately £45 visa fee to the US Embassy. BUNAC deducts the cost of your airfare from your earnings. You get a minimum of $795 in hand spending money for working 6-9 weeks if you are under 21; this rises to $855 if you are over 21.

BUNAC also offers Work America (casual summer work in the USA); KAMP (Kitchen and Maintenance Programme providing behind-the-scenes support work on children's summer camps); and OPT USA (career-related training internships).

Canada

BUNAC's Work Canada and Gap Canada programmes give gap year students the chance to spend 2-12 months working in this beautiful and friendly country. Applicants must be British passport holders aged 18-35. BUNAC will arrange your flexible casual work visa and provide comprehensive pre-departure and arrival orientations.

South Africa

A fantastic opportunity to get involved in one of many volunteer projects based around the beautiful city of Cape Town. Group departures are followed by a one week arrival orientation and eight week placement.

Who can take part? Age: 18+. Nationality: British. Cost: £695. This covers programme literature, placement, 1 week arrival orientation and accommodation for 9 weeks. Additional costs: Flight and insurance.

Ghana

Ghana is considered one of the safest and friendliest countries in West Africa. In conjunction with the Ghanaian student organisation SYTO, BUNAC arranges three month placements (which can be extended up to a total of 12 months).

Who can take part? Age: 18+. Nationality: Any. Cost: £390. This covers programme literature, placement, 5 day arrival orientation plus accommodation during orientation. Additional costs: Flight and insurance plus local payment towards accommodation.

Costa Rica

BUNAC offers three or six month placements in this beautiful and diverse Central American country. Applicants must be able to communicate confidently in Spanish.

Who can take part? Age: 18-32. Nationality: Any permanent resident of the UK. Cost: 3 months £425, 6 months £525. This covers programme literature, placement, one day arrival orientation and arrival accommodation in San Jose. Additional costs: Flight and insurance plus local payment towards accommodation during placement.

Working Abroad | Seasonal work in North America

Peru

BUNAC offers 2 or 3 month placements in this fascinating South American country. All applicants are placed at Flores de Villa, a vibrant community centre on the outskirts of Lima. Applicants must be able to communicate confidently in Spanish. Who can take part? Age: 18+. Nationality: Any permanent resident of the UK. Cost: Two months £695, three months £895 this covers programme literature, placement, three day arrival orientation and arrival accommodation in Lima and all accommodation during placement. Additional costs: Flight and insurance.

Camp America

37A Queen's Gate
London SW7 5HR
UK

Tel: +44 (0) 20 7581 7333
Fax: +44 (0) 20 7581 7377
www.campamerica.co.uk

Each year Camp America sends thousands of young people to work on summer camps and resorts in the States between June and August.

CCUSA

Unit 4CC, Green Dragon House
64-70 High Street,
CR0 9XN Croydon, UK

Tel: +44 (0) 20 8688 9051
Fax: +44 (0) 20 8680 4539
www.ccusa.com

Over the last 16 years, CCUSA have organised safe and secure working holidays for over 100,000 students from all over the world.

If you like working with kids and you have 9 weeks to spare this summer then the CCUSA Camp Counselors USA programme is perfect for you. CCUSA works with over 900 summer camps in beautiful locations in America. You don't need any experience or qualifications but you do need to be at least 18 years old. All CCUSA programmes offer guaranteed placement before departure, free return flights, highest wages, visas, insurance, airport pickup, local orientation, and full-time support before, during and after the programme. CCUSA offers many other programmes, please see their other listings in this chapter in the sections on Seasonal Work in Europe, Seasonal Work in Australia and New Zealand and Internships for full details.

Changing Worlds

11 Doctors Lane
Chaldon
Surrey CR3 5AE, UK

Tel: +44 (0) 1883 340 960
Fax: +44 (0) 1883 330783
www.changingworlds.co.uk

Changing Worlds offers paid work placements in the Canadian Rockies. Demanding hotel work is rewarded by reasonable pay, an excellent social life, accommodation and time to ski on days off. Workers must be capable of working a full 40-hour week and remaining positive. Prices start at £1895 and include return flight, finding a suitable job, assistance with work permits, a one-day UK briefing and assistance from the Changing Worlds representative in-country who will meet you and take you to your work placement. Some work experience is expected. Fundraising advice is available although most workers take paid UK jobs prior to their placement. To be eligible for the placement in Canada you need to be going on to university.

CIEE (Council on International Educational Exchange)
52 Poland Street
London W1F 7AB
UK

Tel: +44 (0) 20 7478 2020
Fax: +44 (0) 20 7734 7322
www.councilexchanges.org.uk

CIEE's Work and Travel USA programme is for up to four months of seasonal work (June to October) in the USA and the deposit is £70. Although most students take seasonal summer jobs, past participants have enhanced their CVs with everything from office temping to career-related summer placements. Check on the CIEE website to read about those who have been and done it or chat to others who are thinking about it on the bulletin boards. The Work and Travel programme gives you far more freedom than the internship programme, although it does entail a certain amount of confidence in your job-seeking abilities. You could do almost any job from bar work in New York to film work in California.

Gap Challenge at World Challenge Expeditions

Black Arrow House,
Chandos Road,
London NW10 6NF, UK

Tel: +44 (0) 20 8728 7272
+44 (0) 20 8728 7200
www.world-challenge.co.uk

Live and work in Canada in the shadow of the breathtaking Rocky Mountains. Gap Challenge offers individuals aged 17-24 two different types of placement, departing three times a year. Each placement is for six months, beginning in September, November or March, working in hotels and ski resorts in and around Banff. The hotels and resorts are high quality and have a well established link with Gap Challenge. They offer between 20 and 50 hours work per week depending on the snow and number of tourists.

Placement fee includes a 12 month date-changeable return ticket to enable you to travel and explore the rest of Canada and North America after your placement. Whilst away, Gap Challengers are offered advice and support from in-country agents and benefit from World Challenge Expeditions' comprehensive 24-hour emergency back-up systems. Applicants must have an unconditional offer from a University to be eligble for the visa.

InterExchange

161 Sixth Avenue
New York NY 10013, USA

Tel: +1 (212) 924 0446
Fax: +1 (212) 924 0575

InterExchange offer two programmes aimed at gappers wanting to work in the USA. You can work on their Camp USA programme for 8-10 weeks either as a member of conssellor (general or speciality, eg tennis, ceramics, swimming) or as a member of the support staff (kitchen, housekeeping, laundry, maintenance and office).

In return you get room and board, a small stipend, round trip transatlantic airfare and the opportunity to travel in the States when you have completed the programme.

You must be at least 19-years-old, fluent in English and either a university student, a teacher, a youth worker or have a specialised skill. The programme begins in June and ends in mid-September. Contact InterExchange direct for information on fees.

The Work & Travel USA programme offers seasonal work in hotels, inns, amusement parks, country fairs, national parks, campgrounds and restaurants in resort areas. Jobs last at least 3 months and you should be prepared to take on menial or physical tasks (cleaning, maintenance etc) in locations away from main cities. You need to be aged 18-28 and a full-time student in tertiary education. Once the job is over your visa allows you to travel within the USA.

change your life forever

Earn cash in amazing places

For details of our paid gap year placements,
visit www.changingworlds.co.uk
or telephone 01892 770000

AUSTRALIA

CANADA

NEW ZEALAND

Seasonal work in Australia and New Zealand

Australasia is still the most popular destination for gappers, so there will be a lot of other backpackers after jobs too - but there are usually plenty of jobs to go round, and many backpackers travel from one casual job to another as a way of paying for their travel. It's a good way to meet people too.

Just surfing the internet from the UK (using keywords like 'Australia jobs' or 'vacation work Australia') gives you an idea of what's on offer. Australian job websites worth a look include:

www.ozsearch.com.au

www.youthjobs.com.au

You may notice that job adverts often carry a note that 'only people with the right to work in Australia may apply for this position'. You can apply or register online, but your chances of getting it before you have a ticket and a visa lined up are not high.

Australian High Commission

Australia House, Strand
London WC2 4LA
Visa enquiries: 090 6550 8900 (£1/min)
www.australia.org.uk

Department of Immigration Australia

www.immi.gov.au

So getting the right type of visa is a priority. The key point is that to do casual work in Australia you will need a Working Holiday Maker (WHM) visa, which costs £65. It allows you to travel and take occasional work (maximum 3 months with each emplyer) for up to a year. The year begins the day you enter Australia, so if you never arrive you don't lose anything - but once you've used up your WHM visa you'll never be allowed another one.

To qualify for a WHM you need to be aged between 18-30 with no dependants, and be a citizen of a country with reciprocal work agreements with Australia (these countries include the UK, Republic of Ireland, Canada and various European and Far Eastern countries). You'll need to prove that you have at least AU$5000 in the bank and enough money for your return fare. Application can be by post (which takes four to five weeks, and you have to send your passport, so you'll be confined to the UK for that period) or you can apply online with your passport number. You can find information on all types of visas, including the Student Visa, on the Australian High Commission website, **www.australia.org.uk**

Many organisations arrange paid work placements in Australia and New Zealand, and some also organise voluntary work assignments in those and other countries. Some of these will also sort out your paperwork such as visas and work permits for you - although you may have to pay extra for this service. Below are listed some useful organisations to check out when you're looking for work in Australasia.

Work opportunities – Australia & New Zealand

Alliances Abroad
2423 Pennsylvania Avenue NW
Washington, DC 20037,
USA

Tel: +1 (202) 467 9467
Fax: +1 (202) 467 9460

The Alliances Abroad Rural Australia work programme will place you in a paid position on a ranch, station, farm or roadhouse in rural Australia. Work positions include farm work, domestic or childcare work on the farm, or rural hospitality. The work programme allows you to experience all that Australia has to offer - backpacking, diving, climbing and journeying throughout the Outback - while earning money!

To start you off there's a 5-day orientation programme on a working farm near Brisbane and then you journey into the Outback for your adventure! Accommodation and meals are provided as well as a salary. Their experienced staff will help you with all of your travel needs, including travel arrangements, recommendations on what to do while abroad, visa/work permit procurement, airport transfers and all that other organisational stuff.

BUNAC (British Universities North America Club)
16 Bowling Green Lane
London EC1R 0QH, UK

Tel: +44 (0) 20 7251 3472
www.bunac.org

BUNAC, best known for its programmes in the USA and Canada, also offers Work Australia and Work New Zealand programmes. BUNAC arranges visas, group departures, an organised stop over, arrival accommodation, orientation and access to a resource office throughout your stay. BUNAC's subsidiary IEP hosts all participants whilst in Australia and New Zealand. Departures are from London and Los Angeles and the extended validity tickets allow trips of up to 18 months' duration.

CCUSA
Unit 4CC
Green Dragon House
64-70 High Street, CR0 9XN Croydon, UK

Tel: +44 (0) 20 8688 9051
Fax: +44 (0) 20 8680 4539
www.ccusa.com

Over the last 16 years, CCUSA have organised safe and secure working holidays for over 100,000 students from all over the world. CCUSA's Work Experience Down Under programme offers a 12-month work and travel visa for both Australia and New Zealand and helps you find a job.

All CCUSA programmes offer guaranteed placement before departure, free return flights, highest wages, visas, insurance, airport pickup, local orientation, and full-time support before, during and after the programme. CCUSA offers many other programmes, please see their other listings in this chapter in the sections on Seasonal Work in North America, Seasonal Work in Europe and Internships for full details.

CCUSA offers many other programmes, please see their other listings in this chapter in the sections on Seasonal Work in North America, Seasonal Work in Europe and Internships for full details.

Changing Worlds

11 Doctors Lane
Chaldon
Surrey CR3 5AE, UK

Tel: +44 (0) 1883 340 960
Fax: +44 (0) 1883 330783
www.changingworlds.co.uk

Changing Worlds offers a variety of paid work placements in New Zealand and Australia. In Queenstown, South Island New Zealand, they will organise work in the most prestigious hotels, you will get local rates of pay, accommodation and a hectic social life. Or you could choose to work in the Bay of Islands region of North Island in a range of jobs including hotel work or farm work. Farm workers get paid pocket money and stay with a local family. In Queensland, Australia, there are paid placements in hotels in Cairns - on the doorstep of the Great Barrier Reef.

Prices start at £1895 and include return flights, finding a suitable job, assistance with work permits, a one-day UK briefing and the support from the Changing Worlds representative in-country who will meet you and take you to your placement. Relevant work experience is always useful particularly for those wishing to work in hotels. Fundraising advice is available although most workers take UK paid jobs prior to their placement. To be eligible you need to be between 18 and 25 for New Zealand and up to 30 for Australia.

Changing Worlds also offers unpaid placements around the world, see their listing under Volunteering Abroad.

Gwendalyne

67-71 Lewisham High Street
SE13 5JX London, UK

Tel: +44 (0)20 8297 3251
Fax: +44 (0)20 8297 0984

Gwendalyne can offer you a work programme in Australia. Included:2 job offers, programme handbook, airport pickup and transfer, 2 nights accommodation with continental breakfast, arrival guide, discount card, bank account preparation, post-arrival orientation, free PC and Internet access, 24 hours emergency line, mail storage service 12 months, discounts across Australia, facsimile receiving, Sydney Walking Tour.

newzealandvisas.com

United Kingdom

Tel: +44 (0) 1270 626626

Cheshire-based newzealandvisas.com specialises in services for travellers to New Zealand/Australia. In particular they Cheshire-based newzealandvisas.com specialises in services for travellers to New Zealand/Australia. In particular they organise working holiday visas for these countries. For a charge of £50 (including Embassy fee) they will post out the application form pack, submit it to New Zealand House then post back (recorded delivery) the passport with visa label. They also offer their own travel insurance which covers young people working in New Zealand/Australia - £211 for fully comprehensive worldwide cover for 12 months. This is helpful as many insurance policies do not cover actually working. The company also offers a Meet & Greet service upon arrival into New Zealand and, last but not least, tax back.

Visas Australia Company

PO Box 1
Nantwich, Cheshire CW5 7PB, UK

Tel: +44 (0) 1270 626 626
Fax: +44 (0) 1270 626 226

Visas Australia Company specialises in processing and issuing all types of visas, particularly for gappers. The Company's service is approved by both the Australian Tourist Board and Australian High Commission.

Visitoz

Grange Cottage, 6 Shipton Road,
Ascott-under-Wychwood, Oxfordshire OX7 6AY , UK

Visitoz programmes allow gap year students or graduates with a working holiday visa to get short-term jobs in Australia to earn money so that they can continue their travels. Jobs range from working on a cattle ranch as a jackeroo or jilleroo to work in tourist stations and trail-riding centres or being a mother's help. They even have places on a crocodile farm. Visitoz says it has over 1000 varied employers on its books, so it can guarantee work in a wide variety of jobs, each job lasting for up to three months. Arrangements are made for bank accounts, Medicare cards (Australian Health Service) and tax file numbers. Pay rates vary (typically about AU$300 a week in hand), and free board and lodging are usually included. Contact William Taunton-Burnet at the address above. Application fee to Visitoz is £25, and the Visitoz programme charge is £570.

Work Oz

First Floor, 68 Plasturton Avenue,
Cardiff CF11 9HJ, Wales

Tel: +44 (0) 29 2022 2211

Work Oz, run by ex-High Commission employees, specialises in helping British gappers work, live and play in Oz. This special Gap-Year Australia package costing £265 per person includes: Working Holiday Visa application fee and application assistance; transport to hostel from airport and first four nights' shared accommodation; four meals during your first four days; membership to the Worldwide Workers network; guaranteed employment within 14 days of registration; free internet access; free phonecard - with AU$5 credit and great rates to the UK and Ireland; social discounts; travel discounts; hop-on hop-off City Harbour Cruise; and a full day exploring the Blue Mountains.

Even if you don't want to take the full Gap-Year Package they will give free work visa advice and can process your visa application for £99 (you also get a useful free Employment Handbook and information about how to register with a doctor in Australia, get a Medicare card and an Australian tax file number). They'll assess your application before it goes off to make sure it's been done correctly (saving you having it sent back if you've made a mistake, which could cost you another five weeks). For an extra £49 you get a World Wide Workers package which gives you an AU$5 phonecard, employment advice and free internet access from the WWW offices in Byron Bay, Cairns, Melbourne and Sydney, travel discounts, discounted jugs of beer with fellow travellers on Fridays and Saturdays and - in Sydney only - a guarantee of work within 14 days of registration.

Chapter 2
Volunteering Abroad

visit: www.gap-year.com

Voluntary work abroad can be one of the most rewarding ways to spend all or part of your gap year. Most gappers who do it come back with memories they never lose and a new perspective on the world.

Taking part in an organised voluntary work project can give you the opportunity to learn about a different culture, meet new friends and learn to communicate with people who may not understand your way of life let alone your language. You will come away with an amazing sense of achievement and, hopefully, pride in what you have done. You could find yourself working with people living in unbelievable poverty, disease, hunger – something which may give you a different perspective on life.

More and more organisations are arranging voluntary placements abroad for gappers, so there's a huge choice of companies and types of voluntary placement. There's also a huge number of people wanting to go on these trips so companies can afford to be picky – you may find you have to prove to them that you should be selected to go before they will accept your money! It can be as much about them choosing you as you choosing them.

The companies have a point: they put a lot of effort into getting you out there and if you can't stick it, everyone loses out, including the gapper who could have been chosen instead of you. Voluntary work can be tough. You may be out in the middle of nowhere, with no western influence to be seen; food, language – the entire culture might be totally different to what you're used to and there may not be many English-speakers around: you will have to cope with culture shock and feeling lonely, isolated and homesick.

Idealist or hedonist?

Because voluntary work is so popular with gappers, commercial companies are starting to get in on the act and the idealism associated with voluntary work is coming under severe commercial pressure. A few organisations offer packages that are little more than tourism dressed up as voluntary work – at a price. Make sure you are clear about what you will be doing before you sign up and part with your money. Also, be honest with yourself about what you want – there's nothing wrong with wanting to travel and have 'a good time'. If you get there, hate it and have to come home early you'll feel so disappointed and have such a sense of failure. If you want to do something 'useful' but you're not sure you want to commit your whole gap year, then why not arrange to join a project for a few months and then go travelling?

When to start applying

Application can close early, particularly for expeditions and conservation projects needing complex funding or tied in with international government

87

programmes. If you'd like to go on one of these projects, planning should usually start about a year ahead, in the autumn term. Others can be taken up at very short notice – Gap Challenge, for example, can take in applications during the August period when you are getting A level results or going through clearing and book you on a project that starts in September. If you don't have much time before your gap year starts (maybe you didn't get the grades you expected, or you've made a last-minute decision to defer uni for a year) it is always worth contacting a voluntary organisation about a project you're interested in in case they've had a last-minute cancellation.

What to expect

Ranging from placements lasting a couple of weeks to teaching for a whole academic year, most placements provide only free accommodation and food – very few provide pocket money.

Both of our schools have a fantastic view of this huge mountain called Mt. Meru, which is Tanzania's second highest mountain. The school is basically a concrete shell - the classrooms have bars on the windows (no glass), concrete floors with massive holes in, a blackboard, some desks and that's it. It's actually cold here in the mornings and evenings and the wind blows straight through the 'windows'. BUT the children are lovely! There are about 50 in each of my classes (I have two) and they are quite keen to learn which is nice. They are loving the stickers I'm giving out and I've brought some soccer balls to play with them at lunch and maybe after school.

We are also teaching adult classes of an evening and they are going really well. The adults are all very nice and are really grateful for the help. They usually last for 2hrs and, as they generally speak quite a bit of English, we are able to have good conversations with them.

My favourite part of the day is walking to and from school and around the local area because all these tiny children come running out yelling 'good morning', 'how are you?' They are so gorgeous.

I am having a wonderful time and am so glad to be here!

Tanya, 29, Australian teacher and 2004 volunteer with MondoChallenge

Gappers expecting cuddly tiger cubs or cute children, a nice apartment with MTV and one long party will soon be on the next flight home. You'll need to be resourceful, be able to teach, build, inspire confidence, communicate and share what you know. Physical and mental fitness, staying power, and the ability to get on with people are essential.

Peter from Africa and Asia Venture explains: "We are looking for self-motivated and reliable positive thinkers. You need to be self-reliant and able to cope when you turn up at a Nepali school and find a basic room, no curtains and that the loo is a 'long-drop' down the garden."

Some other points are worth emphasising. You might feel safer going with a big voluntary organisation because they should be able to offer help in a nasty situation. Experience is certainly important where organisations are concerned. But often a small, specialist organisation is more knowledgeable about a country, a school or other destination. Size and status have little bearing on competence. A charity can be more efficient than a commercial company, and a commercial company can show more sensitivity than a charity. There are few general rules – talk to someone who's been.

Organisations vary as to how much back-up they offer volunteers, from virtually holding your hand throughout your stay and even after you come back, to the 'sink or swim' method. If you're going to get the most out of your volunteering gap year, then be honest with yourself about what you need: if you feel patronised at the slightest hint of advice then you might get annoyed with too much interference from the organisation. Though do bear in mind that they probably know more than you do about the placement, what sort of vaccinations you're going to need, what will be useful to take with you, and how to get the visas and permits you will need. Equally if you're shy or nervous it might be as well to go with an organisation that sends volunteers in pairs or groups. There's nothing wrong with either type of placement – it's about choosing what's right for you.

Talk to a few organisations before you decide which one to go with and, probably more useful, talk to some previous volunteers. They'll be able to tell you what it's really like; don't just ask them if they enjoyed it, get them to describe what they did, what they liked and why, what they didn't like and what they'd do differently – though of course companies are never likely to put you in touch with someone who'll say it was rubbish.

The truth is that over in Tanzania, or wherever you're sent, you can't count on much. Regardless of the reputation of the voluntary work organisation you choose, or the competence of voluntary work co-ordinators in a particular country, it's the luck of the draw whether the school you are put in, for example, really values you – or if a family you stay with treats you well. It's worth checking what training is given and what support there is in-country, but be aware that you may not get what you expect – you need to be adaptable and make the most of whatever situation you find yourself in.

What's the cost?

It varies hugely – some companies just expect you to pay for the airfare – others expect you to raise thousands of pounds for funding. It can be hard to combine raising money with studying for A levels, but there are a lot of ways to do it. As usual, the earlier you start, the easier it will be.

The organisation that you go with should be able to give advice, but options include organising sponsored events (abseiling down a tall building), writing to companies or trusts asking for sponsorship, car-boot sales, or even plain working and saving. The last resort is to go cap-in-hand to your parents, either for a loan or a gift, but this can be unsatisfying and they may simply not be able to afford it. If your parents or relatives do want to help, you could ask for useful items for Christmas or birthday presents – like a rucksack.

Safety first

If you're going with a good organisation they shouldn't send you anywhere too dangerous – but situations change quickly and it's always worth finding out about where you're going for yourself. Check out the Foreign Office's Travel Advice page on **www.fco.gov.uk** or via **www.gap-year.com** The Foreign Office site also has lots of advice on visas, insurance and other things that need to be sorted out before you go, and advice on what to do in an emergency abroad.

"What can I say? It was brilliant!! Perfect!!"

"For my first time travelling alone it was fab – when I arrived at Jo'berg, everything was arranged and it made travelling so much easier than having to find my own way to the reserve. I think it is really good advice to travel with a company for your first time as there are no worries and if there is a problem, you know you have someone you can contact within the country which is reassuring!

"I would just like to say thank you! It was perfect and I had the best time ever"

Heather went on a volunteer project with African Conservation Experience

Voluntary Organisations

Africa & Asia Venture
10 Market Place
Devizes
Wiltshire SN10 1HT, UK

Tel: +44 (0) 1380 729009
Fax: +44 (0) 1380 720 060
www.aventure.co.uk

COMMUNITY, CONSERVATION, SAFARI, TEACHING, TRAVEL

Africa and Asia Venture (AV) is a voluntary work organisation started in 1994 by ex-Army officers Peter Bell and Nigel Warren. AV now takes 500 students per year on teaching placements which consist of three rewarding months in a primary or secondary school in Africa (Botswana, Kenya, Tanzania, Malawi and Uganda), the Indian Himalayas or Nepal and now Mexico, with a month's travel afterwards, including an unforgettable safari.

There are also teaching placements for graduates in Malawi and Tanzania, and a

90

Community and Conservation programme for school-leavers and gaduates in Kenya. AV now offers shorter vacation expeditions from four to six weeks which incorporate shorter projects with a safari.

AV provides a training course first, including advice on teaching, health and safety, language and lifestyle, and full back-up in each country. Cost is about £2,590 including course, accommodation, living allowances, safari, insurance and a contribution towards educating an African or Asian student. Departures are in September, January and April. References provided.

African Conservation Experience

PO Box 28
Ottery St Mary, Devon EX11 1ZN, UK

Tel: 0870 241 5816
www.ConservationAfrica.net

ANIMALS, COMMUNITY, CONSERVATION, CULTURE, ENVIRONMENT, RESEARCH/SCIENCE, SAFARI

African Conservation Experience have been sending volunteers to Africa for over five years and are the original, most experienced organisation for conservation placements in Southern Africa. ACE are able to offer each and every applicant the benefits of their personal experience, and all volunteers receive individual consideration.

African Conservation Experience can offer you the chance to work on game and nature reserves alongside conservationists, zoologists, wildlife vets and reserve managers, making a real contribution to the conservation of African wildlife. Work can involve game capture for tagging and relocation, behavioural and population studies, wildlife veterinary work, anti-poaching patrols and animal rehabilitation.

Volunteers become an integral part of the conservation project, many of which would not be able to run without their input. Placements are from one-three months, and cost from around £2700 for four weeks up to £4000 for 12 weeks. This includes flights, accommodation, all meals and transfers.

African Conservation Trust

PO Box 310
Link Hills, 3652, South Africa

Tel: +27 31 2016180
Fax: +27 31 2016180

ANIMALS, CONSERVATION, ENVIRONMENT

The mission of the African Conservation Trust is to provide a means for conservation projects to become self-funding through active participation by the public. This gives ordinary people a chance to make a positive and real contribution to environmental conservation by funding and participating in the research effort as volunteers.

The trust has initiated the Lake Malawi Hippo Project with the University of Malawi and the University of Natal to quantify and map the entire Hippopotamus (Hippopotamus amphibius) population of the western shore of Lake Malawi. This project is entirely volunteer-funded and staffed. Other projects in Malawi are a reforestation project, an environmental education project and a research base construction project. A three-month period on any of these projects will cost £950.

AFS Community Projects Overseas

Leeming House
Vicar Lane, Leeds LS2 7JF, UK

Tel: +44 (0) 113 242 6136
Fax: +44 (0) 113 243 0631

COMMUNITY, HEALTHCARE, ENVIRONMENT, TEACHING

AFS is part of an international network with 54 partner countries that offers a range of intercultural learning opportunities. Every year AFS places young people, generally from the age of 18-29, on its International Volunteer Programme.

AgriVenture

Avenue M, NAC, Stoneleigh Park,
Kenilworth, Warwickshire CV8 2LG, UK   Tel: +44 (0) 800 7832186

FARM, TRAVEL, AGRIVENTURE, AUSTRALIA, NEW ZEALAND, FARMING

Travel, work, excitement! AgriVenture offers young people aged 18-30 the opportunity to travel and work in Australia, New Zealand, Canada, America and Japan.

AIM (Africa Inland Mission)

Halifax Place, NG1 1QN Nottingham, UK   Tel: +44 0115 9838120

COMMUNITY, CULTURE, RELIGIOUS, TEACHING, TRAVEL

AIM looks for volunteers with a specifically Christian outlook to teach in rural schools in Kenya and Uganda. Usually this is for a full year, starting in late August/September, but volunteers can take time off in the holidays to travel. There are also some two-term placements running from January to August. AIM says the small number of school postings it arranges are thoroughly researched and students are usually placed in pairs. Volunteers need to raise about £3000 for the two-term assignment and £4000 for the full-year one. Apply at least six months in advance.

Akha Heritage Foundation

Matthew McDaniel, Maesai, Chiangrai, Thailand

COMMUNITY, ENVIRONMENT, TEACHING

Based in northern Thailand, the Akha Heritage Foundation offers volunteering opportunities ranging from a month to one year. The Foundation aim is to assist the Akha Hill tribe peoples with projects to aid clean water, nutrition, human rights, literacy and good governance.

Voluntary placements cost $450 per month for food, housing and in-country transport plus $500 per month for the project. Volunteers are encouraged to raise funds for these projects if they do not have full funding, and this has been very successful. Some volunteers bring more funding which allows them to do more in the villages - this can be very rewarding. Volunteers must provide for their health insurance, the air ticket to and from Chiangrai, Thailand and all visas for their stay in Thailand.

The project involves solid, grass roots work and a very close level of community involvement, travelling to villages, working with the Akha on joint projects and living side by side with the Akha communities. These placements are for gappers who are very motivated and self reliant.

Alliances Abroad

2423 Pennsylvania Avenue NW   Tel: +1 (202) 467 9467
Washington, DC 20037, USA   Fax: +1 (202) 467 9460

ANIMALS, COMMUNITY, CONSERVATION, ENVIRONMENT, TEACHING, TRAVEL

Alliances Abroad gears its volunteer programme towards individuals looking for the opportunity to work and be of service in a developing country and makes sure the programme matches your interests, prior experience, abilities and language ability. You can choose from Costa Rica, South Africa, and Hawaii. There's a great variety of placements. In Costa Rica volunteer positions include working in environment and national parks and there's at least a month of language training (if you're not already fluent in Spanish). While in South Africa you can help out the zoologists and vets in the wildlife centre of the world. The Hawaii programme offers volunteer placements from one week to one year on an organic farm. Most of the Alliances Abroad programmes include guaranteed placement before departure, airport pickup, local orientation, and full-time support before, during and after the programme.

Archaeology Abroad
Institute of Archaeology
University College,
31-34 Gordon Square,   Tel: +44 (0) 20 8537 0849
WC1H OPY London, UK   Fax: +44 (0) 20 8537 0849

CONSERVATION, CULTURE, RESEARCH/SCIENCE, TRAVEL, ARCHAEOLOGY
Archaeology Abroad publishes a bulletin twice a year, and lists archaeological field work opportunities abroad. Financial assistance available.

ATD Fourth World
48 Addington Square   Tel: +44 (0) 20 7703 3231
London SE5 7LB, UK   Fax: +44 (0) 207 252 4276

MANUAL WORK
ATD Fourth World is an international voluntary organisation working in partnership with people living in poverty worldwide.

Studio 7
1a Beethoven Street, W10 4LG   Tel: +44 (0) 20 8960 6629
London, United Kingdom   Fax: +44 (0) 20 8962 0126

COMMUNITY, CONSERVATION, ENVIRONMENT
Pioneer Madagascar is a ten-week volunteer scheme that offers first-hand experience of frontline development and conservation work in beautiful and remote areas.

Brathay Exploration Group
Brathay Hall   Tel: +44 (0) 15394 33942
Ambleside, Cumbria LA22 0HP, UK   Fax: +44 (0) 15394 33942

COMMUNITY, CONSERVATION, CULTURE, ENVIRONMENT, RESEARCH/SCIENCE, TRAVEL
Brathay provides 'challenging experiences for young people' aged 15-25. It runs a range of expeditions from one to five weeks long which vary each year.

Bright Light
3 Fentiman Road   Tel: +44 (0) 20 7582 1582
London SW8 1LD, UK   Fax: +44 (0) 20 7582 2379

CULTURE, DANCE, DRAMA, TEACHING
Bright Light is a not-for-profit organisation that runs gap year drama and education projects in Kenya, Uganda, Tanzania and Ethiopia. You get to learn about East African drama, dance and music as well as teaching African children about Western drama and British culture.
The programme lasts three months and is split into three phases. First you spend

93

time working with African theatre professionals, learning about traditional African narrative dance and oral literature, as well as helping with performances. The second phase consists of volunteer teaching in schools. Introducing small groups of children to Western concepts of drama and help them to produce their first play. Finally, you get the chance to produce your own play and then spend time at Lake Naivasha where you can reflect on your experiences. When you return home you may even get the opportunity to workshop your performances at the Old Vic in London. Tours depart in January and May and cost £2440 including all food, travel, accommodation and insurance.

BSES Expeditions

at The Royal Geographical Society   Tel: +44 (0) 20 7591 3141
1 Kensington Gore   Fax: +44 (0) 20 7591 3140
London SW7 2AR, UK   www.bses.org.uk

ANIMALS, CONSERVATION, ENVIRONMENT, RESEARCH/SCIENCE, TRAVEL, EXPEDITIONS

This charitable organisation runs four- to six-week summer expeditions and two- to three-month gap year expeditions to wilderness areas abroad to conduct scientific research on behalf of universities, research institutes or host nations. It also runs conservation and environmental projects combined with exciting adventurous activities from ice climbing to canoeing. BSES sends people aged 16 to 23 abroad (and unpaid leaders aged 21 and over).

In the summer 2005 and 2006 BSES will be visiting the Arctic, Peru, Norway, Greenland and the Amazon rainforest. Their special gap year project for 2005-6, 'Arrival of the Midnight Sun', is a 3-month expedition to the Arctic archipeligo of Svalbard. The financial contribution varies depending on the expedition.

BTCV

Conservation Centre   Tel: +44 (0) 1302 57224
Balby Rd, DN4 0RH Doncaster, UK   Fax: +44 (0) 1302 310167

CONSERVATION

BTCV not only runs working conservation holidays in Britain, but also, by working in partnership with other organisations, runs conservation work holidays abroad in more than 25 countries. These are short, ranging from one-week trips in Europe (about £300) to six weeks turtle research in Thailand (£925 excluding flights). You end up in a mixed group of all ages, but not all of them will be doing conservation work alongside you.

Camphill Communities in the UK

55 Cainscross Road   Tel: +44 (0) 1453 753142
Stroud, Gloacestershire GL5 4EX, UK   Fax: +44 (0) 1453 757469

COMMUNITY, CULTURE, FARMING, TEACHING, CARE FOR THE DISABLED

Camphill is a worldwide network of communities dedicated to work and life with children, adolescents or adults with developmental and other disabilities.

Camps International Limited
Unit 1
Kingfisher Park
Headlands Business Park, Ringwood,
Hampshire BH24 3NX, UK

Tel: +44 (0) 870 2401843
Fax: +44 (0) 1425 485398
www.campsinternational.com

ANIMALS, COMMUNITY, CONSERVATION, CULTURE, ENVIRONMENT, FARMING, RESEARCH/SCIENCE, SAFARI, TEACHING, TRAVEL

Camps International organises expeditions and safaris based in Kenya and Tanzania. You will contribute to all aspects of African life including wildlife conservation, teaching children and building schools and by way of example.

Gappers are drawn predominantly from the UK and you will be living in the bush or on the coast with young people from a broad range of backgrounds. Camps International run their own camps and the staff are permanently on hand to guide you through the experience and ensure you are safe at all times. An experience with camps can last between one to three months; most gappers opt for 3 months. Prices for the camps vary, but on average costs around £1000 per month.

Center for women and children rights (HISANI)
Frednand Fredrick, Makongoro Street, PO Box 1817, Mwanza, Tanzania

CHILDREN, COMMUNITY, HUMAN RIGHTS, TEACHING

HISANI (Kiswahili word meaning 'to nurture one another') promotes children's rights in Tanzania (based primarily on the UN Convention on the Rights of the Child (CRC) and the African Charter on the Rights of the Child). Voluntary placements are available at its Street Children's Centre (SCC) which houses around 18 street children. It also runs an Advocacy Centre which focuses on gaining access, equity, and opportunity for primary school education; working with pregnant teenage girls; and ending corporal punishment in families and schools.

Challenges Worldwide
Scotland

Tel: +44 (0) 131 332 7372

COMMUNITY, ENVIRONMENT

Challenges Worldwide are a registered charity based in Edinburgh, offering volunteers a chance to share their skills and education with communities in developing countries for 3-6 months. A wide range of placements offer the chance to contribute constructively to sustainable projects in environmental protection, poverty alleviation or human development

Changing Worlds
11 Doctors Lane
Chaldon
Surrey CR3 5AE, UK

Tel: +44 (0) 1883 340 960
Fax: +44 (0) 1883 330783
www.changingworlds.co.uk

ANIMALS, COMMUNTY, CONSERVATION, CULTURE, DRAMA, ENVIRONMENT, FARM WORK, TEACHING

Changing Worlds offers challenging voluntary work placements in Tanzania, Chile, Southern India, Nepal, Romania and Latvia. To succeed you must have drive and a desire to make a real contribution. Most volunteers teach although there is a growing number of care work placements in orphanages. Volunteers with sport, music and drama are always popular. After a 2-day UK-based briefing on issues of safety, health and coping with living and working overseas, volunteers travel out as a group to their destinations where they are taken to the orientation course run by the representative. After a few days volunteers go in small groups to live and work in local schools and projects.

For those after a real taste of Australian life, Changing Worlds offers voluntary placements working in the outback. This challenge is not for the faint-hearted - it's hard physical work, but the experience and friends made will remain for a long time in the future. Horse riding experience is useful but not essential.

Changing Worlds also offers voluntary placements working in zoos. These placements would suit those with a genuine interest in animals. There are opportunities to work in conservation eg working with turtles in Queensland and birds in the Bay of Islands, New Zaland.

Changing Worlds prides itself on being a small organisation that knows each volunteer; assistance is always available in-country and in the UK. Volunteers must be aged between 18 and 35 (most are 18-23) and preferably educated to A level. Prices are around £2000 and include return flight and transfer to the placement, courses, accommodation, and all UK and overseas support. Additionally volunteers must budget for visas, insurance, pocket money and food in some cases. Fundraising advice is given at interview.

CMS (Church Mission Society)
Partnership House, 157 Waterloo Road,
London SE1 8UU, UK   Tel: +44 (0) 20 7928 8681

COMMUNITY, CULTURE, RELIGIOUS

Offering more of a learning experience than a giving one, the CMS runs three- to four-week Encounter programmes in Africa, Asia, the Middle East and Eastern Europe for Christians aged 18-30.

Concordia
Heversham House
20-22 Boundary Road, Hove,   Tel: +44 (0) 1273 422 218
East Sussex BN3 4ET, UK   Fax: +44 (0) 1273 421182

COMMUNITY, CONSERVATION, CULTURE, DRAMA, ENVIRONMENT, TEACHING, TRAVEL

Concordia organises international volunteer placements for 16-30 year olds. Standard projects are available in Europe, North Africa, North America, the Middle East and Japan and a limited number of places on projects in Latin America, Asia and Sub Saharan Africa. Volunteers join teams of international volunteers working on conservation, renovation, arts/cultural based or social projects (including children's playschemes and work with adults or children with mental or physical disabilities). There is a registration fee of between £85-£125 depending on the country and volunteers pay their own travel expenses. Board and accommodation is free. Projects last 2-4 weeks and run from June to September with some winter/spring opportunities.

Coral Cay Conservation
The Tower   Tel: +44 (0) 870 750 0668
125 High Street   Fax: +44 (0) 870 750 0667
Colliers Wood, London SW19 2JG, UK   www.coralcay.org

CONSERVATION, ENVIRONMENT, RESEARCH/SCIENCE, TRAVEL

Coral Cay Conservation (CCC) is a not-for-profit organisation that sends teams of volunteers to survey some of the worlds most endangered coral reefs and tropical

visit: www.gap-year.com

forests. CCC volunteers have been responsible for the establishment of numerous World Heritage Sites, marine reserves and wildlife sanctuaries.

CCC currently has expeditions in Fiji, the Philippines, Malaysia and Honduras. Volunteers can split their time between a marine expedition and a forest expedition: dive some of the world's most biodiverse coral reefs, and then spend time in some of the planet's least disturbed and little-known tropical forests. You must be 16 or over, fit, enthusiastic and hardworking but you don't need a scientific background. Marine expeditions start at £700 and rainforests expeditions start at £550. Scuba training is provided on location if required. Costs include meals, expedition accommodation and full science training. Costs do not include international flights and insurance.

Cross-Cultural Solutions

Tower Point 44
North Road
BN1 1YR Brighton, United Kingdom

Tel: +44 (0) 845 458 2781/2782
Fax: +44 (0) 845 458 0258
www.crossculturalsolutions.org.uk

COMMUNITY, CULTURE, TEACHING,TRAVEL, MEDICAL

Experience a country from a whole new perspective through a Cross-Cultural Solutions' volunteer programme in Brazil, China, Costa Rica, Ghana, Guatemala, India, Peru, Russia, Tanzania or Thailand. Cross-Cultural Solutions' programmes give you the opportunity to work side-by-side with local people on locally designed and driven projects, allowing you to see a country through the eyes of its people. Programmes have a flexible three-part structure designed to ensure you to get the most from your international volunteer experience. Programmes range from two to twelve weeks, with monthly start dates running throughout the year. Longer programmes can be arranged. Programme fees are set in US dollars and vary depending on the length of your stay. The programme fee for a 2-week programme is $2,279 which is approximately £1,250. Each additional week is $259, which is approximately £140. This programme fee covers the costs of lodging, meals and ground transportation, plus individual attention and guidance from an experienced and knowledgeable Programme Manager, coordination of your Volunteer Placement, Perspectives Programming activities, a 24-hour emergency hotline in the US, travel and medical insurance, and much more.

Crusaders

2 Romeland Hill
St Albans, Hertfordshire AL3 4ET, UK

Tel: +44 (0) 1727 855 422
Fax: +44 (0) 1727 848 518

CHILDREN, COMMUNITY, RELIGIOUS

Volunteers, who must be committed Christians and aged between 14-20, stay for two to four weeks between July and August in Central or South America, Africa or Asia. Projects involve practical work (such as building) and working with street children, orphans and other evangelistic projects. Successful candidates need to raise £550 to go to Europe or £1700 (depending on your destination) to cover costs if going to other continents. This includes a contribution to the project you'll be working on.

Discover Nepal

GPO Box: 20209
Kathmandu
Nepal

Tel: +977 1 413690
Fax: +977 1 255487
www.discovernepal.com.np

CULTURE, HISTORY, LANGUAGE, SAFARI, TEACHING, WILDLIFE

Discover Nepal's 2-month long teaching projects give you the chance to really learn about your host country. You start with a comprehensive orientation period; as well as a five-day trek in the Kathmandu Valley and a three-day jungle safari, you'll learn about Nepali history, culture and wildlife, get an introduction to the Nepali language, be shown some basic teaching techniques and be treated to a cultural show with Nepali Cuisine.

You will then be put into mixed-nationality groups and placed in secondary schools to help with teaching English and extra-curricular activities. Programmes start in January, April, and October. The basic cost of participation is around US$1600. This doesn't include flights or insurance. Discover Nepal also offers shorter options such as the 3-day Migratory Bird Festival in January, contact them for more details.

Dorset Expeditionary Society/Leading Edge Expeditions

Lupins Business Centre, 1-3 Greenhill,
Weymouth, Dorset DT4 7SP, UK

Tel: +44 (0) 1305 775 599

COMMUNITY, SAFARI, TRAVEL, EXPEDITIONS

Dorest Expeditionary Society is a registered charity promoting up to six adventurous expeditions each year to remote parts of the world open to all from throughout the UK and can qualify for two sections of the Duke of Edinburgh's Gold Award.

Earthwatch

267 Banbury Road
Oxford, Oxfordshire OX2 7HT, UK

Tel: +44 (0) 1865 318 831
Fax: +44 (0) 01865 311383

ANIMALS, COMMUNITY, CONSERVATION, CULTURE, ENVIRONMENT, RESEARCH/SCIENCE

Fancy doing something a bit different this year - saving hippos in Ghana, monitoring Amazon turtles, or looking for hominids in Southern India? International environmental charity Earthwatch currently offers 140 projects in 50 countries: from endangered ecosystems and biodiversity to archaeology, world health and global change. Paying volunteers are given the opportunity to explore remote, rugged and often little-known parts of the world safely whilst helping scientists to carry out vital conservation and cultural research. Prices range from £120 to £2199. Food, accommodation and training are included but flights are extra. Project teams range from three to twenty days and most expeditions are open to anyone over 16.

Eco Africa Experience

Applications Department
Guardian House, Borough Road,
Godalming, Surrey GU7 2AE, UK

Tel: +44 (0) 1483 860 560
Fax: +44 (0) 1483 860 391
www.EcoAfricaExperience.com

ANIMALS, CONSERVATION, ECO TOURISM, MARINE

Do you want to contribute to conservation in Africa? Eco Africa Experience strives to conserve what man is fast destroying - our very own environment. They send 150+ volunteers to several Southern African game reserves and marine projects per year. They set the standards at the selected reserves in order to maintain a degree of uniformity, thus maintaining a high degree of education, training, learning and general hands on experience while fulfilling the core objective - conservation. Placements range from 4 to 12 weeks, during which you can be involved in conservation projects including anti-poaching patrols, monitoring and counting of wildlife, darting and animal capture, bush rehabilitation and the day-to-day maintenance of the reserve. Marine projects may include rescue and rehabilitation of marine species, sampling, tagging, monitoring of marine life, and participating in commercial marine-eco tourism activities which include whale and dolphin watching tours, sea kayaking, township tours, river ferry cruises. Contact Eco Africa Experience direct for information about specific opportunities and prices.

EIL (Experiment for International Living)

Ostega
287 Worcester Road, Malvern,
Worcestershire WR14 1AB, UK

Tel: 0168 45 62577
Fax: 0168 45 62212

COMMUNITY, CONSERVATION, CULTURE, ENVIRONMENT, FARMING, TEACHING, TRAVEL

EIL sends gappers on voluntary placements around the world and places them with local families. Projects last from six weeks to a year and can include anything from helping local children learn new skills to helping on a local farm. Environment work available in Ecuador, Mexico and Kenya. As well as learning new skills and doing something useful, this could be a great way to meet other gappers from around the world. EIL encourages you to learn the local language and gain knowledge about the local culture.

Espero Language Centre

Szkola Jezykow Obcych 'Espero'
al. Jana Pawla II 17/1,   Tel: +48 77 4838325
47-220 Kedzierzyn-Kozle, Poland   Fax: +48 77 4838325

CULTURE, TEACHING, TRAVEL

If you fancy a more unusual teaching experience, what about Poland? The Espero
Language Centre, 50km from the Czech border in the small town of Kedzierzyn-
Kozle, are keen for 'responsible and cheerful' gap year students to teach English.
You would be teaching 15-20 classes a week, mainly conversational English, to
Polish locals from 3.30pm to 7.30pm. The main cost to you will be your travel to
Poland and a bus pass ($18/month). Accommodation and food are free - you stay
with a local Polish 'host' family, so this would be a great way to experience the
culture and learn about Polish traditions and customs as well as day-to-day life.
Write to Barbara Piechocka, Director of Study, if you are interested. She is happy
to put you in touch with one of the gappers teaching there last year.

Euro Academy

2nd Floor
67 -71 Lewisham High Street,   Tel: +44 (0) 20 8297 0505
Lewisham, London SE13 5JX, UK   Fax: +44 (0) 20 8297 0984

LANGUAGES

Though mainly a language school, Euro Academy also organises voluntary
programmes combined with language in Costa Rica.

Frontier

50-52 Rivington Street
London EC2A 3QP, UK

Tel: +44 (0) 20 7613 2422
Fax: +44 (0) 20 7613 2992

CONSERVATION, ENVIRONMENT

Frontier sends 'flexible and committed' volunteers (minimum age 17) on 4-week, 8-week, 10-week or 20-week conservation expeditions to Madagascar, Tanzania, Nicaragua and Cambodia.

Futuresense Ltd

6 Forest Hill
Great Bedwyn
SN8 3LP Marlborough, UK

Tel: +44 (0) 1672 871 661
Fax: +44 (0) 1672 871 661
www.gapguru.com

CULTURE, TRAVEL, WORK

Can't decide whether to work or travel in your Gap year? Combine both with exciting new programmes organised by Futuresense Limited.

The India experience gives a unique insight into India - whilst improving your CV. Opportunities are available to work with multi-national organisations, gaining a greater understanding of how businesses work and what career you would like in the future. Placements are available all over India, and the best bit? you get paid!

Also included is the chance to learn more about Indian culture with combined volunteer projects, living with an Indian family and working to improve the local community. Time is also taken out for tailor-made travel adventures, giving you a totally exclusive but comprehensive Indian experience.

GAP Activity Projects

GAP House
44 Queen's Road, Reading,
Berkshire RG1 4BB, UK

Tel: +44 (0) 1189 594914
Fax: +44 (0) 1189 576 634

ANIMALS, COMMUNITY, CONSERVATION, CULTURE, DRAMA, ENVIRONMENT, FARMING, RELIGIOUS, TEACHING, TRAVEL, ARCHAEOLOGY, LANGUAGES

GAP now places on average 1200 applicants in 32 countries in a year. Placements vary from three to 12 months and include teaching in schools, caring or medical work, environmental placements and camps and outdoor education.

Gap Challenge

at World Challenge Expeditions
Black Arrow House, 2 Chandos
Road, London NW10 6NF, UK

Tel: +44 (0) 20 8728 7272
+44 (0) 20 8728 7200
www.world-challenge.co.uk

CONSERVATION, FARMING, TEACHING, TRAVEL

Gap Challenge provides individuals aged between 18 and 24 with exciting opportunities to take a well-structured gap year, living and working in one of 12 countries around the world and doing something really constructive in their gap year. It is a highly flexible programme that offers the choice of a variety of rewarding and worthwhile paid or voluntary placements ranging from teaching in Tanzania or conservation work in Costa Rica to paid hotel work in the Canadian Rockies. Placements last for between 2 and 9 months and with a 12-month return flight there is plenty of opportunity for independent travel afterwards. Whilst away, Gap Challengers are offered advice and support from in-country agents and benefit from World Challenge Expedition's comprehensive 24-hour emergency back-up systems.

Gap Sports
Willowbank House
84 Station Road
Marlow, Buckinghamshire SL7 1NX, UK

Tel: +44 (0) 870 837 9797
Fax: +44 (0) 1494 769090
www.gapsportsabroad.co.uk

SPORTS
Giving people the opportunity to play, coach, develop, qualify and instruct in sports (and non-sports) overseas.
GAP SPORTS ABROAD
COMMUNITY, CONSERVATION, DRAMA, TEACHING, TRAVEL, SPORT.
5 weeks, 3-12 months and Summer Camps in South Africa, Ghana and Costa Rica.
GAP SNOWSPORTS
∑• Ski/snowboard instructor courses and adventure training in Canada.
∑• International qualifications, outdoor skills, cultural trips and more.
∑• 6 and 10 week courses for beginners and intermediate.
GAP SPOTRTS ACADEMY
∑• Professional tuition from ex-internationals in cricket, rugby, golf and scuba.
∑• Advance your own game, get qualified and get paid to work worldwide.

GIVE Foundation
613-615, JB Tower, Drive-In Road,
Ahmedabad 380054, Gujarat, India

Tel: +91 79 685 3956/685 5667
Fax: +91 79 685 5610

Give India is a non-profit organisation that sets up voluntary work in India.

Glencree Centre for Reconciliation
Glencree, Enniskerry, Co Wicklow, Republic of Ireland   Tel: +353 1282 9711

COMMUNITY

This centre holds workshops on conflict resolution and is an autonomous non-governmental organisation working 'with everybody who tries to bring peace in whatever area of society'. Call for information about short-term volunteer posts (two months in summer, if you like gardening and cooking) or one-year 'Learn and Serve' posts, all at Glencree.

Global Action Nepal
Baldwins. Eastlands Lane, Cowfold,   Tel: +44 (0) 1403 864704
West Sussex RH13 8AY, UK   Fax: +44 (0) 1403 864088

COMMUNITY, CULTURE, DRAMA, ENVIRONMENT, TEACHING

Global Action Nepal was founded in 1996 to improve the education of children in Nepal. GAN's projects and work are always closely in harness with grass roots level needs, focusing on community-led, participatory development. GAN's main activities in Nepal involve working in government schools for sustainable, long-term improvement that will last well beyond the length of the six months that each volunteer spends there.

Volunteers will spend the majority of their time working on our CITE (Clinic for the Improvement of Teachers of English) programme - a programme which enables Nepali English Teachers to work better within their classrooms and gives them the skills and training which they lack. They will also work in conjuction with Nepalese counterparts, and be pivotal in organising the 'children's club' with activities such as environmental work, drama and cultural activities. GAN offers full training and support to volunteers, and aims to keep costs as low as possible while maximising the use of their time spent in Nepal.

Global Adventures Project
38 Queens Gate   Tel: +44 800 085 4197
SW11 5HR London   Fax: +44 207 7590 7444
United Kingdom   www.globaladventures.co.uk

Global Adventures Project is an exciting new Gap Year programme that allows you to design your own truly unique travel experience abroad. It is being organised as a new division of the American Institute for Foreign Study (AIFS) and will enjoy the benefit of the experience and resources of this worldwide organisation.

For a one-off fee, you get a round-the-world ticket with up to 6 or 10 stops and the opportunity to join up to four of our six core programmes in the USA, Brazil, Europe, South Africa, India and Australia/New Zealand with plenty of time for independent travel in between.

Global Vision International
Amwell Farm House, St Albans,
Hertfordshire AL4 8EJ, UK   Tel: +44 (0) 1582 831 300

ANIMALS, CHILDREN, CONSERVATION, ENVIRONMENT, EXPEDITIONS, RESEARCH/SCIENCE

Global Vision International runs conservation expeditions, research projects and independent voluntary work opportunities around the world.

GVI expeditions offers the adventurous individual the chance to work as part of a structured team or as an independent alongside host country organisations. With projects all over the world you can join expeditions as diverse as: turtle protection programmes in Panama, working with street children in Ecuador and China, rainforest expeditions in South America and pioneering wildlife research expeditions in Africa. Further opportunities run all over the world, no experience is necessary and expeditions depart all year round and run from 2 weeks to 12 months.

Global Volunteer Network

| PO Box 2231 | Tel: 0800 096 7864 |
| Wellington, New Zealand | Fax: +64 4 569 9081 |

COMMUNITY, CULTURE, ENVIRONMENT, TEACHING

The Global Volunteer Network supports local community organizations in developing countries through the placement of international volunteers.

Global Volunteers

| 375 East Little Canada Road | Tel: +1 (800) 487-1074 |
| St. Paul, MN 55117-1628, USA | Fax: +1 (651) 482-0915 |

ANIMALS, COMMUNITY, CONSERVATION, CULTURE, ENVIRONMENT

Global volunteers provide gappers with the chance to work on one of over 70 different projects from across the world. The work is hard but very rewarding, and the variety of different projects is very large, from repairing old school houses in third world countries to social work within a Native American village. Costs are around £500 for two weeks, and that includes travel, food and accommodation.

Greenforce

11-15 Betterton Street	Tel: +44 (0) 870 770 2646 / +44 (0) 20 7470 8888
Covent Garden	Fax: +44 (0) 870 7702647 / +44 (0) 20 7470 8889
London WC2H 9BP, UK	www.greenforce.org

ANIMALS, CONSERVATION, ENVIRONMENT, RESEARCH/SCIENCE

Greenforce runs a series of 10-week marine and terrestrial expeditions around the world, all of which are based on wildlife conservation. No previous experience is necessary as they train all volunteers from scratch, and marine volunteers get free diver training.

Choose from tracking large mammals in Zambia, investigating the tree canopy of the Amazon rainforest, or diving the coral reefs of the Bahamas, Fiji or Borneo. There are opportunities to collect data towards a dissertation (provided you agree the topic prior to the expedition). You will learn a wide range of fieldwork techniques, and can get involved in taxonomic classification and data analysis. If you're thinking of developing a career in conservation, ask about the traineeship scheme. Expedition life can be a challenge - be prepared to live a spartan existence, and to pull your weight in a small, well-organised team.

Gwendalyne

| 67-71 Lewisham High Street | Tel: +44 (0)20 8297 3251 |
| SE13 5JX London, United Kingdom | Fax: +44 (0)20 8297 0984 |

Gwendalyne can offer you volunteering programmes in Costa Rica, Peru and South Africa. Choose among conservation projects, Support people in need, help orphans, assist hurt wild animals, or develop new projects.

Habitat for Humanity (Great Britain)
11 Parsons Street
Banbury, Oxfordshire OX16 5LW, UK

Tel: +44 (0) 1295 264240 ext.208
Fax: +44 (0) 1295 264230

COMMUNITY, CULTURE

The Habitat for Humanity's Global Village programme is sending over 25 teams all over the world, including Romania, Zambia, Sri Lanka, Poland and South Africa, to build housing for and with the local population. This is a real way to get to talk to local people from a completely different culture. The aim is not only to provide homes, but also to raise awareness of the need for low cost housing. They are particularly looking for team leaders - training is given. Programmes last for between 3 and 4 weeks. The Habitat for Humanity programmes (such as the Jimmy Carter Work Project, where Jimmy Carter and his wife pitch in with building homes in Africa) are known for their upbeat atmosphere. You can either go along on your own, or make up a team with friends. You do have to pay for your own trip, and costs obviously vary according to location.

Himalayan Light Foundation
GPO Box 1219, Kathmandu, Nepal

Tel: +977 (1) 420 842

COMMUNITY, COMPUTER

The Himalayan Light Foundation (HLF) is a Kathmandu-based non-profit NGO (non-governmental organisation) working to make renewable energy technologies more accessible to rural Nepal. HLF organises programmes that link energy with education, and income-generating activities such as sewing and weaving. Volunteers donate funds to cover a solar electricity system and their in-country costs, then travel to Nepal to install the solar panels themselves after a training course (no prior knowledge of solar power is necessary). Twenty extra systems were installed in a Bongadovan village in one month. Each project is two weeks long and costs about £830. In addition, HLF itself welcomes volunteers who can commit to full-time work for at least five months. Work involves project coordination and development; computer literacy is essential and you have to bring a laptop computer. Volunteers are based in Kathmandu, with occasional field trips into rural Nepal, and cover their own food and accommodation costs, though HLF can help organise a stay with a Nepali family. HLF asks volunteers to contribute £105 to the organisation.

HiPACT
PO Box 770
York House, Empire Way, Wembley,
Middlesex HA9 0PA, UK

Tel: +44 (0) 208 900 1221
Fax: +44 (0) 208 900 0330

COMMUNITY, TEACHING

HiPACT is an association of British universities which aims to widen participation in higher education. It offers opportunities to volunteer both in the UK and abroad. HiPACT has a long-term project in Nigeria, where you could find yourself supporting teachers, development officers or admin staff in local primary and secondary schools. The programme usually lasts between four and 12 weeks between July and September. You pay no fees to HiPACT - you'll have find the money for your flights, insurance, vaccinations and any spending money, but food and accommodation (with local host families, in anything from a jungle hut to a local government official's residence) will be provided for free. HiPACT is keen to emphasise that there is no commitment for you to fundraise - although if you choose to, they're unlikely to stand in your way!

ICYE (Inter Cultural Youth Exchange)

Latin America House
Kingsgate Place
London NW6 4TA, UK

Tel: +44 (0) 20 7681 0983
Fax: +44 (0) 20 7681 0983
www.icye.co.uk

COMMUNITY, CONSERVATION, CHILDREN, CULTURE, ENVIRONMENT,
HUMAN RIGHTS, TEACHING

Do you fancy spending a year abroad getting to know another country and its
culture? Each year ICYE sends young people aged between 18 and 30 to work in
voluntary projects overseas in Africa, Asia, Europe and South America. Volunteers
work in a range of projects including counselling centres, human rights NGOs,
farms, orphanages and schools for the disabled. No specific qualifications,
experience or language skills are required. Instead they are looking for people who
are willing to learn new skills, open to new experiences and committed to intercultural understanding.

Interserve

325 Kennington Road
London SE11 4QH, UK

Tel: +44 (0) 20 7735 8227
Fax: +44 (0) 20 7820 5950

CHILDREN, COMMUNITY, RELIGIOUS

Interserve is a self-financing international missionary society, working mainly in
Asia (Bangladesh, India, Mongolia, Nepal) and in the Arab world. Their gap year
programme 'On Track' places volunteers with local churches and organisations in
a variety of roles.

Interspeak

Stretton Lower Hall
Stretton, Nr. Malpas,
South Cheshire SY14 7HS, UK

Tel: +44 (0) 1829 250 641
Fax: +44 (0) 1829 250596

ANIMALS, COMMUNITY, CONSERVATION, CULTURE, DRAMA, ENVIRONMENT,
TRAVEL

Interspeak organises unpaid work placements in France, Germany and Spain from
between one and six months. You pay a registration fee of £80 up front, then a flat
fee of £320 for arranging the placement. Interspeak will also organise a family for
you to stay with, although you can make your own plans if you prefer. Placement
jobs vary widely, but Interspeak says it can find placements in banking, law,
marketing, media, hotels and restaurants - citing one student working in a fashion
photography studio in France and another for a radio station in Spain.

i-to-i

Woodside House
261 Low Lane
Leeds LS18 5NY, UK

Tel: +44 (0) 870 333 2332
Fax: +44 (0) 113 205 4619
www.i-to-i.com

ANIMALS, COMMUNITY, CONSERVATION, ENVIRONMENT, TEACHING, TRAVEL

i-to-i's volunteer work placements, known as Ventures, are all about cultural
immersion and last from 1 week to 12 months. There are over 300 projects in 24
countries in a variety of schools, orphanages, hospitals, colleges and conservation
centres. You could be reading the news on Radio Ghana or replanting saplings in
the Ecuadorian rainforests. English teaching i-Ventures are available in Bolivia,
China, Costa Rica, Ecuador, Ghana, Honduras, India, Guatemlala, Kenya, Mexico,
Tanzania, Brazil, Vietnam, the Dominican Republic, Peru, Mongolia, Nepal, Sri

Lanka, South Korea (a paid placement) and Thailand; and there are conservation ventures in Croatia, Brazil, Peru, Dominican Republic, Australia, Kenya, Guatemala, Mexico, Tanzania, Bolivia, Costa Rica, Ecuador, Ghana, Honduras, India, Ireland, South Africa, Sri Lanka and Thailand. i-to-i also provides internships in journalism, media and health. For added variety, you can also combine two projects in the same or different countries. Fees for placements range from £495 and include comprehensive insurance, global staff support network, predeparture preparation, TEFL training, airport pick-up, food and accommodation (in most cases).

IVCS
12 Eastleigh Avenue
South Harrow,
Middlesex HA2 0UF, United Kingdom

Tel: +44 (0)20-8864 4740
Fax: +44 (0)20-8930 8338

COMMUNITY, ENVIRONMENT, RURAL DEVELOPMENT
IVCS is a small UK registered charity supporting sustainable development projects in rural India.

IVS (International Voluntary Service)
Old Hall
East Bergholt, Colchester, Essex CO7 6TQ, UK

Tel: +44 (0) 1206 298 215
www.ivs-gb.org.uk

CHILDREN, CONSERVATION, COMMUNITY, SPECIAL NEEDS
IVS exchanges volunteers with over 40 countries, mainly for international voluntary projects (living and working with a group on 2-4 week projects).

Kibbutz Representatives
16 Accommodation Road,
London NW11 8ED, UK

Tel: +44 (0) 20 8458 9235

CHILDREN, FARMING, MANUAL WORK

Kibbutz Representatives is officially part of the kibbutz movement. If you are 18-42 and both physically and mentally fit, KR will organise a place for you either as an individual or as a group.

Kings World Trust for Children
7 Deepdene
Haslemere, Surrey GU27 1RE, UK

Tel: +44 (0) 1428 653504
Fax: +44 (0) 1428 653504

COMMUNITY, FARMING, TEACHING

The Kings World Trust for Children is a UK-based charity which aims to provide a caring home, an education and skills training for orphaned and homeless children and young people in South India.

Language Courses Abroad
67 Ashby Road
Loughborough, Leicestershire
LE11 3AA, UK

Tel: +44 (0) 1509 211612
Fax: +44 (0) 1509 260037

COMMUNITY, HEALTH, LANGUAGES

Language Courses Abroad can arrange for you to do volunteer work alongside some of its language courses, both in Europe and in Latin America. For instance, if you go on a 4-week language course in Guatemala, the company will help arrange volunteer work in local hospitals, orphanages or community projects for a few hours after class each day.

L'Arche
GY/04
Freepost BD 3209
Keighley, West Yorkshire BD20 9BR, UK

Tel: +44 (0) 800 917 1337
Fax: +44 (0) 1535 656426
www.larche.org.uk

COMMUNITY, RELIGIOUS, CARING

L'Arche (French for 'The Ark') began as a small community in a house in Trosly-Breuil in France more than 30 years ago and is now an international movement with 120 communities in 30 countries. Its aim is to provide local communities - a cluster of houses, usually within walking distance of each other and with access to a workshop - for adults with learning disabilities. The work could be weaving, for example, or making candles. L'Arche is 'shaped and guided by the major Christian denominations', but internationally it is multi-faith, predominantly that of the local area. Volunteer 'assistants' are welcome both for its centres in the UK and abroad, to share life with those who need help to learn. To volunteer abroad you need to contact communities in different countries separately, as they will have different requirements - a list of all L'Arche communities worldwide is available.

111

Latin Link Step Teams
Latin Link
175 Tower Bridge Road, SE1 2AB
London, UK

Tel: +44 (0) 20 7939 9014
Fax: +44 (0) 20 7939 9015

COMMUNITY, CULTURE, DRAMA, RELIGIOUS TRAVEL, EVANGELISM

Latin Link sends teams to work in mission with Latin American Christians every spring, from March to July (£2300), and summer, for seven weeks (£1800).

Madventurer
Adamson House
65 Westgate Road,
Newcastle upon Tyne NE1 1SG, UK

Tel: +44 (0) 845 121 1996
www.madventurer.com

COMMUNITY, CONSERVATION, CULTURE, ENVIRONMENT, SAFARI, TEACHING, TRAVEL

Madventurer programmes are flexible and are aimed at gap year students, undergraduates, recent graduates and career breakers. You can choose to join a 5-week or 3-month group project.

Mad Group Projects include building projects, teaching and coaching opportunities, medical placements, environmental projects and tourism projects run in rural areas. They depart throughout the year to Ghana, Togo, Kenya, Uganda, Tanzania, Peru, Bolivia and Trinidad & Tobago. Group Projects cost £1180 for 5 weeks, this includes all food, accommodation, airport pick-up, transfers to the project site, the full support of your Mad Crew, back-up from Mad HQ in the UK and a £200 donation to project materials.

On a 3-month project you also have the opportunity to gain experience in architecture, journalism, media, physiotherapy, care work, law, business and other professional disciplines. 3-month projects cost £1880. Prices include all food, accommodation, airport pick-up, transfers to the project, the full support of your Mad Coordinator, back-up from Mad HQ in the UK.

Madventurer also offers Combo Expedition, which combines project work with community tourism, allowing you to travel around your host country (or countries) and, in return, giving something back to the people. The cost of a Combo Expedition is simply the cost of the Adventure and Project combined (see Madventurer listing in Travel companies).

Marlborough Brandt Group
1a London Road
Marlborough, Wiltshire SN8 1PH, UK

Tel: +44 (0) 1672 514 078
Fax: +44 (0) 1672 514 922

CHILDREN, COMMUNITY, TEACHING

MBG was set up as a link between Marlborough and the village of Gunjur in the Gambia, and has been sending volunteers (from the UK and beyond) to teaching and rural development projects there since 1984. Individual volunteers (you don't have to come from Marlborough) go out for up to six months to the school or to work with TARUD, the local rural development NGO. Selection is by interview; two training weekends are held to prepare volunteers, and there's an induction course on arrival in Gunjur. Costs: about £1500 for the three-month placement and £3000 for the six-month one, all inclusive. MBG say this is a good way to 'experience total immersion in African culture'.

MondoChallenge

Galliford Building
Milton Malsor
NN7 3AB Northampton, UK

Tel: +44 (0) 1604 858225
Fax: +44 (0) 1604 859323
www.mondochallenge.org

COMMUNITY, TEACHING, ORPHANS/STREET CHILDREN, TEACHING,
BUSINESS DEVELOPMENT, WOMEN'S GROUPS, HEALTHCARE

MondoChallenge is a not-for-profit organisation sending volunteers - mostly post-university and career-breakers - to teach in primary and secondary schools in Nepal, North India (Darjeeling and Ladakh known as 'Little Tibet'), Sri Lanka, Tanzania, The Gambia, Kenya and Chile. It is worth noting that the majority of MondoChallenge's volunteers are post-university and career breakers (couples are welcome). Business development programmes are also offered. However Mondo does accept a select few pre-university gap year candidates each year.

The organisation offers three month community-based programmes (flexible from two-six months) giving volunteers the opportunity to learn from, as well as help the local people. Departure dates are at various times of the year and are totally flexible. You make your own travel arrangements and if you want you can spend a little longer by combining two projects, either be in the same country or moving on to another country, or even continent! The cost of around £800 (based on a three-month project) does not include travel. Accommodation is also not included but is organised by MondoChallenge in local families at very low cost.

Oceanic Marine Conservation

Lot 27
Ground floor
Wisma Sabah, Jln haji Saman, 88000,
Kota Kinabula, Sabah, Malaysia

Tel: +60 88256483
Fax: +60 88256483
www.omsf.org

Check out their website for details of their voluntary programmes.

Outreach International

Bartlett's Farm
Hayes Road, Compton Dundon,
Somerset TA11 6PF, UK

Tel: +44 (0) 1458 274957
www.outreachinternational.co.uk

ANIMALS, COMMUNITY, CONSERVATION, ENVIRONMENT,
RESEARCH/SCIENCE, TEACHING, TRAVEL, HUMANITARIAN

Outreach International Projects in Cambodia include working in orphanages, helping a programme for street children, running a centre for landmine and polio victims and teaching English, games and computer skills to the disabled. There are opportunities for both GAP year students and also older people taking a career break.

Projects in Mexico are on the Pacific coast and include conservation work with giant sea turtles & whales. Also working with an eco-tourism company, teaching in coastal schools, helping at an orphanage, running an art, craft & dance project and helping at special needs schools. These projects are ideal for volunteers wishing to immerse themselves in a foreign culture for a period of three or four months and by implication learn Spanish. Outreach offers full training, a language course and full in-country support. There are also a variety of humanitarian and conservation projects in Ecuador.

Outreach International is committed to cross-cultural exchange and education. It combines the desire of young people to travel and work in voluntary projects overseas with the needs of local communities.

Peace River Refuge & Ranch

PO Box 1127, 2545 Stoner Lane,
Zolfo Springs, FL 33890, USA

Tel: +1 863 735 0804

ANIMALS, ENVIRONMENT

Peace River Refuge & Ranch is a non-profit-making exotic animal sanctuary located in Florida. Its all-volunteer staff provides long-term care for confiscated, abused, neglected or unwanted exotic animals (from tigers to bats) to prevent them from being destroyed. Guided tours of the sanctuary are given to educate others about the cruelty that many exotic animals undergo in captivity and the plight of their wild counterparts. Contact the refuge direct for information about fees and accommodation.

People Tree Gap Year Company

105 Westbourne Terrace
W2 6QT London
UK

Tel: +44 (0) 20 7402 557
Fax: +44 (0) 20 7262 7561
www.gapyearinindia.com

COMMUNITY, CONSERVATION, CULTURE, DRAMA, ENVIRONMENT, SAFARI, TEACHING, TRAVEL, WORK PLACEMENTS

People Tree Gap Year Company gives you the chance to experience your dream gap year anywhere in India, Nepal and Sri Lanka. Whether you want to teach, work in conservation, learn to ride an elephant, work in the fashion industry, become a

DJ, or just travel, they are happy to organise it for you. Just tell them your ideas and they will help you design your own unique gap year. Alternatively they run five programmes: teaching placements, conservation placements, work experience placements, learning skills placements and gap year travel. You could mix and match any or all aspects of these placements.

Phenomena Academy

PO Box 225
Te Anau, New Zealand

Tel: +64 (0) 3249 00 88
Fax: +64 (0) 3249 00 87

COMMUNITY, CULTURE

Phenomena Academy has a slightly different approach to volunteering: their aim, through the 30-week Life Design Foundation Course, is to teach you how to approach, enjoy and succeed in life in a completely different way, based on ancient Chinese ideas. An important part of the course is that you will help to build a new health centre for the local community.

Based at Takaro Lodge (where they filmed part of Lord of the Rings) on South Island, the Academy's facilities include a cyber café, a digital cinema, sports facilities and an indoor swimming pool. You can also swim or fish in the nearby river. The course costs US$12,000, half of which is donated to the Health Trust. The price includes accommodation in twin rooms at Takaro Lodge or in Te Anau. Scholarships are available, and the Academy offers a full support service for those who need to fundraise. Courses begin in January, March, June and September.

Project Trust

The Hebridean Centre
Isle of Coll, Argyll PA78 6TE, Scotland

Tel: +44 (0) 1879 230 444
www.projecttrust.org.uk

COMMUNITY, CULTURE, DRAMA, TEACHING, TRAVEL, SOCIAL WORK, MEDICAL, OUTWARD BOUND, DEVELOPMENT

Project Trust offers 12-month placements in over 20 countries across Africa, Latin America, the Middle East, the Caribbean and South and East Asia, departing in August or September. There are also some 8 month placements available on the Winter Programme, departing in January. Projects include teaching English, teaching A level/Higher subjects, work in children's homes, social work, outdoor activities instruction, journalism, conservation and medical projects.

Project Trust places great emphasis on getting the right volunteer in the right project. All applicants attend a 5-day selection course at the headquarters on the Isle of Coll and successful candidates return for a 5- or 6-day briefing and training course in July. Volunteers are expected to raise £3950 from sponsors. This covers selection, training, support overseas, flights, medical insurance, accommodation, food and a small living allowance, and debriefing on return. All volunteers receive ample holiday time to travel and to explore the region they are based in. Apply by Christmas 2005 for departure in August 2006.

Quest Overseas

North West Stables
Borde Hill Estate
Hayward's Heath, West Sussex RH16 1XP, UK

Tel: +44 (0) 1444 47 47 44
Fax: +44 (0) 1444 47 47 99
www.questoverseas.com

ANIMALS, COMMUNITY, CULTURE, ENVIRONMENT, RESEARCH/SCIENCE, SAFARI, TRAVEL, LANGUAGES

Quest Overseas specialise in professionally managed projects and expeditions in

116

Africa and South America.

Gap Year Quest - Three month combined Project and Expedition (and one to one Language Training in South America) - teams aged 18 to 21 - departing between January and April

Expedition Quest - Two and six week Expeditions - teams of Gap Year and University Students - departing June and July

Project Quest - Four to eight week Projects & Placements - teams and individual placements - teams departing June and July

In their tenth year of operations Quest Overseas have four exciting new projects:

Mangueira - children's project and Rio de Janeiro carnival;

Kenya Water Relief Project - small scale water dams and tree planting;

Cairu - safeguarding primary Atlantic rainforest in Brazil;

Namuncahue - Chilean Lake District monkey puzzle forest conservation;

Football Quest - Brazilian football academy and series of friendlies.

Raleigh International

Raleigh House	Tel: +44 (0) 20 7371 8585
27 Parsons Green Lane	Fax: +44 (0) 20 7371 5116
London SW6 4HZ, UK	www.raleighinternational.org

ADVENTURE, COMMUNIOTY, CONSERVATION, CULTURE, ENVIRONMENT, EXPEDITIONS, RESEARCH/SCIENCE, TRAVEL, YOUTH DEVELOPMENT

A Raleigh International is truly unique. You get to choose where and when you go. Additionally you get to choose from a four or seven week Explorer programme or our ten week Expeditions programme. During these periods you complete from one to three different types of projects, environmental, community and adventure. Best of all you get to choose which types you complete. These are developed in partnership with local communities and NGOs to ensure they are both worthwhile and sustainable. We currently have programmes in Malaysia, Chile, Costa Rica and Nicaragua, Fiji, and Namibia. In just a matter of months you could be trekking in Chile, diving in Costa Rica, or building much needed educational facilities in Namibia. 28,000 people have shared this experience. This is your chance.

Rempart

| 1 rue des Guillemites | Tel: +33 (0) 1 42 71 96 55 |
| 75004, Paris, France | Fax: +33 (0) 1 42 71 73 00 |

CONSERVATION, HISTORY, MANUAL WORK

Rempart, a union of conservation associations in France, organises short voluntary work schemes around the world. The projects are all based around restoration and maintenance of historic sites and buildings, from glamorous French chateaux to a garden in Vietnam. You need some previous experience and to be prepared to work hard - usually for 30-35 hours per week. Expect to pay about £10 per day to cover food and lodging, depending on where you are placed. Rempart is strictly a French company, so don't expect to be able to organise the trip in English - you'll need to use appropriate language skills wherever you are on your project.

Senevolu
Senegal

Tel: +221 550 48 85
Fax: +221 855 71 72

COMMUNITY, CULTURE, LANGUAGE, TEACHING

The minimum stay for Senevolu's Volunteer Homestay programme is four weeks, but you can stay as long as a year. During the first five days volunteers stay at a hostel for an orientation period which includes immersion in the Senegalese culture, language courses (French/Wolof) and excursions in the surroundings of Dakar. Volunteers then move to a host family where they participate in all-day activities: trips, celebrations, ataya etc. During the week volunteers work in NGOs (non-governmental organisations), public services, community projects, or primary schools. During the weekend Senevolu organises cultural workshops (African dancing, cooking, djembé, kora, batik etc). Senevolu is also happy to organise weekend excursions for groups of five or more.

Smallpeice Trust
Holly House
74 Upper Holly Walk,
Leamington Spa,
Warwickshire CV32 4JL, United Kingdom

Tel: +44 (0) 1926 333200
Fax: +44 (0) 1926 333202

ENGINEERING, LANGUAGE, WORK PLACEMENT

118

Rachel Wilde, 18, gap year student

My brother went on a Raleigh International expedition in Chile and the stories that I heard certainly whet my appetite for travel and adventure - Raleigh style, and by that I mean I wanted more than just an extended sightseeing trip. What Raleigh could provide was a diverse experience with the chance to work on so many different and worthwhile projects and to meet people from a range of backgrounds. Before signing on the dotted line I had a look at other organisations to see what the competition had on offer but it didn't stand up against Raleigh.

I tried not to have any expectations of what the expedition would be like - I'd never done anything like this before so it was almost impossible to imagine anyway - I just knew I would enjoy it but be challenged at the same time - mentally and physically. I also wanted to travel (but not to spend a whole year wandering aimlessly) and starting my gap year with something structured would give me more confidence to carry on. I suppose if I did have expectations at all, they were that I would have been more uncomfortable for more of the time. I think that for most of this expedition the weather has been kind!

I have done things that have made me feel very proud this expedition - from installing the plumbing in the medical centre we refurbished to building a path up a steep mountain. On a personal level, I have learned how to work with a group of people having just met them and how to be a person for others to lean on when they need a shoulder.

Time on expedition is time speeded up! I have got to know people in three weeks better than some of my friends from back home that I've know since primary school - it really is incredible. And the days whiz by - partly because each one is so different to the one before and almost every day I am learning something new, and also because there is always some challenge to overcome or problem to solve to keep the mind engaged.

There have been challenges, of course. Working out how best to get on and work with people who have such different opinions to mine. It has helped me to put pettiness into perspective and I can now take a more mature approach to teamwork and get on and work with people even if we disagree.

I will remember Chile as being a place I was very happy in - always laughing and meeting wonderful people. The Chileans have been so warm and welcoming and the Raleigh volunteers have been such fun to spend three months with. Chile is such a beautiful country.

A Raleigh expedition is hard work, emotionally and physically, but the environment is so supportive that you feel you can get over any difficulties - and the rewards are huge. I've had a fantastic time.

119

The Smallpeice Trust runs the European Engineering Foundation Programme, a gap year for students who defer their entry to university on an engineering-related degree course.

SPW (Students Partnership Worldwide)

17 Dean's Yard   Tel: +44 (0) 20 7222 0138

COMMUNITY, CONSERVATION, ENVIRONMENT, HEALTH

Each year SPW recruits, trains and supports nearly 300 volunteers aged 18-28 to work on various health education or environment projects in partnership with local volunteers.

STEN (Save the Earth Network)

PO Box CT 3635   Tel: +233 21 667791
Cantonments-Accra, Ghana   Fax: +233 21 669625

CULTURE, CONSERVATION, ENVIRONMENT, ECO/CULTURAL TOURISM, FARMING, TEACHING

STEN organises voluntary placements in Ghana in line with its policy for promoting sustainable development, agro-forestry, environmental conservation, eco-tourism and cultural tourism. Their aim is to help reduce poverty, hunger, malnutrition, disease, illiteracy, drug abuse, unemployment, and environmental degradation whilst offering travellers the most socially responsible, exciting and affordable alternative to mass tourism. You could find yourself teaching English to primary kids, educating local youth on the dangers of drug abuse or planting fruit trees at an agro-forestry farm.

Placements last between one and four months (you can stay longer if you're teaching) and cost between £100 and £175. Accommodation is with local host families and food is mainly Ghanian dishes - this is true immersion in Ghanian culture. You may well spend your whole placement without contact with another European. According to gappers who've been on STEN placements, the director, Eben Mensak, is one of the friendliest people you'll meet, but admin and organisation is relaxed and you may not know what or where your placment is until you arrive in Ghana. These placements are for gappers who are mature, independent and able to stand on their own two feet. Eben can be reached by e-mail at ebensten@yahoo.com if you don't want to phone Ghana!

Svezhy Veter Travel Agency

Karla Marxa 228-a
Izhevsk 426057, Russia

Tel: +7 (3412) 45 00 37
Fax: +7 (3412) 45 00 38

TEACHING

Svezhy Veter Travel Agency, based in Izhevsk in Russia, places teachers at a local school. You'll be teaching for up to 15 hours a week, both during the day (7-17 year-olds) and in the evening (13-45 year-olds).

Teaching & Projects Abroad

Aldsworth Parade
Goring
Sussex BN12 4TX, UK

Tel: +44 (0) 1903 708300
Fax: +44 (0) 1903 501026
www.teaching-abroad.co.uk

ANIMALS, COMMUNITY, CONSERVATION, ENVIRONMENT, RESEARCH/SCIENCE, SAFARI, TEACHING, TRAVEL

Teaching & Projects Abroad organises voluntary work placements, mostly teaching, in such far flung places as Bolivia, Chile, China, Ghana, India, Mexico, Mongolia, Nepal, Peru, Romania, Russia, Senegal, South Africa, Sri Lanka, Swaziland, Thailand and Togo.

Other voluntary work opportunities include medicine, veterinary medicine, social work, archaeology, conservation, business and architecture. There is a range of business opportunities in Shanghai, including advertising, human resources, electronics, engineering, IT, accountancy and finance. The medical placements (in China, India, Ghana, Mexico, Mongolia and Romania) include anything from dentistry to physiotherapy. Placements start any time and last from one month to a year. Costs range from £995 to around £1800, and include food, lodging, travel, insurance and local back-up. Teaching & Projects Abroad holds several open days so you can meet staff and previous volunteers.

The Leap Overseas Ltd

121 High Street
Marlborough, Wiltshire SN8 1LZ, UK

Tel: 0870 240 4187
Fax: +44 (0) 1672 519944

ANIMALS, COMMUNITY, CONSERVATION, ENVIRONMENT, SAFARI, TRAVEL

The leap organises voluntary placements in Kenya, Tanzania, Malawi, Botswana, Namibia, South Africa, Zambia and Nepal for gappers and 'career breakers'. Placements are in bush camps, safari lodges, private ranches and boutique hotels, situated in game parks, conservation areas, bush and coastal locations.

The Year Out Group
Queensfield
28 King's Road, Easterton,
Wiltshire SN10 4PX, UK

Tel: +44 (0) 7980 395789
www.yearoutgroup.org

ANIMALS, COMMUNITY, CONSERVATION, CULTURE, DRAMA, ENVIRONMENT, RELIGIOUS, RESEARCH/SCIENCE, TEACHING, TRAVEL

The Year Out Group is an association of leading Year Out organisations that was formed in 1998 to promote the concept and benefits of well-structured year out programmes, to promote models of good practice and to help young people and their advisers in selecting suitable and worthwhile projects. In 2003, the then 28 members of the Group accounted for 23,000 structured year out placements. There are now 32 members (listed below) with several applications in the pipeline.

The Group's member organisations provide a wide range of Year Out placements in the UK and overseas that cover courses and cultural exchanges, expeditions, volunteering and structured work placements. All members have agreed to adhere to the Group's Code of Practice and more detailed operational standards for each of the four sectors mentioned above all of which were published in the website. The Group's website also contains guidelines for students and advisers. These include questions that potential 'gappers' should ask providing organisations as they look for the programme that best suits their needs. Year Out Group monitors information published by its members for accuracy.

Year Out Group members are expected to put potential clients and their parents in contact with those that have recently returned. Year Out Group considers it important that these references are taken up at least by telephone and, where possible, by meeting face to face. Group members include their complaints procedure in their contracts. Year Out Group can advise on making complaints but is not itself able to deal with them. Nor is Year Out Group able to 'police' the 22,000 placements provided by its members but it can take action if any member is shown to be consistently negligent.

There will always be less-than-perfect organisations among members of a trade association and good ones that are not. There are some small specialist organisations with excellent reputations that cannot afford the membership fees. Whether or not an organisation is a member of Year Out Group, the questions in the student guidelines can be used to advantage.

Year Out Group Membership (January 2004): Academic Year in the USA & Europe; Asia Venture; Africa Conservation Experience; Art History Abroad; BSES Expeditions; BUNAC; CESA Languages Abroad; Coral Cay Conservation; Council Exchanges; CSV (Community Service Volunteers); Flying Fish; Frontier Conservation; GAP Activity Projects; Gap Challenge/World Challenge Expeditions; Greenforce; i-to-i International Projects; Outreach International; Project Trust; Quest Overseas; Raleigh International; Students Partnership Worldwide; Teaching & Projects Abroad; Travellers Worldwide; Trekforce Expeditions; The International Academy; The Smallpeice Engineering Gap year; The Year in Industry; Year Out Drama.

Time for God

2 Chester House
Pages Lane, Muswell Hill,
London N10 1PR, UK

Tel: +44 (0) 20 8883 1504
Fax: +44 (0) 20 8365 2471

COMMUNITY, CONSERVATION, CULTURE, ENVIRONMENT, RELIGIOUS,
YOUTH WORK, CARE WORK

Time for God co-ordinates national and international projects, including youth and community work, homeless and rehabilitation projects in the UK, USA, Europe, Australia, Ghana etc. Start dates are January and September. Fees apply.

Travellers Worldwide

7 Mulberry Close
Ferring
West Sussex BN12 5HY, UK

Tel: +44 (0) 1903 502595
Fax: +44 (0) 1903 500364
www.travellersworldwide.com

CONSERVATION, TEACHING, WORK PLACEMENTS

Travellers provides voluntary placements overseas. Volunteers don't need any qualifications apart from enthusiasm, dedication and a sense of humour. The projects include Teaching, Conservation, Work Experience and Community Development, as well as Language and Cultural courses. Prices start at £895 (excluding airfare) for three months, though placements can last for any length of time from two weeks to one year. Placements are currently available in Argentina, Brazil, Brunei/Borneo, China, Cuba, Ghana, Guatemala, India, Kenya, Malaysia, Nepal, Russia, South Africa, Sri Lanka, Ukraine, Vietnam and Zimbabwe; the list of couintries and projects is ever expanding.

Examples of programmes include:

Teaching projects: English, IT, football, music, drama workshops.

Conservation: working with orang-utans, elephants, lions, rhinos, dolphins, coral and plants.

Work Experience: law, journalism, medicine, veterinary, tourism, radio.

Language courses: Spanish, Russian, Mandarin,

plus: Tango, photography, music.

Most importantly, Travellers Worldwide tailors placements to individual requirements - just let them know what you want and they will see what they can do for you.

Trekforce Expeditions

34 Buckingham Palace Road
London SW1W 0RE
UK

Tel: +44 (0) 20 7828 2275
Fax: +44 (0) 20 7828 2276
www.trekforce.org.uk

COMMUNITY, CONSRVATION, CULTURE, ENVIRONMENT,
RESEARCH/SCIENCE, TEACHING, TRAVEL

Trekforce is a long-established charity that organises adventurous 8-20 week expeditions to Central and South America and East Malaysia. Working with local partners, their projects concentrate on rainforest conservation, scientific research and local communities. Their extended programmes of three to five months combine working as a team to complete a valuable project with additional optional phases of learning Spanish in a second country and teaching in a rural community. Applications are welcome throughout the year.

UNA Exchange

Temple of Peace
Cathays Park, CF10 3AP Cardiff, Wales

Tel: +44 (0) 29 202 23088
Fax: +44 (0) 29 20222540

COMMUNITY, CONSERVATION, CULTURE, ENVIRONMENT

UNA Exchange arranges international volunteer projects in over 60 countries: from Armenia to Zambia. Projects last 2-3 weeks and include environmental protection, construction, renovation, organising arts and cultural events, and projects working with disadvantaged children, refugees, and people with special needs.

VAE Kenya

c/o Simon C D Harris (Director)

Tel: +44 (0) 1568 750 329

COMMUNITY, TEACHING

VAE Kenya places well-motivated school leavers or graduates as volunteer teachers in extremely poor, rural schools experiencing a shortage of local staff and resources.

Ventureco Worldwide

The Ironyard
64-66 The Market Place
Warwick, CV34 4SD, UK

Tel: +44 (0) 1926 411 122
Fax: +44 (0) 1926 411 133
www.ventureco-worldwide.com

ANIMALS, COMMUNITY, CONSERVATION, CULTURE, ENVIRONMENT, SAFARI, TRAVEL

VentureCo's concept: is the ideal travel combination for Gap Year and Career Gap travellers who want to explore off the beaten track, learn about the host country while they are there and give something back before they return home. Each Venture combines three modules in one massive four-month programme: language school, voluntary work and a wilderness expedition.

South & Central America

Inca Venture (Ecuador, Peru, Bolivia and Chile)
Patagonia Venture (Peru, Bolivia, Chile, Argentina and Tierra del Fuego)
Aztec & Maya Venture (Guatemala, Belize, Mexico, Cuba and Costa Rica)

Africa

Rift Valley Venture (Kenya, Uganda and Tanzania)

Southeast Asia

Himalaya Venture (India and Nepal)
Indochina Venture (Cambodia, Vietnam, Laos and China)

Experienced VentureCo Leaders accompany each team of between 10 and 16; preparation gets under way ten weeks before departure from the UK with a build-up weekend; full in-country expedition training is provided. Planning, leadership and organising roles throughout the Venture are shared amongst the team and each Venturer will lead a leg of the expedition.

As expedition travel professionals our price is all-inclusive (the build-up weekend, international flights, personal travel insurance, taxes, trekking permits & mountain fees, language tuition, all expedition activities, aid project donation and all domestic flights/travel are included). We have no kitties and no local payments. Prices from £4,500. VentureCo hold ATOL license 5306 and are members of the Year Out Group. VentureCo have separate Ventures for school leavers and individuals on a career break.

Applications are welcome throughout the year.

Village Educational Project
(Kilimanjaro), c/o Miss Katy Allen MBE,
Mint Cottage, Prospect Road,
Sevenoaks, Kent TN13 3UA, UK   Tel: +44 (0) 1732 459 799

COMMUNITY, TEACHING, TRAVEL

Students teach English to children in rural primary schools in the Marangu region of Mount Kilimanjaro in Tanzania. It costs about £2000 including airfare but excluding visa, spending money and insurance.

Volunteer Galapagos
58 Springfield Park Avenue   Tel: +44 (0)700 593 8521
Chelmsford, Essex Cm2 6en, UK   Fax: +44 (0) 870 122 9029

COMMUNITY, HEALTH, RESEARCH/SCIENCE, TEACHING, WORK PLACEMENTS

The Galapagos Volunteer Programme places volunteers in a variety of vacancies which contribute to the development of the local community. Placements include teaching, fishing, events organizing, nursing, scientific research and marketing tasks. The organisation works hard to ensure you get a placement that suits your interests and makes the most of your skills. Placements last at least a month, though they recommend at least three and you can stay for up to a year (if you stay for at least five months you get a cruise around the Galapagos Islands).

The programme costs $49.70 per day for the first month, then $22.70 per day for subsequent months. Prices include all food, accommodation, national park entrance fee, return air flight from mainland Ecuador to the Galapagos Islands. Applications are welcomed throughout the year.

VSO (Voluntary Service Overseas)

317 Putney Bridge Road	Tel: +44 (0) 20 8780 7500
London SW15 2PN,	Fax: +44 (0) 20 8780 7300
UK	Minicom: 020 8780 7254

COMMUNITY, CULTURE, ENVIRONMENT

VSO's Youth for Development programme (for ages 18-25) sends volunteers to placements in the developing world. You spend 10-12 months in the host country doing work which is both useful to the host organisation and relevant to your interests. All volunteers complete a Global Education Project to share their learning. Participants are usually undergraduates from UK universities who have a long-term interest in international development or young people with experience of volunteering or community work who are keen to pursue a career in social welfare or international development.

VSO also runs the six-month World Youth programme for 17-25 year olds. Volunteers spend three months in the UK and three months in a developing country, living with a counterpart from a developing country with a local family and volunteering together with local community organisations. YFD follows the academic year, while World Youth is currently running programmes starting in February and August. Volunteers are expected to raise a minimum of £500 (for WY) and £700 (for YDF) respectively. In return VSO will provide medical insurance, training, vaccinations, visas, travel costs, living allowance and rent.

Workaway.info
Spain

ANIMALS, COMMUNITY, CONSERVATION, CULTURE, ENVIRONMENT, FARMING, SAFARI, TEACHING, TRAVEL

Workaway's philosophy is simple: 5 hours of work per day in exchange for food and accommodation with friendly hosts in varying situations and surroundings. The aim is to promote cultural understanding between different peoples and lands throughout the world and enable people travelling on a limited budget to fully appreciate living and working in a foreign environment. Its particularly good for language learners who can immerse themselves in their target language whilst living abroad.

Workaway.info is rather like an international volunteering dating agency! The organisation holds a database of families, individuals or organizations in different countries who are looking for help in a range of different fields - from painting to planting, building to baby-minding or shopping to sheep shearing. Workaway matches up volunteers and 'hosts' according to skills and job type and introduces them.

Workwaway recommends that travellers arrange an initial trial period (5 days or so) with the view of extending should both parties wish to (some workers end up staying for up to a year and become life long friends!)

127

WorldWide Volunteering for Young People

7 North Street Workshops   Tel: +44 (0) 1935 825588
Stoke Sub Hamdon   Fax: +44 (0) 1935 825775
Somerset TA14 6QR, UK   www.wwv.org.uk

ANIMAL, COMMUNITY, CONSERVATION, CULTURE, DRAMA, ENVIRONMENT,
FARMING, RELIGIOUS, RESEARCH/SCIENCE, SAFARI, TEACHING, TRAVEL,
CHILDREN, YOUTH WORK, CARE WORK, HEALTHCARE, HERITAGE/ARCHAEOLOGY
Worldwide Volunteering publishes the UK's most authoritative on-line and CD-
ROM database of volunteering opportunities for 16-35 year olds. They match
volunteers' wishes to the requirements of 1,00 organisations with over 300,000
annual placements throughout the UK and worldwide.

Projects last anything from a week to a year and range from those that cost nothing
and provide pocket money to those that cost thousands. Your school, library or
careers centre may have the database or you can find free access points near you
on our website. Alternatively contact WorldWide Volunteering at the above
address.

WWOOF (World Wide Opportunities on Organic Farms)

PO Box 2675   Tel: +44 (0) 1273 476 286
Lewes   Fax: +44 (0) 1273 476 286
East Sussex BN7 1RB, UK   www.wwoof.org.uk & www.wwoof.org

ANIMALS, COMMUNITY, CONSERVATION, CULTURE, ENVIRONMENT,
FARMING, TRAVEL

WWOOF places member volunteers on about 280 organic farms in the UK and
many more abroad, on working weekends or longer stays. Voluntary help is usually
on small farms that cannot afford to take on paid employees but like having
volunteers to stay.

YAP (Youth Action for Peace)

8 Golden Ridge   Tel: 01983 752557
Freshwater, Isle of Wight PO40 9LE, UK   Fax: 01983 756900

ANIMALS, COMMUNITY, CONSERVATION, CULTURE, DRAMA, ENVIRONMENT,
FARMING, RELIGIOUS, RESEARCH/SCIENCE, SAFARI, TEACHING, TRAVEL

YAP organises short term international voluntary work projects, youth
exchanges and workcamps through a network of national branches and
partner organisations in Europe, The Middle East, Africa, Asia, Asia and
America. YAP brings together a temporary community of 10-20 international
volunteers from different backgrounds to provide services to local community
projects. The volunteers carry out unskilled tasks that would not otherwise be
possible without paid labour. Each workcamp is managed by the local
community organisation.

Chapter 3
Learning Abroad

Learning Abroad

Your gap year is the ideal opportunity to combine the experience of living in a different culture and studying. You might want to continue learning something that interested you at school – a language or history. But 'learning' doesn't have to be academic; there are loads of sport 'schools' around the world that cater for all sports and all levels. For culture vultures, why not enrol on an art course in Florence or a film course in New York?

There's a huge variety of courses and you should be able to find something to fit your interests, budget and schedule. To make this chapter a bit easier to follow we've split it into section by type: **Academic year abroad; Arts & Culture (Art, Culture, Design & Fashion, Drama, Music, Photography); Languages (Language courses, TEFL); and Sport.**

An academic year abroad

Another way of getting to know a place and its people in depth is to spend a whole year 'living the language and culture' at a foreign school, in Europe, the USA, or even further afield. You could spend the academic year before you go to university in a French Lycée or German Gymnasium, in a school in Spain, or a Spanish-speaking school in Argentina, for example – which still leaves several months free for travel.

European Union   **http://europa.eu.in**

The website homepage has portals in the 20 different languages now spoken in the EU following recent enlargement.

EUROPASS   **www.europass-uk.co.uk**

Europass is a method of recording the training carried out and skills acquired during a period of work experience, undertaken as part of an on-going training programme, in another European country.

Although it does not represent formal accreditation, the standard format of this passport-style document is intended to ensure a consistent framework for the recognition of skills by training providers and employers throughout Europe.

All the information contained within the Europass is endorsed by sending and receiving organisations. This information includes details such as the name and level of the course being followed in the UK and the training and practical work undertaken abroad.

Organisations offering academic placements abroad

AFS Community Projects Overseas

Leeming House
Vicar Lane, Leeds LS2 7JF, UK

Tel: +44 (0) 113 242 6136
Fax: +44 (0) 113 243 0631

AFS Schools Programme (ages 15-18) gives you the opportunity to live abroad for a year and learn about a country's culture and language through immersion in its way of life. You can choose from 54 countries.

Au Pair in America (APIA)

37 Queen's Gate
London SW7 5HR, UK

Tel: +44 (0) 20 7581 7311
www.aupairamerica.co.uk

Don't just live in America for 12 months, be an American student! APIA's EduCare programme gives you a taste of US college life. You will be considered a non-degree student and have the freedom to study whatever you like. Live with an American family and, in exchange for up to 30 hours of childcare, you will receive a $1000 study allowance and a $105 weekly payment plus room and board. A local APIA community counsellor will link you up with other au pairs and EduCare participants in the area and will assist you in selecting and registering for your courses. Most placements are made in late summer and you must be aged 18-26 with a driving licence.

CESA Languages Abroad

CESA House
Pennance Road
Lanner, Cornwall TR16 5TQ, UK

Tel: +44 (0) 1209 211 800
Fax: +44 (0) 1209 211 830
www.cesalanguages.com

See Learning Abroad: Languages: Multi-languages for more info.

Challenge Educational Services

101 Lorna Road
Hove
East Sussex BN3 3EL, UK

Tel: +44 (0) 1273 220261
Fax: +44 (0) 1273 220376
www.challengeuk.com

Challenge Educational Services is a specialist provider of academic year courses at the universities of the Sorbonne, Angers, Nantes, Poitiers and Grenoble. Prices vary for the French university academic year, eg in the region of £5000 at the Universite de Poitiers, including tuition and accommodation.

An opportunity in the USA is currently an academic exchange programme for 15-18 year olds, ideal as part of a gap year. Students live in the USA for 5 or 10 months and study at an American High School. Prices are from £3495 for a ten-month academic year and £2995 for a 5-month semester.

ESU (English-Speaking Union)

Dartmouth House
37 Charles Street
London W1J 5ED, UK

Tel: +44 (0) 20 7529 1550
Fax: +44 (0) 20 7495 6108
www.esu.org

The English-Speaking Union was set up to promote understanding between nations. It organises educational exchanges in high schools (mostly boarding) in the US and Canada, awarding up to 40 scholarships a year to gap year students.

You could end up in a school in the middle of New York or in the middle of an Indiana field. Tuition and board are free, but you need to allow around £2500 for fares and spending money.

Fulbright Commission

US Educational Advisory Service	Tel: +44 (0) 20 7404 6994
62 Doughty Street	Fax: (0)20 7404 6874
London WC1N 2TZ, UK	www.fulbright.co.uk

If you want to take a full four-year degree at a US university or college, you will need to start planning at least a year before entry. Get in touch with The Fulbright Commission's US Educational Advisory Service (EAS) in London the summer before you want to start a US degree. You will then need to write to US universities, applying for the fall (autumn) term starting at the end of August or beginning of September (application forms available from the university the previous year). Each October The Fulbright Commission holds a 'College Day' for prospective undergraduates: more than 100 US universities are usually represented. The Fulbright Commission's Beginner's Guide to Undergraduate Study in the USA is a good booklet to help get you started. Their offices are open Mondays: 1.30pm-7pm; and Tuesdays to Fridays: 1.30pm-5pm (they are closed for most UK and US national holidays).

Institute of International Education

| 809 United Nations Plaza, New York, | |
| NY 10017-3580, USA | Fax: (US) 212-984-5358 |

The Institute of International Education runs a service called IIEPassport which offers a comprehensive search for study programmes abroad. You can search for international education opportunities by country, language, subject and many other criteria; you then get a list of study abroad programmes that specifically match your needs as well as a list of other programmes you might be interested in.

Office of International Education, Iceland

Neshaga 16	Tel: +354 525 4311
107 Reykjavík	Fax: +354 525 5850
Iceland	www.hi.is

Don't worry if your Icelandic isn't up to scratch: most institutions offer courses in English and if none are available then you can usually get private tutoring.

University of Iceland: The faculty of Natural Sciences offers a one-year course in English for Foreign Students in Earth Sciences covering topics in geology, geography and geophysics. Emphasis is put on aspects of Icelandic geology such as volcanic and geothermal activity, glaciers and plate tectonics, as well as physical and human geography. The course is suitable for ERASMUS exchange students from the EU and others wanting to spend a year in Iceland as a part of their university education. A minimum background of a year's undergraduate study in earth sciences is assumed. The faculties of Social Sciences and Humanities jointly offer courses in Northern Culture providing a general perspective on Icelandic history, society and culture and introducing the Icelandic language to students.

The Icelandic College of Engineering and Technology (ICET): The Department of Industrial Business Administration offers a one-year programme in English, leading to a BSc degree in International Marketing Management, which is open to exchange students. You need to have a diploma in Industrial Business Administration.

133

Bifröst business school: Exchange students may study at Bifröst in the spring semester when courses are taught in English. During the spring semester, the students complete a project or a dissertation, fulfilling general requirements for similar assignments or a thesis at the final stage of the undergraduate level of education.

Iceland University of Education: To meet the need of incoming exchange students the University offers ten courses taught in English.

Arts and Culture

Attracted to art? Moved by music? Hooked on history? There are some mouth-watering courses across Europe for students interested in art, literature, history and other cultural pleasures.

Accademia del Giglio

Art

| Via Ghibellina 116 | Tel: +39 055 23 02 467 |
| 50122, Florence, Italy | Fax: +39 055 23 02 467 |

This language school also offers classes in fresco painting.

Accademia Italiana

| Piazza Pitti 15 | Tel: +39 055 284 616 |
| 50125, Florence, Italy | Fax: +39 055 284486 |

An international design, art and language school, the Accademia Italiana puts on summer (one to three months) language courses as well as full-year and longer academic and Masters courses.

Art Under One Roof

| Via dei Pandolfini | Tel: +39 055 2478867 |
| 46r, 50122, Florence, Italy | Fax: +39 055 2478867 |

Art Under One Roof, in the centre of Florence, is an undergraduate-level art institute specialising in foundation art programmes.

British Institute of Florence

Piazza Strozzi 2	Tel: +39 (0) 55 2677 8200
50123	Fax: +39 (0) 55 2677 8222
Florence, Italy	info@britishinstitute.it

The British Institute of Florence runs a thriving and successful school which offers many courses including watercolour painting and life drawing.

Centro Machiavelli

| Piazza Santo Spirito 4 | Tel: +39 (0) 55 2396 966 |
| Florence 50125-I, Italy | Fax: +39 (0) 55 280 800 |

This small language school in a quiet square 10 minutes away from the tourist-crammed Ponte Vecchio offers the usual full range of language courses, quite reasonably priced. Apprenticeship courses can be organised in local artists' and artisans' workshops nearby.

Challenge Educational Services

101 Lorna Road
Hove
East Sussex BN3 3EL, UK

Tel: +44 (0) 1273 220261
Fax: +44 (0) 1273 220376
www.challengeuk.com

Challenge Educational Services organises a 12-week programme in Paris, combining language tuition with classes at a French Art school. Ideal for those with a reasonable standard of French and at least GCSE Art.

See Learning Abroad: Languages: French for more information about their languages courses.

Euro Academy

2nd Floor
67 -71 Lewisham High Street,
Lewisham, London SE13 5JX, UK

Tel: +44 (0) 20 8297 0505
Fax: +44 (0) 20 8297 0984

Though mainly a language school, Euro Academy offers many specialist courses which you can combine with language studies such as art in Florence, with use of their 800sqm art studio for budding da Vincis.

Il Sillabo

Via Alberti
31, 52027 San Giovanni, Valdarno (AR), Italy

Tel: + 39 055 9123238
Fax: + 39 055 942439

See Il Sillabo's listing in Learning Abroad: Languages: Italian.

Culture

Art History Abroad (AHA)

179c New Kings Road
London SW6 4SW
UK

Tel: +44 (0) 20 7731 2231
Fax: +44 (0) 20 7731 2456
www.arthistoryabroad.com

Art History Abroad (AHA) offer six weeks travelling and studying the masterpieces of western art and civilization in the company of experts. Venice, Verona, Florence, Siena, Rome and Naples.

A year out is a time to broaden your horizons, both physically and intellectually. You too can do AHA - 70% of our students join us because they have not had the opportunity to study the history of culture in depth before. We have brilliant tutors who are clear, patient, energetic and great fun and they will illuminate your world. Our method of on-site study in tutorials of eight is unique to AHA. It is a 'hands on' and unforgettable experience of art.

Italy might change your life - it is all at once stylish, energetic and brimming with life, day and night. The food is pretty fantastic too!

You can choose from Year Out courses running in the Autumn (Oct-Dec), Spring (Jan-Mar) and Early Summer (Apr-May) to fit with your other Gap year plans. We also offer two week summer courses (Jul-Aug) that are perfect for those with less time available on their Year Out, or indeed for those who must go straight on to university. These include a Classics trip to Sicily, the Amalfi Coast, Naples and Rome, Art History courses in Venice, Florence and Rome as well as two London based courses with optional weekend visits to Paris and Amsterdam, one focusing on the Contemporary Art scene in the capital, the other looking to discover the wealth of Art History in Britain (London, Oxford and Manchester)

Prices range from £800 - £5100 per course and there is a scholarship worth £1950 (only applicable to Italy based courses). For further details of the scholarship please contact the office.

British Institute of Florence

Piazza Strozzi 2
50123
Florence, Italy

Tel: +39 (0) 55 2677 8200
Fax: +39 (0) 55 2677 8222
www.britishinstitute.it

The British Institute of Florence offers many courses including opera, Dante, film appreciation, Tuscan cooking, wine appreciation, watercolour, life drawing.

Centro Studi Europeo (Europass)

Palazzo Guadagni, Piazza Santo Spirito 9,
50125, Florence, Italy

Tel: +39 055 213 030

Centro Studi Europeo, based in the Eurocentres Firenze, is part of a network of Eurocentres Foundation language schools, with 30 others in Europe, the USA, Canada and Japan. The school takes 150-200 students in the high season and offers a good range of language and cultural courses.

Cross-Cultural Solutions

Tower Point 44
North Road
BN1 1YR Brighton, UK

Tel: +44 (0) 845 458 2781/2782
Fax: +44 (0) 845 458 0258
www.crossculturalsolutions.org.uk

Cross-Cultural Solutions offers international Volunteer Programmes with a strong emphasis on cultural exchange. Through working with local people on locally designed and driven projects, volunteers experience real immersion in the local culture and have access to extraordinary people and places rarely seen by the average traveller. The Perspectives Programme activities, including an in-depth orientation, insights into cultural norms, language assistance, guest speakers and special events, all serve to enhance the cultural experience of volunteers.

Cultural Exchange Group of Argentina

Hidalgo 95
Capital Federal, C1405BBA Buenos Aires, Argentina

Tel: +54 11 49025153
Fax: +54 11 49025153

Cultural Exchange Group of Argentina www.gicarg.org: GICArg specialises in intensive Spanish language programmes as well as other study abroad programmes and internships. GICArg offers programmes in partnership with five top universities in different locations throughout Argentina, Uruguay and Chile. GICArg also offers Tango and cooking courses, internships and volunteer work placements.

DIKEMES - International Center for Hellenic and Mediterranean Studies

5 Plateia Stadiou
PO Box 17176, GR - 10024, Athens, Greece

Tel: +30 210 7560749
Fax: +30 210 7561497

The International Center for Hellenic and Mediterranean Studies is a not-for-profit educational institution which promotes the study of the culture of Greece (ancient, medieval and modern) and the Mediterranean world.
See Learning Abroad: Languages: Greek for more info.

Don Quijote

PO Box 218
Stoneleigh
Epsom, Surrey KT19 OYF, UK

Tel: +44 (0) 20 8786 8081
Fax: +44 (0) 20 8786 8086
www.donquijote.org

Don Quijote offers Spanish and Activities courses including flamenco dancing, wine tasting, cuisine and literature.
See Learning Abroad: Languages: Spanish for more info.

EIL (Experiment for International Living)

Ostega
287 Worcester Road, Malvern,
Worcestershire WR14 1AB, UK

Tel: 0168 45 62577
Fax: 0168 45 62212

EIL provides a way of learning a language without having to sit in a classroom. Going on a cultural exchange means you can spend time with a foreign family, not only learning the language but also soaking in the local culture. Take a look at the section on volunteering abroad for their voluntary projects such as helping on a local farm to educating the local children.

THE JOHN HALL
PRE-UNIVERSITY COURSE
FIRST IN THE FIELD AND **STILL** FIRST IN THE FIELD

London VENICE Florence Rome

- entirely different from any other cultural programme in Italy

January to March annually for Students of the Arts and Sciences.

Lectures / on-site visits given by a team of
writers, artists, musicians and university lecturers.
Art History, Music, Architecture, Conservation,
History, Opera, Literature, Design, Cinema.
Visits include Padua, Ravenna, Villas and
gardens near Venice, Florence and Rome.

Private visits in Venice to S.Marco, in Florence to the Uffizi
Gallery and Accademia and in Rome to the Vatican Museums,
Sistine Chapel and the Keats Shelley Museum.

Classes: Life Drawing, Photography, Italian Language.

Information from: The Secretary
12 Gainsborough Road, Ipswich IP4 2UR
Tel: 01473-251223 fax: 01473-288009

email: info@johnhallpre-university.com

www.johnhallpre-university.com

El Casal

Balmes 163
3/1, 08008 Barcelona, Spain

Tel: +34 (93) 217 90 38
Fax: +34 (93) 217 90 38 (phone first)

Based in Barcelona, El Casal offers the chance to soak in Catalan culture through a programme that combines study, travel and community service. You will have the opportunity to stay with a host family or in an apartment of your own. Whilst in Barcelona, El Casal provides excursions and seminars.

They will also help you get involved in local community projects or an internship with a local company. Each stay is around four months and the basic cost of the trip is around £5,000 to stay with a host family. There are other costs for excursions and trips or any travel arrangements to or from Barcelona.

Euro Academy

2nd Floor
67 -71 Lewisham High Street,
Lewisham, London SE13 5JX, UK

Tel: +44 (0) 20 8297 0505
Fax: +44 (0) 20 8297 0984

Though mainly a language school, Euro Academy offers many specialist courses such as Découverte de la Provence and Decouverte de la Cuisine Provençale courses in Aix-en-Provence which combine language with culture by including a full programme of excursions, wine tasting and cookery lessons. In Malaga students can combine Spanish and dance with Sevillanas and Salsa lessons.

Il Sillabo

Via Alberti
31, 52027 San Giovanni, Valdarno (AR), Italy

Tel: + 39 055 9123238
Fax: + 39 055 942439

See Learning Abroad: Languages: Italian.

Istituto di Lingua e Cultura Italiana Michelangelo

Via Ghibellina 88, 50122, Florence, Italy

Tel: +39 055 240 975

Please contact the school direct for more information.

Istituto Donatello

Via Galliano 1
50144, Florence, Italy

Tel: +39 055 354 112
Fax: +39 055 355 686

In a very friendly and familial environment you can learn the Italian language as well as learn about Italian art history, cooking, wood carving and theatre. The institute organises accommodation with other students or Italian families.

Istituto Europeo

Piazza delle pallottole n. 1 (duomo)
1-50122 Florence, Italy

Tel: +39 05523 81071
Fax: +39 05528 9145

See Learning Abroad: Languages: Italian for more details.

Italian Cultural Institute (Istituto di Cultura Italiano)

39 Belgrave Square, London SW1X 8NX, UK

Tel: +44 (0) 20 7235 1461

The Italian Cultural Institute has a bookshelf brimming with free leaflets on courses of all sorts in Italy (including Italian cookery, music, culture and fashion, for example).

PETERSBURG STUDIES

Winter in St Petersburg - A Six Week Course

An exceptional opportunity for students with an interest in Russia.

Study the culture, history and present day life of this intense and remarkable city.

Accomodation in a Swiss owned hotel, a skilfully designed programme, excellent lecturers, guides and local contacts.

Volunteer in the Hermitage Museum or for St Petersburg charities
Improve your Russian
Follow a workshop in a Russian film studio
Practice printmaking, academic drawing or Russian cooking
Ski, skate and sled in the frozen landscape

PETERSBURG STUDIES GmbH
www.petersburgstudies.com
Inmaculada de Argumosa (41) 1 461 3630
Alexandra Samarine (44) 0 20 7727 6751
alexandra@petersburgstudies.com

**PETERSBURG
STUDIES**

John Hall Pre-University Course

12 Gainsborough Road	Tel: +44 (0) 1473 251 223
Ipswich	Fax: +44 (0) 1473 288 009
Suffolk IP4 2UR, UK	www.johnhallpre-university.com

John Hall Pre-University courses, running from January to March, start with an introductory week in London based at the National Gallery, that includes visits to Simon Dickinson (to learn about the art trade), the Richard Rodgers Studios (architecture) and the Saatchi Collection (modern art). Then a party of about 50 students (mostly gappers) travels to Venice for six weeks of visits and lectures, given by nearly 30 different lecturers, on Italian history, European art (from Byzantine through Renaissance to modern), Architecture, Literature, Music, Opera, and World Cinema. Students can practise life drawing and photography; Italian language lessons are extra.

There's also an optional extra week in Florence and five days in Rome. The seven-week course costs around £6100, which includes travel, half-board and a one-month vaporetto pass.

Lorenzo de' Medici

Via Faenza 43, Florence, Italy	Tel: +39 055 287 143 50123

The Lorenzo de' Medici offers language courses (7 levels) and cultural courses and has a large library in the adjoining San Iacopo di Corbolini church.

Petersburg Studies

8 Larkhall Lane	Tel: +44 (0) 20 7727 6751
SW4 6SP London, UK	Fax: +44 (0) 20 7229 8242

Russia made accessible is the idea behind the six week course for gap year students set up by Petersburg Studies GmbH. St Petersburg's extraordinary history, its architecture, museums, music, literature and contemporary life are opened up through lectures, guided tours, workshops and volunteer schemes. These include the option to work in a film studio, for charity, for a local newspaper and for the Hermitage Museum itself.

The course runs from the end of January to the beginning of March - and costs around £4,850, including accommodation in a comfortable and central hotel. The programme is full and challenging - it also includes Russian language classes.

Petersburg Studies GmbH has the active support of the UK Friends of the Hermitage.

TASIS, The American School in Switzerland

CH-6926 Montagnola-Lugano,	Tel: +41 91 960 5151
Switzerland	Fax: +41 91 993 2979

Each year, the TASIS schools and summer programmes attract over 2400 students representing more than 40 nationalities who share in a caring, family-style international community. The PG Year, established in 1965, enrols a select group of students who wish to participate in a unique educational opportunity, which draws on the academic strengths of TASIS and the cultural resources of Europe.

3

Learning Abroad | Culture

141

Design & Fashion

Accademia Italiana

Piazza Pitti 15
50125, Florence, Italy

Tel: +39 055 284 616
Fax: +39 055 284486

The Accademia Italiana is an international design, art and language school. Every year it puts on summer language courses which last from one to three months.

Italian Cultural Institute (Istituto di Cultura Italiano)

39 Belgrave Square, London SW1X 8NX, UK   Tel: +44 (0) 20 7235 1461

The Institute has a bookshelf brimming with free leaflets on courses of all sorts in Italy (including Italian cookery, musical, culture and fashion).

Film, Theatre & Drama

Bright Light

3 Fentiman Road
London SW8 1LD, UK

Tel: +44 (0) 20 7582 1582
Fax: +44 (0) 20 7582 2379

Bright Light is a not-for-profit organisation that runs gap year drama and education projects in Kenya, Uganda, Tanzania and Ethiopia. You get to learn about East African drama, dance and music as well as teaching African children about Western drama and British culture.

The programme lasts three months and is split into three phases. First you spend time working with African theatre professionals, learning about traditional African narrative dance and oral literature, as well as helping with performances. The second phase consists of volunteer teaching in schools. You introduce small groups of children to Western concepts of drama and help them to produce their first play. Finally, you get the chance to produce your own play and then spend time at Lake Naivasha where you can reflect on your experiences. When you return home you may even get the opportunity to workshop your performances at the Old Vic in London. Tours depart in January and May and cost £2440 including all food, travel, accommodation and insurance.

Istituto Donatello

Via Galliano 1
50144, Florence, Italy

Tel: +39 055 354 112
Fax: +39 055 355 686

In a very friendly and familial environment you can learn the Italian language as well as learn about Italian art history, cooking, wood carving and theatre. The institute organises accommodation with other students or Italian families.

Metropolitan Film School

125 Bolingbroke Grove
SW11 1DA London, UK

Tel: +44 (0) 845 658 4400
Fax: +44 (0) 20 7228 1098

Practical courses for aspiring filmmakers. All students leave with a calling card - their own script or movie! We can offer distribution through our partners, Picturehouse cinemas.

NYFA (New York Film Academy)
100 East 17th Street
New York, NY 10003, USA

Tel: +1 212 674 4300
Fax: +1 212 477 1414

Whether you want to be the next Tarantino, Nick Park or Halle Berry the New York Film Academy runs programmes all year round in New York City and at Universal Studios in Hollywood, California as well as summer workshops at: King's College in London; Princeton University; the Harvard Faculty Club; Disney-MGM Studios, Florida; FEMIS, the French National Film School, Paris; and the ITESM Campus in Mexico City, Mexico.

Programmes offered include 4, 6 and 8-week intensive filmmaking workshops, 12-week evening classes, a comprehensive one-year filmmaking, one-week Movie Camp ($1500), 4-week intensive Acting for Film ($2500), 4-week 3D Animation ($3500) and evening screenwriting workshops during the summer months. There's a good balance of theory and practical. Teaching standards are high - some of the tutors can even boast an Oscar on their mantelpiece! Don't worry if you've got no experience - all you need is to be talented and keen - the Academy has an open door policy for applications, but they do expect total commitment.

PCFE Film School
The Prague Center for Further Education,
Karmelitska 18, 118 00 Prague 1, Czech Republic

Prague-based PCFE Film School offers 3-week workshops, semester and year programmes in filmmaking including directing, screenwriting, cinematography, editing and film history and theory. Teachers at PCFE Film School come from Prague's prestigious National Film Academy and from among Europe's leading film directors. Students at the film school come from all over the world.

Their programmes will appeal to gap year students eager to explore their interest in film before starting university or a career. Those completing PCFE programmes can use their Prague experience to further their applications to film academies back in their home countries, apply for film industry-related jobs, or use their newly acquired skills to make films on their own regardless of their career choice. PCFE Film School programmes are highly intensive and structured.

Music

Istituto Europeo
Piazza delle pallottole n. 1 (duomo)
1-50122 Florence, Italy

Tel: +39 05523 81071
Fax: +39 05528 9145

See Learning abroad: Languages: Italian for more details.

Italian Cultural Institute (Istituto di Cultura Italiano)
39 Belgrave Square, London SW1X 8NX, UK   Tel: +44 (0) 20 7235 1461

The Italian Cultural Institute has a bookshelf brimming with free leaflets on courses of all sorts in Italy (including Italian cookery, musical, culture and fashion, for example).

143

Photography

Nigel Turner Photographic Workshop
948 Osterville Street, Unit D,
Henderson, NV 89052, USA   Tel: +1 (702) 804 8962

Nigel Turner, a professional landscape photographer in the West of the US, offers one- and two-week workshops on photographic technique. You will be based in Las Vegas and have the chance to capture some of the most breathtaking scenery the US has to offer, from Death Valley to Yosemite National. Contact Nigel direct for prices and more information.

Steve Outram Crete Photo Tours & Workshops
D.Katsifarakis Street   Tel: +30 28210 32201
Galatas, Chania 73100, Crete, Greece   Fax: +30 28210 32201

Professional photographer Steve Outram uses his local knowledge of Zanzibar, Lesvos and Western Crete to show you how to make the most of photographic opportunities and develop your skill as a photographer.

Languages

Language is part of our everyday lives. We use it constantly to communicate with one another – but of course if we don't speak the same language as another person, it becomes a barrier rather than a bridge. Even if you don't want to study a language academically, being able to speak even the smallest amount of a foreign language opens opportunities.

There's more to a language than just words: most language courses will include local culture, history, geography, religion, customs and current affairs – as well as food and wine. A language also involves more than just translating your own thoughts into someone else's words. A new language brings a whole new way of thinking with it, and therefore a much deeper understanding of the people who shaped it and use it. Why do some languages have no future tense – is there a different way time is conceived? Most people will know that the Icelanders have lots of words for 'snow', but did you know that they have 85 words for 'storm'?

Think laterally when you decide where you want to study. Spanish is spoken in many countries around the world, so you could opt for a Spanish course in Brazil, rather than Spain, and then go travelling around South America. Many cities with a particular international flavour will offer a variety of language courses: in Brussels, capital of the European Union, courses in other languages such as German, Spanish, Italian or even Russian can be found in a number of institutions. As everyone knows, Belgium is partly Dutch/Flemish-speaking and partly French-speaking: the Belgian Embassy in London will let you have a free list of Flemish and French language schools throughout Belgium.

Belgian Embassy   103 Eaton Square
                                         London NW1 6PU, England
                                         Tel: +44 (0) 207470 3700

Sheets and pieces

Languages are fun, especially if you're the teacher. While strangling perfectly good verbs, nouns and adjectives beyond recognition, students often provide the best entertainment of all. Indeed, language lessons are rarely more enjoyable than when your student inadvertently says something that perhaps, well, they shouldn't have.

One great example used to be my lesson where a low-level student had to learn the names of various bits of office equipment. It sounds dull – surely there is only limited interest in teaching people how to say 'pen', 'pencil', 'computer', 'printer' and 'cupboard'? But before you jump to any conclusions, mull this conundrum over for a second: as an English teacher of French students, do you teach them to say a 'piece of paper' or a 'sheet of paper'? Say it out loud in your best French accent. You understand the dilemma.

My favourite ever mistake in English was at a company of headhunters. I had a welcome class with a group where we were introducing ourselves. Instead of each person introducing themselves in turn, I asked each person to introduce someone else. That way, the other person could correct any mistakes, and a conversation would hopefully develop.

So I learnt that Stéphanie was an accountant who lived in Chartres and liked mountain-biking. Stéphanie told us that Sébastian worked as a recruitment consultant on the third floor and was married. And then, Sébastian spoke:

"This is Françoise. She is a secretary on the sixth floor. She lives in promiscuity."

"Sorry?" I looked around the room for some explanation. Genuinely lost for words, I didn't know whether to laugh or put a stop to this slander immediately. To my horror, four faces nodded and smiled in agreement with their colleague.

"It is true," added Françoise, without the slightest hint of shame or embarrassment.

"Really?" I asked, my mind racing to try to decipher why anyone would tell this to the English teacher.

"Oh yes," said Sébastian. "She lives in the next street, actually. In promiscuity. You know, en proximité."

"Oh, I see," I said, relieved. "Nearby..."

Josh

145

Volunteer placements

Be aware though that if you learn a language outside its original country you may learn a particular accent and dialect that is only spoken there and may be considered inferior by some people (or even not be understood) elsewhere, eg Spanish in South America, French in Belgium, Canada and Switzerland, German in Austria and Switzerland.

There's a whole section in this book about voluntary work abroad *(see Volunteering Abroad)*, whether arranged under the umbrella of a gap year organisation in the UK or independently and directly between the volunteer and the project itself. Some language course organisers also arrange volunteer placements after a language course, which can equip volunteers better for their work, and you can find details on their websites.

Living with a family

If enrolling on a language course sounds too much like school, another way of learning a language is staying with a family as an au pair or tutor (giving, say, English or music lessons to children) and going to part-time classes locally. *(See Working Abroad, for more details on au pair work.)*

Finding the right place to learn

You can try universities, which often have international summer school centres or courses for foreign students. For those who would prefer to dip their toes in gently, there is the popular network of British Institutes abroad. And there's a plethora of independent language colleges to choose from, either directly or through a language course organiser or agency in the UK. The advantage in dealing with a UK-based organisation is that if something goes wrong, it is easier to get it sorted out within easy reach and under UK law.

Language course organisers, consultancies and agencies will provide advice, book courses and organise your accommodation for you, usually getting their income from the commission they receive from language schools. Always ask the agency or language school to put you in contact with one or two students who have done the course you have in mind, so that you can get their views of what it's like before you sign up for anything.

Using the internet

As with most subjects the first place to go for extra information on language courses is the internet. Use search engines like **www.freeserve.co.uk**, **www.google.com**, **www.lycos.com**, **www.msn.com** and **www.yahoo.com**. If you're looking for courses

The following are some international language course websites that we have found:

www.europa-pages.co.uk

www.ialc.org

www.goabroad.com

www.languagesabroad.com

Language courses

Courses at language schools abroad can be divided into as many as ten different levels, ranging from tuition for the complete beginner to highly technical or specialised courses at postgraduate level. The usual classification of language classes, however, into 'beginner' or 'basic', 'intermediate' and 'advanced' works well. Within each of these levels there are usually subdivisions, especially in schools large enough to move students from one class to another with ease. When you first phone a school from abroad or send in an application form, you should indicate how good your knowledge of the language is.

When you arrive, you may be tested before being allocated to your class, or you may be transferred from your original class to a lower or higher one as soon as they find you are worse or better than expected.

Different schools will use different methods of teaching: if you know that you respond well to one style, check that is what your course offers. Foreign language lessons are often attended by a variety of nationalities so they are almost always conducted in the language you are learning, forcing you to understand and respond without using English. In practice, however, most teachers can revert to English to explain a principle of grammar if a student is really stuck.

The smaller the class the better, though the quality of the teaching is most important – at more advanced levels, well-qualified graduate teachers should be available. Language schools and institutes show a mass of information, photographs and maps on their websites, so it's easy to find out if the school is near to other places that interest you, whether it's a city centre or a coastal resort. The admissions staff should be happy to give you references from previous students.

Over the next few pages we've listed some of the organisations offering language opportunities to gappers, from formal tuition to 'soaking it up' while you live with a family. We've split the organisations according to the languages they offer: **Arabic, Chinese, Dutch, French, German, Greek, Indonesian, Italian, Japanese, Portuguese, Russian, Spanish**). Some of the larger companies offer several languages – you'll find the full details of these companies listed under the Multi-languages section, and just their contact details under each individual language that they offer.

Multi languages

AFS Community Projects Overseas

Leeming House
Vicar Lane, Leeds LS2 7JF, UK

Tel: +44 (0) 113 242 6136
Fax: +44 (0) 113 243 0631

AFS Schools Programme (for ages 15-18) offers the opportunity to live abroad for a year, from a choice of 54 countries, and learn a language through immersion in the way of life.

Alliances Abroad

2423 Pennsylvania Avenue NW
Washington, DC 20037, USA

Tel: +1 (202) 467 9467
Fax: +1 (202) 467 9460

Alliances Abroad offers language programmes in Costa Rica, Spain and Ecuador and will ensure they find you the best language school available. They supply relevant information on the country you have chosen and provide comprehensive pre-departure support.

Cactus Language

4 Clarence House
30-31 North Street, Brighton,
East Sussex BN1 1 EB, UK

Tel: +44 (0) 845 130 4775
Fax: +44 (0) 1273 775868

Cactus Language offers residential intensive group and individual courses lasting from a week to a year in Europe, Latin America, Asia and Africa. All classes are taught by native teachers, with students from around the world. Accommodation is with host families, in halls of residence or in shared or private apartments. Multi-destination, work experience and volunteer courses are also available worldwide and TEFL (CELTA) courses are offered in England and Spain. Airline tickets can also be arranged (including round-the-world tickets).

Caledonia Languages Abroad

The Clockhouse
Bonnington Mill, 72 Newhaven Road,
Edinburgh EH6 5QG, Scotland

Tel: +44 (0) 131 621 7721/2
Fax: +44 (0) 131 621 7723
www.caledonialanguages.co.uk

Caledonia Languages Abroad provides tailor-made advice and a personalised booking service for courses at 42 language schools around the world. Founder/owner Kath Bateman says: 'We have travelled to the countries we recommend and are always ready to discuss ideas with gap year students, whether they want to go away for one month or one year.' CLA can organise your course and accommodation and give you practical advice on all aspects of your trip.

Caledonia Languages Abroad arranges French courses in Aix-en-Provence, Biarritz, Bordeaux, Chambery, Montpellier, Nice or Paris. Prices range from £325 for two weeks in Nice (20 group lessons a week) to £930 for a four-week combination course of 20 group lessons and five individual lessons per week. The individual lessons can be focused on specific areas of professional interest, such as business, legal or political French.

You can learn Spanish as far away as Argentina, Cuba, Costa Rica, Bolivia, Ecuador, Mexico or Peru; Barcelona, Benalmadena, Cordoba, Granada, Madrid, Salamanca, Tenerife, Mallorca, Malaga, San Sebastian or Seville in Spain. In Peru a course in Cusco can be followed by a course in the Sacred Valley of Urubamba, near Inca ruins and trekking routes, or on an island in the middle of Lake Titicaca. Individual lessons cost £200 per week plus accommodation. In Malaga, students can study at the beautiful 'beachside centre', in a mansion set in lush gardens beside the beach. This centre is ideally suited for younger students on a budget. Courses are for two or four weeks. Two weeks costs £340 for 40 lessons, and includes accommodation in a student flat.

Caledonia Languages Abroad runs German courses in Berlin or Stuttgart. Also available are Russian in St Petersburg or Moscow and Portuguese in Lisbon, Faro or Brazil and Arabic in Egypt. Caledonia's Italian language school in Siena is in a beautiful building in the oldest part of this walled medieval city. Forty lessons over 2 weeks costs £270. Accommodation with a host family on a half-board basis from £350 for 2 weeks for a single room. Schools also in Rome, Florence, Sicily and Sorrento and CELTA courses are available in Edinburgh, London and Spain all year round.

CESA Languages Abroad

CESA House	Tel: +44 (0) 1209 211 800
Pennance Road	Fax: +44 (0) 1209 211 830
Lanner, Cornwall TR16 5TQ, UK	www.cesalanguages.com

CESA Languages Abroad are a family company, this year celebrating 25 years in business. They arrange programmes in language colleges in Europe and beyond (Japan, Morocco and China for example) and offer advice on the most appropriate course for you. Of all the languages CESA offers, Spanish and Italian most in demand. You can choose from Spanish courses in Costa Rica (San Jose), Ecuador (Quito and Cuenca), Mexico (Cuernavaca or Playa del Carmen) and Spain (Granada, Madrid, Marbella, Malaga, Nerja, Salamanca, Barcelona or Seville for one week to nine months.

Three months' tuition plus a flat share in Seville starts at £2035. CESA also runs one-week Easter French and Spanish revision courses (30 lessons) in Nice and Madrid for AS and A2 level students.

CESA's German courses in Berlin are becoming increasingly popular, particularly the Work Experience option for Gap and university students. Courses are also run in Cologne, Lindau, Munich (München) and Vienna or Kitzbühel (Austria). Italian courses are offered in cities such as Rome, Milan and Florence and also smaller locations such as Viarregio and San Giovanni from one to 36 weeks. You can choose to improve your French in the Caribbean (Guadeloupe in January has definite attractions!) or in a wonderful selection of locations in France. If your language ambitions lie further afield, CESA also offers courses in Japanese, (Okazaki, near Nagoya), Russian (at language schools in St Petersburg and Mosow), Chinese (close to the Forbidden City, in Beijing) and Greek (in the capital city, Athens or the beautiful island of Crete).

CIEE (Council on International Educational Exchange)

52 Poland Street	Tel: +44 (0) 20 7478 2020
London W1F 7AB	Fax: +44 (0) 20 7734 7322
UK	www.councilexchanges.org.uk

CIEE arranges Language Study Abroad programmes with language schools in several countries, offering tuition in flexible blocks (£350 upwards including homestay) in Cuba and Ecuador as well as France, Germany, Italy and Spain.

149

EF International Languages
74 Roupell Street
London SE1 8SS, UK

Tel: +44 (0) 8707 200735
www.ef.com

On an EF International Language Schools programme you will immerse yourself in the language and culture of some of the world's most exciting cities. Choose from Nice, Barcelona, Munich, Rome, Quito, St Petersburg or Shanghai. All the schools except the one in Rome are EF owned. Rome is an excellent partner school with the EAQUALS accreditation. You can study for as little as two weeks (from £620 including accommodation and meals) or for a complete academic year (from £6250 including flights, accommodation and meals). Courses start throughout the year and are open to all levels, from complete beginner to advanced. All courses include accommodation and meals; courses within Europe over 12 weeks also include return flight. In selected locations EF offers work placements and voluntary projects to run in conjunction with the language programme.

Euro Academy
2nd Floor
67 -71 Lewisham High Street,
Lewisham, London SE13 5JX, UK

Tel: +44 (0) 20 8297 0505
Fax: +44 (0) 20 8297 0984

Euro Academy has over 30 years' experience in arranging language courses for all ages at all levels at its partner schools throughout Europe and South America. You can study French in Paris, Nice, Bordeaux, Tours or Aix-en-Provence; German in Berlin, Hamburg, Frankfurt or Munich; Spanish in Spain (Nerja, Benalmadena, Alcala de Henares, San Sebastian, Granada, Madrid, Salamanca, Alicante, Seville, Barcelona, Malaga, El Puerto or Valencia) or South America (Ecuador, Costa Rica,

Peru, Bolivia, Guatemela or Cuba); Italian in Rome, Milan, Florence, Siena or Bologna; Russian in St Petersburg or Moscow; Portuguese in Lisbon or Faro; or Greek in Hania (Crete), Athens or Thessaloniki. Most Euro Academy schools offer courses from one week upwards (some students stay for over 6 months) for beginners to advanced level students. Courses are flexible and Euro Academy is happy to try to accommodate your needs. They offer one-on-one tuition as well as group language courses.

Type of accommodation varies, catering for all budgets: you can choose from well-appointed student residences, hotels and hostels, or you can opt to live with a local family. Euro Academy also offers specialist courses, such as the Decouverte de la Provence and Decouverte de la Cuisine Provençale courses in Aix-en-Provence which combine language with culture by including a full programme of excursions, wine tasting and cookery lessons. In Malaga students can combine Spanish and dance with Sevillanas and Salsa lessons. The Florence school boasts a large art studio for budding da Vincis. It also offers three Italian and cookery courses. Or if you are facing exam stress, why not try one of their exam revision courses in Bordeaux or Biarritz?

Euro Academy also arranges unpaid work placements for up to six months in France, Germany, Spain and Italy.

Eurolingua Institute

Havre St Pierre 265 Allée du Nouveau Monde,	Tel: +33 4 67 15 04 73
34000, Montpellier, France	Fax: +33 4 67 15 04 73

Eurolingua is a network of 70 institutes teaching nine languages in 35 countries. For summer A level revision or gap year study the best courses are probably the standard 'group programmes' with 15 hours of tuition a week in a group (any length from 2 to 50 weeks). You are tested on arrival to slot you into a Beginner, Intermediate or Advanced level group. In Montpellier in France, for example, a pretty university town with a medieval centre and narrow streets, you pay about £690 for a four-week French course at the Eurolingua Institute, with half-board homestay accommodation about £110 a week extra.

Language Courses Abroad

67 Ashby Road	Tel: +44 (0) 1509 211612
Loughborough, Leicestershire LE11 3AA, UK	Fax: +44 (0) 1509 260037

Language Courses Abroad offers courses in French, German, Greek, Italian, Portuguese, Russian and Spanish in venues throughout Europe and South America, inluding Cuba. They specialise in arranging tailor-made course combinations to suit individual needs - so, for example, you could study one language in several locations, or several languages in one location. Twelve weeks learning Spanish in Quito (Ecuador), Cusco (Peru) and Sucre (Bolivia) costs £2181 including accommodation but excluding airfares. Course lengths vary from one week to nine months, and accommodation is with host families (half board) or in self-catering student or private studio apartments.

Many course venues offer excursions and supplementary courses. So in Cuba you might want to take guitar lessons (£37 per week) or learn samba, rumba, salsa or mambo (£26 per week). Other options include creole cooking in the Dominican Republic, ice fishing from St Petersburg, volcano visiting or white water rafting in Costa Rica or wine tasting in Venice.

Learn Languages Abroad
'Sceilig'
Ballymorefinn
Glenasmole, Dublin 24, Republic of Ireland

Tel: +353 1 451 1674
Fax: +353 1 451 1636
www.languages.ie

Learn Languages Abroad will help you find the course best suited to your needs - whatever your age or language ability. They work with a number of language schools across Europe, all chosen after extensive research to identify high quality, reasonably priced language schools in excellent locations. Using regular visits and feedback from students they continually monitor the performance of the schools.

They organise your application to the school and take care of the whole booking process for you. The best bit is that their service is absolutley free to gappers who book a course of 12 weeks or more (others pay a booking fee of €50).

Courses available range from two weeks to a full academic year. You can decide upon the intensity - from four hours per day upwards. There are discounts on longer courses in several schools.

Guide prices: four week course, including family bed & breakfast accommodation: (Prices shown in Pounds Sterling and may fluctuate with currency)

French: Nice £1,000, Paris £1,000, Vichy £1,000

German: Hamburg £670, Heidelberg £900

Italian: Florence £900, Milan £900, Rome £900, Siena £900

Spanish: Alicante £1,125, Barcelona £1,145, Cadiz £790, Denia £990, Granada £970, Madrid £1,145, Malaga £900, Ronda £725, Salamanca £1,075, San Sebastian £925, Vitoria £975

If you want to learn with friends, Learn Languages Abroad can also arrange for special rates for groups of five or more.

OISE
90 Great Russell Street   Tel: 020 7631 3674
London WC1B 3PS, UK   Fax: 020 7631 3679

OISE provides language courses in the Germany, France and Spain. The courses can be as cheap as £325 and go up to the £600 per week. The courses range between one and twelve weeks.

Arabic

AFS Community Projects Overseas
Leeming House   Tel: +44 (0) 113 242 6136
Vicar Lane, Leeds LS2 7JF, UK   Fax: +44 (0) 113 243 0631

For further details see main listing under Multi-languages.

British Council
10 Spring Gardens   Tel: +44 (0) 20 7930 8466
London SW1 2BN, UK   www.britishcouncil.org

The British Council in Cairo has courses in Arabic - contact the British Council in London for details.

Caledonia Languages Abroad
The Clockhouse, Bonnington Mill   Tel: +44 (0) 131 621 7721/2
72 Newhaven Road,   Fax: +44 (0) 131 621 7723
Edinburgh EH6 5QG, Scotland   www.caledonialanguages.co.uk

For further details see main listing under Multi-Languages

Embassy of the UAE (Resource Centre)
30 Princes Gate, SW7 London, UK   Tel: +44 (0) 20 7581 1281

The Embassy of the United Arab Emirates (UAE) in London can send you a list of language institutes, colleges and universities that teach Arabic in the Emirates, particularly Dubai, the city-on-a-creek that combines the heritage of the middle East with the customs of the West plus Abu Dhabi and Sharjah.

SOAS (School of Oriental and African Studies)
SOAS Language Centre   Tel: +44 (0) 20 7898 4888
University of London, Thornhaugh Street,
Russell Square, London WC1H 0XG, UK   www.soas.ac.uk

The SOAS is part of the University of London and can arrange for you to study in an Arabic-speaking country.

153

Chinese

AFS Community Projects Overseas
Leeming House
Vicar Lane, Leeds LS2 7JF, UK

Tel: +44 (0) 113 242 6136
Fax: +44 (0) 113 243 0631

For further details see main listing under Multi-languages.

EF International Languages
74 Roupell Street, London SE1 8SS, UK

Tel: +44 (0) 8707 200735

For further details see main listing under Multi-languages.

WorldLink Education
Storgatan 24
302 43 Halmstad, Sweden

Tel: +46 35 106680
Fax: +46 35 106685

WorldLink Education's Chinese language programme immerses you in Mandarin Chinese through class instruction, after-class tutoring, language exchanges with native speakers and a range of optional extra activities including: Chinese character writing, songs, traditional massage, traditional medicine, painting, calligraphy and Taiji Quan (T'ai chi). There are social events (Peking Duck feast, bowling nights, games nights, karaoke, basketball, Chinese movies, touch rugby) and half- or full-day excursions to sites of interest such as the Great Wall, Summer Palace, Temple of Heaven, Lama Temple, Tian'anmen Square and the Forbidden City.

Based in Beijing, the programmes cater for all levels from beginner to advanced, and course lengths vary from four weeks ($2220 to $2800) to a full semester or academic year ($8660 to $11250). Prices include accommodation, tuition and all optional extras. You can also combine the language programme with learning martial arts *(see Learning Abroad: Sport)*. WorldLinkEdu can also arrange subsidised guided trips around China for its students to places such as Shanghai, Xian, Inner Mongolia, Datong and Tibet. *(see Travel: tour companies)* for more details.

Dutch

CERAN Lingua International
Avenue des Petits Sapins 27
B-4900 SPA, Belgium

Tel: +32 8779 1122
Fax: +38 87 791 188

CERAN runs weekly intensive residential language programmes in Dutch, French, German, Spanish and Japanese with 'complete immersion' in the language from 8am to 10pm.

French

Global Adventures Project
38 Queens Gate
SW11 5HR London
UK

Tel: +44 800 085 4197
Fax: +44 207 7590 7444
www.globaladventures.co.uk

Actilangue

2 rue Alexis Mossa
06000, Nice, France

Tel: +33 (0) 493 96 3384
Fax: +33 (0) 493 443716

Actilangue is located in the heart of Nice, near the beach and the famous Promenade des Anglais. Courses are conducted solely in French by experienced instructors.

AFS Community Projects Overseas

Leeming House
Vicar Lane
Leeds LS2 7JF, UK

Tel: +44 (0) 113 242 6136
Fax: +44 (0) 113 243 0631
www.afsuk.org

For further details see main listing under Multi-languages.

Alliance Française

1 Dorset Square, London NW1 6PU, UK

Tel: +44 (0) 20 7723 6439

Alliance Française is a non-profit-making organisation funded by a trust with a network of Alliances in 138 countries. UK teaching centres are spread throughout the country, from Jersey to Glasgow, and many of them regularly run trips to France. These are aimed at giving you a taste of French cuisine and culture as well as the opportunity to improve your language skills. Their two-week trip to Provence (£1330 all inclusive) consists of language activities in the morning and workshops/excursions in the afternoon. Check out their website for details of other Alliances around the world.

Alliances Abroad

2423 Pennsylvania Avenue NW
Washington, DC 20037, USA

Tel: +1 (202) 467 9467
Fax: +1 (202) 467 9460

For further details see main listing under Multi-languages.

Belgian Embassy

103 Eaton Square
London SW1W 9AB, UK

Tel: +44 (0) 20 7470 3700
www.diplobel.org/uk

It's always worth contacting the local embassies as they will be able to give you lists of language schools, they may even organise their own courses or summer schools.

BLS French Courses

42 rue Lafaurie de Monbadon,
33000 Bordeaux, France

Tel: +33 (0) 556 51 0076

If you like the sound of the Bordeaux area, with its warm, open countryside and vineyards, you could try BLS French courses, based in the heart of Bordeaux. You will be put up in a modest hotel or, more likely, with a host family, perhaps with another student.

British Institute in Paris

11 rue de Constantine,
75007, Paris, France

Tel: +33 1 4411 7383
www.bip.lon.ac.uk

The British Institute in Paris is part of the University of London, and is the only British university institute in continental Europe. It does not run a specific gap year course, but there are courses available covering grammar, translation, and French

155

literature and civilisation which last from ten weeks to one academic year, with between two and eight hours of teaching per week. Course costs depend on the value of the pound - but, roughly speaking, if you do a whole term with eight hours a week tuition, it will cost you around £900.

Cactus Language

4 Clarence House, 30-31 North Street,
Brighton, East Sussex BN1 1 EB, UK

Tel: +44 (0) 845 130 4775
Fax: +44 (0) 1273 775868

For further details see main listing under Multi-languages.

Caledonia Languages Abroad

The Clockhouse
Bonnington Mill, 72 Newhaven Road,
Edinburgh EH6 5QG, Scotland

Tel: +44 (0) 131 621 7721/2
Fax: +44 (0) 131 621 7723
www.caledonialanguages.co.uk

For further details see main listing under Multi-languages.

CERAN Lingua International

Avenue des Petits Sapins 27
B-4900 SPA, Belgium

Tel: +32 8779 1122
Fax: +38 87 791 188

CERAN runs weekly intensive residential language programmes in Dutch, French, German, Spanish and Japanese with 'complete immersion' in the language from 8am to 10pm.

CESA Languages Abroad

CESA House
Pennance Road
Lanner, Cornwall TR16 5TQ, UK

Tel: +44 (0) 1209 211 800
Fax: +44 (0) 1209 211 830
www.cesalanguages.com

For further details see main listing under Multi-languages.

Challenge Educational Services

101 Lorna Road
Hove
East Sussex BN3 3EL, UK

Tel: +44 (0) 1273 220261
Fax: +44 (0) 1273 220376
www.challengeuk.com

Challenge Educational Services organises French courses at several French universities and private language institutes. Prices vary from £875 for a four-week summer programme at the Université de Grenoble (20 hours tuition a week) to £5000 for a full academic year at the Université de Poitiers, including tuition and accommodation. One semester (1 October to 31 January) at the world famous Université de la Sorbonne, in the heart of left-bank Paris, costs £6690 and summer courses there run from four to eleven weeks (from £1490).

Courses are also available throughout the year at private language schools in Paris, Bordeaux and Antibes lasting from one to 26 weeks. The personal attention, intensive tuition and small class sizes make this type of course ideal for students who have limited time available to study abroad.

CIEE (Council on International Educational Exchange)

52 Poland Street	Tel: +44 (0) 20 7478 2020
London W1F 7AB	Fax: +44 (0) 20 7734 7322
UK	www.councilexchanges.org.uk

For further details see main listing under Multi-languages.

College Northside

CP480, 916 14ème Avenue,	Tel: +1 819 322 1133
Val-Morin, Québec JOT 2RO, Canada	Fax: +1 819 322 2111

Northside offers an intensive French immersion camp through the summer geared towards gappers aged between 16 and 20, located in the mountains in the French-speaking village of Val-Morin about an hour's drive north of Montreal.

Ecole SKI-EXP-AIR School

770 Colonel Jones	Tel: +418 654 9071
Ste Foy	Fax: +418 654 9071
Quebec City, Canada	www.ski-exp-air.com

Ski Exp Air runs courses in Canada, designed to get you a ski/snowboard instructor qualification whilst you improve your French. As the sport course progresses, more and more classes are taught in French and there are weekly French conversation sessions.

You will be based on a college campus in Quebec City where you can mix with French-speaking students. The accommodation has TV/internet facilities and you would have the use of a swimming pool, a gymnasium and tennis, volleyball and badminton courts.

For more information about the courses see Ski Exp Air in the Learning Abroad section under Sport.

EF International Languages

74 Roupell Street	Tel: +44 (0) 8707 200735
London SE1 8SS, UK	www.ef.com

For further details see main listing under Multi-languages.

ELFCA (Institut d'Enseignement de la Langue Française sur la Côte D'Azur)

66 Avenue de Toulon	Tel: +33 (0) 4 9465 0331
83400 Hyères,	Fax: +33 (0) 4 9465 8122
France	www.elfca.com

The ELFCA institute is located in Hyères on the Mediterranean coast. Tutition is in small groups, 22 to 30 hours per week, with courses ranging from 1 week at 265 euros to 22 weeks at 200 euros per week. Students can take the Alliance Française exams or prepare for the DELF exams.

The school is in smart air-conditioned premises with a restaurant. Accommodation can be in hotels or apartments, though ELFCA always recommends that you truly immerse yourself in the French way of life by living with a host family. This is probably the best option as the French are well-known for their cuisine, and those from the southern regions pride themselves on their hospitality and conviviality, so you will be well looked after.

The local area is well-known for its beauty and Hyères is an attrative medium-sized town of 55,000 inhabitants offering modern facilities as well as more than 20km of

157

wonderful beaches. Its central position between Provence and the Riviera, makes it easy to visit other well-known towns and interesting sites such as Monaco, Nice, Cannes, Marseilles, Camargue, The Verdon Canyon, Avignon etc.

En Famille Overseas
4 St Helena Road
60b Maltravers Street,
Colchester, Essex CO3 3BA, UK

Tel: +44 (0) 1206 546 741
Fax: +44 (0) 1206 546 740

En Famille Overseas arranges for you to stay with a family in France as a paying guest. You can attend a suitable language course nearby or have private coaching from your host. Prices start from £200 a week for full board accommodation, including excursion expenses. Tuition costs are extra - around £12 an hour. You can use your 'homestay' as a springboard for finding a local job and you can stay with a family for a week to a year, with the board and lodging costs negotiable if you stay more than a month. En Famille usually needs about a month's notice to fix it up.

Euro Academy
2nd Floor
67 -71 Lewisham High Street,
Lewisham, London SE13 5JX, UK

Tel: +44 (0) 20 8297 0505
Fax: +44 (0) 20 8297 0984

For further details see main listing under Multi-languages.

Fondation 9
485 Avenue Louise
Brussels 1050, Belgium

Tel: + 32 (0) 2 627 52 52
Fax : + 32 (0) 2 627 51 00

Founded in 1989 by the Université Libre de Bruxelles, the Chamber of Commerce and Industry of Brussels and the city of Brussels, Foundation 9 offers courses on its campus in Brussels with accommodation in the campus halls of residence, with families or in studio flats.

Institut Cunéiforme
3, Rue Maguelone, 34000, Montpellier, France

Tel: +33 4 6706 5690

The Institut Cunéiforme runs intensive courses in Montpellier lasting between two weeks and three months. Accommodation is with local families (although hotels can be arranged on request), and the aim is to immerse you completely in the life of the city. So as well as having French tuition, you can go to classes on subjects ranging from cheese to poetry. Visits are organised to local museums, markets and buildings, and Montpellier is an excellent base from which to investigate some wilder pursuits: you can try skiing, snow sports, horse riding, canoeing, trekking and rafting.

Institut Français
17 Queensberry Place,
London SW7 2DT, UK

Tel: +44 (0) 20 7581 2701

About 6000 students pass through the Institut Français each year - it's the official French government centre of language and culture in London. The Cultural Centre Library at the Institut has a booklet with comprehensive information on language courses in France, Cours de Français Langue Etrangère (in French), which lists beginner, intermediate and advanced level courses.

Institut Savoisien

Institut Savoisien d'Etudes Françaises pour Etrangers
Domaine Universitaire de Jacob Bellecombette,   Tel: +33 4 7975 8414
F 73011 - BP 1104, Chambery Cedex, France   Fax: +33 4 7975 8416

Among the host of universities in France offering language courses to students from abroad is the Université de Savoie: its language institute offers courses throughout the year. Your level of French is assessed on arrival and you are placed with the appropriate group. Among the many courses offered, there is a three-week summer course (20 hours per week) costing €490 excluding accommodation. Situated in Chambéry, about 50km from Annecy near the Swiss border with southeast France, the Institut is also the region for ski enthusiasts who prefer to study in winter.

Language Courses Abroad

67 Ashby Road   Tel: +44 (0) 1509 211612
Loughborough   Fax: +44 (0) 1509 260037
Leicestershire LE11 3AA, UK   www.languagesabroad.co.uk

For further details see main listing under Multi-Languages.

Learn Languages Abroad

'Sceilig'   Tel: +353 1 451 1674
Ballymorefinn   Fax: +353 1 451 1636
Glenasmole, Dublin 24, Republic of Ireland   www.languages.ie

For further details see main listing under Multilanguages.

Lyon Bleu International

3 Grande Rue des Feuillants, 69001, Lyon, France   Tel: +33 4 7839 7690

Lyon Bleu International language school is located in a UNESCO-designated World Heritage site in central Lyon. It offers programmes for all levels of French, and teaches for the usual range of recognised French language certificates, including Alliance Française exams. Guided tours and excursions are arranged and are free to participants of general French classes.

There's also a language exchange programme which enables you to meet French people and practise your French.

Point3 Centre de Langues

404 St-Pierre Street, Suite 101,
Montréal, Quebec H2Y 2M2, Canada   Tel: +1 514 840 7228

If you like the idea of learning French in Canada, the Point3 language centre in Montréal, Quebec, promises to limit its class size to ten and runs courses ranging from two to 36 weeks. Culturally one of the liveliest cities in Canada, Montréal is also near the US border and within reach of New York and Boston as well as Toronto, Ottawa and the Niagara Falls.

Four weeks' tuition (22 hours per week) costs CAN$924 (approx £375). Accommodation is charged separately, and prices vary according to where you stay - options include a host family, a student residence or a fully-furnished apartment.

Vis-A-Vis
2-4 Stoneleigh Park Road,
Epsom, Surrey KT19 0QT, UK

Tel: +44 (0) 20 8786 8021

Vis-A-Vis offer French courses in nine locations worldwide including Annecy, Bruxelles, Montréal, Montpellier, Nice, Royan, Vichy and Paris. Various other accommodation options are available, and there is the usual range of course length, level and intensity.

Global Adventures Project
38 Queens Gate
SW11 5HR London
UK

Tel: +44 800 085 4197
Fax: +44 207 7590 7444
www.globaladventures.co.uk

German

AFS Community Projects Overseas
Leeming House
Vicar Lane, Leeds LS2 7JF, UK

Tel: +44 (0) 113 242 6136
Fax: +44 (0) 113 243 0631

For further details see main listing under Multi-languages.

Alliances Abroad
2423 Pennsylvania Avenue NW
Washington, DC 20037, USA

Tel: +1 (202) 467 9467
Fax: +1 (202) 467 9460

For further details see main listing under Multi-languages.

British-German Youth Exchange
British Council (Central Bureau),
German Embassy, UK

Tel: +44 (0) 20 7723 6439

Contact for details of programmes.

BWS Germanlingua
Bayerstr. 13
80335 Munich, Germany

Tel: +49 (0) 89 599 892 00
Fax: +49 (0) 89 599 892 01

BWS Germanlingua is based in Munich and Berlin; all staff are experienced teachers, and class have a maximum of 12 students.

Caledonia Languages Abroad
The Clockhouse
Bonnington Mill, 72 Newhaven Road,
Edinburgh EH6 5QG, Scotland

Tel: +44 (0) 131 621 7721/2
Fax: +44 (0) 131 621 7723
www.caledonialanguages.co.uk

For further details see main listing under Multi-languages.

CERAN Lingua International
Avenue des Petits Sapins 27
B-4900 SPA, Belgium

Tel: +32 8779 1122
Fax: +38 87 791 188

CERAN runs weekly intensive residential language programmes in Dutch, French, German, Spanish and Japanese with 'complete immersion' in the language from 8am to 10pm.

CESA Languages Abroad

CESA House
Pennance Road
Lanner, Cornwall TR16 5TQ, UK

Tel: +44 (0) 1209 211 800
Fax: +44 (0) 1209 211 830
www.cesalanguages.com

For further details see main listing under Multi-languages.

CIEE (Council on International Educational Exchange)

52 Poland Street
London W1F 7AB
UK

Tel: +44 (0) 20 7478 2020
Fax: +44 (0) 20 7734 7322
www.councilexchanges.org.uk

For further details see main listing under Multi-languages.

Deutsch-Institut Tirol

A-6370 Kitzbühel
Am Sandhugel, Austria

Tel: +41 53 56 71274
Fax: +41 53 56 72363

The Deutsch-Institut Tirol has been offering German courses combined with skiing, in Kitzbühel, Austria, for over 20 years. For the last three years we have run a specific programme for gappers. No previous knowledge of German is required. German classes for all standards are offered. The intensive German lessons are followed by skiing or snowboarding tuition, sufficient to enable you to take the instructors' exam, leaving you free to work as a ski/snowboard instructor for the whole winter season. Some experience in skiing/snowboarding is recommended. One week out travelling around Eastern Europe is included in the programme.

EF International Languages

74 Roupell Street, London SE1 8SS, UK

Tel: +44 (0) 8707 200735

For further details see main listing under Multi-languages.

Euro Academy

2nd Floor
67 -71 Lewisham High Street, Lewisham,
London SE13 5JX, UK

Tel: +44 (0) 20 8297 0505
Fax: +44 (0) 20 8297 0984

For further details see main listing under Multi-languages.

German Academic Exchange Service

34 Belgrave Square
London SW1X 8QB, UK

Tel: +44 (0) 20 7235 1736
Fax: +44 (0) 20 7235 9602

The German Academic Exchange Service is the largest academic exchange service in the world, granting over 60,000 scholarships per year. Its booklet Sommerkurse in Deutschland lists summer courses at German universities in language, literature, regional studies, music and other subjects. The list is designed for university students, but there's no reason why gap year students can't apply too.

German Embassy (Cultural Department)

23 Belgrave Square
London SW1X APZ, UK

Tel: +44 (0) 20 7824 1300
www.german-embassy.org.uk

Goethe Institut
Languages Department, 50 Princes Gate,
Exhibition Road, London SW7 2PH, UK   Tel: +44 (0) 20 7596 4004

The Goethe Institut is probably the best-known international German language school network, with 125 centres in 76 countries. It is a non-profit organisation funded by the German government, and it offers a wide variety of courses as well as having a lending library and multimedia centre in London. It will happily send you information on studying in Germany, including the booklets Learn German in Germany and Sommerkurse in Deutschland.

The Goethe Institute has 16 course locations in Germany, including Bonn, where you can, for example, go on a 4-week intensive course for €945 (tuition only) or €1355 (single room accommodation included). There's also a 3-week summer course aimed specifically at those aged between 18 and 20. It takes place in Berlin and Hersshing and costs €1915 all inclusive.

Language Courses Abroad
67 Ashby Road   Tel: +44 (0) 1509 211612
Loughborough   Fax: +44 (0) 1509 260037
Leicestershire LE11 3AA, UK   www.languagesabroad.co.uk

For further details see main listing under Multi-Languages.

Learn Languages Abroad
'Sceilig'   Tel: +353 1 451 1674
Ballymorefinn   Fax: +353 1 451 1636
Glenasmole, Dublin 24, Republic of Ireland   www.languages.ie

For further details see main listing under Multilanguages.

Greek

AFS Community Projects Overseas
Leeming House   Tel: +44 (0) 113 242 6136
Vicar Lane, Leeds LS2 7JF, UK   Fax: +44 (0) 113 243 0631

For further details see main listing under Multi-languages.

CESA Languages Abroad
CESA House   Tel: +44 (0) 1209 211 800
Pennance Road   Fax: +44 (0) 1209 211 830
Lanner, Cornwall TR16 5TQ, UK   www.cesalanguages.com

For further details see main listing under Multi-languages.

DIKEMES - International Center for Hellenic and Mediterranean Studies
5 Plateia Stadiou   Tel: +30 210 7560749
PO Box 17176, GR - 10024, Athens, Greece   Fax: +30 210 7561497

DIKEMES, in collaboration with its North American associate, College Year in Athens, brings more than 300 university students to Athens each year to study Ancient Greek Civilization and the East Mediterranean Area.

A range of university-level summer programmes is also available, including

Intensive Modern Greek Language, which attracts participants from Europe and North America., DIKEMES has now developed continuing education programmes in collaboration with the University of Birmingham, UK in the fields of Archaeology, Ancient History and Byzantine Studies.

Euro Academy
2nd Floor
67 -71 Lewisham High Street,   Tel: +44 (0) 20 8297 0505
Lewisham, London SE13 5JX, UK   Fax: +44 (0) 20 8297 0984

For further details see main listing under Multi-languages.

Greek Embassy Education Department
1a Holland Park   Tel: +44 (0) 20 7221 0093
London W11 3TP, UK   www.greekembassy.org.uk

Go to the Greek Embassy website to link to the Greek Ministry of Education. Here you can find a list of universities and schools in Athens, Thessalonika, Crete and the Greek islands among other places where modern Greek is taught, in combination with civilisation and culture courses (ancient and modern).

Indonesian

Language Courses Abroad
67 Ashby Road, Loughborough,   Tel: +44 (0) 1509 211612
Leicestershire LE11 3AA, UK   Fax: +44 (0) 1509 260037

For further details see main listing under Multi-Languages.

Italian

AFS Community Projects Overseas
Leeming House   Tel: +44 (0) 113 242 6136
Vicar Lane, Leeds LS2 7JF, UK   Fax: +44 (0) 113 243 0631

For further details see main listing under Multi-languages.

Global Adventures Project
38 Queens Gate   Tel: +44 800 085 4197
SW11 5HR London   Fax: +44 207 7590 7444
UK   www.globaladventures.co.uk

Accademia del Giglio
Via Ghibellina 116   Tel: +39 055 23 02 467
50122, Florence, Italy   Fax: +39 055 23 02 467

This quiet, small school takes about 30 students, taught in small classes. As well as Itaian language courses, they offer classes in fresco painting.

Accademia Italiana
Piazza Pitti 15
50125, Florence, Italy

Tel: +39 055 284 616
Fax: +39 055 284486

An international design, art and language school, the Accademia Italiana puts on summer language courses as well as full-year and longer academic and Masters courses.

AFS Community Projects Overseas
Leeming House
Vicar Lane, Leeds LS2 7JF, UK

Tel: +44 (0) 113 242 6136
Fax: +44 (0) 113 243 0631

For further details see main listing under Multi-languages.

Alliances Abroad
2423 Pennsylvania Avenue NW
Washington, DC 20037, USA

Tel: +1 (202) 467 9467
Fax: +1 (202) 467 9460

For further details see main listing under Multi-languages.

British Institute of Florence
Piazza Strozzi 2
50123
Florence, Italy

Tel: +39 (0) 55 2677 8200
Fax: +39 (0) 55 2677 8222
www.britishinstitute.it

Established in 1917 to promote the cultures and language of Great Britain and Italy, The Institute offers an extensive range of courses in Italian Language, Art History, Practical Art and Italian Culture as well as teaching English to the local Italian population.

visit: www.gap-year.com

Types of Course: 'Living Italian' 3 month language courses, History of Art, Life Drawing, Watercolour, Italian Opera, Cinema & Film, Tuscan Cooking, University credits available.

Timing & Length of Course: courses are from two days to one year; most run monthly. Summer School in August.

Destinations: Florence & Massa Marittima near the Tuscan coast.

Costs: Tuition only costs from 90 euro for one week and from 295 euro for four weeks. Help is given to find and book accommodation. Students have the use of the Library and free email and internet for the duration of the course.

Eligibility: The minimum age is 18.

Cactus Language
4 Clarence House
30-31 North Street, Brighton,   Tel: +44 (0) 845 130 4775
East Sussex BN1 1 EB, UK   Fax: +44 (0) 1273 775868

For further details see main listing under Multi-languages.

Caledonia Languages Abroad
The Clockhouse   Tel: +44 (0) 131 621 7721/2
Bonnington Mill, 72 Newhaven Road, Fax: +44 (0) 131 621 7723
Edinburgh EH6 5QG, Scotland   www.caledonialanguages.co.uk

For further details see main listing under Multi-languages.

Centro Linguistico Italiano Dante Alighieri
Piazza della Repubblica 5   Tel: +39 (0) 55 21 0808
I-50123 Florence   Fax: +39 (0) 55 28 7828
Italy   www.clida.it

Recognised as a premier international language school and by the Italian Ministry of Public Education, Centro Linguistico Italiano Dante Alighieri (CLIDA) has, since 1965, offered courses that can be taken as credit for a number of US and European Universities.

The school enjoys comfortable surroundings and offers students easy access to all of its services. CLIDA's teaching staff is composed of highly qualified professors from various international backgrounds. CLIDA specialises in offering its language and cultural instructions in various forms. We offer language group courses, from beginners to those wishing to teach Italian abroad. Course vary in length - from four weeks to nine months.

CLIDA also offers an Academic Year that comes in the form of Italian group courses with complementary cultural and artistic courses and an internship programme that is specifically designed to offer valuable international working experience.

The school can place students in accommodation including shared flats, but tries to avoid placing them with others of the same nationality to make sure that they practice their language skills.

Centro Machiavelli
Piazza Santo Spirito 4   Tel: +39 (0) 55 2396 966
Florence 50125-I, Italy   Fax: +39 (0) 55 280 800

This is a delightful small language school in the Santo Spirito district of Florence, in a quiet square 10 minutes away from the tourist-crammed Ponte Vecchio. Machiavelli has the normal range of language courses, quite reasonably priced.

165

Apprenticeship courses can be organised in local artists' and artisans' workshops nearby and there is always the chance for conversation with local students.The school has a happy atmosphere, all ages, with mainly young continental European and some Japanese students.

Centro Studi Europeo (Europass)
Palazzo Guadagni, Piazza Santo Spirito 9,
50125, Florence, Italy   Tel: +39 055 213 030

Centro Studi Europeo, based in the Eurocentres Firenze, is part of a network of Eurocentres Foundation language schools, with 30 others in Europe, the USA, Canada and Japan. The school takes 150-200 students in the high season and offers a good range of language and cultural courses.

CESA Languages Abroad
CESA House	Tel: +44 (0) 1209 211 800
Pennance Road	Fax: +44 (0) 1209 211 830
Lanner, Cornwall TR16 5TQ, UK	www.cesalanguages.com

For further details see main listing under Multi-languages.

CIEE (Council on International Educational Exchange)
52 Poland Street	Tel: +44 (0) 20 7478 2020
London W1F 7AB	Fax: +44 (0) 20 7734 7322
UK	www.councilexchanges.org.uk

For further details see main listing under Multi-languages.

Euro Academy
2nd Floor

67 -71 Lewisham High Street,	Tel: +44 (0) 20 8297 0505
Lewisham, London SE13 5JX, UK	Fax: +44 (0) 20 8297 0984

For further details see main listing under Multi-languages.

Il Sillabo
Via Alberti	Tel: + 39 055 9123238
31, 52027 San Giovanni, Valdarno (AR), Italy	Fax: + 39 055 942439

Il Sillabo, a small, family-run school, offers a relaxed, warm and friendly environment blending language instruction, and cultural experiences. Il Sillabo offers a wide variety of Italian language courses for all levels, which can be taken alongside additional courses such as cookery, drawing, painting, ceramics and archaeology. It also offers an intensive cultural and social programme.

Courses start throughout the year. Il Sillabo offers generous discounts for long term enrolment, eg €2079 for the 24-week intensive course instead of €2790. Il Sillabo also helps its students find cheap, convenient accommodation with local host families, in self-contained apartments, on farms or in local hotels. Accommodation in a shared apartment, in a single room for 24 weeks would cost around €2040.

Istituto di Lingua e Cultura Italiana Michelangelo
Via Ghibellina 88, 50122, Florence, Italy   Tel: +39 055 240 975

Housed in the 15th-century Palazzo Gherardi close to Michelangelo's house and Florence University, the Michelangelo Institute offers cultural courses (mainly eight two-hour sessions) on Art History, Literature (Boccaccio, Dante, Petrarch, plus

Giacomo Leopardi, Allesandro Manzoni, Pier Paolo Pasolini), Commerce and Commercial Correspondence, and 'L'Italia oggi', a current affairs course that covers the Italian political system, political parties, north/south issues, the media and EU/Italy relationships.

Istituto Donatello

Via Galliano 1   Tel: +39 055 354 112
50144, Florence, Italy   Fax: +39 055 355 686

In a very friendly and familial environment you can learn the Italian language as well as learn about Italian art history, cooking, wood carving and theatre. The institute organises accommodation with other students or Italian families.

Istituto Europeo

Piazza delle pallottole n. 1 (duomo)   Tel: +39 05523 81071
1-50122 Florence, Italy   Fax: +39 05528 9145

Istituto Europeo offers Italian language courses lasting from a week (20 hrs, €202) to a year (960 hrs, €3998). There are three language schools: two in Italy (Florence and Chieti) and one in Japan (Osaka). As well as running courses on Italian wine and food (€120 each for 16 hrs), Istituto Europeo also has an art and music school. Trips and excursions can be arranged to local museums. Fees include tuition, materials, use of a piano and cultural and recreational extra curricular activities. Accommodation is available in individual apartments (€690-140), shared apartments (€380-E470 for single room; €280-€370 double room) or hotels. Prices are for 4 weeks excluding bills.

Italian Cultural Institute (Istituto di Cultura Italiano)

39 Belgrave Square,
London SW1X 8NX, UK   Tel: +44 (0) 20 7235 1461

The Italian Cultural Institute has a bookshelf brimming with free leaflets on courses of all sorts in Italy (including Italian cookery, musical, culture and fashion).

Italian Embassy

N14 3 Kings Yard   Tel: +44 (0) 20 7312 2200
London WIK 4EH, UK   www.embitaly.org.uk

Includes a list of Italian language schools.

Language Courses Abroad

67 Ashby Road   Tel: +44 (0) 1509 211612
Loughborough, Leicestershire LE11 3AA, UK   Fax: +44 (0) 1509 260037

For further details see main listing under Multi-Languages.

Learn Languages Abroad

'Sceilig'   Tel: +353 1 451 1674
Ballymorefinn   Fax: +353 1 451 1636
Glenasmole, Dublin 24, Republic of Ireland   www.languages.ie

For further details see main listing under Multilanguages.

Lorenzo de' Medici

Via Faenza 43, Florence, Italy   Tel: +39 055 287 143 50123

The Lorenzo de' Medici's intake peaks in spring at about 600 students, with many of them coming from the USA to do cultural courses linked to US university programmes. Its language teaching method is to 'systematically develop the four principal linguistic abilities: speaking, listening, reading and writing.' It also offers the usual combinations of language courses (seven levels) and cultural courses and has a large library in the adjoining San Iacopo di Corbolini church. Also two sparkling professional kitchens where aproned students can be seen making pasta the Italian way.

Scuola Leonardo da Vinci
Via Bufalini 3   Tel: +39 055 261181
50122, Florence, Italy   Fax: +39 055 294820

Very near the Hospidale and the Piazza del Duomo in the centre of Florence, this relaxed school offers standard (2 to 24 weeks, 20 lessons a week on six ability levels, starting every two weeks, about €570 for 4 weeks), intensive and intensive plus courses in Italian. Also has schools in Rome (+39 066 889 2513) and Siena (+39 057 724 9097).

Torre di Babele
Via Bixio 74   Tel: +39 067008434
00185 Rome, Italy   Fax: +39 0670497150

Torre di Babele is officially authorized by the Italian Ministry of Education and is also a member of ELITE (Excellent Language Institutions Teaching in Europe) and ASILS (Associazione Scuole di Italiano come Lingua Seconda).

Courses run all year round and are led by highly-qualified teachers. The school, which is also a teacher training centre, aims to use dynamic teaching methods and stimulating texts in order to incorporate the personal interests of students as well as diverse aspects of Italian life. All courses are taught in small groups (maximum 12), giving students individual attention in a friendly and relaxed atmosphere.

The school offers a rich and interesting extra-curricular programme with guided tours and seminars on art, architecture, cinema, literature, politics, Italian cooking and wines. At weekends there are excursions to sites of interest including Pompeii, Naples, Orvieto and Florence. An intensive course (4 hours a day for 2 weeks) costs €310. Accommodation is available in private homes, student apartments and hotels. Two weeks' accommodation in a single room costs €207; a double room costs €145, there is a reduction for longstay.

Japanese

AFS Community Projects Overseas
Leeming House   Tel: +44 (0) 113 242 6136
Vicar Lane, Leeds LS2 7JF, UK   Fax: +44 (0) 113 243 0631

For further details see main listing under Multi-languages.

CERAN Lingua International
Avenue des Petits Sapins 27   Tel: +32 8779 1122
B-4900 SPA, Belgium   Fax: +38 87 791 188

CERAN runs weekly intensive residential language programmes in Dutch, French, German, Spanish and Japanese with 'complete immersion' in the language from 8am to 10pm.

CESA Languages Abroad

CESA House
Pennance Road
Lanner, Cornwall TR16 5TQ, UK

Tel: +44 (0) 1209 211 800
Fax: +44 (0) 1209 211 830
www.cesalanguages.com

For further details see main listing under Multi-languages.

Japan Foundation London Language Centre

27 Knightsbridge
London SW1X 7LY, UK

Tel: +44 (0) 20 7838 9955
www.nihonjocentre.org.uk

The Japan Foundation London Language Centre does not organise courses itself, but it provides a list of Japanese language centres in the UK, for groups, individuals or tailor-made courses at all levels.

Japanese Embassy

101-104 Piccadilly
London W1J 7JT, UK

Tel: +44 (0) 20 7465 6500
www.uk.emb-japan.go.jp

The Japanese Embassy website has information about studying in Japan as well as information about visas you'll need if you want to study, teach (usually TEFL) or work there.

SOAS (School of Oriental and African Studies)

SOAS Language Centre
University of London, Thornhaugh Street,
Russell Square, London WC1H 0XG, UK

Tel: +44 (0) 20 7898 4888
www.soas.ac.uk

SOAS offers part-time evening classes for beginners. But if you want to study Japanese more intensively there are full-time one-year courses - although these are run in London, once you have successfully passed the three-term course (around £7,500) you are given the chance of a work placement in Japan.

Portuguese

Caledonia Languages Abroad

The Clockhouse
Bonnington Mill, 72 Newhaven Road,
Edinburgh EH6 5QG, Scotland

Tel: +44 (0) 131 621 7721/2
Fax: +44 (0) 131 621 7723
www.caledonialanguages.co.uk

For further details see main listing under Multi-languages.

Canning House

2 Belgrave Square
London SW1X 8PJ, UK

Tel: +44 (0) 20 7235 2303
www.canninghouse.com

The Canning House Education and Cultural Department provides information about Latin America, Portugal and Spain. Among various information leaflets (all £4) it publishes a list of universities and language centres offering language courses in these countries, with prices and dates, and another leaflet about employment and work experience opportunities for young people in Latin America, Portugal or Spain. This includes organisations and useful contacts for teaching posts, summer jobs, international voluntary work camps and au pair work in each country. You can use the centre's library, which houses over 60,000 books, to research your trip. Library membership costs £20. Membership of Canning House

(£40 a year, £30 for students) gets you involved in all sorts of London-based Hispanic/Latin events, such as film, poetry readings and talks.

CIAL Centro de Linguas
Av da Republica   Tel: +351 217 940 448
41 - 8th Floor, Lisbon 1050-187, Portugal   Fax: +351 217 960 783

With schools in Lisbon and Faro, CIAL organises courses in Portuguese including group courses with either 3 hours' tuition (€240 per week) or 6 hours' tuition (€432 per week), a two-week teachers training course (€450), individual lessons (€30 per hour) and private groups of two (€45 per hour), as well as specialist courses in Brazilian or African Portuguese. Accommodation is in private homes at an extra cost of €108 per week, which includes breakfast.

Euro Academy
2nd Floor, 67 -71 Lewisham High Street,   Tel: +44 (0) 20 8297 0505
Lewisham, London SE13 5JX, UK   Fax: +44 (0) 20 8297 0984

For further details see main listing under Multi-languages.

Language Courses Abroad
67 Ashby Road Loughborough,   Tel: +44 (0) 1509 211612
Leicestershire LE11 3AA, UK   Fax: +44 (0) 1509 260037

For further details see main listing under Multi-Languages.

Russian

AFS Community Projects Overseas
Leeming House   Tel: +44 (0) 113 242 6136
Vicar Lane, Leeds LS2 7JF, UK   Fax: +44 (0) 113 243 0631

For further details see main listing under Multi-languages.

Caledonia Languages Abroad
The Clockhouse   Tel: +44 (0) 131 621 7721/2
, Bonnington Mill, 72 Newhaven Road,   Fax: +44 (0) 131 621 7723
Edinburgh EH6 5QG, Scotland   www.caledonialanguages.co.uk

For further details see main listing under Multi-languages.

CESA Languages Abroad
CESA House   Tel: +44 (0) 1209 211 800
Pennance Road   Fax: +44 (0) 1209 211 830
Lanner, Cornwall TR16 5TQ, UK   www.cesalanguages.com

For further details see main listing under Multi-languages.

EF International Languages
74 Roupell Street, London SE1 8SS, UK   Tel: +44 (0) 8707 200735

For further details see main listing under Multi-languages.

Euro Academy

2nd Floor, 67 -71 Lewisham High Street,   Tel: +44 (0) 20 8297 0505
Lewisham, London SE13 5JX, UK   Fax: +44 (0) 20 8297 0984

For further details see main listing under Multi-languages.

Language Courses Abroad

67 Ashby Road
Loughborough,   Tel: +44 (0) 1509 211612
Leicestershire LE11 3AA, UK   Fax: +44 (0) 1509 260037

For further details see main listing under Multi-Languages.

Obninsk Humanities Centre

Dubravushka, 249020 Kaluga Oblast, Obninsk,
Pionersky Proezd 29, Russia

The Obninsk Humanities Centre is an independent boarding school two hours from Moscow offering intensive and reasonably priced Russian courses. A week costs $300 (or $200 if you're a student), including 20-25 hours tuition, full board and lodging, emergency medical treatment, transport to and from the airport and sightseeing trips.

You also get access to sport and leisure facilities including volleyball grounds, ping-pong tables, a football pitch which doubles as a skating-rink in winter, scenic cross-country skiing pistes in the surrounding forest and mountain-skiing slopes. If you agree to teach some English your fees may be waived completely. For further information contact the UK representative, Lara Bushell, at: 143 Langton Way, London SE3 7JS, England, Tel: +44 (0) 20 8858 0614; Fax: +44 (0) 20 8305 0405.

Russian Language Centre

11 Coldbath Square   Tel: +44 (0) 20 7689 5400
London EC1R 5HL, UK   www.russiancentre.co.uk

The Russian Language Centre in London offers a flexible approach to learning this language, with a range of courses available. Courses of any length from two weeks to a year, including summer courses, can be arranged in Russia, at the Grint Educational Centre which used to be part of Pushkin University in Moscow, at Moscow State University or at St Petersburg State University. Accommodation can be arranged for you, either in Russian student halls or with a family.

Russian Language Centre of Moscow M V Lomonosov State University

Rooms 3 and 4, Building 9, Khokhlova Str,
Moscow State University by M V Lomonosov,   Tel: +7 (095) 939-5692
Moscow, Russia   Fax: +7 (095) 939-5692

Founded by Moscow State University in 1990, the Russian Language Centre specialises in providing individual tuition. Courses are held at all levels and range from 12-24 hours per week. The individual nature of the tuition means you can have 'practical' lessons with your tutor, visiting local museums, theatres, exhibitions and cafés.

Tuition is billed per 'academic hour' (ie 45 minutes), and ranges from US$12 for a one-on-one lesson at a location of your choice to US$4 for a lesson on campus in a group of 5-8. Accommodation is either in a hotel on campus (US$16-US$23 per day) or with host families (US$11-US$16 per day). Excursions are arranged to sites of interest including St Petersburg, Irkutsk (lake Baikal) and Petrozavodsk. For a small fee, the centre will provide you with visa support, airport pickup and transfer.

Spanish

Academia Hispanica - Ih Córdoba

Rodriguez Sanchez
15, 14003 Córdoba, Spain
Tel: +34 957 488 002
Fax: +34 957 488 199

Academia Hispanica offers language tuition in small groups (max: 8 per class) in the historic centre of Córdoba. There are courses to suit all levels. If you want to learn as much as possible in a short time, the two-week General Intensive Course costs €265 for 20 lessons per week; the one-week Intensive Plus (€422) combines 20 group lessons with 10 one-to-one tuition sessions. Both intensive courses are available to beginners and advanced Spanish speakers.

The DELE course (€673) runs for four weeks and prepares you for the Diploma de Español como Lengua Extranjera (Spanish as a Foreign Language Diploma) examination. Be prepared to work hard as the course includes 20 intensive Spanish lessons and 6 exam preparation lessons per week! Tailor-made private lessons for 1 or 2 people (€29 per lesson) and Business Spanish are also available. All students joining the language school take a basic test to establish their profiency.

Accommodation is located in the historic city centre, prices vary depending on availability: a single room with a Spanish host family including breakfast, lunch and weekly laundry service will cost around €240 per fortnight. Single rooms in self-catering flats or apartments are also available.

Global Adventures Project

38 Queens Gate
SW11 5HR London
UK
Tel: +44 800 085 4197
Fax: +44 207 7590 7444
www.globaladventures.co.uk

Academia de español, Simon Bolivar

Leonidas Plaza 353 y Roca, Quito, Ecuador
Tel: +593 22 504977

The Simon Bolivar Spanish is one of the biggest Spanish schools in Ecuador with an average of 40 students per month. Individual Spanish lessons are offered at the main building in Quito and group lessons are given at centres in the Amazon jungle and on the coast.

Prices are from US$980 to US$1120 for 4 weeks, including: 20 hours of individual Spanish lessons per week, homestay with private room and meals, all taxes, airport pickup, unlimited internet usage, all weekdays activities (incl. salsa lessons!) and some study materials. The school is located in a quiet residential area of Quito and all host families are located within walking distance of the school.

AFS Community Projects Overseas

Leeming House
Vicar Lane, Leeds LS2 7JF, UK
Tel: +44 (0) 113 242 6136
Fax: +44 (0) 113 243 0631

For further details see main listing under Multi-languages.

Alliances Abroad

2423 Pennsylvania Avenue NW
Washington, DC 20037, USA
Tel: +1 (202) 467 9467
Fax: +1 (202) 467 9460

For further details see main listing under Multi-languages.

Learning Abroad | Languages/Spanish

visit: www.gap-year.com

Cactus Language
4 Clarence House
30-31 North Street, Brighton,   Tel: +44 (0) 845 130 4775
East Sussex BN1 1 EB, UK   Fax: +44 (0) 1273 775868

For further details see main listing under Multi-languages.

Caledonia Languages Abroad
The Clockhouse   Tel: +44 (0) 131 621 7721/2
Bonnington Mill, 72 Newhaven Road,   Fax: +44 (0) 131 621 7723
Edinburgh EH6 5QG, Scotland   www.caledonialanguages.co.uk

For further details see main listing under Multi-languages.

Canning House
2 Belgrave Square   Tel: +44 (0) 20 7235 2303
London SW1X 8PJ, UK   www.canninghouse.com

The Canning House Education and Cultural Department provides information about Latin America, Portugal and Spain. Among various information leaflets (all £4) it publishes a list of universities and language centres offering language courses in these countries, with prices and dates, and another leaflet about employment and work experience opportunities for young people in Latin America, Portugal or Spain. This includes organisations and useful contacts for teaching posts, summer jobs, international voluntary work camps and au pair work in each country.

You can use the centre's library, which houses over 60,000 books, to research your trip. Library membership costs £20. Membership of Canning House (£40 a year, £30 for students) gets you involved in all sorts of London-based Hispanic/Latin events, such as film, poetry readings and talks.

CERAN Lingua International
Avenue des Petits Sapins 27   Tel: +32 8779 1122
B-4900 SPA, Belgium   Fax: +38 87 791 188

CERAN runs weekly intensive residential language programmes in Dutch, French, German, Spanish and Japanese with 'complete immersion' in the language from 8am to 10pm.

CESA Languages Abroad
CESA House   Tel: +44 (0) 1209 211 800
Pennance Road   Fax: +44 (0) 1209 211 830
Lanner, Cornwall TR16 5TQ, UK   www.cesalanguages.com

For further details see main listing under Multi-languages.

CIEE (Council on International Educational Exchange)
52 Poland Street   Tel: +44 (0) 20 7478 2020
London W1F 7AB   Fax: +44 (0) 20 7734 7322
UK   www.councilexchanges.org.uk

For further details see main listing under Multi-languages.

Cursos Internacionales de la Universidad de Salamanca
Patio de Escuelas Menores,
s/n 37008, Salamanca, Spain   Tel: +34 923 294 418

The Universidad de Salamanca offers summer courses in subjects like Spanish cookery, Spanish guitar, flamenco dance, and The World of the Bull: a complete guide to Bullfighting.

Don Quijote
PO Box 218   Tel: +44 (0) 20 8786 8081
Stoneleigh   Fax: +44 (0) 20 8786 8086
Epsom, Surrey KT19 OYF, UK   www.donquijote.org

Don Quijote has language schools in Spain and Latin America. In Spain the school offers courses in Barcelona, Granada, Madrid, Malaga, Salamanca, Seville, Puerto de la Cruz in Tenerife, and Valencia (where you can take a two-week course for £426, including staying in a self-catering flat).

Latin America is very popular for gap year Spanish studies: cheap airfares if you're lucky. There is a don Quijote school in Guanajuato, Mexico. A 2-week course including staying in a student flat is £346.

Don Quijote also offers Spanish and Activities courses including flamenco dancing, wine tasting, scuba diving, cuisine and literature.

EF International Languages
74 Roupell Street, London SE1 8SS, UK   Tel: +44 (0) 8707 200735

For further details see main listing under Multi-languages.

En Famille Overseas
4 St Helena Road   Tel: +44 (0) 1206 546 741

60b Maltravers Street, Colchester,
Essex CO3 3BA, UK   Fax: +44 (0) 1206 546 740

En Famille Overseas arranges for you to stay with a family in Spain as a paying guest. You can attend a suitable language course nearby or have private coaching from your host. Prices start from £200 a week for full board accommodation, including excursion expenses. Tuition costs are extra - around £12 an hour. You can use your 'homestay' as a springboard for finding a local job and you can stay with a family for a week to a year, with the board and lodging costs negotiable if you stay more than a month. En Famille usually needs about a month's notice to fix it up.

Euro Academy
2nd Floor   Tel: +44 (0) 20 8297 0505
67 -71 Lewisham High Street,
Lewisham, London SE13 5JX, UK   Fax: +44 (0) 20 8297 0984

For further details see main listing under Multi-languages.

GALA
Woodcote House
8 Leigh Lane, Farnham,   Tel: +44 (0) 1252 715 319
Surrey GU9 8HP, UK   Fax: +44 (0) 1252 715 319

GALA acts as an agent for several private language schools in Spain and Latin America. Courses range from two weeks with half-board accommodation in Seville to full nine-month courses. Accommodation is available. Work experience in Spanish hotels is offered.

Hispalingua
General Yague 3, 33004, Oviedo, Asturias, Spain   Tel: +34 98 524 3186

Hispalingua in Oviedo offers four- or eight-week summer courses which will leave you with an understanding of the region as well as the Spanish language. It is about three hours by public transport from Bilbao, (go see the 'sardine-can' Guggenheim museum), and five hours from Madrid.

Instituto Chac-Mool
Privada de la Pradera #108, Colonia Pradera,
Cuernavaca, 62170 Morelos, Mexico   Tel: +52 (777) 317-1163

Instituto Chac-Mool in Cuernavaca, Mexico offers Spanish immersion courses that include 25 hours of weekly Spanish instruction, culture classes, extra-curricular activities, Sunday excursions, and a homestay with a local Mexican family. All instructors are college graduates, native Spanish speakers, and have been trained for 6 months in a method that will have students speaking and understanding Spanish quickly - emphasizing conversation and staying away from tedious grammar drills.

Instituto Chac-Mool is so confident you will learn Spanish quickly that they offer a

175

money back guarantee. Special programmes are also available for medical, business and law enforcement students, contact the institute direct for pricing and more information.

Students of all skill levels can enrol to begin studies any Monday throughout the year and they can study up to 26 weeks. If you mention **www.gap-year.com**, you will get discounts on programmes of 4 weeks or longer. A 4-week programme costs US$1100, (for each additional 4-week programme add US$1000). Price includes tuition and housing with 3 daily meals; small additional charge if you want a private room or to study during June and July.

Language Courses Abroad
67 Ashby Road
Loughborough, Leicestershire LE11 3AA, UK

Tel: +44 (0) 1509 211612
Fax: +44 (0) 1509 260037

For further details see main listing under Multi-Languages.

Learn Languages Abroad
'Sceilig'
Ballymorefinn
Glenasmole, Dublin 24, Republic of Ireland

Tel: +353 1 451 1674
Fax: +353 1 451 1636
www.languages.ie

For further details see main listing under Multilanguages.

Spanish Embassy Education Department
20 Peel Street
London W8 7PD
UK

Tel: +44 (0) 20 7727 2462
Fax: +44 (0) 20 7229 4965
www.sgci.mec.es/uk/

Spanish Study Holidays
67 Ashby Road
Loughborough, Leicestershire LE11 3AA, UK

Tel: +44 (0) 1509 211 612
Fax: +44 (0) 1509 211612

Spanish Study Holidays offers Spanish courses throughout Spain and central and south America lasting from a week to nine months, with 12-30 Spanish lessons a week. Courses are run at all levels and weekend excursions are arranged. Accommodation is in flats, student rooms or with a host family. A two-week intensive course in Madrid (20 lessons per week) in self-catering accommodation costs £425; (a bit more if you stay with a host family). A similar 12-week course costs £1787 (self-catering) or £2380 (host family). Other course centres in Spain include Salamanca, Granada, Seville, Malaga, Madrid, Alicante and Barcelona.

Courses are also available in Bolivia, Costa Rica, Cuba, Ecuador, Guatemala, Mexico and Peru. A two-week course in Guatemala (20 lessons per week) costs £349, including tuition and full board with a host family.

TEFL

Inlingua International
Belpstrasse 11
3007 Bern, Switzerland

Tel: +41 31 388 7777
Fax: +41 31 388 7766

Inlingua International runs TESOL (Teaching English to Speakers of Other Languages) in its colleges throughout Europe. For example, for a cost of £995 you could take the five-week full-time TESOL course leading to a Trinity TESOL certificate at its college in Cheltenham. Once you are qualified, you can make use of the Inlingua recruitment service and the many jobs listed on its website to start earning yourself some money. Inlingua does point out that it can't absolutely guarantee to find you a job.

Prague Schools s.r.o

Na Sekyrce 1392/2	Tel: +42 (0) 233 322 742
160 00 Praha 6	Fax: +42 (0) 233 323 779
Czech Republic	www.tefl.cz

Prague Schools is a dynamic private TEFL school based in Prague 6, specializing in the Trinity Certificate in TESOL (Teaching English to Speakers of Other Languages) courses. Their 4-week, intensive TEFL Certificate course is a practical and theoretical training course designed to produce teachers with the skills and techniques needed to teach English.

Their TEFL/TESOL course is validated by Trinity College London and is internationally recognised, the school stresses their course is not a self-validated TEFL course.

Sport

There are sports courses for all types at all levels, from scuba diving for beginners to advanced ski instructor qualification courses, in pretty much every country in the world. Of course if you manage to get qualified as an instructor you may be able to use it to get a job for the rest of your gap year.

Make sure the course offers the qualifications that will be useful to you and check that the instructors are properly qualified. Most important is to make sure that you have the necessary insurance – take a look at any of the sport websites and you'll find out that accidents do happen (**www.bungeezone.com** disasters page is particularly scary) and if you slip whilst up a mountain injuries tend to be a bit more serious – and expensive – than a sprained ankle. That said, learning a sport abroad is a great way to meet new people, experience the local culture and have a really energetic, fun gap year.

Sport Courses & Qualifications

Ale Corte
6A Dale Grove, N12 8EA London, UK   Tel: +44 (0) 20 86329829

Ale Corte is an experienced snowboarder and instructor who has trained the Argentine National Ski Team and helped compile the techniques and standards used to examine snowboard instructors. His clinics are designed for all levels and are aimed at helping you improve a particular aspect of your technique or progress towards instructor level (though you can't actually take the instructor qualifications).The instructor will complete specially prepared tuition appraisal forms and produce video analysis of progress.

Clinics: 1 or 2 weeks for a minimum of 4 people. The price of £850 pp per week includes accommodation half board, 6 day lift pass, transfers from airport, 6 hours day clinic, material assessment and video correction. Personal tuition: £1500 pp per week.

Allabroad
5 The Square, Marina Bay, Gibraltar, UK   Tel: +350 50202

Allabroad offers friendly expert tuition, tidal certificates, introductory courses to Yachtmaster and sailing from Gibraltar to North Africa and Spain.

Allan Dive
Tel: +60 88 711 715
Borneo, Malaysia   Fax: +60 88 711 715

The Allan Dive school on the island of Borneo in Malaysia offers both PADI and SSI (Scuba School International) Instructors training facilities doing basic training to instructor level, marine conservation projects etc. They also offer internship programmes taking beginners to instructor level in six months to a year. Course prices range from £1500 to £3000 depending on the course you choose. Cost includes training, accommodation & certification. There may be an opportunity for employment.

Base Camp Group
Unit 30, Baseline Business Studios,   Tel: +44 (0) 20 7243 6222
Whitchurch Road, W11 4AT London, UK   Fax: +44 (0) 20 7243 6222

At Base Camp the ski and snowboard instructor courses provide a blend of adventure and training to help you achieve your goals and qualify as an instructor.

BASI (British Association of Snowsport Instructors)
Glenmore   Tel: +44 (0) 1479 861 409
Aviemore, Invernesshire PH22 1QU, Scotland   Fax: +44 (0) 1479 861 718

BASI runs a full-time ten-week course for potential instructors (you need to be an intermediate skier) from January to April for approx. £5000 in Switzerland, Italy, Andorra, France and America.

Bear Creek Outdoor Centre
R R#3 Campbell's Bay   Tel: +1 819 453 2127
Quebec J0X 1K0   Fax: +1 819 453 2128
Canada   www.bearcreekoutdoor.com

Bear Creek Outdoor Centre near Ottawa offers a ten-week outdoor adventure leadership programme aimed at all levels. You must be at least 18 years of age, be able to swim and consider yourself to be in good health.

The programme focuses on nationally (Canadian) and internationally recognised qualifications including kayak instructor and swiftwater rescue technician. Skills are taught in mountain bike guiding, raft guiding, riverboarding, provisioning and backcountry cooking, navigation, group dynamics and leadership. The instructors are highly experienced and you're likely to find yourself being taught to kayak by members of the Canadian Whitewater freestyle team!

The cost of CAN$8000 (about £3700) includes instruction and certification, transportation from Ottawa, room and board, equipment, accommodation on field trips and personal safety equipment. The price does not include travel to and from Ottawa.

Bermuda Sub Aqua Club

P. O. Box, HM3155,
HM NX Hamilton, UK   Tel: + 1 441 291 5640

The Bermuda Sub Aqua Club is a branch of the British Sub Aqua Club and offers members a varied programme of club-organised dives; a safe, structured, proven training programme (BSAC), social activities; access to the club's compressor for air fills and a club newsletter. The club is also active in the community, regularly participating in such events as the Keep Bermuda Beautiful Marine Clean-up dives. The club offers British Sub Aqua Club training courses and welcomes divers from other training agencies (PADI, NAUI, SSI, etc) to 'cross-over' at an equivalent level to their current certification.

Big Squid Scuba Diving Training and Travel

72 Hubert Grove, Clapham, London SW9 9PD, United Kingdom   Tel: +44 (0) 20 7733 6966

Big Squid offers a variety of dive courses using the PADI and TDI systems of diver education. Beginners can start with Discover Scuba courses (a trial dive in the pool) or go straight on to the Open Water Diver course.

Blue Dog Adventures

Amwell Farmouse

Nomansland, Wheathampstead, St. Albans,	Tel: (0)1582 831302
Hertfordshire AL4 8EJ, UK	Fax: (0)1582 834002

Blue Dog offers a variety of adventures, but focuses mainly on equestrian adventures catering for all levels of horsemanship.

Christchurch Parachute School

P O Box 16625	Tel: +64 3 343 5542
Hornby, Christchurch, New Zealand	Fax: +64 3 348 4366

If you would like to learn how to skydive in New Zealand then The Christchurch Parachute School could be the place to do it. They offer many different types of skydiving, including tandem and sports diving. The most expensive jump available, with training included is £100. Accommodation is also available.

Deutsch-Institut Tirol

A-6370 Kitzbühel	Tel: +41 53 56 71274
Am Sandhugel, Austria	Fax: +41 53 56 72363

The Deutsch-Institut Tirol has been offering German courses combined with skiing, in Kitzbühel, Austria, for over 20 years. For the last three years we have run a specific programme for gappers. No previous knowledge of German is required. German classes for all standards are offered. The intensive German lessons are followed by skiing or snowboarding tuition, sufficient to enable you to take the instructors' exam, leaving you free to work as a ski/snowboard instructor for the whole winter season. Some experience in skiing/snowboarding is recommended. One week out travelling around Eastern Europe is included in the programme.

179

Don Quijote

PO Box 218
Stoneleigh
Epsom, Surrey KT19 OYF, UK

Tel: +44 (0) 20 8786 8081
Fax: +44 (0) 20 8786 8086
www.donquijote.org

Fancy diving into the Spanish language and into the clear blue Atlantic Ocean? Don Quijote offers a Spanish language/scuba diving package in Tenerife. Cost, including a 2-week Spanish course and staying in a student flat, is £742.

Eco Africa Experience

Applications Department
Guardian House, Borough Road,
Godalming, Surrey GU7 2AE, UK

Tel: +44 (0) 1483 860 560
Fax: +44 (0) 1483 860 391
www.EcoAfricaExperience.com

Do you want to contribute to conservation in Africa? Eco Africa Experience strives to conserve what man is fast destroying - our very own environment. They send 150+ volunteers to several Southern African game reserves and marine projects per year. They set the standards at the selected reserves in order to maintain a degree of uniformity, thus maintaining a high degree of education, training, learning and general hands on experience while fulfilling the core objective - conservation. Placements range from 4 to 12 weeks, during which you can be involved in conservation projects including anti-poaching patrols, monitoring and counting of wildlife, darting and animal capture, bush rehabilitation and the day-to-day maintenance of the reserve.

Marine projects may include rescue and rehabilitation of marine species, sampling, tagging, monitoring of marine life, and participating in commercial marine-eco tourism activities which include whale and dolphin watching tours, sea kayaking, township tours, river ferry cruises. Contact Eco Africa Experience direct for information about specific opportunities and prices.

Ecole SKI-EXP-AIR School

770 Colonel Jones	Tel: +418 654 9071
Ste Foy	Fax: +418 654 9071
Quebec City, Canada	www.ski-exp-air.com

Ski-exp-air is a Canadian ski and snowboard school serving an international clientele and offering quality, professional instruction in a fun atmosphere. They are located in the Quebec City Region, the wintersport capital of Canada. Using the four surrounding major mountain resorts and friendly, personalized instruction, they will teach you to be an excellent skier and snowboarder - regardless of whether you have ever been on snow or not! Ski-exp-air's three month programme is designed to ensure that you reach the level of certification of your choice as ski, snowboard instructor or racing coach. Canadian instructors and coaches have a world wide reputation of excellence. Ski-exp-air invite you to join them as a valued member of their team: ìWe have proven success in making dreams, your dreams, a reality.î

Exp-air-guide

770 Colonel Jones	Tel: +418 654 9071
Ste Foy	Fax: +418 654 9071
Quebec City, Canada	www.ski-exp-air.com

Become an expert in outdoor trip leadership: Exp-Air-Guide is a Canadian wilderness school that provides, through a variety of great outdoor experiences, the knowledge, skill and attitude you need to become an outdoor adventure leader.

Students come to the exp-air-guide course from all over the world, for the high quality, safe, professional instruction in a fun atmosphere. The highly qualified instructors teach you to canoe, kayak, and hike in a variety of wilderness settings - even if you had little or no experience. You will canoe and kayak both fast and flat water. You will paddle close enough to whales in the mighty Saguenay fjord to practically reach out and touch them! You will trek along historic paths through Canada's forests! Canada's white waters, wildlife, lakes, scenic mountains and valleys will be your classroom and your home. ìWe have proven success in making dreams, your dreams, a reality!î

Flying Fish

25 Union Road	Tel: +44 (0) 1983 280 641
Cowes	Fax: +44 (0) 1983 281821
Isle of Wight PO31 7TW, UK	www.flyingfishonline.com

Flying Fish trains and recruits over 600 people each year to work as yacht skippers and galley chefs and as sailing, diving, surfing, windsurfing, kitesurfing and snow sports instructors. Combine professional training with international adventure and the chance to make money while having fun. Taking advantage of some of the best training locations in the world, watersports courses are run in the UK, Australia, Greece, Cyprus and Egypt whilst ski and snowboard instructor training takes place in Canada.

Flying Fish offers the opportunity to become qualified in a range of sports. What the company calls its Three Year Plan enables students to train, work and travel in the gap year and to pick up interesting jobs in the long vacations during their degree. Flying Fish has its own career advisors to place students, once qualified, in jobs. Courses range from two to 18 weeks and are available to complete beginners and for those who already have some experience.

Gibraltar Sailing Centre

Queensway Quay Marina   Tel: +350 78554
Ragged Staff Warf, Gibraltar, UK   Fax: +350 70652

Expert tuition with the full range of RYA courses.

Greenforce

11-15 Betterton Street   Tel: +44 (0) 870 770 2646 / +44 (0) 20 7470 8888
Covent Garden   Fax: +44 (0) 870 7702647 / +44 (0) 20 7470 8889
London WC2H 9BP, UK   www.greenforce.org

Greenforce runs a series of 10-week marine and terrestrial expeditions around the world, all of which are based on wildlife conservation. No previous experience is necessary as all volunteers get trained from scratch, marine volunteers also get free diver training. You can choose from tracking large mammals in Zambia, investigating the tree canopy of the Amazon rainforest, or diving the coral reefs of the Bahamas, Fiji or Borneo. Expedition life can be a challenge - be prepared to live a spartan existence, and to pull your weight in a small, well-organised team.

Ionian Sailing School

Universal Marina, Crableck Lane, Sarisbury Green,
SO31 7ZN Southampton, UK   Tel: +44 (0) 1489 572054

The Ionian Sailing School is based in Corfu and is a fully RYA recognised teaching establishment. They offer the full range of theory and practical courses from Competent Crew to Yachtmaster. Teaching by qualified instructors is relaxed and fun on their fully MCA safety coded yachts.

London Scuba Diving School

Rabys Barn, New Chapel Road, Lingfield,
Surrey RH7 6LE, UK   Tel: +44 (0) 700 027 2822

The London Scuba Diving School walks you underwater on the floors of swimming pools in Battersea and Bayswater. It also arranges one-week diving holidays in the Red Sea where divers can explore the wreck of the merchant ship Dunraven (sunk in 1876). Diving limit 30 metres. Accommodation is in a 13-cabin cruiser where night dives are possible. Prices £600-£700.

Marine Divers (British Sub-Aqua Club School 388) Hong Kong

3E, Block 18, Dynasty View, 11 Ma Wo Road,
Tai Po, New Territories, Hong Kong, China   Tel: +852 2656 9399

Become a BSAC Open Water Instructor. In 6-8 weeks train from beginner to instructor. Training and fun in Hong Kong (The City of Life), with optional 5-day trip to the Philippines. Various packages. Possible employment opportunities.

National Mountaineering Centre

Plas-y-Brenin, Capel Curig, Bettws-y-Coed,
Gwynedd LL24 OET, Wales   Tel: +44 (0) 1690 720 214

For those hoping to reach dizzy heights, the National Mountaineering Centre offers a vast range of activities and courses. There are 170 courses in Wales, Scotland

and the Swiss Alps priced from £99 upwards. The recommended course for those wanting to gain experience in all outdoor pursuits is the week-long multi-activity course. Priced at £310, it includes indoor climbing, skiing, kayaking, navigation and mountain walking. This price includes accommodation for the week (and there's also a weekend course at £145).

Neptune's Diving & Sports Center

Km 14.5, Miguel de la Madrid, Manzanillo, Tel: +11 52 314 334 3001
Colima 28850, Mexico Fax: +11 52 314 334 3002

Neptune's Diving and Sports Center's intensive diving programme encompasses classroom, confined water, open water and hands-on learning experience leading to both the PADI and NAUI Divemaster qualifications. You must be at least 18-years-old, in good physical condition, know how to swim and have attended a basic first aid and CPR course (Neptune's can provide this at an additional cost). You will also need to provide a medical clearance for diving dated no more than 30 days prior to attending the course.

Courses are based in Manzanillo and either Cancun or Cozumel (depending on which course dates you choose) and taught in English and Spanish. You will have the opportunity to complete or surpass the minimum number of open water dives required for certification as a Divemaster. Once you've completed the Divemaster programme you travel to Cancun, Mexico for the Instructor Development Course run at a PADI CDC facility. You can start the course at any stage depending on your experience.

The complete 8-week course (novice to Divemaster) costs $1600; the 9-day instructor course is an extra $1200. Fees include course training, cost of boat trips, scuba tanks, air fills, weight belts, weights, all the dives required to meet your Divemaster requirements (most interns dive a minimum of 65 dives during the programme) and accommodation.

New Zealand Skydiving School

Control Tower Tel: +64 3 343 5542
Wigram Aerodrome, Christchurch, New Zealand Fax: +64 3 348 4366

Learn to skydive in New Zealand, the adventure capital of the Southern Hemisphere. NZ Skydiving School offers a Diploma in Commercial Skydiving; includes 200 skydives and industry experience, available to international students.

Nonstopski

79 Leatherwaite Road Tel: 0870 241 8070
London SW11 6RN, UK Fax: +44 (0) 20 7801 6201

Nonstopski is a family run company that offers 3-week and 11-week instructor training courses in the Canadian Rockies.

Ocean Republic

1 The Watertower, Palmerston Road,
BH1 4HT Bournemouth, UK Tel: +44 (0) 1202 469132

Ocean Republic specialises in training watersports enthusiasts who wish to gain professional qualifications and work in the watersports industry. Instructor qualifications are offered in Diving (PADI), Windsurfing (RYA) and Kitesurfing (IKO and BKSA). The training takes place at their 'intensive training base' on a tropical island in the Philippines, and is run by UK trainers. Courses vary in length from 4 to 12 weeks depending on the candidates previous experience in a particular discipline. Work experience is available along with Ocean Republic's 'instructor placement programme'. As well as training candidates, Ocean Republic can organise all-inclusive holidays to their watersports locations in the Philippines with all budgets catered for.

Peak Leaders

Mansfield
Strathmiglo
Fife KY14 7QE, Scotland

Tel: +44 (0) 1337 860 079
Fax: +44 (0) 1338 868 176
www.peakleaders.com

Peak Leaders run winter programmes in Canada, Argentina and New Zealand which include ski and snowboard instructor training, mountain safety, first aid, avalanche awareness, language, management, work experience and leadership.

PJ Scuba

Level 13, Country Tower B,
225/274 Sumpwut Road,
Bang Na, Bangkok 10260, Thailand

Tel: +166 864 4490
Fax: +166 720 7520

P J offers gap year students the chance to study scuba diving to instructor level (PADI) and then teach in Thailand, Vietnam or Cambodia upon graduation through their 'internship programme'. There is no entry qualification apart from good interpersonal skills and the ability to swim. On graduation you will be internationally recognized as a PADI dive professional allowing you to work worldwide in exotic places. P J Scuba also offers additional courses FREE of charge tailored to the individual needs of the applicant such as underwater photography, marine life studies or deep diving.

The programme costs US$5000 (less if you already have diving experience or your own equipment). Included in the price are accommodation, insurance and one meal per day, as well as a full set of scuba diving equipment (tools of the trade), all certification fees, manuals, training aids and full training. They have a pro-active job placement scheme at the end of the training programme to help you find work. The programme is ongoing and can be joined at any time convenient to you.

Planet Subzero,
UK

Tel: +44 (0) 7905 097 087
Fax: +44 (0) 479 071211

Planet Subzero's ski programme includes loads of added extras such as the opportunity to attend avalanche courses, heli-skiing and getting involved in the ski/snowboard competition circuit. They cater for everyone from complete beginners through to people who have done several seasons before and provide help, guidance and support at the resorts.

It is an opportunity for you to live away from home, immersed in another culture, improve your skiing/boarding, as well as your language skills - the all-round gap year experience. Prices range from £650 for a month to £2200-£2500 for the season (depending on the resort).

Portugal Sail & Power

Meadow House
Limekiln Close, Claydon,
Ipswich, Suffolk IP6 0AW, UK

Tel: +44 (0) 1473 833001
Fax: +44 (0) 1473 832989

Portugal Sail & Power offers all RYA Tidal practical sailing courses from 'Competent Crew' to 'Coastal Skipper' as well as shore-based RYA theory courses. They take a relaxed approach, making sure the course is a proper cruise as well as a learning experience. For those wishing to extend their knowledge further the Yachtmaster Preparation course is specifically designed for the Yachtmaster exam.

For those people who only have limited time, 5-day courses are available for a more intensive learning experience. On the longer courses you have the chance to complete one or more of the 60 mile passages required to move up to Yachtmaster level. The sailing school is happy to help with booking flights and will organise all transfers.

Pro Dive Academy
International Student Services, TAFE NSW - Northern Sydney Institute, 213 Pacific Highway, St Leonards, Sydney NSW 2065 , Australia

Pro Dive Academy offers an extensive range of courses focussed on providing internationally-recognised qualifications. Based in Australia, you'll be diving among some of the most beautiful coral reefs in the world. A truly great experience whether pursuing a career or not.

Saracen Sailing Mallorca
Apartado de Correos 84   **Tel: 0845 330 1357**
E-07510 Sineu, Mallorca, Spain   **Fax: 0034 971 509 064**

The Saracen Sailing School in Mallorca is an RYA approved sea school and offers a broad range of practical tidal sailing courses aboard their yachts based in North East Mallorca all year round. Cost varies according to the course, for example the 5-day RYA Competent course costs £450. Price includes accommodation, breakfast and lunch, fully qualified professional instruction and all boat expenses (eg fuel & berthing), but not air fares or insurance.

Ski Instructor Training Co
Queenstown, Otago, New Zealand   **www.skiinstructortraining.co.nz**

Ski Instructor Training Co offers you the opportunity to train for your ski instructor qualification with the New Zealand Snow Sports Instructors Alliance Stage 1 ski instructors exam. The 11-week programme, based out of Queenstown, costs around £3200 including accommodation, lift passes, mountain transport, three days a week on-snow training from a New Zealand examiner, evening sessions with the use of video analysis, Heliski/board trip, an off-piste awareness course and the NZSIA Stage One Exam. The organisers are well-qualified - in fact they're examiners for the NZSIA (New Zealand Snow Sports Instructors Alliance). You will need full medical and snow sports insurance cover to be allowed to participate.

Ski le Gap
220 Wheeler   **Tel: +1 819 429 6599**
Mont-Tremblant, Quebec J8E 1V3, Canada   **Fax: +1 819 425 7074**

Ski le Gap offers ski and snowboard instructor training courses based at the popular Canadian resort of Tremblant. The three-month programme prepares you for the level I qualification through tuition in small groups, videos, clinics, seminars, lectures and individualised daily goals.

The four-week Minigap is an opportunity to get your instructor's qualification at the very beginning of the season. Be warned - this course is not for beginners! Minigap costs £600 including half board accommodation, lift pass, ski/snowboard instruction, Level I ski/snowboard exam fee, transport to and from Dorval airport. The fee does not include airfare, personal medical insurance or equipment.

185

Activities and trips arranged by Ski le Gap include visits to Quebec, Ottawa and Montréal, and an 'outdoor experience' programme which involves cross-country skiing and igloo building. Some students stay on to teach for the Tremblant Ecole de Neige.

Snowboard Instructor Training Co
Queenstown, Otago, New Zealand   **www.snowboardinstructortraining.co.nz**

Snowboard Instructor Training Co offers you the opportunity to train for your ski instructor qualification with the New Zealand Snow Sports Instructors Alliance Stage 1 snowboard instructors exam. The 11-week programme, based out of Queenstown, costs around £3200 including accommodation, lift passes, mountain transport, three days a week on-snow training from a New Zealand examiner, evening sessions with the use of video analysis, Heliski/board trip, an off-piste awareness course and the NZSIA Stage One Exam. The organisers are well-qualified - in fact they're examiners for the NZSIA (New Zealand Snow Sports Instructors Alliance). You will need full medical and snow sports insurance cover to be allowed to participate.

Sunsail
The Port House
Port Solent, Portsmouth,   **Tel: +44 (0) 23 9222 2224**
Hampshire PO6 4TH, UK   **Fax: +44 (0) 23 9221 9827**

Sunsail offers the full range of RYA yacht courses as well as their own teaching programmes. Their instructors are RYA qualified. They have bases in the UK, the Canaries and Thailand.

Surfing Queensland
13 Durham Cres, Buderim, Qld 4556, Australia   **Tel: + 61 075445 4870**

Surfing Queensland is affiliated with Surfing Australia nationally and the International Surfing Association, recognised by local, state and national levels of government. They offer education in surf safety/surf awareness, surf instruction for beginners/elite, coaching accreditation, event management amateur/professional and officiating of the same. Their courses are under the NCAS accreditation system.

Taupo Bungee
202 Spa Road   **Tel: +64 7 377 1135**
PO Box 919, Taupo, New Zealand   **Fax: +64 7 3771136**

Taupo Bungee programme enables you to be registered as a Jumpmaster. You start out working at a registered jump site as a member of the site crew in the office, and as you learn you progress to more difficult jobs. After about 12 months you become a Jump Officer helping the Jumpmaster on the platform and learning the ropes, so to speak. After a further 6 months you can take the exam to be be registered as a Jumpmaster. Assuming you are successful the world will be your oyster as most countries recognise the New Zealand registration.

The School of Wilderness Arts & Technology
RR#1 Box 79, Palmer Rapids,
Ontario K0J 2E0, Canada   **Tel: +1 613 758 1092**

The school's 15-week 'LEAD semester' programme leads to internationally-recognised qualifications. You start with a minimum of 10 weeks' training in

186

whitewater canoeing, whitewater kayaking, canoe tripping, sea kayaking, rock climbing, rapelling, navigation, sailing, mountain biking, SCUBA and wilderness first aid; followed by five weeks of student-organised international expeditions.

The Summer (June-Oct), and Fall (August-Dec) programmes are based in Canada with expeditionary components in Canada, the US and Mexico. The Winter programme (Jan-April) is based in Mexico with expeditionary components in Mexico, Belize and Honduras. The price, CAN$10,695 - CAN$12,645, includes accommodation in dorm style rooms and all meals except on travel days. Transport to expedition locations in the Fall and Winter programmes cost extra.

UKSA (United Kingdom Sailing Academy)

West Cowes, Isle of Wight, UK

Tel: +44 (0) 1983 203014
Fax: +44 (0) 1983 295938

The United Kingdom Sailing Academy (UKSA), based in Cowes, trains watersport instructors, professional skippers and crews for yachts. The Academy has modern facilities, including residential accommodation and a fleet of over 300 craft.

Gappers train with UKSA for six months, in Cowes and Barbados, to become multi-qualified water sport instructors just at the time when major water activity holiday companies are recruiting staff for the summer season (600 companies worldwide recruit directly through the Academy). If you have a yachting background you can complete the Professional Crew and Skipper Training (PCST) course in the first six months, before seeking employment. Qualifications gained last from 2 to 4 years so you can use them to find further employment in the international holiday market in the future.

WorldLink Education

Storgatan 24
302 43 Halmstad, Sweden

Tel: +46 35 106680
Fax: +46 35 106685

WorldLink Education teaches Chinese martial arts in the land of its origins under the guidance of Chinese national Wushu (Kung Fu) champions. Training forms offered include Changquan (long fist), Nanquan (southern fist), Daoshu (broad sword), Jainshu (straight sword), Gunshu (staff), Qiangshu (spear), Taiji Quan (Taichi), Taiji Sword, Nan Dao (southern sword), Sanshou (Sanda - full contact fighting), Tanglang quan (praying mantis), Ditang quan (Tumbling boxing) and other arts such as Qigong.

Optional extra activities include afternoon classes in character writing, songs, traditional massage, traditional medicine and painting. There are social events (Peking Duck feast, bowling night, karaoke, basketball, Chinese movie, touch rugby) and half- or full-day excursions are organised to sites of interest including the Great Wall, Summer Palace, Temple of Heaven, Lama Temple, Tian'anmen Square and the Forbidden City.

Courses are available at all levels and last between one week ($700 - $1240) to a full academic year ($8290 - $14,860). Prices include accommodation, training and all optional extras. You can also combine the martial arts programme with learning Mandarin Chinese, see Learning Abroad: Languages: Chinese. WorldLinkEdu can also arrange subsidised guided trips around China for its students to places such as Shanghai, Xian, Inner Mongolia, Datong and Tibet. *(see Travel: tour companies)* for more details.

Conservation

The Bush Academy

PO Box 5478
Durban 4000
KwaZulu-Natal, South Africa

Tel: 00 27 31 3609300
Fax: 0027 31 3609333
www.bushacademy.co.za

A career in the exciting Field Guiding and Game Lodge Management industry is both practical and rewarding, ideal for those who prefer the great outdoors to the chaos of city life.

The Bush Academy courses are ideally suited to gappers wanting an introduction to conservation in Southern Africa and those wishing to pursue a conservation oriented career, as well as improving their personal knowledge of wildlife.

The Bush Academy has many courses on offer: from the one year course for those seeking either a career in this field, or alternative gap-year experience to 1-, 3- and 6-month Ranger Training experience courses. For more information, visit their website.

188

Chapter 4
Tips for Travellers

Loophole

I went into the yacht club in Sydney harbour and signed on as a crew member on an American yacht – about 40 feet with a crew of five. The skipper was a nuclear submarine captain, a bit of a nutter. We sailed up the coast north from Sydney for about five days and ran into the first reef. One night we attached ourselves to a buoy and we woke up at 3am, smashed against the reef. We scrambled up the mast and as the sun rose we found ourselves lying on the side of the reef with a big hole in the side of the boat.

We were rescued by people from the next door resort island and then we lived it up as shipwrecked mariners for three days. I lost quite a lot of stuff, and things I did get back were soaked in seawater and diesel.

When I put in an insurance claim I got nothing. It turned out that my tourist policy didn't cover me if I worked.

Rupert, Balliol, Oxford University

This section covers travel in general: whether you have a pre-arranged voluntary work placement already set up or you're just intending to go with the flow, this chapter should help you plan a problem-free trip. There's lots of practical advice for those who haven't been on long trips abroad before, with information on useful internet sites – take a look at **www.gap-yearshop.com** at the back of the book for kit and accessories you might need to take with you. The next chapter lists travel companies and you'll find useful information about individual countries, including embassy phone numbers in *Appendix 2: Country Info.*

When to go

Before starting university may well be the easiest time in your life to go abroad – you haven't started your career, you're unlikely to have a mortgage to pay, you probably don't have children yet. In short, you have less responsibilities.

If your finances aren't going to stretch to a year-long round-the-world tour then you're not alone. You could start the year by working (in the UK or abroad) and saving your earnings to pay for your travels. Money is not the only consideration – you may find other commitments dictate when you can travel. Perhaps you want to fit in retakes, or other courses like learning to drive. And you definitely don't want to have to come back from a sunny beach just to sort out your university entrance.

If you go travelling in the summer straight after A levels – and you haven't got an unconditional offer – you may have to come home in time for the crucial A level results in mid-August to enter clearing. And if you apply for university entrance while on your gap year, you may need to apply before you go travelling and/or return in time to make decisions and sort out all the paperwork.

After graduation also provides a natural break in life – before focusing on your career (and paying off your student loan!). The main problem at this point will be financial – but you could take a temping job and save up for your travels.

Anytime at all.

This is not as strange as it sounds. So-called 'career breaks' are becoming more and more popular. Employer's attitudes to sabbaticals are changing (slowly) so you might be able to persuade them to give you a sabbatical and hold your job for your return. Or, perhaps, you're feeling stale in your current job and want a change. If you do something constructive with your time out then future employers should view this as an asset. Once you have a mortgage/spouse/children it will take more effort to organise your gap-year, but it is still possible.

The only rule is to go for it – if you want to go, then it's the right time.

Be prepared

Leave someone in charge at home

Leave someone reliable and trustworthy in charge of sorting things out for you – especially the official stuff that won't wait. Get someone you really trust to open your post and arrange to talk to them at regular intervals in case something turns up that you need to deal with. But some things you just have to do yourself, so make sure you've done everything important before you go and won't be needed to sign or apply for anything while you're away.

Know where you're going

The more you know about your destination, the easier your trip will be: India, for example, is unbearably hot in April and May. It's also worth finding out when special events are on. It would be a shame to turn up in Hong Kong for example and have just missed the annual Dragon Boat race – check out **www.whatsonwhen.com** which lists all sort of events around the world.

Before visiting any country that has recently been politically volatile or could turn into a war zone check with the FCO for the current situation (Tel: 0870 606 0290 / **www.fco.gov.uk**) for up-to-date information.

Identity crisis

If you do need to get yourself a passport for the first time, application forms are available from Post Offices. A standard adult ten-year passport costs £42 and you'll need your birth certificate and passport photos. It should take no more than a month from the time you apply to the time you receive your passport, although it's sensible to allow some leaway.

You can send the form direct to the Passport Office or use their 'Check and Send' service (extra £5) at one of the 2300 Post Offices and Worldchoice travel agents throughout the UK. The 'Check and Send' service gets your application checked for completeness (including documentation and fee) and given priority by the UK Passport Services (UKPS) – they are usually able to process these applications in two weeks.

If your passport application is urgent you can use the guaranteed same-day (Premium) service or the guaranteed one-week (Fast Track) service. Both services are only available by appointment (phone the UKPS Adviceline on +44 (0) 870 521 0410), and both are expensive (£89 for Premium, £70 for Fast Track). The Premium service is for renewals and amendments only.

This may seem complicated, but the UKPS website, **www.ukps.gov.uk**, is very helpful. It's a good idea to leave a complete photocopy of your passport at home before you go travelling and also to keep a photocopy with you – this can make a lost or stolen passport much easier to cope with.

Passport Agency

Globe House, 89 Eccleston Square
London SW1V 1PN, UK
Tel: +44 (0) 870-521 0410
www.ukps.gov.uk

It is useful to join the International Youth Hostels Association (YHA): they run over 4000 hostels in over 50 countries offering reasonably priced accommodation. YHA membership for one year costs £14.00 for 18-year-olds and over, and £7.00 for under-18s.

YHA (England & Wales)	Dimple Road, Matlock, Derbyshire DE4 3YH, UK Tel: +44 (0) 1629 592600 Fax: +44 (0) 1629 592702 www.yha.org.uk

An ISIC (International Student Identity Card – www.isiccard.com) costs £7 (valid for 15 months from September to the following December). Simply pick up the application form from your local Students' Union, Student Travel Office, college or school and is available from STA Travel, either online (www.statravel.co.uk/c_flights/discountcards.asp) or by calling +44 (0) 870 1600 599. It identifies you as a student and entitles you to over 900 student discounts in the UK alone. Discounts include everything from museum entrance and restaurant bills to flights and international phonecalls. You also get access to a 24-hour ISIC travel helpline. You qualify for an ISIC if you are in full time education (15 hours per week, 26 weeks per year). If you are on a gap year and have a confirmed place in higher education you are eligible for a card in the calendar year in which you are due to start your higher education place. If you don't qualify for an ISIC, then the IYTC (International Youth Travel Card, £7) is valid for a year and offers similar discounts to anyone under 26, and is available from the same places as an ISIC.

Planning the route

Do you feel lured to a particular area? Latin America? Scandinavia? ...or to a particular climate? Snow? Monsoon? ...or to unexplored territory? Mongolia via the Trans-Siberian Express? ...what about a particular purpose? Surfing? Learning a language? ...or all these ingredients, wrapped up in one journey?

You need to get a framework clear in your mind – or let a cheap round-the-world ticket decide the framework for you. Bear in mind that it's safer to travel with someone you know, and having contacts lined up along the route is a big help. The more remote a place is, the more useful it is to have company. If you have six months or so to spare, you can arrange travel that takes you all the way round the world, although you may find it interesting to spend more than half your time in one region, like Africa or the USA.

Following the herd

There are well-trodden backpacking routes: through south-east Asia and Australia; across Russia to China and Hong Kong by rail; from the USA to central America; or through Spain and Africa and back to the UK. You may feel that following the same routes everyone else is taking is boring – but there's probably a reason that they've become popular over the recent years – they're interesting, exciting and varied.

If you want to be more explorer than follower of fashion, then why not try countries that have recently opened up to foreign visitors – though they tend

Tips for Travellers | Be prepared

The Gap-Year Guidebook 2005/2006

to charge a lot for visas (check visa costs through a travel agent, who may be able to arrange it for you).

Obviously avoid danger zones and check with contacts who know a country as well as the Foreign Office (**www.fco.gov.uk**). The political situation around the world as we go to press is serious stuff and can't be ignored – the point of your gap year travels is to have fun, experience different cultures, meet new people – not to end up in the middle of a war zone with your life in danger. The Foreign Office updates its danger list regularly as new areas of unrest emerge, but it's not, and never can be, a failsafe, as was illustrated by the Bali bombing in 2002.

Travel guides

The *Rough Guide* and *Lonely Planet* books are probably the best-known guides and are excellent – whatever your interests, these books will give you relevant information about the places you are going to – as well as copious information on towns, travel routes and budget hotels in the countries they cover.

Insurance

Your insurance needs to be fixed before you go, but it's a far from simple matter. The range of policies is vast – and they all cover different things. The basic things to check if an insurance policy covers are: medical, legal, passport loss, ticket loss, cash loss, luggage, cancellation, missed flights, working abroad, hazardous sports, medical conditions. Also see if they provide a 24-hour helpline.

It is important to make sure that you are covered for the activities you are likely to take part in. Be aware that companies may make a distinction between doing a hazardous sport once (eg going skiing during your brief trip to the Stubai Glacier) and spending your whole time doing them (eg six months intensive skiing in the Rockies). Some insurance policies also have age limits.

Some banks provide cover for holidays paid for using their credit cards, but their policies may not include all the essentials. Banks also offer blanket travel insurance (medical, personal accident, third party liability, theft, loss, cancellation, delay and more). You may be able to get reductions if you have an account with the relevant bank or buy foreign currency through it. Beware of 'free' insurance provided with your ticket. 'Free' can mean 'not very useful'.

Medical Insurance

There are reciprocal agreements between EEA (formerly EU) member states to treat each other's medical emergencies free or at a reduced cost, usually where sudden illness or an accident means an immediate operation. You need to take an E111 ("E one eleven") form with you, which entitles you to free or reduced state medical care while you're in certain countries. Pick one up from a post office, fill it in and take it back to the post office to get it stamped. Your E111 lasts you as long as your personal details are still correct – so if you change address, for example, you need to get a new one.

194

Countries with no health care agreements with the UK include Canada, the USA, India, most of the Far East, the whole of Africa and Latin America. Wherever it happens a serious illness, broken limb or injury you cause someone else can be very expensive.

Medical insurance is usually part of an all-in travel policy, costs vary widely by company, destination, activity and level of cover. Make sure you have generous cover for injury or disablement, know what you're covered for and when you've got the policy read the small print carefully (for example, does it cover transport home if you need an emergency operation that cannot be carried out safely abroad?).

Some policies won't cover high risk activities like skiing, snowboarding, bungee jumping etc so you'll need to get extra specific cover. If you have a condition that is likely to recur, you may have to declare this when you buy the insurance. Also, check whether the policy covers you for the medical costs if the condition does recur.

Already covered?

If you're going abroad on a voluntary work assignment you may find that the organisation arranging it wants you to take a specified insurance policy as part of the total cost. You may also find you have a 'clash of policies' before you even start looking for the right policy. For example, if your family has already booked you a one-year multi-travel insurance policy to cover travel with the family at other times of the year, you may find you are already covered for loss of life, limb loss, permanent disablement, some medical expenses, theft and so on. These multi-trip policies can be basic as well as quite cheap, and it's essential to check the small print of what the policy covers before you decide whether you need extra cover.

You are very likely to need extra cover if you'll be doing sports or anything dangerous like bungee-jumping. In this case you can start by finding out (through the broker or agent who sold you the policy) if any additional cover can be tacked on to your existing policy, though this can be expensive and most off-the-shelf policies won't do it.

Try to find a policy that doesn't already duplicate what is covered by an existing policy (they don't pay out twice), but some duplication is unavoidable and it's obviously better to be covered twice than not at all.

Making a claim

Read through the small print carefully before you travel and make sure you know what to do if you need to make a claim – most policies will insist that you report a crime to the police (often within a certain time period) and send in the police report with your insurance claim. What you don't want to happen is to have a claim dismissed because you don't have the right paperwork to back it up.

Insurers are unlikely to trip over themselves to pay you money: 'Some [insurers] will do almost anything to avoid paying a claim. Many travel policies impose conditions which are virtually impossible to meet' (*The Sunday*

The Gap-Year Guidebook 2005/2006

196

Telegraph, 6 Jan 2002). For example, some policies demand that you report not only theft of items but also loss of items. Fine, but the police are likely to be pretty reluctant to write a crime report because you think you may have accidentally left your camera in the loo! The Foreign Office website, **www.fco.gov.uk/travel**, has a good page about insurance and is worth checking out for advice and links.

Who to choose?

Since travel agents were banned from making you buy their favourite insurance policy as part of a travel package, there has been intense competition between insurance companies. There are now several insurers offering tailor-made insurance policies for gap year students.

Companies offering Gap-Year insurance

24Dr Travel
South Lodge, Slaugham, West Sussex RH17 6AQ, England

Boots Insurance
Freepost (SCE 12060), GU34 3BR Alton, England   Tel: +44 (0) 845 840 2020

£299 12 months worldwide
£69 3 months in Europe
£129 3 months in Europe with 21 days winter sports coverage

Down Under Worldwide Travel Insurance
Downunder Insurance Services Ltd   Tel: +44 (0) 800 393 908
3 Spring Street   Fax: +44 (0) 207 402 9272
Paddington, London W2 3RA, England   www.duinsure.com

Endsleigh
Shurdington Road   Tel: +44 (0) 800 028 3571
Cheltenham, Gloucestershire GL51 4UE, England   www.endsleigh.co.uk

£202.55 - Single 'Gap Year' worldwide, £354.46 - Couple, £115.08 - Single 'Gap Year' Europe, £207.15 - Couple, £305.85 - Single 'Gap Year Plus* worldwide, £535.25 - Couple, £149.61 - Single 'Gap Year Plus* Europe, £269.30 - Couple

Go Travel Insurance
Crowley House, Bentalls,
Basildon SS14 3BY, England   Tel: +44 (0) 870 152 5840

£124.79 Backpacker policy: 1 yr Europe (£155.99 with baggage cover)
£164.83 Backpacker policy: 1 yr Australia & New Zealand
(£206.04 with baggage cover)
£210.65 Backpacker policy: 1 yr Worldwide
(£263.92 with baggage cover)
Cover includes cancellation, medical, legal, cash, cancellation, missed departure. A winter sports policy is also available.

visit: www.gap-year.com

MRL Insurance
Enterprise House
Station Parade, Chipstead,
Surrey CR5 3TE, England

Tel: +44 (0) 870 876 7677
www.MRLInsurance.co.uk

Navigator Travel Insurance
19 Ralli Courts
West Riverside
M3 5FT Manchester, England

Tel: +44 (0) 161 973 6435
Fax: +44 (0) 161 973 6418
www.navigatortravel.co.uk

Norwich Union/HSBC
PO Box 4, Surrey Street, Norwich,
Norfolk NR1 3NG, England

Tel: +44 (0) 800 092 9561

Options Travel Insurance
Lumbry Park, Selborne Road, Alton,
Hampshire GU34 3HF, England

Tel: +44 (0) 800 917 1091

Planet Travel Insurance
PO Box 4379, BN14 0WB Worthing, England

Tel: +44 (0) 845 458 4587

STA Travel
52 Grosvenor Gardens
Victoria, London SW1, England

Tel: 0870 160 6070
www.statravel.co.uk

199

What to Take

Start thinking early about what to take with you and write a list – adding to it every time you think of something. Then sit down and rationalise – cross off everything you don't really need. Pack the essentials and enough clothes to see you through – about five changes of clothing should last you for months if you choose carefully. Don't take anything that doesn't go with everything else and stick to materials that are comfortable, hard-wearing, easy to wash and dry and don't crease too much. Make sure you have clothes that are suitable for the climates you are visiting. And relax – you can't prepare for every eventuality if you're living out of a rucksack. The best way to know what you need is to ask someone who's already been what they took, what they didn't need and what they wished they had taken.

Religious customs

Women wear long sleeves and cover their legs in Muslim countries: don't wear a bikini top and shorts in city streets. Uncovered flesh, especially female, offends Islam. Similarly in Buddhist countries the head is sacred and so it is unconventional to touch it. Even in Europe you'd be expected to cover your head, and be dressed respectfully if you go into a church. Each culture or religion has its own holy 'laws', and casual Anglo-Saxon habits can offend and you could find yourself in real trouble. Do some research first.

Maps, directions and vital information

Unless you're going trekking you won't need anything too flash: the ones in guidebooks are usually pretty good. A good pocket business diary can be very useful – one that gives international dialling codes, time differences, local currency details, bank opening hours, public holidays and other information. Take a list with you of essential information like directions to voluntary work postings, key addresses, medical information, credit card numbers (try to disguise these in case everything gets stolen), passport details, contact numbers in case of loss of travellers cheques and insurance and flight details – and leave a copy with someone at home as well.

Another way of keeping safe copies of your vital documents (even if everything you have is lost or stolen) is to scan them before you leave and e-mail them as attachments to your internet-based e-mail address.

Tickets and money

Leave photocopies of serial numbers of tickets, passports and credit cards at home. It's also worth keeping copies on you, separate from the rest of your valuables, and one travellers' cheque separate from the others (useful if all the rest get stolen). Waist money pouches worn under clothes are really good.

Take widely-accepted travellers cheques like those issued by big international banks – but don't make the mistake of taking American Express travellers' cheques to Cuba or any other country on less than friendly erms with the US – and don't carry much cash. Cheques in pounds sterling are widely accepted, but US dollars more so. It is worth recording the numbers of the travellers cheques that you spend, as it helps if you need to replace lost or stolen ones. It can help to arrive with some local currency in notes and coins. Be careful at foreign exchange shops or kiosks: they often charge extortionate commissions or make the equivalent amount of money on very wide exchange rates.

Credit cards

Essential back-up. Both Visa and Mastercard are useful for getting local currency cash advances, sometimes from a cash dispenser, at banks abroad. You can then use the cash to buy more travellers cheques – safer than walking around with suitcases of money. If you're using your credit card to get money over the counter then you're likely to need some form of ID (eg passport). The problem with a credit card is not losing it or having it stolen – keep a note of the numbers and how to report the loss of the card.

Wiring money

If all else fails and you find yourself stranded with no cash, no travellers cheques and no credit cards, then having money wired to you could be a lifesaver. Two major companies offer this service: MoneyGram (**www.moneygram.com**) and Western Union (**www.westernunion.com**). Both have vast numbers of branches worldwide – MoneyGram has 55,000 in 155 countries and Western Union has 140,000 in 185 countries.

The service allows a friend or relative to transfer money to you almost instantaneously. Once you have persuaded your 'guardian angel' to send you the money, all they have to do is go to the nearest MoneyGram or Western Union, fill in a form and hand over the money (in cash). It is then transferred to the company's branch nearest to you, where you in turn fill in a form and pick it up. Both you and the person sending the money will need ID, and you may be asked security questions.

Kit

Where to buy

Some overseas voluntary organisations (such as SPW) arrange for their students to have discounts at specific shops, like the YHA. The best advice on equipment usually comes from specialist shops, although they may not be the cheapest: these include YHA shops, Blacks, Millets and Camping and Outdoors Centres. Take a look at **www.gap-yearshop.com** for a specialist selling over the internet (see the back of this book).

Rucksacks

Advice from students who have collapsed under the weight of 65- to 70-litre rucksacks: think carefully before buying so big. There is no need to look like a walking sack of coal, sweating under the weight of bottles of shampoo that will take two months to use. Thailand does have shampoo. For hot countries a 30-

to 35-litre rucksack (excluding sleeping bag) is usually big enough. In cold countries you are obviously going to need a bigger rucksack, but you can keep bags light by packing clothes made of special lightweight fabrics.

Try not to set off with a totally full bag – you're bound to buy stuff along the way and you don't want to be trekking across the world with a handful of plastic bags. If you really can't resist and end up buying too many souvenirs to carry you can always post them home, but be warned: postage is expensive, so that 'cheap' souvenir could end up costing more than you bargained for. You could always start off with a bigger bag, but remember, the longer you walk the heavier it gets.

Rucksacks that take a sleeping bag at the bottom are popular, and so are ones that open laterally like suitcases so you don't have to pull out all your worldly possessions just to find a pair of socks. You might want to go for one with zips and tiny padlocks for security, but remember that this doesn't give real protection, as a determined thief will happily slash your bag open.

A well-stitched 65-litre rucksack will cost between £60 and £90, and a 35-litre rucksack between £40 and £50, but prices vary greatly. Remember, the most expensive is not necessarily the best – get what is most suitable for your trip.

You can get all sorts of trendy attachments such as 'an integral pocket for your hydration bladder' but don't hand over money for stuff you won't need. If you go to a good outdoor store, they should be able to advise you on exactly what you need for your particular trip. Most of these stores have websites with helpful hints and lists of 'essential' items. Best of all talk to someone who's been before and ask them what they wish they'd taken or left at home.

A must is an extra small day bag or rucksack to carry valuables and things you need in a hurry, as well as bottles of water, guidebooks, camera and so on. You should be able to leave your rucksack in most hostels or guest houses if you are staying for more than a day (most thieves won't be interested in nicking your socks), or in a locker at the train station. ALWAYS take camera, passport, important papers and money with you everywhere, zipped up, preferably out of view.

Footwear

It's worth investing in something comfortable if you're heading off on a long trip. In hot countries, a good pair of sandals is the preferred footwear for many and there's a great range of sports sandals available. They might seem a bit pricey (£30-£70), but a good strong pair will last and be comfortable. If you're going somewhere cheap, you could just pick up a pair out there, but you're likely to be doing a lot more walking than usual – even if you're only sight-seeing – so comfort and durability are important.

Some people like chunky walking boots, others just their trainers, but it's best to get something that won't fall apart when you're halfway up Mount Kilimanjaro. Take more than one pair of comfortable shoes in case they don't last, but don't take too many – they'll be an unnecessary burden, and take up precious space in your rucksack.

Sleeping bags

First, are you sure you even need one? For hot countries you may just want to take a sheet sleeping bag (basically just a sewn-up sheet). If you do take a sleeping bag, think about what you'll be doing. The more active your holiday, the more you need a decent bag; go to a specialist shop where you can get good advice.

Take into account weight and size and the conditions you'll be travelling in – you might want to go for one of those dinky compression sacs that you can use to squash sleeping bags into. Sheet bags are useful, and you can usually rent down bags for treks in, say, Nepal – but don't assume you'll always be able to do this. For cold countries, you need bulky heat-retaining materials. If you're going to be doing a lot of sleeping outdoors, a roll-mat is probably a good idea too.

The main thing is that you can carry it and that you will be comfortable. No way are you going to have enough energy to look around art galleries, let alone climb Mt Kilimanjaro (however comfortable your shoes are), if you're not getting any sleep.

Prices vary hugely and you can sometimes find a four-season bag cheaper than a one-season bag – it's mostly down to quality: at the cheaper end expect to pay around £10 for a sheet bag; £30 for a one-season sleeping-bag (suitable to 5°C); £30-40 for a two-season sleeping-bag (suitable to 0°C); £45 for a three-season sleeping-bag (suitable to -5°C). You can pay more than two or three times as much for better gear.

Not all trips go as planned..

Max, 18, joined a project on the Nicoya Peninsula, West Costa Rica, with Raleigh International. The aim of the project was to build an eating area for visiting children, and a fire look-out tower for the reserve. Fire is a major problem in the tropical dry forest, where temperatures reach 40C:

For the next two weeks we acted as general labourers for the local builders, carrying sand, cement, gravel, and aluminium girders to the top of a steep hill, where the builders constructed the lookout tower.

There were howler monkeys that kept us awake at night, leaf-cutter ants that ate through our tents and clothing, scorpions in our eating area, and a puma that circled our camp. I had a tick on my manhood, I was stung on my ear, sunburnt, and repeatedly bitten by a swarm of black ants. My luck did not increase; I contracted a fungal infection in my eye, which developed into a corneal ulcer. I was unfortunately hospitalised for a week in San José and then flown home for further treatment. It sounds grim, but I'd do it all over again if I could.

Although I can only imagine the amazing experiences that would have followed if I had lasted the expedition, I know that the short time that I spent in Costa Rica with Raleigh International was extremely worthwhile and enjoyable. Think therefore what an experience you could have volunteering if you manage to last the whole expedition!"

First-aid kit

There is no need to take a whole chemist's shop with you. Ask your GP for advice, but useful basics are rehydration sachets (to use after diarrhoea); waterproof plasters; TCP; corn and blister plasters for sore feet; cotton buds; a small pair of straight nail scissors (not to be carried in your hand luggage on the 'plane); safety pins; insect repellent; antiseptic cream; anti-diarrhoea pills (only short term; they stop the diarrhoea temporarily but don't cure you); water sterilisation tablets; and anti-histamine cream.

You can get a medical pack from most chemists or travel shops, by mail order from MASTA (Tel: +44 (0) 113 238 7575; **www.masta.org**). Homeway (see **www.gap-yearshop.com**) also specialises in medical kits for travellers: the contents vary from sting relief, tick removers, blister kits, sun block and rehydration sachets to complete sterile medical packs with needles and syringe kits (in case you think the needle someone might have to inject you with may not be sterile). You can also get dual-voltage mosquito killer plugs, various types of mosquito net, water purification tablets and filters, money pouches, world receiver radios, travel irons and kettles. Not to mention a personal attack alarm. If you take too much kit though, you'll need a removal van to take it with you.

Handy items

The list of useful things to take varies from person to person, but the following are generally considered very helpful: string that can double as a washing line and is handy for putting up mosquito nets; a universal sink plug; a torch; and a padlock and chain to secure your rucksacks on long journeys and double-lock hostel rooms. A penknife with different functions is also extremely useful (remember that since 11 September 2001 you can no longer pack any sharp items in your hand luggage when travelling by 'plane) as are water purifying tablets (if bottled mineral water is available check that the seal is intact). Masking tape has also been recommended to us as a vital piece of survival kit; apparently it's handy for mending slashed rucksacks, sealing ant nests, fixing doors, sticking up mosquito nets...

Cameras

For most people, being able to record their trip is a vital part of the experience. Remember to be very careful to keep cameras and film safe from damage (usually sand and water) and theft. Keep all your negatives in a safe place because most travellers agree there is nothing more gutting than losing either your developed photos or undeveloped films – they're irreplaceable. Getting photos developed as you go along is an option worth considering; it may work out cheaper, and stops you looking at stacks of photos long after taking them and asking yourself "Which mountain is that?" If you are one of those people who considers every new view to be a photo opportunity, then you may not want to carry the extra weight around in your already-heavy rucksack, but you can always post them home either as pics or as undeveloped films. Take a few moments to label them so you know what you're looking at when you get home.

The new APS (Advanced Photo System) films are small and get rid of the need for negatives, as the film can be developed repeatedly. But they are expensive to develop and can be hard or impossible to get hold of in some countries. Of course, the ultimate is the digital camera; you can download your photos and e-mail them home. You can buy quite small digital cameras for as little as £40 – but you need to be sure you can download your pics as they don't tend to be able to store many images at a time.

Health & Safety

Note: Although we make every effort to be as up-to-date and accurate as possible, the following advice is intended to serve as a guideline only. It is designed to be helpful rather than definitive, and you should always check with your GP what you need for your trip, preferably at least eight weeks before going away.

It's not only which countries you'll be going to, but for how long and what degree of roughing it: six months in five-bottle-top hostels puts people at higher risk than two weeks in a five-star Mandarin Hotel. Tell your doctor your proposed travel route and the type of activities you will be doing and ask for advice not only about injections and pills needed, but symptoms to look out for and what to do if you suspect you've caught something. Some immunisations are free under the NHS but you may have to pay for the more exotic/rare. Some, like the Hepatitis A vaccine, can be very expensive, but this is not an area to be mean with your money – it really is worth being cautious with your health.

If you are going abroad to do voluntary work, don't assume the organisation will give you medical advice first or even when you get there, though they often do. Find out for yourself, and check if there is a medically-qualified person in or near the institution you are going to be posted with. People who've been to the relevant country/area are a great source of information.

It is important to keep a record of any treatment, such as courses of antibiotics, that you have when overseas to tell your doctor when you get back. Also be wary of needles and insist on unused ones; it's best if you can see the packet opened in front of you, or you could take a 'sterile kit' (containing needles) with you. Also, many people recommend that you know your blood type before you leave the country, to save time and ensure safety. Your GP might have it on record – if not, a small charge may be made for a blood test.

Some travellers prefer to go to a dedicated travel clinic to get pre travel health advice. This may be especially worthwhile if your GP/Practice nurse does not see many travellers. British Airways has three travel clinics in London where you can get jabs – call 020 7606 2977 for more information about this service. The Medical Advisory Services for Travellers Abroad (MASTA) has travel clinics around Britain. To find your nearest clinic check the website **www.masta.org** or contact the Location Line (Tel: 01276 685 040).

Alternatively you can do your own research and take the information to your doctor or nurse. MASTA has a 'Travellers Health Line' on 0906 8224 100. Travellers leave details of their proposed journey to obtain a health brief by first class post. This brief provides information on the recommended vaccines, malaria tablets, disease outbreak information and safety advice. Calls cost 60p/min and last approximately 4-5 minutes depending on how many countries you request details on.

There are also some websites offering good free advice about vaccinations etc:

Tips for Travellers | Health & safety

www.e-med.co.uk   www.fitfortravel.scot.nhs.uk

www.travelhealth.co.uk

For safety advice try the Foreign and Common Wealth Office:
www.fco.gov.uk/travel.

Department of Health Freefone Health Information Service
(Tel: 0800 665 544) and their website: **www.dh.gov.uk/home/fs/en**

Make sure you have a sensible First Aid kit with you, organise your medical insurance and, if you don't speak the language, have the basic words for medical emergencies written down so you can explain what is wrong.

Accidents / Injuries

Accidents and injuries are the greatest cause of death in young travellers abroad. Alcohol / drug use will increase the risk of these occurring. Travellers to areas with poor medical facilities should take a sterile medical equipment pack with them. As highlighted earlier, make sure that you have good travel insurance that will bring you home if necessary.

AIDS

The HIV virus that causes AIDS is caught from: injections with infected needles; transfusions of infected blood; sexual intercourse with an infected person, or possibly cuts (if you have a shave at the barber's, insist on a fresh blade, but it's probably best to avoid the experience altogether). It is NOT caught through everyday contact, insect bites, dirty food or crockery, kissing, coughing or sneezing.

Protect yourself: always use condoms during sex, make sure needles are new (you can take your own sterile pack for medical emergencies) if you need a blood transfusion make sure blood has been screened, and don't get a tattoo or piercing until you're back home and can check out the tattoo shop properly. Remember this is a fatal disease and though medical advances are being made there is no preventive vaccination and no cure.

Asthma and allergies

Whether you are an asthmatic or have an allergy to chemicals in the air, food, stings, or antibiotics, ask your GP for advice before you go. You will be able to take some treatments with you.

Chronic conditions

Asthmatics, diabetics, epileptics or those with other conditions should always wear an obvious necklace or bracelet or carry an identity card stating details of their condition. Tragedies do occur due to ignorance, and if you are found unconscious, a label can be a life saver. See **www.medicalert.org.uk/** for information on obtaining these items.

You should also keep with you a written record of your medical condition and the proper names (not just trade names) of any medication you are taking. If you are going on an organised trip or volunteering abroad, find out who the responsible person for medical matters is and make sure you fully brief them about your condition.

Contraceptives

If you are on the pill it is advisable to take as many with you as possible. Remember that contraceptives go against some countries' religious beliefs so they may not be as readily available as you might think. Antibiotics, vomiting and diarrhoea may inhibit the absorption of the pill, so use alternative means of contraception until seven days after the illness. Condoms: unprotected sex can be fatal, so everyone should take them even if they are not likely to be used (not everyone thinks about sex the whole time). Keep them away from sand, water and sun. If buying abroad, make sure they are a known make and have not been kept in damp, hot or icy conditions.

Dentist

Pretty obvious but often forgotten: get anything you need done to your teeth before you go. Especially worth checking up on are wisdom teeth and fillings - you don't want to spend three months in India with toothache.

Diabetics

Wear an obvious medical alert necklace or bracelet or carry an ID card stating your condition (preferably with a translation into the local language). Take enough insulin for your stay, although it is unlikely that a GP will give you the amount of medication needed for a full year of travelling – three to six months is usually their limit, in which case, be prepared to buy insulin abroad and at full price. Ring the BDA Careline to make sure the brand of insulin you use is available in the particular country you are planning to visit. Your medication must be kept in the passenger area of a plane, not the aircraft hold where it will freeze.

Diabetes UK   10 Parkway, London NW1 7AA, UK
Tel: +44 (0) 207 424 1000
Careline: 0845 1202960
E-mail: careline@diabetes.org.uk
www.diabetes.org.uk

Diabetes UK produces a general travel information booklet as well as specific travel packs for about 70 countries. Ring or e-mail the Careline (Mon-Fri 9am-5pm) or check out the website for expert advice and all information for diabetic travellers, including info on travel insurance.

Diarrhoea

By far the most common health problem to affect travellers abroad is travellers' diarrhoea. This is difficult to avoid but it is sensible to do the best you can to prevent problems. High risk food / drinks include untreated tap water, shellfish, unpasteurised dairy products, salads, raw / undercooked meat and fish. Take a kit to deal with the symptoms of travellers' diarrhoea (your doctor or nurse should be able to advice on this). Remember to take plenty of 'safe' drinks if you are ill and rehydration salts to replace lost vitamins and minerals.

Eyes

Wearers of contact lenses should stock up on cleaning fluid before going, especially if venturing off the beaten track, and be careful what water is used for cleaning; ask your optician for advice.

Dust and wind can be a real problem, so carrying refreshing eye drops to soothe itchy eyes and wash out grit can be really useful. Also most travel and camping shops sell plastic bottles of mildly medicated hand cleanser that dries instantly and are small and light to carry. You only use a small amount each time so it's worth packing a couple. They're really useful for cleaning hands before putting in contact lenses if the local water supply is suspect. It's also worth making sure you have glasses as a back-up, as it's not always possible to replace lost or broken contacts.

If you wear glasses consider taking a spare pair – they don't have to be expensive and you can choose frames that are flexible and durable. Keep them in a hard glasses case in a waterproof (and more to the point sandproof) pouch.

Malaria

Caught from the bite of an anopheles mosquito, and mosquitoes are vicious and vindictive. Highest risk areas are tropical regions like Sub Saharan Africa, the Solomon islands and Vanuatu (Pacific), the Amazon basin in South America and parts of Asia. There's no jab, but your GP will give you a course of pills to take.

Bra-less with worms

We were about to go trekking and it looked like I had a huge verruca on my foot, so I wasn't sure if I'd be able to walk. I got it checked out at a clinic in Kathmandu, and as they'd never heard of a verruca, they just decided to chop the dead skin off. I sat there as they sawed and proceeded to pull out a huge sack of worms from inside my foot. The Western doctor said he'd never seen anything like it and he later told me that I must have picked it up from sandflies on a beach in Zanzibar.

While we were trekking I got severe fever which turned out to be typhus contracted from my nits. While I was lying semi-delirious in the lodge, the owner's daughter came into my room and started rummaging under my bed. I was too ill to do anything and I later discovered she'd nicked my bra. I had to trek all the way home bra-less – because being a minimalist trekker I'd only brought one with me.

Catherine

The Gap-Year Guidebook 2005/2006

Water needs respect

Water. Seems so simple. Yet if only I had understood how it really can affect the body.

Having decided on joining many like-minded people on an 'adventure of a lifetime', rather than listen to all the horror stories I wanted to hear about all the amazing places and people I could meet. I didn't want to be bombarded by all the Health and Safety information that doctors and parents give, as it all seemed too serious.

Not only that, it all seemed so expensive at the time, especially when I was scrimping and saving every last penny so I could spend an extra night on that stunning beach I visualised in my mind.

But be warned. I am not alone in the troubles faced when returning. If you survive your entire trip without a doggy stomach then you're one of the few. When I got home, taking into account that it would take a while to adjust back to 'normal living' I made excuses for my general ill health. As time went on my parents and I started to ask questions and sought the help of The Hospital for Tropical Diseases. I was diagnosed with Giardia, a parasite found in water.

How I got it? Simple. Not treating the water properly. Looking back, when travelling you relish the simplicity of living, eating and drinking what and when you like. No one is looking over your shoulder and in this carefree existence you begin to forget the simple rules. All it takes is one lapse, a local ice pop to cool you down in that scorching heat, a lump of ice in your rather warm coke, a sip of someone else's water. In short un-purified water.

And the cost? Well I'm still suffering from the long term effects associated with the parasite and the treatment needed. Not only do I still feel unwell but financially it continues to be very costly. Don't get me wrong, those six months I spent travelling are the best days so far of my life, but, given what I know now, would I change anything? Yes. Simple, I will always treat water with the respect it deserves, which does mean spending money on buying proper equipment to purify water. After all, it's about your long-term health, you don't want to be fighting the after effects like I have been for the last four years: where's the fun in that?

Felicity

It may sound obvious, but try to avoid getting bitten as much as possible. Use insect repellent, preferably containing either DEET (diethyltoluamide), or extract of lemon eucalyptus oil. Keep your arms and legs covered between dusk and dawn and use a 'knockdown' spray to kill any mosquitoes immediately.

Mosquito nets are useful, but they can be hard to put up correctly. It is often worth carrying a little extra string and small bits of wire so that the net can be hung up in rooms that don't have hanging hooks. Ideally the net should be impregnated with an insecticide, you can buy nets that are already treated from specialist shops and travel clinics (see **www.gap-yearshop.com** for a full range). For a long trip, the pills can cost a lot. And some people, particularly on long trips, stop taking their pills, especially if they're not getting bitten much. Don't. Malaria can be fatal.

Your GP, practice nurse or local travel clinic should know which of a variety of anti-malarials is best for you, depending on your medical history (e.g. for epileptics) and the countries you are visiting. Your travel health adviser will also be able to tell you what the symptoms of malaria are, and that you must seek treatment quickly. The combination of paludrine plus chloroquine is recommended for some countries. In areas where the malaria shows significant drug resistance, mefloquine, doxycyline or Malarone will be recommended.

All the anti-malarial tablets have various pros and cons, and some of them have rather significant side-effects. If you are going to try the weekly mefloquine tablets, MASTA recommends that you start taking the course two and a half to three weeks before departure. Most people who experience unpleasant side effects with this drug, will notice them by the third dose. This trial will allow you time to swap to an alternative regime before you go, if you do have problems.

Doxycycline can also be started two days before departure and is taken every day until one month after return. For paludrine and chloroquine start the course one week before you leave and continue it for four weeks on your return. Don't think that this means you can leave it until a week before you go – the earlier you see your GP the better.

As there are a number of different antimalarials, it's important to make sure you're taking the right variety. Visit your GP or travel clinic a couple of months before you go to discuss the options.

It's worth doing a little research of your own before going to your GP or Practice nurse! Very occasionally we here stories of unsuitable drugs being recommended – this can be from the GP, practice nurse travel agent or pharmacist.

Sunburn

Avoid over-exposure, especially on first arrival in a sunny country, and use sun creams and sun-block frequently.

Estimates of the number of cases of non-malignant skin cancer a year range from 45,000 to the British Association of Dermatologist estimate of as many as 100,000 a year.

It is the third most common cancer in 15-39 year-olds and it is the second most common cancer in the country. Malignant melanoma is one of the most common cancers among 20-35 year olds.

Don't think you're safe if you're spending three months as a skiing instructor, either – snow can increase the amount of exposure to the sun's harmful rays significantly.

Vaccinations

Hepatits (A&B), Japanese Encephalitis, Meningitis, Polio, Rabies, Tetanus, Tuberculosis, Typhoid, Yellow Fever

Ask your GP for advice on vaccinations/precautions at least six to eight weeks before you go (some may be available on the NHS). Keep a record card on you of what you've had done.

SAFETY:

boring and a bit obvious,
but really important

- Travel in pairs if you can
- Never hitch-hike or accept lifts from strangers
- Avoid badly-lit streets after dark
- Never discuss your own or your family's financial situation with strangers
- Never try unknown substances
- Never carry unopened parcels for people, especially when you fly
- Always let people know where you are going and stay in touch with people back home regularly.
- Don't swim in strong currents or heavy waves: several gap year students have drowned this way
- Check fire exit routes in hostels or other buildings where you plan to stay
- Shake out clothes and shoes before you put them on: snakes, scorpions or allergy-causing plants may have got inside
- If you don't like the look of some of the other people in a hostel, put your bed against the door at night
- Keep windows open if you are in a room with a gas water heater or other source of carbon monoxide to let gases escape if the equipment is faulty

Seeking Medical Advice Abroad

You can expect to be a bit ill when you travel just due to the different food and unsettled lifestyle (paracetamol and loo paper will probably be the best things you've packed). But if vomiting and/or diarrhoea continue for more than 4 to 5 days or you run a fever, have convulsions or breathing difficulties (or any unusual symptoms), get someone to call a doctor straight away. Seek advice on the best doctor to call, the British Embassy or a five-star hotel in the area may be able to offer some advice here.

If the doctor advises being sent home for treatment and you have an insurance policy with a repatriation arrangement, get someone to call the insurance company's headquarters or office in the relevant country for help as soon as possible. If your treatment is not free you should be able to pay by credit card, but check first with your insurers – they may cover the costs upfront. If you do pay yourself, make sure the details are written out on a receipt and keep all bills or receipts so you can claim on your insurance policy when you get home.

Staying safe

Before you do anything or go anywhere think about the consequences – this isn't about not having a good time, or being boring – it's about getting through your gap year alive and not getting mugged, raped or murdered. If people hassle you you can usually crack a joke and move on. If you are offered strange drinks or drugs be sensible and think about your safety first.

One of the biggest dangers in accepting a drink is that someone can slip in the so-called "date rape" drug (Rohypnol). It doesn't taste of anything and you won't know you're taking it. Combined with alcohol, it can induce a blackout with memory loss and decrease your resistance, leaving you open to attack. About ten minutes after ingesting the drug, you may feel dizzy and disoriented, simultaneously too hot and too cold, or nauseous. You might have difficulty speaking or moving and then pass out. Victims have no memory of what happened while under the drug's influence. Another drug that can be use in a similar way is GHB (gamma-hydroxybutate) also known as "liquid ecstacy", "somatomax", "scoop" or "grievous bodily harm".

If you are tempted to try the local variety of cannabis in the belief that it is relatively harmless and universal, know what the local drug laws are and don't take risks. In many places in South Asia, for example, it is illegal and possession carries stiff penalties in prisons where conditions are not remotely like they are in the UK.

Remember also, that if you are speaking English with a local inhabitant, they may not understand or use a word with the same meaning as you do. Particularly in the fraught area of emotional relationships and dating, remembering this, and understanding the local religion, customs and morality can save a lot of misunderstanding, misery and heartache.

If someone keeps pestering you with unwanted sexual advances after you have said no, get to somewhere where there are other people within earshot.

213

Only use violence as a last resort – it's not worth fighting back against violent muggers. They're likely to be stronger than you and may be carrying a gun or a knife.

Remember in many third world countries, where there are no social security or welfare systems, life can be cheap and people desperate and what may seem like a cheap trinket to you may be enough to buy them a square meal for which they are desperate enough to steal from you violently, so it is sensible not to wear too much jewellery.

Another good tip is to try to always carry a supply of small change and small notes in a pocket (trousers or jeans with deep pockets can be very useful) and not reveal that you are carrying larger notes. Do not keep all your money in one place, distribute it between, say, a small daytime backpack, your rucksack or suitcase and a hidden belt bag so that if you are robbed, you still have some money in reserve.

If someone tries to snatch your bag throw it at them – it keeps as much space between you and them and puts them off guard, giving you time to get away. Anyway you'll have wisely hidden any money, passports or tickets in a bag under your clothes. Stick close to other people while you get back to base.

Meeting places

Your first impression of some countries will be the swarm of people that descends on you, hassling you to take a taxi or buy something – at night it can be quite scary. Remember, anyone can get lost. When you are on the road don't panic. Always agree meeting places before you go somewhere and play safe by having a double back-up plan. "If I don't see you outside the Latino Roxy at 1.00, I'll see you at the Lufthansa office at 4.00. Then I'm going back to the hostel." Try looking behind you occasionally.

Safety courses have been available for business travellers for years – companies are now offering courses specifically designed for gappers. These are by no means boring – you won't be sitting at a desk taking notes!

Learning to be safe

British Red Cross
9 Grosvenor Crescent, London SW1X 7EJ, England   Tel: 020 7245 6315

The Red Cross offers first aid courses around the UK lasting from one to four days depending on your experience and the level you want to achieve. Prices are from £20 for a two hour 'save a life course' to £160 for a four-day course. Contact them directly to find your nearest course.

Expedition Advisory Centre
Royal Geographical Society (with IBG)   Tel: +44 (0) 20 7591 3030
1 Kensington Gore, London SW7 2AR, England   Fax: +44 (0) 20 7591 3031

The Expedition Advisory Centre provides information, training and advice to anyone embarking on a scientific or adventurous expedition overseas.

International Remote Trauma

Pegaxis House
Suite 144, 61 Victoria Road, Surbiton,   Tel: + 44 (0) 208 398 4242
Surrey KT6 4JX, England   Fax: + 44 (0) 208 398 4242

International Remote Trauma runs a first aid training course designed especially for gappers, covering the many situations that may occur whilst travelling in the more hostile regions of the world. The course lasts two days at a cost of £160 plus VAT.

I-Survive.
South West Survival School
Barliabins, Bullen Street, Thorverton,   Tel: +44 (0)7771 752 507
Devon EX5 5NG, England   Fax: 01392 861184

I-survive runs many different survival courses, including a first aid course, ranging from 2-day courses to a two-week trip to Sweden. They will teach you how to build shelters, cook food, navigate and create a fire in the wilderness. This could be very good for anyone planning on camping whilst on their travels. Prices start at £145 for the two day course rising up to £1100 for the trip to Sweden.

Objective Team
Bragborough Lodge FarmBraunston,   Tel: +44 (0) 1788 899 029
Nr Daventry, Northants NN11 7HA, England   Fax: +44(0)1788 891 259

Objective Team offers a one-day safety awareness course for gappers. Instructors include ex British Army SAS and intelligence officers. The course is designed to teach you how to recognise, evaluate and avoid dangerous situations.

St John Ambulance
National Headquarters, 27 St John's Lane,   Tel: +44 (0) 8700 10 49 50
London EC1M 4BU, England   Fax: +44 (0) 8700 10 40 65

The St John Ambulance Association runs first aid courses throughout the year around the country. Courses last a day and are suitable for all levels of experience. To find out more contact 08700 104950.

Suffolk Sailing
Unit 75, Claydon Business Park,
Gipping Road, Great Blakenham,   Tel: +44 (0) 1473 833010
Ipswich, Suffolk IP6 0NL, England   Fax: +44 (0) 1473 833020

Although mainly suppliers of sailing safety equipment, Suffolk Sailing does offer a one-day RYA/DOT Basic Sea Survival Course for Small Craft.

The course includes:

Preparation for sea survival - survival, difficulties and requirements; equipment available; training drills; actions prior to abandonment.

Practical wet drill - liferaft launching, boarding; survival whilst in water; capsize drill; final abandonment.

Principles of survival - protection in both hot and cold conditions; location; water rationing and collection; food rationing; survival craft ailments.

Lifejackets and liferafts - life jacket design, construction,wearing and use; safety harness design and use; liferaft standards, design, launching, equipment; actions taken whilst in liferaft.

Search and rescue - rescue by helicopter; coastguard, SAR organisation.

Tips for Travellers | Health & safety

215

The Knowledge Gap
Pitt Farmhouse   Tel: +44 (0) 117 974 3217
Chevithorne, Devon EX16 7PU, England   Fax: +44 (0) 117 974 3307

The Knowledge Gap, set up by a group of former SAS soldiers and experienced travellers, offers gappers practical advice on travel safety through a three day residential course based on Exmoor. Students stay in youth hostel accommodation (part of the learning experience) and receive a mixture of indoor and outdoor instruction. The course is designed to make you aware of common dangers associated with gap year travel and to demonstrate that these can generally be avoided with a little prior planning and preparation. In no way is the course all theory - it demands both participation and a sense of humour. It is best to arrive with few assumptions!

Stop thief!

If you have money, a camera or a passport stolen abroad (and the chances of this are high), report the theft immediately to the nearest police station and make sure you have some written record from them giving the date that you did so with all relevant details .

Police in popular budget destinations may have had to deal with hundreds of insurance scams in the past and may not be sympathetic. Dress smartly (and cover up; going in a bikini is not a good idea), stay polite and calm, but firm. It is very unlikely anyone will catch the thief or get your stuff back – all you need is a record of the police report for your insurance claim. Ask someone back home to notify insurers and post or fax a copy of the police notification home. Many insurers will not pay up for loss or theft unless the police are notified (some policies won't pay out if you don't do this within 24 hours). This also applies if you are involved in any accident likely to result in an insurance claim. Keep records of everything that might be important – better to throw it away later than not to have it when needed.

Getting about:
Trains, buses, planes

Trains

Inter-Railing

If you want to visit a lot of countries, one of the best ways to travel is by train on an Inter-Rail ticket. With Inter-Rail you have the freedom of the rail networks of Europe (and a bit beyond), allowing you to go as you please in 28 countries. From the northern lights of Sweden to the kasbahs of Morocco, you can call at all the stops. Inter-Rail takes you from city centre to city centre – avoiding airport hassles, ticket queues and traffic jams, and giving you more time to make the most of your visit. Inter-Rail passes are available for both under and over 26s, but you need to have lived in Europe for at least six months.

Overnight trains are available on most major routes, saving on accommodation costs, allowing you to go to sleep in one country and wake up in another! Supplements apply so ask when you book. You will have to pay extra to travel on some express inter-city trains or the Eurostar. Most major stations such as Paris, Brussels, Amsterdam and Rome have washing facilities and left luggage.

Inter-Rail divides Europe into eight zones: you can opt to travel in as many zones as you want (see the table below), but your ticket won't include travel in the UK.

Zone A: Republic of Ireland

Zone B: Norway, Sweden, Finland

Zone C: Austria, Denmark, Germany, Switzerland

Zone D: Croatia, the Czech Republic, Hungary, Poland

Zone E: Belgium, France, Luxembourg, The Netherlands

Zone F: Spain, Portugal, Morocco

Zone G: Italy, Greece, Turkey

Zone H: Bulgaria, Romania, Macedonia, Yugoslavia.

Inter-Rail Prices

		Under 26	Over 26
Any **1** zone	16 days	£159	£223
Any **2** zones	22 days	£215	£303
All zones	One month	£295	£415

(Prices correct at time of going to press.) For further details on how to buy an Inter-Rail pass, visit their website **www.inter-rail.co.uk**.

Eurostar

The Eurostar train is a quick, easy and relatively cheap way to get to Europe. You can get from London to Calais for £69, and the trains are comfortable and run frequently. Tickets can be purchased online at **www.eurostar.com**, in an approved travel agency, or at any Eurostar train station.

Trans-Siberian express

If you're looking for a train adventure then you're unlikely to beat the Trans-Siberian Express. It will cost you about £500 for train transport only. On top of this you will need some money for food and drink, visas, air fare etc. For China, Russia and Mongolia you'll need to have a visa for your passport to allow you into each country. Contact each relevant embassy to find out what type of visa you will need (ie visitor's or transit).It's probably easiest to arrange for all your train tickets, visas and hotel accommodation through a specialist agency, about six months before you leave. Your journey will be a lot easier if you have all your paperwork in order before you leave – although it will cost you more to do it this way.

The trains can be pretty basic, varying according to which line you're travelling

217

on and which country owns the train. On some trains you can opt to upgrade to first class for about an extra $200. This should give you your own cabin with shower, wash basin and more comfort – though you'll be more comfortable, you may find it more interesting back in second class with all the other backpackers and traders.

If you're traveling in Autumn or winter make sure you take warm clothes – the trains have rather unreliable heating. If you travel in late November/December you may freeze into a solid block of ice, but it will be snowing by then and the views will be spectacular. If you go in September it will be warmer and a bit cheaper.

If you want to read up about it before you go, try the *Trans-Siberian Handbook* by Bryn Thomas. It is updated frequently and it has details about the towns you'll be passing through and the timetables. But go to **www.trans-siberia.com** for the best and most comprehensive information about the Trans-Siberian Express anywhere. It will answer all your questions and give you useful hints. It's run by someone who has personally travelled on the trains, so he knows what he's talking about.

Buses/Coaches

Getting on a bus or coach in a foreign country, especially if you don't speak the language, can be a voyage of discovery in itself. UK bus timetables can be indecipherable, but try one in Patagonia! Get help from a local you trust, hotel/hostel staff, or the local police station if all else fails. In developing countries, locals think nothing of transporting their livestock by public transport, so be prepared to sit next to a chicken!

That said, some buses and coaches can be positively luxurious and they do tend to be cheaper than trains.

Greyhound International

Greyhound Lines Inc
PO Box 660689, MS490 Dallas
TX 75266-0689, USA
Tel: +1 800 229 9424
www.greyhound.com

Greyhound buses now have air conditioning, tinted windows and a loo on board, as well as a strict no smoking policy. Greyhound also arranges a 'GoHostelling' package that combines bus travel and hostel accommodation. There's the usual 10% discount for ISIC and Euro 26 ID cardholders. The bus company operates outside America too, with Greyhound Pioneer Australia and Greyhound Coach Lines Africa. Check out their website or contact them for information about their various ticket options.

Planes

Travel is one area where the internet has definitely grown up – you can search for ticket information, timetables, prices and special offers whether you're travelling by air, sea, train or bus. Often you can book and pay online and pick up your ticket at the airport. Make sure you read the 'Terms and Conditions' to see what you're paying for and whether you can get your money back.

Because the internet gives customers so much information to choose from, travel companies have to compete harder to win your booking. Because it shows you what flexibility is possible (a lot), you could also find your decision-making turned upside down. Instead of planning a round-the-world trip, for example, by deciding on your destinations and then finding the cheapest flight path through them, you could look at the special offers available first, see how far in advance you can book a ticket, and decide what to do with the destinations you've got when you've booked. One of the destinations – for example, a voluntary work assignment beginning in Tanzania in February – may have to be on a fixed date; the others may not. The route you have in mind may be different from the samples on offer, but you can usually have one tailor-made for you and the prices you find on the web, with simple maps, can act as a benchmark.

Make sure you check out the company making an offer on the web before you use internet booking procedures (does it have a verifiable address and phone number?), and read all the small print in a booking contract before you agree to buy – just as you would outside the virtual world.

Bargain flights

Scheduled airlines often offer discount fares for students under 26, so don't rule them out. Other cheap flights are advertised regularly in the newspapers and on the web (see above). All sorts of travel agents can fix you up with multi-destination tickets, and student travel specialists often know where to find the best deals for gap year students.

Above all, travel is an area where searching the internet for good deals should be top of your list – though it works best for single-destination trips rather than complex travel routes where you have to change several times. Here are some useful websites – the prices are examples we found in December 2003:

Airline Network   www.airline-network.co.uk

Flight search engine and booking service for low cost scheduled flights. Sample flight: London, Gatwick to Los Angeles, California with Virgin Atlantic from £266 including tax.

Austravel   www.austravel.net

Combines scheduled and charter flights to produce RTW itineraries. Information about and flights to Australia, New Zealand, Asia and the South Pacific.

Bargain Holidays   www.bargainholidays.co.uk

Not really for students en route to a backpacking trail, but worth a look in case there's a cheap offer that takes you close to where you're heading.

Bridge the World   www.b-t-w.co.uk

Website that gives RTW routes using a variation of different airlines. For example, the 'Star Alliance' Tour 2 goes from London - Vienna - Istanbul (overland) Cairo - Dubai - Ho Chi Minh - Singapore - Auckland - Raratonga - Los Angeles - Miami - Santiago - Rio - London for £1695.

British Midland
www.flybmi.com

Low cost flights to Europe and America.

Cheap Flights
www.cheapflights.co.uk

Flights and destinations, special deals, holiday offers, round-the-world tickets, last minute bargains. Sample flight: Edinburgh to Barcelona for £99.

Deckchair.com
www.deckchair.com

Aims to find you the best available fare. Key in where you want to leave from and go to, plus dates and other details, and wait to see what happens! We keyed in London Heathrow to Delhi and found it for £390.90 (indirect).

EasyJet
www.easyjet.co.uk

Easyjet offers cheap flights to European destinations with further reductions if you book over the internet.

Flightbookers
www.flightbookers.com

Cheap online flights can be booked from this site. They also offer many deals, such as one-way from Gatwick to Bangkok for £334.

Last Minute
www.lastminute.com

Finds tickets from 24-hours' notice to a few weeks ahead. Negotiates discount flights with various airlines. Sample flight: London to Lisbon return from £125.60 including tax. They also offer sporting tickets, entertainment etc.

Last Stop
www.laststop.co.uk

Another site for last-minute bargain holidays.

One World
www.oneworldalliance.com

Alliance between Aer Lingus, American Airlines, BA, Cathay Pacific, Finnair, Iberia, LanChile & Qantas. Their programmes include 'oneworld explorer' and 'circle trip explorer' both of which are good if you want to cover lots of miles and stopovers.

Ryanair
www.ryanair.com

Low cost airline to European destinations - many outward flights are actually free! - but make sure you check how much the return flight will be.

STA Travel
52 Grosvenor Gardens
Victoria, London SW1, UK

Tel: 0870 160 6070
www.statravel.co.uk

STA Travel are specialists in travel for students and those under 26, offering low-cost flights, accommodation, insurance, gap-year travel, overland & adventure tours, ski & snowboard, round-the-world tickets, discount cards, city breaks and international travel help.

They offer students and those under 26 exclusive discounts on travel with quality airlines. Most airline tickets are valid for one year, so its often impossible to finalise all your plans before you leave the UK. With this in mind STA Travel tickets are designed to offer the greatest possible flexibilty. You can usually change your dates of travel and even your route for little cost.

STA Travel have Travel Help branches or agents in over 50 countries worldwide and if you can't get into a local STA Travel branch, then there is a Help Desk telephone service, which provides you with essential backup for travellers on the move. With over 450 branches worldwide and well-travelled, experienced staff, STA Travel can assist you with all your travel plans for your trip.

Their round the world tickets are cheap and very easy to organise. For example: London - Kuala Lumpur - Sydney - Melbourne - Mexico City - London costs £735 plus tax.

Thomas Cook   www.thomascook.com

General travel agent with high street branches offering flights and late deals.

Travelocity   www.travelocity.co.uk

Key in destination and budget and see what Travelocity's search engine finds. Also has destination guide, flight timetables, maps and weather.

www.cheaponlineflights.com   www.cheaponlineflights.com

Great travel website offering some very low prices, especially if you are prepared to go last minute.

www.germanwings.com   www.germanwings.com

Once in Europe this is a great company to get flights to other European cities. They also offer special deals for limited flights for €19.

Car

Another popular option is to travel (mostly around Europe) by car. It means you can kip in it when necessary, save money on train fares and you don't have to lug your rucksack into cafés.

Make sure you know the motoring regulations of the countries you'll be visiting – they vary from country to country. Check that you are insured to drive abroad and that this is clear on the documentation you carry with you. The AA advises that you carry your vehicle insurance, vehicle registration documents and a current tax disc in the car and, of course, take your driving licence with you. If you still have an old paper licence you might want to consider getting it updated to a photo licence before you go, but make sure you leave enough time for this – the DVLNI isn't known for its speedy processing. You can pick up a DL1 form from most Post Offices, your local Vehicle Licencing office or call the DVLNI on +44 (0) 28 7034 1469.

It is also advisable to take an International Driving Permit (IDP) as not all countries accept the British driving licence. In theory you don't need one in any of the EC member states, Iceland, Liechtenstein or Norway, but the AA recommends having an IDP if you intend to drive in any country other than the UK. And as it only costs £5.50 it's better than getting into trouble and being fined for driving without a valid licence.

An International Driving Permit is valid for 12 months and can be applied for up to three months in advance. Applying is easy – The AA and RAC issue the permits – you must be over 18 and hold a current UK driving licence. You'll need to fill in a form and provide your UK driving licence, passport and a recent passport-sized photo of yourself, which you can take to a participating Post Office or post them to the AA or RAC (see below for address), allowing at least ten working days. Both the AA and RAC websites have loads of info about the permit and driving abroad in general, and you can even download the application form.

It's a good idea to put your car in for a service a couple of weeks before you leave and, unless you're a mechanic, it is worth getting breakdown cover specifically for your trip abroad with any of the major recovery companies such as the AA, RAC or Green Flag. If you end up stuck on the side of the road it could end up an expensive experience.

The RAC recommends taking a first aid kit, fire extinguisher, warning triangle, headlamp beam reflectors and spare lamp bulbs. These are all required by law in many countries and make sense anyway.

The Automobile Association

Fanum House, Erskine
Renfrewshire PA8 6BW, UK
Tel (IDP): +44 (0) 800 55 00 55
(Other motoring enquiries): +44 (0) 8705 500 600
www.theaa.com

The RAC

Motoring Services
Travel Administration
PO Box 1500
Bristol BS99 2LH, UK
Tel (IDP): +44 (0) 800 550055
(Other motoring enquiries): +44 (0) 906 471740
www.rac.co.uk

Ships

If you want to get to the continent, then taking a ferry across to France or Belgium can be cheap – but why not sail free as a working crew member on ships? Contact head offices of shipping companies to find out the procedures before you leave the UK and find out how to book a passage from a foreign port.

A useful book on this subject is *Working on Yachts and Super Yachts* Price £10.99 (plus £1.50 p&p), published by Vacation Work Abroad, 9 Park End Street, Oxford OX1 1HJ, Tel: +44 (0) 1865 241 978, Fax: +44 (0) 1865 790 885.

Telepassport-Bulgaria
Str. Floor 1, Suite 1
8000 Bourgas, Bulgaria   Tel: +359 56 816 277

Telepassport-Bulgaria is a crew manning agency, so if you're interested in spending your year out on a ship travelling the world then it could be worth your while getting in touch. A huge range of jobs are available.

Bicycles

Of course, if you're feeling hyper-energetic, you could cycle around the place. This is really popular in north Europe, especially Holland, where the ground tends to be flatter. Most travel agents would be able to point you in the right direction, or you can just rely on hiring bikes while you are out there – make sure you understand the rules of the road.

Florence by Bike Via San Zanobi 120-121   Tel: +39 055 488 992
50129 Firenze, Italy   see: www.gap-year.com

Florence by Bike is a well-organised bike rental company operating in Tuscany. To see what they offer, take a look at their impressive website.

Accommodation

Hostels are to backpackers what eggs are to bacon, and there are masses to choose from. How safe they are (from fire, flood, drugs, prostitution, theft, rip-off scams etc) obviously varies widely and gappers often rely on *Rough Guide* or *Lonely Planet* guidebooks or the word-of-mouth recommendations from other backpackers to find a suitable one. Check out **www.hostelworld.com** for hostels pretty much anywhere.

No-one expects five-star conditions and most backpackers don't care too much about the usual drawbacks (from cockroaches to back-breaking beds) as long it's cheap – most hostels would have to double their prices to conform to rigorous health and safety regulations.

Use your common sense and always check where the fire exits are when arriving at a hostel – it's too late to look if there's already a fire and you're trying to get out if the building. This may sound odd, but don't have a bath without some ventilation – faulty water heaters give off lethal and undetectable carbon monoxide fumes and will kill you without you realising it as you fall gently to sleep, never to wake up again. Use your instincts – if you the think the hostel's dodgy or simply not up to scratch, go and find another one.

Accommodation

Comité Parisien de L'Association Catholique des Services de Jeunesse Feminine
63 Rue Monsieur le Prince   Tel: +33 1 44321290
75006, Paris, France   Fax: +33 1 44321291

This organisation publishes a brochure with addresses of Foyers de Jeunes à Paris et dans la region Paisienne.

Natives
39-43 Putney High Street   Tel: +44 (0)8700 463377
SW15 1SP London, England   Fax: +44 (0) 8451 275 048

Natives help gappers looking for somewhere to live during the ski season. They can find you accommodation in a number of European ski resorts including Val d'Isere, Chamonix, Les Arcs, Meribel/Mottaret, Avoriaz and Tignes; and there are private rentals available in resorts such as Courchevel, Les Menuires and Les Deux Alpes. Accommodation includes one-bedroom apartments, shared studio apartments or private chalets. If you are not already in a group and are looking for flatmates to share with, they will do their best to find a match you up with other gappers.

Prices start from £1059 per person for a furnished apartment for 5 people in Chamonix including bills (water, electricity, heating, tourist taxes) for the season. Season dates in all resorts are from early January to mid April - this cuts out the expensive Christmas/new year. Earlier or later dates can be arranged.

Keeping in touch:
phone, e-mail, snail mail

Spare a thought for those you're leaving behind – friends as well as family. Not only will they be worried about your safety, but they may actually be interested in your travels – most are probably jealous and wish they could go too.

You might find your parents are panic-stricken at the thought of you going off into the wide world without them, especially if you are travelling under your own steam rather than on an organised project. Their way of showing they care may be to treat you like you're six years old again – they can't help it – humour them. Try to reach a compromise about how often you will get in touch with them – once a fortnight seems reasonable.

It's not just about keeping them happy: make sure you tell them where you are and where you are going – that way if something does happen to you, at least

they know where to start looking. Backpackers do go missing, climbers have accidents, trekkers get lost; at least if someone is concerned by you not getting in touch when expected they can then alert the police. Of course if you don't stick to what you agreed, don't be surprised if the international police come looking for you.

On the receiving end

You probably can't wait to get away, but you'll be surprised how homesickness can creep up on you when you're thousands of miles away. Getting letters or e-mails can be a great pick-me-up if you're feeling homesick, weary or lonely, so distribute your address widely to friends and family before you go in order to ensure a steady supply of mail. If you're not able to leave behind an exact address then you can have letters sent to the local Poste Restante, often at a main post office, and collect them from there. Also, parcels do usually get through, but don't send anything valuable.

Phone

Use a credit card if you can. If you walk into any international hotel you should be able to use a Visa or Mastercard to pay for an international phone call, but watch out for overcharging. Or you can reverse the charges: if the international operator doesn't understand, try using the American term 'collect call'.

One alternative is to take a chargecard with you. This avoids having to get to grips with local phonecards, operators who don't speak your language and having enough local currency coins to feed the payphone. If you do a search on the internet you will find various offers and schemes – check what you're getting before you give your credit card details.

You can use BT's Chargecard to phone home from abroad from any phone – just call the operator and quote your pin number. The calls are charged to your BT phone account back home and are itemised on the bill; weekly limits can be set in advance. There are different types of Chargecard accounts you can set up, including limiting card use to one number or a set of numbers. For further details on BT Chargecards call: Freephone +44 (0) 800 345 144.

Mobiles

If you're one of those people who needs to be attached to your mobile day and night, you'll probably want to take it with you. Make sure you've set up your account to allow you to make and receive calls and text messages in all the countries you'll be travelling to (and e-mails if you've got a WAP phone).

Try to limit use of your mobile to emergencies – they usually cost a fortune to run abroad as you pay for all the incoming calls at international rates too. It's worth insuring the handset as mobile theft is common and if it's the latest model, try not to flash it around

But don't rule out using your mobile phone as gap year kit; it might save your life if you break your leg half way up a mountain and need to call for help (make sure you keep the battery charged).

225

Snail mail

Aerogrammes are a cheap way of writing from most countries. Registering letters usually costs only a few pence (or equivalent) from third world countries, and is definitely worthwhile. Postcards are quick, cheap and easy – though not very private.

E-mail

Really useful technologies are rare, but e-mailing is one of them. What's more, you can now send e-mails free from almost any web-connected computer to almost any other, using services like Hotmail or Yahoo. These are usually free because they are being paid for by advertising or telephone line rental charges. All you do is get the free e-mail website up on a computer screen before you leave the UK and key in your registration details to get a free account.

Then, if you can get to a cybercafé or internet kiosk in an airport, hotel, university, office or home when you're abroad you can simply log in to your mailbox (remember your 'User ID' and password if these are part of the package) and receive messages or send them back home.

It beats picture postcards for speed, and you can write much more. If you're a techie with a digital camera and access to computer equipment, you can send your photos 10,000 miles home as e-mail attachments minutes after you've taken them. Here are the most well-known free e-mail providers:

www.altavista.com	www.lycos.co.uk
www.excite.co.uk	www.postmaster.co.uk
www.freeserve.co.uk	www.talk21.co.uk
www.hotmail.com	www.yahoo.co.uk

Hotmail is the best known of these, although in practice there is little difference between the services. Most give the opportunity to redirect mail from other e-mail addresses, so you don't need to worry about telling everyone what your new e-mail address is.

If you think getting to a cybercafé is going to be hard there are always WAP phones (you need to register your e-mail address before you leave). Air Mail (www.airmail.co.uk) will forward e-mails to you as text messages on your mobile, and you can send e-mails by simply sending them a text message which they will forward as an e-mail. Check their website for their up-to-date tariff. In practice, however, if there are no internet facilities in the area then the chances are there won't be a mobile phone signal either, and you may have to resort to more traditional methods of communication.

Having said that, thousands of cybercafés now sprinkle the globe, and even nuns in Bolivia have got wired up to the Net, so you'll probably find somewhere that you can e-mail home from at some point. This has got to be the quickest and most reliable way to communicate.

Chapter 5
Travel Companies

visit: www.gap-year.com

The names of exotic travel agents can be found in advertisements in the national daily and Sunday newspapers. Voodoo Ventures, say, may promise three weeks of throbbing thrills in Haiti. Make sure you get references and talk to a gapper who has been on their gap year before you hand over hard cash or sign up for anything.

If you're not sure about a company you can contact the Year Out Group and see if they're a member or if the YOG have heard of them – **www.yearoutgroup.org**, Tel: +44 (0) 7980 395 789.

As gap years become more popular and so become big business, more travel companies are offering travel deals specifically aimed at gappers. The following travel companies are just some of the ones we found that are used to dealing with independent travellers and students:

Travel companies, tour operators & expedition organisers

AAHA Adventure Trekking & Expedition
PO Box 12205   Tel: +977 1 357135
Kathmandu, Nepal   Fax: +977 1 357135

Nepal-based AAHA offers trekking, mountaineering, climbing, mountain flights, jungle safaris, river rafting, hiking, sightseeing, hot air ballooning, mountain biking and various specialised tours including: pilgrimage, cultural, religious, anthropological, and buddhist. AAHA is committed to the preservation of the environment, the safeguarding of ecological balance, and the emancipation and economic advancement of women in more remote parts of the country. AAHA prides itself on its customer service and promises to 'definitely put every ounce of effort to make your holiday a remarkable memory, an unforgettable one forever!'

Adventure Alternative
31 Myrtledene Road, BT8 6GQ Belfast, N Ireland   Tel: +44 (0)2890 701476

Adventure Alternative focuses on higher altitude expeditions but also offers safaris and desert treks and expeditions in Kenya and Nepal specifically designed for gappers. The trips are designed to be quite demanding, so these are the people to go to if you are looking for a real test. Adventure Alternatives organising one-off expeditions to conquer some of the world's toughest terrain, including Mount Everest. Most of the regular trip are priced at under £2,000.

Alliances Abroad
2423 Pennsylvania Avenue NW   Tel: +1 (202) 467 9467
Washington, DC 20037, USA   Fax: +1 (202) 467 9460

If you're looking for something a bit different, tailored to your needs, time frame,

229

budget, skills, interests etc, Alliances Abroad will design a customized programme for you or your group. Their vast range of packages include teaching English (in China or Spain); internships and work placements in the US; working in rural Australia on a ranch or farm; volunteer placements in Costa Rica (environment and national parks), South Africa (helping out zoologists and vets), Hawaii (organic farm work).

Their experienced staff will help you with all of your travel needs, including travel arrangements, recommendations on what to do while abroad, visa/work permit procurement, airport transfers and all that other organisational stuff. Most of their programmes offer guaranteed placement before departure, airport pickup, local orientation and full-time support before, during and after the programme.

Blue Dog Adventures
Amwell Farmouse, Nomansland, Wheathampstead,   Tel: (0)1582 831302
St. Albans, Hertfordshire AL4 8EJ UK   Fax: (0)1582 834002

Blue Dog offers a variety of adventures, but focuses mainly on equestrian adventures catering for all levels of horsemanship.

Bridge the World
45-47 Chalk Farm Road   Tel: +44 (0) 870 444 7474
Camden, London NW1 8AJ UK   www.b-t-w.co.uk

Bridge the World organises tailor-made RTW trips and has experience with gap year travellers. If you're interested in visiting Australia, there's a 'wine and canapé' meeting on the first Thursday of every other month at their West End office (4 Regent Place, W1B 5EA) where you'll get the chance to discuss your plans with consultants. Phone in advance as places are limited.

BSES Expeditions
at The Royal Geographical Society   Tel: +44 (0) 20 7591 3141
1 Kensington Gore   Fax: +44 (0) 20 7591 3140
London SW7 2AR UK   www.bses.org.uk

This charitable organisation runs four- to six-week summer expeditions and 2- to 3-month gap year expeditions to wilderness areas abroad. The expeditions combine adventure activities with environmental and scientific research on behalf of universities, research institutes or host nations. In 2005/6 the proposed summer destinations are Peru, Arctic Svalbard, Greenland and the Amazon rainforest. The gap year expeditions will be to the Arctic archipeligo of Svalbard, Norway. Your financial contribution varies depending on the expedition destination.

Bukima Expeditions
29 Hamilton Road,   Tel: 0870 7572230
West Norwood, SE27 9RZ London UK   Fax: 0870 7572231

Bukima operates overland expeditions and safaris from 10 to 28 days across Africa, South America and the Middle East. In every tour they offer the amount of land they cover is vast, so getting an idea of a countries overall culture is a priority. An average price for a month is £500 but that does not include the activities intinery.

Camps International Limited

Unit 1, Kingfisher Park
Headlands Business Park, Ringwood,
Hampshire BH24 3NX UK

Tel: +44 (0) 870 2401843
Fax: +44 (0) 1425 485398
www.campsinternational.com

Camps International organises expeditions and safaris based in Kenya and Tanzania. You will contribute to all aspects of African life including wildlife conservation, teaching children and building schools and by way of example.
Gappers are drawn predominantly from the UK and you will be living in the bush or on the coast with young people from a broad range of backgrounds. Camps International run their own camps and the staff are permanently on hand to guide you through the experience and ensure you are safe at all times. An experience with camps can last between one to three months; most gappers opt for 3 months. Prices for the camps vary, but on average costs around £1000 per month.

College Northside

CP480, 916 14ème Avenue, Val-Morin,
Québec JOT 2RO, Canada

Tel: +1 819 322 1133
Fax: +1 819 322 2111

CTS Travel

44 Goodge Street, London W1 UK

Tel: +44 (0) 20 7290 0620

Student travel specialists offering adventure tours, worldwide flights, budget accommodation, rail and coach passes and student travel cards, insurance, budget car rental and lots of other travel stuff.

Cultural Hi-Ways

PO Box 4191, Wallingford,
Connecticut 06492 - 7560, USA

Tel: +1 203 949 0277

Cultural Hi-Ways arranges short trips around America and Canada for people aged 18+. Their excursions are particularly aimed at gappers and au pairs already in the States who would like to see more of the country. Destinations include California, Boston, Washington and Niagra Falls. An all-inclusive 2-day trip to Niagara Falls including the 'Maid of the Mist' boat ride costs around $220.

Dorset Expeditionary Society/Leading Edge Expeditions

Lupins Business Centre, 1-3 Greenhill,
Weymouth, Dorset DT4 7SP UK

Tel: +44 (0) 1305 775 599

Dorest Expeditionary Society is a registered charity promoting up to six adventurous expeditions each year to remote parts of the world. Expeditions are open to all from throughout the UK and can qualify for two sections of the Duke of Edinburgh's Gold Award. Leaders and helpers are all volunteers, and all-inclusive costs range from £500 - £2200. The expeditions take place during July and August. Destinations vary each year - you may climb Mt Kenya, help with a local school community project, white-water raft, then Safari in the Masai Mara - all in Kenya, or trek through the Moonlands of Ladakh in the Himalayas of India, or learn alpine skills in the Cascade mountains of the USA. No prior experience necessary as training and team-building weekends take place in the UK. Age range 15-21+.

Travel Companies | Travel companies

5

Eco Africa Experience

Applications Department, Guardian House   Tel: +44 (0) 1483 860 560
Borough Road, Godalming,   Fax: +44 (0) 1483 860 391
Surrey, GU7 2AE UK   www.EcoAfricaExperience.com

Do you want to contribute to conservation in Africa? Eco Africa Experience strives to conserve what man is fast destroying - our very own environment. They send 150+ volunteers to several Southern African game reserves and marine projects per year. They set the standards at the selected reserves in order to maintain a degree of uniformity, thus maintaining a high degree of education, training, learning and general hands on experience while fulfilling the core objective - conservation. Placements range from 4 to 12 weeks, during which you can be involved in conservation projects including anti-poaching patrols, monitoring and counting of wildlife, darting and animal capture, bush rehabilitation and the day-to-day maintenance of the reserve. Marine projects may include rescue and rehabilitation of marine species, sampling, tagging, monitoring of marine life, and participating in commercial marine-eco tourism activities which include whale and dolphin watching tours, sea kayaking, township tours, river ferry cruises. Contact Eco Africa Experience direct for information about specific opportunities and prices.

Encounter

2001 Camp Green, Debenham,   Tel: +44 (0) 1728 862222
Stowmarket, Suffolk IP14 6LA UK   Fax: +44 (0) 1728 861127

Encounter organises overland trips in groups of 8-23 people, usually with a wide spread of nationalities. Your main mode of transport is a truck, which you could ride all the way from London to Cape Town or even to Kathmandu via Nairobi. Trips last between two and 26 weeks and are also run to South America. It's mainly camping, with hostel stays in big centres. There are also shorter tours like the six-day trek in Borneo. You can book from the UK or when you're out there.

Exodus Travels

Grange Mills   Tel: +44 (0) 20 8675 5550
Weir Road, London SW12 0NE UK   Fax: +44 (0) 20 8673 0779

Exodus organises adventure trips for groups of between 8 and 22 people. Their tours range from one-week multi-activity holidays in Europe to overland expeditions across Africa, Asia, South America and Australia, as well as treks to most of the world's great mountain ranges. Brochure hotline: +44 (0) 20 8673 0859.

Footloose Travel

3 Springs Pavement   Tel: +44 (0)1943 604030
Ilkley, West Yorkshire LS29 8HD UK   Fax: +44 (0)1943 604070

Footloose specialises in organising tailor-made trips for groups and individuals. You can tap into their expertise and knowledge to make sure you plan exactly what you want.
Contact Footloose direct for fees.

Four x 4 Safaris

PO Box 312   Tel: + 27 11 958-1746
1735 Strubensvalley, South Africa   Fax: + 27 11 958-1084

Four x 4 Safaris arranges guided, self-drive safaris in Botswana game reserves. You should get to see the 'safari big five' (lions, leopards, buffaloes, elephants, rhinos) as well as lots of other species. Even though the trips only last up to two weeks, it could be a great way to either start or finish your travels or to do after you've been on a voluntary placement. Prices are around £1500 not including flights.

Go Differently Ltd
UK   **Tel: +44 (0) 1799 521950**

We offer small-group, short-term volunteering and tailor-made holidays based on the appreciation and respect of the local environment and people throughout India and SE Asia.

Goaway
                                                Tel: +44 (0) 20 7224 7070
UK   **Fax: +44 (0) 20 7224 5353**

Goaway specialises in organising travel to India, which has a population of over one billion people and diversity like you've never seen before; it's often described as more like a continent than a country. Wherever you go, north, south, east or west, you'll come across a vast array of different people, different customs, different religions and different languages. You can use your journey to take in many of the must-see places of the world. Some of the most popular sights include the Taj Mahal in Agra, the beaches in Goa, wildlife parks of Kerala, the Himalaya mountains, Dharmsala - you might even catch a glimpse of Bollywood stars in Mumbai.

Greyhound International
Greyhound Lines Inc
PO Box 660689, MS490, TX 75266-0689 Dallas,   **Tel: +1 800 229 9424**
USA   **www.greyhound.com**

America's legendary bus company Greyhound offers the International Ameripass (from $135 for four days to $437 for 60 days) for routes on the US mainland and selected points in Canada, and there's a separate pass for Canada with some connecting journeys between the two countries. You can travel when you want, but you must show your Ameripass/Canada Pass to a terminal or station ticket agent for validation when you start each journey.

Greyhound buses now have air conditioning, tinted windows and a loo on board as well as a strict no smoking policy. Greyhound also arranges a 'GoHostelling' package that combines bus travel and hostel accommodation. There's the usual 10% discount for ISIC and Euro 26 ID cardholders. The bus company operates outside America too, with Greyhound Pioneer Australia and Greyhound Coach Lines Africa.

High & Wild
1 Heritage Courtyard   **Tel: +44 (0)1749 671777**
Sadler Street, BA5 2RR Wells UK   **Fax: +44 (0)1749 670888**

High and Wild plan some of the most unusual and exciting adventures to destinations worldwide. They have contact with many very different bona fide organisations in over 200 locations worldwide with gap year projects to suit you. They can plan something outrageous as a short-term adventure, but equally well can also place you in a longer-term conservation project for example.

233

From Banking To Biking!

Dickon, aged 28 from London, was enjoying a successful career in banking when he decided it was time for a change. "I'd gone straight from university to the city. I felt that I needed a broader perspective on life, in terms of my own personal development."

Dickon certainly picked a challenging placement. For 3 months, he supported AIDS orphans and children with AIDS in Cambodia. His experiences were deeply moving, uplifting, and on occasions, traumatic.

"Essentially I was a flying doctor, but on a bike, with provisions consisting of little more than soap or vitamin pills. It was humbling to see the gratitude of the people we tried to help. For so long nobody had cared. There were many moments of utter tragedy, as well as plenty filled with the laughter and warmth of the amazing people that I had the privilege to support."

AIDS is rife throughout the country, and with little or no government support in place, suffering and discrimination is commonplace.

"I can honestly say that volunteering has changed my life. I feel a lot more grounded as a person. The simple things in life mean so much more. I'd encourage anyone to take time out to volunteer, it's amazing how a comparatively short period of time can give you an utterly new steer on life."

Cathy, 25 from UK.

"Half way through the project in Tanzania I caught malaria! We had gone hiking, but after doing 20 miles on the first day I started aching. On the following day I was sweating, had headaches and was feeling sick. It just got progressively worse.

I had taken the right precautions, I was just unlucky, but clearly I had malaria! I collapsed at the side of the road and flagged down a car that took us to the nearest hospital at the next village. We couldn't find a doctor. In the end we found a nurse who told us that the doctor had gone home and no-one was on call.

We eventually found a hospital in Tanga. The staff were absolutely brilliant and looked after me well. The organisation I went with, MondoChallenge, also looked after me well. After a week or so I was fine, and on the upside, I lost a stone and a half!"

Journey Latin America

12/13 Heathfield Terrace
London W4 4JE UK

Tel: +44 (0) 20 8747 3108
Fax: +44 (0) 20 8742 1312

JLA is the UK's major specialist in travel to Latin America. Its 'Open-Jaw' transatlantic tickets permit you to fly into one country and out of another.

Kumuka

40 Earls Court Road
Earls Court Road London UK

Tel: +44 (0)207 937 8855
Fax: +44 (0)207 937 6664

Kumuka offers over 150 tours in 52 different countries, ranging from 4 days to 35 weeks. They hold film nights around the UK to give you a taste of the sort of tours they offer: anywhere from Johannesburg to Cancun in Mexico. Prices tend to be the good side of £1000 for around a month, but do not include flights.

Madventurer

Adamson House
65 Westgate Road,
Newcastle upon Tyne NE1 1SG UK

Tel: +44 (0) 845 121 1996

www.madventurer.com

Madventurer programmes, specifically for gappers, university students and career breakers, take you on a fully-equipped 4x4 overland vehicle, to explore those out-of-the-way places that you would otherwise not be able to reach safely on your own either in Africa or Latin America. Programmes include the Gorilla Trek Safari (22 days through Kenya and Uganda) and the Andes to Amazon adventure, following in the footsteps of the Incas by hiking to the mysterious ruins of Machu Picchu. Each adventure group has two expedition leaders who are fully trained mechanics and have a wealth of travelling experience. You help with daily tasks such as setting up the camp and shopping for fresh supplies in local markets.

Madventurer also offers Combo Expedition, which combines project work (see Madventurer's listing in Volunteering Abroad) with community tourism, allowing you to truly experience your host country (or countries) and, in return, give something back to the people. Each group project lasts for between 4 to 5 weeks and solo projects can last from between 3 months and a year.

Migration Overland Ltd

North Lodge, Main Street, Edmondthorpe,
Leicestershire LE14 2JU UK

Tel: +44 (0) 7817 710209

Migration Overland organises 16-week overland trips from UK to West Africa. Mountain bikes, all terrain boards and kayaks are carried on a fully-prepared expedition vechicle, allowing you to explore, discover and interact with everything around.

The emphasis of the the overland trips is on involving every single group member in the running of the trip. Not just in the day-to-day workings, but a real input in to where you go, what you do and how long you stay there. With a maximum of ten group members, backed by the knowledge and experience of you group leaders, you really will be part of making the decisions. There is no set itinerary; you will decided that! Flexibility is the key... a local festival? let's join in! An unsoilt beach - why not stay a while? An invitation from a local family - let's stay for dinner!

Camp under the stars, drink tea with desert nomads and come away with more than just stamps in your passport!

Mountain Beach Activity Holidays

13 Church Street
Ruddington, Nottingham NG11 6HA UK

Tel: +44 (0) 115 921 5065
Fax: +44 (0) 1159 216 182

One company offering mountain biking holidays (with first-aid trained guides) is Mountain Beach Activity Holidays. With holidays in Greece, Portugal, Costa Rica, Brazil, Chile, Mexico, New Zealand, Scotland, Canada or France, it aims to 'emphasise the holiday element, rather than an enforced regime, and ensure a great experience.'

Most of the bikers are 20-somethings. Prices vary: two weeks in Greece for £549 (excl. flights) to two weeks in Costa Rica for £1,495 (excl. flights). Bike hire and shared accommodation included. Insurance extra.

Overland Club

Salters House, Salters Lane,
Sedgefield, TS21 3EE Stockton-on-Tees UK

Tel: 0845 658 0336
Fax: 0845 658 0337

Overland Club provide the ultimate in adventure style group tours and expeditions. They have over 50 tours and expeditions, ranging from four days to 28 weeks throughout Africa, the Middle East, South America, New Zealand, Australia and Asia, with new trips being introduced each year!

Overland Club supply everything from short safari style tours to epic journeys across entire continents! With over ten years experience and pioneers of many of the routes used today, Overland Club remain at the forefront of overland adventure style travel. It's not just where you're going, its how you get there!

Peak Leaders

Mansfield
Strathmiglo
Fife KY14 7QE, Scotland

Tel: +44 (0) 1337 860 079
Fax: +44 (0) 1338 868 176
www.peakleaders.com

Peak Leaders run winter programmes in Canada, Argentina and New Zealand which include ski and snowboard instructor training, mountain safety, first aid, avalanche awareness, language, management, work experience and leadership.

People Tree Gap Year Company

105 Westbourne Terrace
W2 6QT London
UK

Tel: +44 (0) 20 7402 557
Fax: +44 (0) 20 7262 7561
www.peopletree@gapyearindia.com

People Tree Gap-Year Company gives you the chance to experience your dream gap year anywhere in India, Nepal and Sri Lanka. Whether you want to teach, work in conservation, learn to ride an elephant, work in the fashion industry, become a DJ, or just travel, they are happy to organise it for you. Just tell them your ideas and they will help you design your own unique gap year.

Alternatively they run five programmes: teaching placements, conservation placements, work experience placements, learning skills placements and gap year travel; so you could also mix and match any or all aspects of these placements.

Phoenix Expeditions

College Farm, Far Street, Wymeswold,
Leicestershire LE12 6TZ UK

Tel: +44 (0) 1509 881818
Fax: +44 (0) 1509 881822

Phoenix Expeditions specialises in safaris and expeditions in Africa, Turkey and the Middle East. Trips range from 18 days to 20 weeks.

STA Travel

52 Grosvenor Gardens
Victoria, London SW1 UK

Tel: 0870 160 6070
www.statravel.co.uk

STA Travel are specialists in travel for students and those under 26, offering low cost flights, accommodation, insurance, gap year travel, overland & adventure tours, ski & snowboard, round-the-world tickets, discount cards, city breaks and international travel help.

They offer students and those under 26 exclusive discounts on travel with quality airlines. Most airline tickets are valid for one year, so it's often impossible to finalise all your plans before you leave the UK. With this in mind STA Travel tickets are designed to offer the greatest possible flexibility. You can usually change your dates of travel and even your route for little cost.

STA Travel have Travel Help branches or agents in over 75 countries worldwide and if you can't get into a local STA Travel branch, then there is a Help Desk telephone service, which provides you with essential backup for travellers on the move. With over 450 branches worldwide, with 65 of those in the UK, and well-travelled, experienced staff STA Travel can assist you with all your travel plans for your trip.

STEN (Save the Earth Network)

PO Box CT 3635
Cantonments-Accra, Ghana

Tel: +233 21 667791
Fax: +233 21 669625

STEN organises eco-tourism programmes in Ghana in conjunction with a network of tour operators there. The trips, in small groups led by a guide, include hiking, river rafting and canoeing, mountaineering, villages and beaches, culture and photo tours, traditional stories, historic sites, traditional drumming and dances, traditional houses, trekking, touring environmental conservation projects, animal sanctuaries and nature tourism. Accommodation is with local host families or in hotels. The cost of $140 a week includes room and board, but doesn't cover transport or health insurance.

The Bush Academy

PO Box 5478
Durban 4000
ZwaZulu-Natal, South Africa

Tel: 00 27 31 3609300
Fax: 0027 31 3609333
www.bushacademy.co.za

A career in the exciting Field Guiding and Game Lodge Management industry is both practical and rewarding, ideal for those who prefer the great outdoors to the chaos of city life.

The Bush Academy courses are ideally suited to gappers wanting an introduction to conservation in Southern Africa and those wishing to pursue a conservation oriented career, as well as improving their personal knowledge of wildlife.

The Bush Academy has many courses on offer: from the one year course for those seeking either a career in this field, or alternative gap-year experience to 1-, 3- and 6-month Ranger Training experience courses. For more information, visit their website.

The Expedition Company

PO Box 17
Wiveliscombe, TA4 2YL Taunton UK

Tel: +44 (0)1984 624780
Fax: +44 (0)1984 629045

The Expedition Company takes gappers on photographic tours to Iceland, Greenland or the Himalayas. The tours can last up to four weeks and will take you to some of the most stunning scenery on the planet, for you to photograph. Contact the company direct for prices and more info.

Tiger Trails

Dale Cottage	Tel: +44 (0)1946 841495
Calderbridge, Cumbria CA20 1DN UK	Fax: +44 (0)1946 841495

Tiger Trails specialises in tailor-made safaris to see and photograph tigers, leopards and other wildlife in India, Nepal and Sri Lanka. Bengal Tigers can be seen stalking prey in the National Parks of India and Nepal by elephant or jeep safari. Leopards are found throughout India and Nepal, but Sri Lanka offers the best chance of tracking these elusive big cats.

Trailfinders

215 Kensington High Street,	
London W8 6BD UK	Tel: +44 (0) 20 7937 1234

Trailfinders offers a one-stop service for independent travellers - including visa and medical arrangements. It is more expensive to get your vaccinations done here rather than with your GP but the service is much more efficient. You don't need to make an appointment, but try to avoid lunch time if you can as this is the busiest time. The London Travel Clinic is at 194 Kensington High Street (Tel: +44 (0) 20 7938 3999) and is open Friday-Wednesday 9am-5pm, Thursday 9am-6pm and Saturday 10am-5.15pm.

For flight information, call +44 (0) 20 7937 1234 (European flights); +44 (0) 20 7937 5400 (Transatlantic flights); +44 (0) 20 7938 3939 (Long-haul flights); +44 (0) 20 7938 3848 (Visa and Passport Service).

TrekAmerica

16/17 Grange Mills	Tel: +44 (0) 870 444 TREK (8735)
Weir Road	Fax: +44 (0) 870 444 8728
London SW12 0NE UK	www.trekamerica.co.uk

TrekAmerica - Offering more than 60 itineraries from one to nine weeks in TrekAmerica's fun, free, and flexible small group adventure tours are the ideal way to explore North America.

Lets Trek Australia & NZ - TrekAmerica goes down under. Whether snorkeling on the Great Barrier Reef, off-roading around Fraser Island, exploring the vast Australian outback, or visiting the North and South Islands of New Zealand, with Lets Trek Australia & NZ you will get more adventure than you can handle.

TrekAdventures - TrekAdventures unique concept of flexible itineraries, private transport and the use of local suppliers will ensure you get the most out of your holiday and enjoy all the breathtaking natural beauty and incredibly varied culture Central and South America have to offer.

Why travel with TrekAmerica? Exclusive 10% Gap - Year Guidebook discount; explore the hard to reach national parks and Indian lands; experience the big cities and small towns; perfect for individuals and friends alike; wide variety of tours throughout North America, Central and South America, Australia, and New Zealand.

Trekforce Expeditions

34 Buckingham Palace Road
London SW1W 0RE
UK

Tel: +44 (0) 20 7828 2275
Fax: +44 (0) 20 7828 2276
www.trekforce.org.uk

Trekforce is a long-established charity that organises adventurous 8-20 week expeditions to Central and South America and East Malaysia. Working with local partners, their projects concentrate on rainforest conservation, scientific research and local communities.

Their extended programmes of three to five months combine working as a team to complete a valuable project with additional optional phases of learning Spanish in a second country and teaching in a rural community. Applications are welcome throughout the year.

Truck Africa

Wissett Place, Norwich Road, Halesworth,
Suffolk IP19 8HY UK

Tel: +44 (0) 1509 881509
Fax: +44 (0) 1986 874114

Organises long haul adventure camping safaris for people aged 18-30. For example, the 'Trans Africa' trip lasts five months and travels from the UK to Tanzania, via (amongst other places) Marrakesh, the beaches of the Ivory Coast, the stilted villages of Benin, the Rift Valley lakes of Kenya and the Serengeti National Park.

The trip costs £2100 per person (plus £550 kitty money), which works out as £129 per week. Trips leave in October. Their UK agent is Phoenix Expeditions (Tel: +44 (0) 1509 881818).

Ventureco Worldwide

The Ironyard, 64-66 The Market Place,
WarwickCV34 4SD UK

Tel: +44 (0) 1926 411 122
Fax: +44 (0) 1926 411 133

VentureCo's concept is the ideal travel combination for Gap Year and Career Gap travellers who want to explore off the beaten track, learn about the host country while they are there and give something back before they return home. Each Venture combines three modules in one massive four-month programme: language school, voluntary work and a wilderness expedition.

South & Central America

Inca Venture (Ecuador, Peru, Bolivia and Chile)
Patagonia Venture (Peru, Bolivia, Chile, Argentina and Tierra del Fuego)
Aztec & Maya Venture (Guatemala, Belize, Mexico, Cuba and Costa Rica)

Africa

Rift Valley Venture (Kenya, Uganda and Tanzania)

Southeast Asia

Himalaya Venture (India and Nepal)
Indochina Venture (Cambodia, Vietnam, Laos and China)

Experienced VentureCo Leaders accompany each team of between 10 and 16; preparation gets under way ten weeks before departure from the UK with a build-up weekend; full in-country expedition training is provided. Planning, leadership and organising roles throughout the Venture are shared amongst the team and each Venturer will lead a leg of the expedition.

239

As expedition travel professionals our price is all-inclusive (the build-up weekend, international flights, personal travel insurance, taxes, trekking permits & mountain fees, language tuition, all expedition activities, aid project donation and all domestic flights/travel are included). We have no kitties and no local payments. Prices from £4,500. VentureCo hold ATOL license 5306 and are members of the Year Out Group. VentureCo have separate Ventures for school leavers and individuals on a career break.

Applications are welcome throughout the year.

Walks Worldwide

| 12 The Square | Tel: +44 (0)1524 242000 |
| Ingleton, Carnforth, Lancashire LA6 3EG UK | Fax: +44 (0)1524 242657 |

Walks Worldwide offers different types of walking expeditions around the world, from walking across the Swedish coastal peninsulas to trekking to Everest base camp. They can help groups organise their own trip or you can join one of the existing groups.

Wild at Heart Youth Safari Adventures

| 15 Plantation Road, 15 Plantation Road, Kwazulu, | Tel: +27 31 765 2947 |
| Natal 3650, South Africa | Fax: +27 31 765 7248 |

Wild at Heart Youth Safari's is a well-established South African Based Youth Adventure company. From helping at a monkey sanctuary to working at a reptile farm there are many different opportunities available.

They also offer more holiday-type safari tours in different locations around southern Africa, including the Kruger national Park; 'African Adventures' includes a safari on quad bikes or hiking in the Drakensburg mountain range. Contact them direct for more details and prices.

World Challenge Expeditions

Black Arrow House	Tel: +44 (0) 20 8728 7272
2 Chandos Road	Fax: +44 (0) 20 8961 1551
London NW10 6NF UK	www.world-challenge.co.uk

World Challenge Expeditions has been organising placements and expeditions to some of the most remote and culturally diverse places on Earth for over 15 years. They currently offer the following programmes:

Team Challenge: the opportunity to plan and lead your own expedition (4 - 6 weeks) to the developing world, to East Africa, the Andes and Amazon, Borneo, India and the Himalayas or Central America. Accompanied by a highly-qualified and experienced Expedition Leader, you'll be trekking in some of the most amazing scenery in the world and completing worthwhile project work.

First Challenge: offers students a range of eight- and fourteen-day expeditions including First Challenge Learning to Lead, designed specifically to develop leadership potential in students aged 18-20. Under the discreet guidance of a highly-qualified leader you will be responsible for planning and leading your own adventurous journey to Morocco, Poland, Romania or Andalucia.

Close Encounters

"I had several 'close encounters' with the African wildlife - being charged by a protective mother elephant, a nose-to-nose meeting with an inquisitive hyena, tracking rhino on foot and being in the path of male lions, all of which have been memorable 'highlights' of my trip. I have also learnt an awful lot about the bush, and made a worthwhile contribution to the conservation projects. On a personal note, my African Conservation Experience was an all-round fantastic time and introduced me to some good friends. From recognising the sounds of different birdsong, to simply sitting and enjoying the natural quiet and stillness; my three months soaking up the atmosphere of the bush and working hard for conservation have taught me most of all that I want to go back!"

Nikki

Chapter 6

Office Skills

Office Skills

Office work is based on information technology, so being trained in this field can seriously help your chances of earning that quick cash. Office temping is a very common job that pays reasonably well and there is plenty of it around.

In this chapter we try and steer you in the right direction to getting that first job, including listings for colleges that run short information technology courses.

Work experience asap

The big question is 'how do I get work experience when everywhere I go rejects me because I haven't got work experience?' This could

seriously ruin the whole gap year plan. For simple menial work, such as stacking shelves or fruit picking then it shouldn't be too much of a problem, but those types of jobs don't pay particularly well. If you need money fast then you might have to look elsewhere.

Gap year recruiters tend to expect their clients to have no work experience at all, so it could be a good idea to get ahead of the game and get some experience under your belt before you leave school. If you're reading this whilst you're in the lower VIth then you have quite a lot of time left and we advise you to use it to get as much work experience as possible. Or perhaps take that computer course during the school holidays. This will seriously impress your future employers.

Even if the work is basic (filing, making the tea), it shows that you can function within a working environment. Ask your school for some help organising some work placements. We're not saying that you have to spend every week of your holidays working, perhaps just two or three weeks. And remember you can always do with that a bit more cash. It may seem like a drag now, but think how much more impressive you'll be at job interviews later on with a fatter CV and references in hand.

245

Skills for work

What are the skills that you need in order to get that vital job? Don't forget that you only have a limited time, so you don't want to be training for too long as that will cut down on your earning time and therefore enjoyment time. This is why many people choose to go into trades such as bartending or retail, where the company tends to provide the training. Though this might not prove to be nearly as lucrative as office work.

If you've done a computer based course during VIth form then that could well prove to be enough. If you can type at around 40-45 words per minute or you're comfortable designing websites then you stand a good chance of landing a fairly well paid job.

"We have quite a lot of 18-year-olds, coming through us," says Louise Billington of Henderson Recruitment. "Most stay in a job for three or four months and save themselves a few thousand to go abroad with… The most important thing they need is 40-45 wpm touch-typing. You can teach yourself with a computer package… You'll be tested on your skills and you'll need to understand how to format a document as well. A good telephone manner and a knowledge of Microsoft Office software (Access, Excel, Powerpoint and Word) are a big help."

Qualifications – who needs them?

Qualifications are needed when you can't otherwise prove that you're capable of whatever the job involves. For example, if you're not French and have never lived in France, then you'll have to have a qualification showing that you can speak French, if that's what the job involves. In office work the agency that you go through will put you through some tests to show your skills to the employer.

"More important than any paper qualification is that your typing speed and accuracy are strong enough to take you through the tests which your agencies will ask you to undertake. Practice is vital in building up your speeds but don't despair if you don't reach that magic 45 words per minute in the test, there are other options available which will help you build up your speeds while you are working," says James Reed, Chief Executive, Reed Employment Services.

Many offices, especially the smaller ones, will offer a trial, for around three days, just to make sure that you have what it takes. This saves them from sorting through an array of paperwork and qualifications.

What if I'm just no good?

Well, you'll just have to get good then won't you. Training for information technology has dramatically changed recently. Skills that used to take a full year now can take as little as one month. The prices have dropped too. Evening courses at a local FE college can be under £100 and public libraries also run courses on the internet. IT is already very firmly in schools' curricula so most of you should already have the skills to cope within the office. If not, then get going and get trained.

246

Which college?

There are lots of different things to look at when choosing a college. Convenience (location, hours) is very important, along with price. However, you don't want to compromise the quality of qualification you will receive because of practical concerns. A good idea might be to check with an agency about the value of a qualification from particular colleges. Or check with the actual college on the employment record of their past students.

Finding the right course

Of course you want to start earning as soon as possible so is it worth spending a longer time studying for a qualification that you don't really need? How do you know which course is best for you? Can you compare different word processing courses against each other; surely word processing is just word processing? Also, you don't want to pay to learn something that you already know how to do. To help with this little dilemma the City & Guilds, which awards over a million certificates a year, defines the levels of its qualifications (which continue up to Level 7).

Level 1: introductory awards for those new to the area covering routine tasks or basic knowledge and understanding

Level 2: qualifications for those with some knowledge of and ability in the areas which acknowledge individual responsibility

Level 3: qualifications that recognise complex work involving supervisory ability

If you think that you already know level two, for example, then its worth your while going straight onto level 3.

How much to pay?

The most important thing here is not to get ripped off. Of course the better the course the more expensive it's likely to be, but what things can you check for to make sure that you're not being conned? Be aware of the VAT and any other hidden costs that there might be. To test the value of the course compare the total hours of tuition to the price. Check out each course and just be sure that what you are going to do will be of benefit, before parting with any money.

Over the next pages you'll find a list of colleges from all over the country which run intensive business skills courses. It is only an indicator of what's available, not a guarantee of quality. We're happy to hear from (and reports about) any training centres that offer short courses in office skills.

247

Colleges

KEY

Size of college (number of full-time students):
L Large (100+)   **M** Medium (50-100)   **S** Small (0-50)

Course types:
I Intensive, usually 12 weeks or less
Md Modular
Flex Mix of tuition and practice time with flexible timing
Cert Lead to recognised certificated qualifications
DIY One or two modules studied at college/training centre. Student can enter exam for individual elements or full set of modules including ones that have been self-taught

Course contents:
WP	Word processing	**SS**	Spreadsheets
TT	Touch-typing	**EM**	E-mail
DB	Databases	**Web**	Web design

ENGLAND

Bedfordshire

Barnfield College (FE)

Rotherham Avenue, Luton,
Bedfordshire LU1 5PP
Tel: +44 (0) 1582 569 700

L / Flex, Cert
WP, TT, DB, SS, EM, Web

Birmingham

Bournville College

www.bournville.ac.uk

Bristol Road South, Northfield,
Birmingham B31 2AJ
Tel: +44 (0) 121 483 1000

L / Flex, Cert
WP, TT, DB, SS, EM, Web

Bristol

City of Bristol College

www.cityofbristol.ac.uk

College Green Centre, St Georgeís Road,
Bristol BS1 5UA
Tel: +44 (0) 117 904 5000

L / Flex, Cert, DIY
WP, TT, DB, SS, EM, Web

Emma Hall Business & Secretarial College

7 Duchess Road, Clifton, Bristol B58 2LA
Tel: +44 (0) 117 973 4783

S / Flex, Cert, DIY
WP, TT, DB, SS, EM

248

Cambridgeshire

Huntingdonshire Regional College

www.huntingdon.ac.uk

California Road, Huntingdon,
Cambridgeshire PE18 7BL
Tel: +44 (0) 1480 379 100

L / Flex, Cert, DIY
WP, TT, DB, SS, EM, Web

Isle College

Ramnoth Road, Wisbech,
Cambridgeshire PE13 0HY
Tel: +44 (0) 1945 582 561

L / Flex, Cert, DIY
WP, TT, DB, SS, EM

Peterborough Regional College

Park Crescent, Peterborough,
Cambridgeshire PE1 4DZ
Tel: +44 (0) 1733 767 366

L / Flex, Cert, DIY
WP, TT, DB, SS, EM, Web

Cheshire

Newton Secretarial School

12L Saltney House, Chesterbank Business Park,
River Lane, Saltney, Chester, Cheshire CH4 8SL
Tel: +44 (0) 1244 681 814 / +44 (0) 1244 537265

S / I, Flex, Cert, DIY
WP, TT

South Trafford College

www.stcoll.ac.uk

Manchester Road, West Timperley,
Altrincham, Cheshire WA14 5PQ
Tel: +44 (0) 161 952 4600

L / Flex, Cert, DIY
WP, TT, DB, SS, EM, Web

Cleveland

www.cleveland.ac.uk

Redcar & Cleveland College, Corporation Road,
Redcar, Cleveland TS10 1EZ
Tel: +44 (0) 1642 473 132

L / Flex, Cert, DIY
WP, DB, SS, EM, Web

Cornwall

Cornwall College

www.cornwall.ac.uk

Trevenson Road, Redruth,
Cornwall TR15 3RD
Tel: +44 (0) 1209 611 611Fax: +44 (0) 1209 616161

L / Flex, Cert, DIY
WP, TT, DB, SS, EM, Web

Penwith College

www.penwith.ac.uk

St Clare Street, Penzance,
Cornwall TR18 2SA
Tel: +44 (0) 1736 335 000Fax: +(0)1736 335 100

L / Web, Flex, Cert
WP, TT, DB, SS, EM

249

County Down

East Down Institute of Further and Higher Education

Market Street, Downpatrick,
County Down BT30 6ND
Tel: +44 (0) 1396 615 815

L / Flex, Cert, DIY
WP, TT, SS, EM

Denbighshire

Coleg Llysfasi

www.llysfasi.ac.uk

Ruthin, Denbighshire LU15 2LB
Tel: +44 (0) 1978 790 263

Flex, Cert, DIY
WP, TT, DB, SS, EM, Web

Derbyshire

Derby College

www.mackworth.ac.uk

Prince Charles Avenue, Mackworth,
Derby DE22 4LR
Tel: 0800 028 0289

L / Flex, Cert, DIY
WP, TT, DB, SS, EM, Web

Devon

Plymouth College of Further Education

www.pcfe.ac.uk

Kings Road, Devonport, Plymouth,
Devon PL1 5QG
Tel: +44 (0) 1752 305 300Fax: +44(0)1752 305 342

L / Flex, Cert, DIY
WP, TT, DB, SS, EM, Web

Dorset

Broadlands Training

121a Old Christchurch Road, Bournemouth,
Dorset BH8 0AL
Tel: +44 (0) 1202 552 161

S / Flex, Cert, DIY
WP, TT, DB, SS, EM

East Sussex

Hove College

www.hovecollege.co.uk

Medina House, 41 Medina Villas, Hove,
East Sussex BN3 2RP
Tel: +44 (0) 1273 772577Fax: +44 (0)1273 208 401

M / Flex, Cert
WP, TT, DB, SS, EM, Web

Plumpton College

www.plumpton.ac.uk

Ditchling Road, Plumpton, Nr Lewes,
East Sussex BN7 3AE
Tel: +44 (0) 1273 890 454

L / Flex, Cert
WP, DB, SS, EM, Web

East Yorkshire

Bishop Burton College
www.bishopburton.ac.uk

Bishop Burton, Beverley,
East Yorkshire HU17 8QG
Tel: +44 (0) 1964 553 000

L / Cert
WP, DB, SS, Web

Hull College
www.hull-college.ac.uk

Queen's Gardens Site, Hull,
East Yorkshire HU1 3DG
Tel: +44 (0) 1482 329 943

L / Flex, Cert
WP, TT, DB, SS

Essex

Havering College
www.havering-college.ac.uk

Ardleigh Green Road, Hornchurch,
Essex RM11 2LL
Tel: +44 (0) 1708 455 011

L / Flex, Cert
WP, TT, DB, SS, EM, Web

South-East Essex College (F&HE)
www.se-essex-college.ac.uk

Luker Road, Southend, Essex SS1 1ND
Tel: +44 (0) 1702 200 400

L / Flex, Cert
WP, TT, DB, SS

Thurrock & Basildon College (FE)
www.thurrock.ac.uk

Woodview Grays, Essex RM16 2YR
Tel: +44 (0)8456 015 746

L / Flex, Cert
WP, TT, DB, SS, EM, Web

Gloucestershire

Hartpury College
www.hartpury.ac.uk

Hartpury House, Hartpury, Gloucester,
GL19 3BE
Tel: +44 (0) 1452 700 283

L / Flex, Cert
WP, DB, SS, EM, Web

Hampshire

Cricklade College
www.cricklade.ac.uk

Charlton Road, Andover,
Hampshire SP10 1EJ
Tel: +44 (0) 1264 360 036

L / Flex, Cert, Split
WP, TT, DB, SS, EM, Web

Havant College (FE)
www.havant.ac.uk

New Road, Havant, Hampshire PO9 1QL
Tel: +44 (0) 239 271 4040

L / Flex, Cert
WP, TT, DB, SS, EM, Web

Highbury College

Dovercourt Road, Cosham, Portsmouth,
Hampshire P06 2SA
Tel: +44 (0) 23 9238 3131

L / Flex, Cert, DIY
WP, TT, DB, SS, EM, Web

South Downs College www.southdowns.ac.uk

College Road, Waterlooville, L / Flex, Cert
Hampshire PO7 8AA WP, TT, DB, SS, EM, Web
Tel: +44 (0) 23 9279 7979

Sparsholt College www.sparsholt.ac.uk

Winchester, Hampshire SO21 2NF L / Cert
Tel: +44 (0) 1962 776 441 WP, DB, SS, EM

Herefordshire

Herefordshire College of Art & Design www.hereford-art-col.ac.uk

Folly Lane, Hereford, L Web
Herefordshire HR1 1LT
Tel: +44 (0) 1432 273 359

Hertfordshire

Barnet College www.barnet.ac.uk

Wood Street, Barnet, L / Flex, Cert, Md, I
Hertfordshire EN5 4AZ WP, DB, SS
Tel: +44 (0) 20 8440 8300 / +44 (0) 20 8440 6321

Kent

Bromley College of F&HE www.bromley.ac.uk

Rookery Lane, Bromley, L / Flex, Cert
Kent BR2 8HE WP, DB, SS, EM, Web
Tel: +44 (0) 20 8295 7000

Mid-Kent College of F&HE

Horsted Centre, Maidstone Road, L / Flex, Cert, DIY
Chatham, Kent ME5 9UQ WP, DB, SS, EM, Web
Tel: +44 (0) 1634 830 633

Orpington College

The Walnuts, Orpington, Kent BR6 0TE L / Flex, Cert, DIY
Tel: +44 (0) 1689 899 700 www.orpington.ac.uk WP, TT, DB, SS, EM, Web

West Kent College (FE) www.wkc.ac.uk

Brook Street, Tonbridge, Kent TN9 2PW L / Flex, Cert, DIY
Tel: +44 (0) 1732 358 101 WP, TT, DB, SS, EM

Lancashire

Accrington & Rossendale College www.accross.ac.uk

Sandy Lane Centre, Sandy Lane, L / Flex, Cert, DIY
Accrington, Lancashire BB5 2AW WP, TT, DB, SS, EM, Web
Tel: +44 (0) 1254 389 933

Leicestershire

Leicester College (FE)

www.leicestercollege.ac.uk

Freemanís Park Campus, Aylestone Road,
Leicester LE2 7LW
Tel: +44 (0) 116 224 2000

L / Flex, Cert, DIY
WP, TT, DB, SS, EM, Web

Lincolnshire

Boston College

www.boston.ac.uk

Skirbeck Road, Boston,
Lincolnshire PE21 6JF
Tel: +44 (0) 1205 365 701

L / Flex, Cert, DIY
WP, DB, SS, EM

Grantham College (FE)

www.grantham.ac.uk

Stonebridge Road, Grantham,
Lincolnshire NG31 9AP
Tel: +44 (0) 1476 400 200 Fax: +44 (0)1476 400291

L / Flex, Cert, DIY
WP, TT, DB, SS, EM, Web

London

City College

www.citycollege.ac.uk

University House, 55 East Road,
London N1 6AH
Tel: +44 (0) 20 7253 1133

L / Flex, Cert, DIY
WP, TT, DB, SS, EM, Web

CRTS International College (London N17)

United Kingdom Tel: +44 (0) 20 8801 0371

Enfield College (FE)

www.enfield.ac.uk

73 Hertford Road, Enfield, London EN3 5HA
Tel: +44 (0) 20 8443 3434

L / Flex, Cert, DIY
WP, TT, DB, SS, EM, Web

Holburn College (London SE7)

Tel: +44 (0) 020 7385 3377

Institut Français

17 Queensberry Place, London SW7 2DT
Tel: +44 (0) 20 7581 2701

Interlink College of Technology (London E15)

Tel: +44 (0) 20 8522 0622

Islamic College for Advanced Studies (London NW10)

Tel: +44 (0) 20 845 9993

253

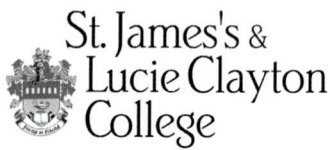

St. James's & Lucie Clayton College

Executive Business & Secretarial Courses in Your Gap Year

One Term Gap Course

- In-depth IT training, a grounding in Media subjects & Teeline shorthand
- Tutor led, excellent results
- Emphasis on confidence building & careers advice
- Associated Recruitment Consultancy
- Commercial language options
- Courses start in January, April & September

Short, Intensive Touch Typing & IT Courses

- Up to date MS Office packages
- Courses start every Monday; from two to six weeks

Fun Summer Courses

- One to two week Image Courses including Make-up & Style, Confidence & Interview Techniques

Please contact us for a prospectus

St. James's & Lucie Clayton College, 4 Wetherby Gardens, London SW5 0JN
Tel: **020 7373 3852** · Fax: **020 7370 3303** · Email: **information@sjlccollege.co.uk**

www.sjlccollege.co.uk

London School of Management (London W5)

Tel: +44 (0) 20 8567 4355

Merton Adult Education

www.mertonadultcollege.ac.uk

Whatley Avenue, London SW20 9NS
Tel: +44 (0) 20 8543 9292 Fax: +44 (0) 20 8544 1421

L / Flex, Cert, DIY
WP, DB, SS, EM, Web

Pitmans Training Centre

www.pitmantraining.com

288 Regent Street, London W1R 5HE
Tel: +44 (0) 20 242 4590

M / Flex, Cert, DIY
WP, TT, DB, SS, EM, Web

Queen's Business & Secretarial College

www.qbsc.ac.uk

24 Queensberry Place, London SW7 2DS
Tel: +44 (0) 20 7589 8583

L / I, Cert
WP, TT, DB, SS, EM

After university, graduates are facing increasing competition for jobs and employers can afford to favour those with the most extensive portfolio of relevant work experience. Well-organised students will begin to build this portfolio during their gap year and continue throughout the long vacations during their time at university.

Exotic travel plans require financing, which means most gap year students will need to find a job. Many, however, do not appreciate just how important that job can be for their future careers.

Taking an intensive course at Queen's can equip students with the IT and business skills they need to gain this experience and to help boost finances during vacations. Fast keyboarding and good computer skills are also an obvious advantage at university. In addition, job-search skills are an integral part of all courses at Queen's. Students are given a thorough training in preparing a CV, writing covering letters, interview technique and the importance of personal presentation.

St James's & Lucie Clayton College

www.sjlccollege.co.uk

4 Wetherby Gardens, London SW5 OJN
Tel: +44 (0) 20 7373 3852 Fax: +44 (0) 20 7370 3303

M / I, Md, Flex, Cert
WP, TT, DB, SS, EM

St James & Lucie Clayton College offers a one term Pre/Post University Course which is ideal for school leavers during their gap year. It equips the gap year student with the necessary confidence and training required to gain competitive temping rates within a commercial office environment, skills which will be invaluable for university course work too. The course, offered in September, January & April, covers the following essential areas - IT (MS Office, e-learning, keyboard training etc), practical business development (effective writing skills, team building, shorthand etc) personal development & life skills (careers guidance, interview techniques, self defence etc), and marketing skills (an introduction to creative advertising, PR). Intensive touch typing and IT courses (one to six weeks) prove particularly popular with gap year students wishing to only take short courses in these fundamental skills.

The Collegeís established links with London-based companies and its own associated recruitment consultancy helps to ensure that students find temporary assignments, many of which offer attractive rates of pay, enabling the student to gain commercial experience and fund their travel or other plans in their gap year.

255

Londonderry

North West Institute of F&HE   www.nwifhe.ac.uk

Strand Road, Londonderry BT48 7AL   L / Flex, Cert, DIY
Tel: +44 (0) 28 7127 6000   WP, TT, DB, SS, EM

Manchester

Manchester College of Arts & Technology (FE)   www.mancat.ac.uk

Ashton Old Road, Openshaw, Manchester M11 2WH   L / Flex, Cert, DIY
Tel: +44 (0)161 953 5995   WP, TT, DB, SS, EM, Web

Merseyside

Knowsley Community College   www.knowsleycc.ac.uk

Rupert Road, Ruby, Merseyside L36 9TD   Flex, Cert, DIY
Tel: +44 (0) 151 477 5777   WP, TT, DB, SS, EM, Web

Middlesex

Stanmore College (FE)   www.stanmore.ac.uk

Elm Park, Stanmore, Middlesex HA7 4BQ   L / Flex, Cert, DIY
Tel: +44 (0) 20 8420 7700   WP, TT, DB, SS, Web

West Thames College (FE)   www.west-thames.ac.uk

London Road, Isleworth, Middlesex TW7 4HS   L / Flex, Cert, DIY
Tel: +44 (0) 20 8326 2020   WP, TT, DB, SS, EM, Web

Norfolk

Great Yarmouth College

Southtown, Great Yarmouth, Norfolk NR31 0ED   L / Flex, Cert, DIY
Tel: +44 (0) 1493 655 261   WP, TT, DB, SS, EM, Web

College of West Anglia   www.col-westanglia.ac.uk

Tennyson Avenue, Kingís Lynn, Norfolk PE30 2QW   L / Flex, Cert, DIY
Tel: +44 (0) 1553 761 144Fax: +44 (0) 1553 764 902   WP, TT, DB, SS, EM, Web

North Yorkshire

Selby College (FE)   www.selbycollege.co.uk

Abbottís Road, Selby, North Yorkshire YO8 8AT   L / Flex, Cert, DIY
Tel: +44 (0) 1757 211 000   WP, TT, DB, SS, EM, Web

Nottinghamshire

Broxtowe College (F&HE)   www.broxtowe.ac.uk

High Road, Chilwell, Nottingham NG9 4AH   L / Flex, Cert, DIY
Tel: +44 (0) 115 917 5252   WP, TT, DB, SS, EM, Web

Oxfordshire

Abingdon College

www.abingdoncollege.ac.uk

Wooton Road, Abingdon, OX14 1GG
Tel: +44 (0) 1235 555 585

Flex, Cert
WP, TT, DB, SS, EM

Oxford Media & Business School

Rose Place, Oxford OX1 1SB
Tel: +44 (0) 1865 240 963

Flex, Cert
WP, TT, DB, SS, EM, Web

Oxford Media & Business School offers 6-week gap year ëLife Skillsí courses starting four times a year: January, April, July and September. The gap year ëLife Skillsí course is designed to help you make the most of your gap year. First, it will give you an early taste of a university style environment, so when the time comes to start your degree youíll quickly feel at home. Second, it will give you useful training in key ëLife Skillsí such as the use of the latest IT software - invaluable both for later degree submissions and for earning useful extra cash for the rest of your gap year. Finally, it will actually help you find well-paid gap year temping work through the OMBS Careers Direct placement bureau - great for your CV and great for funding your gap year travelling.

Pembrokeshire

Pembrokeshire College (FE)

www.pembrokeshire.ac.uk

Haverfordwest, Pembrokeshire SA61 1SZ, Wales
Tel: +44 (0) 800 716 236

L / Flex, Cert
WP, TT, DB, SS, EM, Web

Shropshire

Shrewsbury College of Arts & Technology

www.shrewsbury.ac.uk

London Road, Shrewsbury, Shropshire SY2 6PR
Tel: +44 (0) 1743 342342

Flex, Cert, DIY
WP, TT, DB, SS, EM, Web

Somerset

Bridgewater College

www.bridgewater.ac.uk

Bath Road, Bridgewater, Somerset TA6 4PZ
Tel: +44 (0) 1278 455464

L / Flex, Cert, DIY
WP, TT, DB, SS, EM, Web

Cannington College (FE)

Cannington, Bridgwater, Somerset TA5 2LS
Tel: +44 (0) 1278 65500

L / Flex, Cert, DIY
WP, TT, DB, SS, EM

Staffordshire

Cannock Chase Technical College

www.cannock.ac.uk

The Green, Cannock, Staffordshire WS11 1UE
Tel: +44 (0) 1543 462 200 www.cannock.ac.uk

L / Flex, Cert, DIY
WP, TT, DB, SS, EM, Web

Rodbaston College (F&HE)
www.rodbaston.ac.uk

Rodbaston, Penkridge, Staffordshire ST19 5PH
Tel: +44 (0) 1785 712 209

L / Flex, Cert, DIY
WP, DB, SS, EM, Web

Suffolk

Leiston Training Centre (FE)

47 High Street, Leiston, Suffolk IP6 4EL
Tel: +44 (0) 1728 831 464

S / Flex, Cert, DIY
WP, TT, DB, SS, EM, Web

Rendlesham Training Centre (FE)

Building 164, AIA Rendlesham,
Woodbridge, Suffolk IP12 2TW
Tel: +44 (0) 1394 461 438

S / Flex, Cert, DIY
WP, TT, DB, SS, EM, Web

Surrey

Guildford College of Further and Higher Education
www.guildford.ac.uk

Stoke Park, Guildford, Surrey GU1 1EZ
Tel: +44 (0) 1483 448 500

Flex, Cert
WP, DB, SS, Web

Guildford Secretarial & Business College
www.g-s-c.co.uk

17 Chapel Street, Guildford, Surrey GU1 3UL
Tel: +44 (0) 1483 564 885

Flex, Cert, DIY
WP, TT, DB, SS, EM, Web

Merton College
www.merton.ac.uk

Morden Park, London Road, Morden, Surrey SM4 5QX
Tel: +44 (0) 20 8408 6500

L / I, Flex, Cert
WP, TT, DB, SS, EM, Web

Nescot
www.nescot.ac.uk

Reigate Road, Ewell, Epsom, Surrey KT17 3DS
Tel: +44 (0) 20 8394 3038

L / Flex, Cert, DIY
WP, TT, DB, SS, EM, Web

Tyne & Wear

Newcastle College
www.ncl-coll.ac.uk

Rye Hill Campus, Scotswood Road,
Newcastle-upon-Tyne NE4 7SA
Tel: +44 (0) 191 200 4000

L / Flex, Cert, DIY
WP, TT, DB, SS, EM, Web

Warwickshire

Stratford-upon-Avon College (FE)
www.strat-avon.ac.uk

The Willows North, Alcester Road,
Stratford-upon-Avon, Warwickshire CV37 9QR
Tel: +44 (0) 1789 266 245

L / Flex, Cert
WP, DB, SS, EM

Warwickshire College

www.warkscol.ac.uk

Warwick New Road, Leamington Spa,
Warwickshire CV32 5JE
Tel: +44 (0) 1926 318 000

L / Flex, Cert, DIY
WP, TT, DB, SS, EM

West Lothian

West Lothian College (FE)

Almondvale Cresent, Livingston,
West Lothian EH54 7EP, Scotland
Tel: +44 (0) 1506 418181Fax: +44 (0)1506 409980

Flex, Cert, DIY
WP, TT, DB, SS, EM, Web

West Midlands

Coventry Technical College (FE)

Butts, Coventry, West Midlands CV1 3GO
Tel: +44 (0) 2476 526700

L / Flex, Cert, DIY
WP, TT, DB, SS, EM, Web

Dudley College

www.dudleycol.ac.uk

The Broadway, Dudley, West Midlands DY1 4AS
Tel: +44 (0) 1384 363 000
West Sussex

L / Flex, Cert, DIY
WP, TT, DB, SS

West Sussex

Crawley College (FE)

www.crawley-college.ac.uk

College Road, Crawley, West Sussex RH10 1NR
Tel: +44 (0) 1293 442200 Fax: +44 (0)1293 442739

L / Flex, Cert, DIY
WP, TT, DB, SS

West Yorkshire

Dewsbury College

www.dewsbury.ac.uk

Halifax Road, Dewsbury, West Yorkshire WF13 7AS
Tel: +44 (0) 1924 465 916

L / Flex, Cert, DIY
WP, DB, SS, EM, Web

Park Lane College (FE)

www.parklanecoll.ac.uk

Park Lane, Leeds, West Yorkshire LS3 1AA
Tel: +44 (0) 113 216 2000

L / Flex, Cert, DIY
WP, TT, DB, SS, EM, Web

Shipley College (FE)

Exhibition Road, Bradford, West Yorkshire BD18 3JW
Tel: +44 (0) 1274 757 222

L / Flex, Cert, DIY
WP, TT, DB, SS, EM, Web

Westfield College of FE
www.wakcoll.ac.uk

Margaret Street, Wakefield, West Yorkshire WF1 2DH
Tel: +44 (0) 1924 789 789

L / Flex, Cert, DIY
WP, TT, DB, SS, EM, Web

Wiltshire

Salisbury College
www.salisbury.ac.uk

Southampton Road, Salisbury, Wiltshire SP1 2LW
Tel: +44 (0) 1722 344 344

L / Flex, Cert, DIY
WP, DB, SS, EM, Web

Wiltshire College
www.lackham.ac.uk

Lacock, Nr Chippenham, Wiltshire SN15 2NY
Tel: +44 (0) 1249 466 800Fax: +44 (0) 1249 444474

L / Flex, Cert, DIY

Worcestershire

Evesham College
www.evesham.ac.uk

Davies Road, Evesham, Worcestershire WR11 1LP
Tel: +44 (0) 1386 712 600

L / Flex, Cert, DIY
WP, DB, SS, EM, Web

I did the gap year course at OMBS to earn some money to finance my gap year travels to Australia.

Learning to touch type was also invaluable. I had always been fascinated by people that could sit there, staring at the screen, while their fingers swept across the keyboard in a flurry of digits. Once I'd completed the course I was a lot more confident about using a computer, and I too could type whilst staring at the screen.

I got a temporary job at a company that makes computer games. My job wasn't glamorous: I typed up letters, I answered the phone and I sent mail, but I did enjoy myself nonetheless. When I left two weeks later I had a big fat cheque in my pocket and a grin on my face

Since then the skills I learnt have been invaluable to my university career in that I can set up my essays the way I want them to look, graphs etc for projects look the way I want them to look; and I can get all my essays typed up so much quicker because I don't have to look at the keyboard.

Ellie

Chapter 7
Learning in the UK

Frustrated that hardly anything you were taught at school seemed relevant to your life? Why not use your gap year to learn new skills that you choose yourself - you can make them as useful as you want.

Archaeology

Are you an avid watcher of Time Team or fascinated by the Sutton Hoo treasure? Would you love to find an ancient relic? You could get yourself on an actual archaeological dig.

Archaeological Organisations

Archaeology Abroad
Institute of Archaeology
University College, 31-34 Gordon Square,   Tel: +44 (0) 20 8537 0849
WC1H OPY London, UK   Fax: +44 (0) 20 8537 0849

For info on digs abroad try the Archaeology Abroad bulletin and web pages.

Council for British Archaeology
St Mary's House   Tel: +44 (0) 1904 671 417
66 Bootham   Fax: +44 (0) 1904 671 384
York, Yorkshire YO30 7BZ, UK   www.britarch.ac.uk

The best starting point for archaeological digs in the British Isles is a magazine called British Archaeology which contains information about events and courses as well as digs.

Museum of London
London Wall   Tel: +44 (0) 20 7814 5777
London EC2Y 5HN, UK   www.museumoflondon.org.uk

The Museum of London runs four archaeology courses from September to March and one from April to July ('Field archaeology and the Roman-British period in southern Britain'). These run on one evening a week (with a break at Christmas and Easter), and cost £166 (student discounts) for the whole course.

Art

If you're seriously interested in painting, sculpting or other artistic subjects, but don't know if you want to carry it through to a full degree, there is the useful option of a one-year art foundation course, available from a wide variety of art colleges. A foundation course at art college doesn't count towards an art degree in the sense that you can then skip the first year of your three-year degree course.

263

Competition for undergraduate places is based on the volume and standard of work in a candidate's 'entry portfolio', having a portfolio from your foundation course puts you at a natural advantage. Course providers also advise against specialising in one discipline, say sculpture, before covering the more wide-ranging syllabus of a foundation course.

Art

Blake College
162 New Cavendish Street
London W1W 6YS
UK

Tel: +44 (0) 20 7636 0658
Fax: +44 (0)207 436 0049
www.blake.ac.uk

Bristol School of Animation
UWE, Faculty of Art, Media and Design,
Bower Ashton, Kennel Lodge Rd,
BS3 2JT Bristol, UK

Tel: +44 (0)117 344 4810
Fax: +44 (0)117 344 4820

Run by UWE's Faculty of Art, Media and Design, The Bristol School of Animation runs a wide range of animation courses aimed at budding animators of all levels and abilities. For beginners and younger animators there are some comprehensive introductory animation summer schools. For more mature and experienced animators they offer a three-month animation course which provides intensive 3D (model) or 2D (drawn) animation training. They also run an MA in animation, life drawing for animation classes and a selection of short computer animation courses.

Camberwell College of Arts
Peckham Road
London SE5 8UF
UK

Tel: +44 (0) 20 7514 6302
Fax: +44 (0)20 7514 6310
www.camb.linst.ac.uk

Established 100 years ago, Camberwell College of Arts, London has a long tradition of teaching art, design and conservation. Today it offers a blend of heritage and new thinking at foundation studies, undergraduate and postgraduate level.

Cardiff School of Art and Design
University of Wales Institute
Llandaff Campus, Western Avenue, Cardiff CF5 2YB

Tel: +44 (0) 2920 416 637
www.uwic.ac.uk/csad

Central Saint Martins College of Art and Design
Southampton Row
London WC1B 4AP
UK

Tel: +44 (0) 20 7514 7000
Fax: +44 (0) 20 7514 7254
www.csm.linst.ac.uk

Chelsea College of Art and Design
Manresa Road
London SW3 6LS, UK

Tel: +44 (0) 20 7514 7750
www.chel.linst.ac.uk

Heatherley School of Art

80 Upcerne Road
Chelsea
London SW10 0SH, UK

Tel: +44 (0) 20 7351 4190
Fax: +44 (0)20 7351 6945
www.heatherleys.org

The Heatherley School of Art in Chelsea runs a full-time one-year foundation/portfolio course and other courses include a two-year diploma in figurative sculpture, a two-year diploma in portraiture, art A level (one-year intensive course), printmaking, watercolour/pastel, general drawing and painting, life drawing, oil painting and figurative sculpture. There are also plenty of Saturday and evening classes.

Slade School of Fine Art (Summer School)

University College
Gower Street, WC1E 6BT London, UK

Tel: +44 (0) 20 7679 7772
www.ucl.ac.uk/slade

The Slade Summer School runs a unique Fine Art Foundation Course, which runs full-time, five days a week for ten weeks. During the first five weeks students are given a thorough grounding in drawing, painting and sculpture. In the second part of the course, students are given space to develop their own work, with advice and guidance from course tutors. The course culminates in a private view of students' work. The basic course fee is £2,600, accommodation is available in halls of residence at extra cost. Other one and two-week courses in Fine Art also available during the ten weeks of the Summer School.

Wimbledon School of Art

Merton Hall Road
London SW19 3QA
UK

Tel: +44 (0) 20 8408 5000
Fax: 020 8408 5050
www.wimbledon.ac.uk

Cookery

You probably spend more than 500 hours a year eating, but can you cook? There are really two types of cookery courses for gappers: basic skills and how to earn money.

The basic skills courses are for those who want to be able to feed themselves more than baked beans or packet soup. These courses can take you from boiling water through to quite a reasonable level - you may not be able to cook for a dinner party of 12, but you should leave being able to cook a variety of tasty meals without poisoning anyone. Cheap and cheerful cookery courses (standard, ethnic, exotic) can be found at day or evening classes at local colleges of further education. Usually the fees are low but you have to pay for ingredients.

The second type of course is aimed at teaching you the skills needed to work as a cook during your gap year. Working as a cook in ski resorts, on yachts in the Caribbean or in villas in Tuscany or the South of France not only allows you to see the world, but pays you while you see it.

"The majority of those who want to work after doing our Essential Cookery course do find cooking work," says Hilary McFarland from Cookery at the Grange. "What's involved in being a chalet cook depends on what a ski company or employer wants. Usually the day starts with cooked breakfast for

265

the ski party, then possibly a packed lunch, tea and cake when hungry skiers get back, possibly canapés later, and a three- or four-course supper. The food does need more than the usual amount of carbohydrate."

That doesn't mean dropping a large pile of pasta on a plate - ski companies expect high standards and may ask for sample menus when you apply for chalet cooking jobs. Sometimes the menus are decided in advance and the shopping done locally by someone else; sometimes the cook has to do the shopping.

Perhaps surprisingly, ski companies and agencies rarely ask about language skills - the cooks seem to manage without. *(see Chapter 1: Working Abroad)* for ideas on making use of your new skills.

Cookery

Belle Isle School of Cookery
Lisbellaw
County Fermanagh BT94 5HG, UK

Tel: 028 66387231
Fax: 028 66387261

Essential Cooking is an intensive four week course designed for people who are interested in learning the key skills for a gap year job in cooking, for instance, as chalet cooks. It offers the students a chance to create their own style and enhance their repertoire, as well as gaining confidence. The course costs £2,000 and includes accommodation. Successful students receiving the diploma, which is accredited by a local college, will be introduced to companies that are looking to recruit.

Aldeburgh Cookery School
84 High Street, Aldeburgh,
Suffolk IP15 5AB, UK

Tel: +44 (0) 1728 454 039

Courses range from one to five days and cover a range of themes, from shellfish and pacific cuisine to exotic spices.

Annette Gibbons Cookery
Ostle House, Mawbray, Maryport,
Cumbria CA15 6QS, UK

Tel: +44 (0) 1900 881 356

Annette Gibbons offers a one-day How to Cope at University cookery course. In the morning she demonstrates how to cook a nutritious lunch, then you sit down to eat it, afterwards you learn how to shop and eat wisely and cheaply.

CookAbilty
Tricia Samways & Venetia Cameron-Rose
Furze House, Nicholashayne,
Somerset TA21 9QY, UK

Tel: 01823 461374
Fax: 01884 840304

CookAbilty caters (excuse the pun) for all types of gap year students, from those who just want to know how to prepare more than beans on toast to budding gourmets who might be looking for a career in the culinary arts. Courses run from 10 o'clock on Monday morning until after lunch on the Friday. The £325 course fee includes accommodation, tuition, all ingredients and meals.

Cookery at The Grange

The Grange, Whatley, Frome,
Somerset BA11 3JU, UK

Tel: +44 (0) 1373 836 579
www.cookeryatthegrange.co.uk

Cookery at the Grange in Somerset offers immensely popular four week residential cookery courses. Working in kitchens around a Somerset farmhouse courtyard, local and home grown organic ingredients are used wherever possible. A sense of fun and plenty of hands on work ensures a good understanding of food and cooking by the end of the month. The course leads on to cooking for family and friends or to working professionally - in chalets, on boats or outside catering - ideal for generating a little cash.

The intensive Essential Cookery Course costs £2,520 to £2,940 (depending on the time of year), including accommodation in twin-bedded rooms and particularly suits gap year students.

Cookery School at Little Portland Street

15B Little Portland Street,
London W1W 8BW, UK

Tel: +44 (0) 20 7631 4590

Cookery School at Little Portland Street aims to turn out confident, inspired cooks rather than restaurant chefs. Courses specially tailored for university and pre-university students run during the summer holidays.

Cutting Edge Food & Wine School

Hackwood Farm, Robertsbridge, East Sussex TN32 5ER, UK   Tel: +44 (0) 1580 881 281/+44 (0) 7900 583 150

Based in a 16th century farmhouse at Robertsbridge vineyard, Cutting Edge offers a range of cookery courses in modern kitchens. The foundation course provides a practical introduction to subjects like 'healthy eating on a budget', 'hygiene' and 'cooking for friends'. The chalet cooking course gives you tips on cooking for groups, shopping, storage and quantities, and helps you develop a wide repertoire of recipes. You will be taught in small groups (maximum 10) by Tom Kime, who has an excellent reputation and who cooked for Jamie Oliver's wedding! Courses last a week (Mon-Fri) and cost £349 including accommodation, meals and all equipment. The chalet course can be extended to two weeks, costing £649.

Edinburgh School of Food and Wine

The Coach House
Newliston
Edinburgh EH29 9EB, Scotland

Tel: +44 (0) 131 333 5001
Fax: +44 (0) 131 335 3796
www.esfw.com

Courses of interest to gappers are the four week Intensive Certificate Course which is geared towards chalet work, and the 1 week Survival Course which is ideally suited to those leaving home for the first time. Course fees vary in price - £95 for a one day cookery class, £395 for the Survival Course and £2000 for the 4 week Intensive Course.

The School works closely with both large and small companies within the travel and tourism market and can offer a personal introduction to agents and ski companies based in Scotland, England and Europe.

269

Kilbury Manor Cookery Course
Colston Road, Buckfastleigh,
Devon TQ11 0LN, UK   Tel: +44 (0) 1364 644079

Kilbury Manor offers personally designed and intensive short courses, for a maximum of four people. The courses are designed to suit individual needs, including chalet and crew cooks, and cater for all ranges of ability: professional as well as amateur cooks are welcomed. Courses cost £325 (one-on-one) for a 2-day course with 12 hours tuition per day; £225 per person for 2 people and £200 per person for 3 people. The cost of the course is fully inclusive of accommodation, food, notes and recipes. Contact the school for their full range of courses and prices.

Le Cordon Bleu
114 Marylebone Lane   Tel: +44 (0) 800 980 3503
London W1U 2HH, UK   www.cordonbleu.edu

Le Cordon Bleu has courses ranging from their famous diplomas in 'Cuisine and Pâtisserie', to the shorter Gourmet Sessions featuring regional French cuisine, fusion, pâtisserie à la carte and bread baking. They also run an intensive version of their standard ten-week professional programme, allowing students to study on a fast track system. The four-week Essentials Course, geared specifically to gappers, is full time and includes a trip to Paris. The price is £1940 and includes the minimum uniform required. Contact the institute for brochures covering all their courses.

Leiths School of Food & Wine
21 St Alban's Grove   Tel: +44 (0) 20 7229 0177
London W8 5BP   Fax: +44 (0) 20 7937 5257
UK   www.leiths.com

Leiths runs a four-week Foundation Course (£2060) starting in mid-July, five days a week. The most popular gap year courses, useful for chalet-people-to-be, are the three-month Beginner's Certificate in Food and Wine (£4600, September to December) and the Basic Certificate in Practical Cookery (£2055, four weeks, full-time from August.

Murray School of Cookery
Glenbervie House   Tel: +44 (0) 1420 23049
Holt Pound, Farnham, Surrey GU10 4LE, UK   Fax: +44 (0) 1420 23049

The Murray School of Cookery offers two courses for gappers: the Cookery Certificate Course and the Chalet Chef Course. The intensive 4-week Cookery Certificate Course covers the skills required for anyone wanting to work on luxury yachts, at premier ski chalets or at small restaurants and hotels. The course costs £1500, which does not cover accommodation.

The one-week Chalet Chef Course, designed in conjunction with major ski operators, teaches students to prepare recipes ideal for catered ski chalets, as well as menu planning, accounting, hygiene and other knowledge needed to be a successful chalet host. The non-residential course costs £395 per person including all ingredients and equipment. Successful students also have access to the Murray School of Cookery database of ski companies and job vacancies.

271

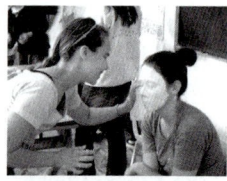  

Natives

39-43 Putney High Street
SW15 1SP London, UK

Tel: +44 (0)8700 463377
Fax: +44 (0) 8451 275 048

Natives run a 5-day chalet cookery course for those planning to work as a chalet host at a ski resort. Taught by experienced season workers who know what the job involves, the course gives you the opportunity to experience cooking for large numbers before you start your season. Held at St Teresa's School for Girls in Surrey on four dates in July, August and October, the course costs £379, which includes all tuition, materials and full-board accommodation.

Tante Marie

Woodham House
Carlton Road
Woking, Surrey GU21 4HF, UK

Tel: +44 (0) 1483 726957
Fax: +44 (0) 1483 724173
www.tantemarie.co.uk

Tante Marie School of Cookery offers a variety of courses suitable for gappers. The 11-week certificate course (£4500) provides an internationally recognised qualification and is particularly suitable for students who wish to work the ski and yacht season. The 4-week Essential Skills Course (£1,950) offers a good grounding in cookery.

Drama

So, you want to be an actor... Your parents may be quaking in the background, telling you it's insecure and you'll never know where your next pay packet's coming from. One way to find out if you really can make it in acting (or if you're more suited to being a barrister or a bricklayer) is to try a drama course in your gap year.

Drama

Metropolitan Film School

125 Bolingbroke Grove
SW11 1DA London, UK

Tel: +44 (0) 845 658 4400
Fax: +44 (0) 20 7228 1098

Practical courses for aspiring filmmakers. All students leave with a calling card - their own script or movie! We can offer distribution through our partners, Picturehouse cinemas.

Emerson College

Forest Row, East Sussex RH18 5JX, UK

Tel: +44 (0) 1342 822238

Emerson College

Orientation Gap Year Programme

Emerson College is an international centre for adult education and research based on the work of Rudolf Steiner (after whom Steiner schools are named), set in beautiful grounds in the Ashdown Forest area of rural Sussex.

The Orientation Gap Year gives young people a chance to place themselves in cultural history, look at the dynamics of working as an individual and part of a group and evaluate their own capacities and ideals. From study, artistic work and volunteer work, students are given the opportunity to see how their own inner world meets the outer world and what challenges and opportunities this presents. All this within the context of community life at the college.

THE OXFORD SCHOOL OF DRAMA

Six Month Foundation Course

Open to students aged 17+

Spend September to March in the lively, creative environment of one of the UK's leading drama schools.

The course includes:
Acting
Movement
Voice
Improvisation
Musical Theatre
Film & TV
Stage Fighting

To find out more contact:
The Oxford School of Drama
Sansomes Farm Studios
Woodstock
Oxon OX20 1ER
Tel: **(01993) 812883**
Email: **info@oxforddrama.ac.uk**
Website: **www.oxforddrama.ac.uk**

Three Year and One Year Courses accredited by the National Council for Drama Training.

Oxford School of Drama

Sansomes Farm Studios
Woodstock
Oxford, Oxfordshire OX20 1ER, UK

Tel: +44 (0) 1993 812883
Fax: +44 (0) 1993 811220
www.oxforddrama.ac.uk

The Oxford School of Drama six-month (September to March) Foundation Course for students (age 17+) includes acting technique, movement and voice. Entry is by audition, so if you enjoy performing but haven't taken exams in Drama or English you can still apply. Foundation Course graduates have gone on to train at leading drama schools including the Royal Academy of Dramatic Art, The London Academy of Music and Dramatic Art, the Guildford School of Acting, further courses at the Oxford School of Drama and to study at Oxford, Cambridge and other leading universities. Entry is by audition.

RADA (Royal Academy of Dramatic Art)

62-64 Gower Street
WC1E 6ED London, UK

Tel: +44 (0) 20 7636 7076
Fax: +44 (0) 20 7323 3865

This legendary drama college runs summer school courses. No audition is needed for the RADA Summer School (July-Aug) with its four weeks of intensive 'Shakespeare-based' workshops. There's also a two-week practical theatre set design course (£630) in July where you will design the scenery and costumes for a Shakespeare play. RADA Technical courses run open days throughout the academic year where you are welcome to see work in progress and meet staff and students.

Stratford-upon-Avon College

CV37 9QR Stratford-upon-Avon, UK

Tel: +44 (0) 1789 266 245
Fax: +44 (0)1789 267 524

Stratford-upon-Avon College runs a Year Out Drama gap year course, providing an exciting and challenging opportunity with a Theatre company. During the intensive course you will encouraged to develop extra curricular work, for example in directing, writing and performing. Fees are available on application.

Driving

There are two reasons to learn to drive: first, unless you're intending to live in an inner city indefinitely, you'll need a driver's licence to get a job; secondly, it will give you independence and you won't have to rely on everyone else (especially your parents) to give you lifts everywhere. Even though you might not be able to afford the insurance right now, let alone an actual car, your gap year is an ideal time to take driving lessons.

The test comes in two parts, theory and practical: and you need to pass the theory test before you apply for the practical one. However, you can start learning practical driving before you take the theory part, but to do that you need a provisional driving licence. You need to complete driving licence application form D1 and photocard application form D750 (available from most post offices). Send the forms, the fee of £29 and original documentation confirming your identity such as your passport or birth certificate (make sure you keep a photocopy) and a passport sized colour photograph to the DVLA. You also need to check that you are insured for damge to yourself, other cars or other people, and if you are practising in the family car, your parents will have to add cover for you on their insurance.

Theory test

The theory test is a 40-minute touch-screen test where you have to get 30 out of 35 multiple-choice questions right. You don't have to answer the questions in turn and the computer shows how much time you have left. You can have 15 minutes practice before you start the test properly. If you have special needs you can get extra time for the test - ask for this when you book it.

Since November 2002, the theory test has also included a hazard test, in which you are shown a number of video clips filmed from a car, each containing one or more developing hazards. You have to indicate as soon as you see a hazard developing which may result in the driver taking some action, such as changing speed or direction. The sooner a response is made the higher the score.

Test results and feedback information are given within half-an-hour of finishing. The test fee is £15.50. Your driving school, instructor or local test centre should have an application form, although you can book your test over the phone (0870 240 0009) or online at DSA Online booking.

275

Practical test

You have two years to pass the practical test once you have passed the theory part. The practical test will cost £39, unless you choose to have it in the evening or on Saturday in which case the cost will increase to £48. You can book the practical test in the same way as the theory test. The bad news is that the tests are tough and it's quite common to fail twice or more before a pass. The practical test requires candidates to drive on faster roads than before - you'll need to negotiate a dual carriageway as well as a suburban road. You'll fail if you commit more than 15 driving faults. Once you pass your practical test, you can exchange your provisional licence for a full licence for £12.

Instructors

Of course some unqualified instructors (including parents) are experienced and competent, as are many small driving schools - but some checking out is a good idea if a driving school is not a well-known name. You can make sure

Driving

that it is registered with the Driving Standards Agency and the instructor is qualified. AA and BSM charges can be used as a benchmark if you're trying other schools.

AA (Automobile Association)   Tel: +44 (0) 8706000371
UK   www.theaa.co.uk

Routes you to an AA centre near you. The website has lots of useful information on driving in the UK and abroad, including stuff about breakdown, insurance and travel planning. You can find hotels, good places to stop whilst driving and you're even able to find out about up-to-date traffic news.

Driving Standards Agency   Tel: +44 (0) 870 010 1372
UK   www.driving-tests.co.uk

Information on theory and practical driving tests, fees and other relevant information. Also has a driving test booking service.

DVLA (Driver and Vehicle Licencing Agency)
Longview Road   Tel: +44 (0) 870 240 0009
Morriston   Fax: 01792 783071
GA6 7JL Swansea, UK   www.dvla.gov.uk

RAC (Royal Automobile Club)   Tel: +44 (0) 800 55 00 55
UK   www.rac.co.uk

The RAC website has lots of useful information on driving in the UK and abroad, with breakdown, insurance and other services.

Languages

Even if the job you are applying for doesn't require them, employers are often impressed by language skills. With the growth of the internet, most companies like to think of themselves as having international potential at the very least. If you didn't enjoy language classes at school, that shouldn't necessarily put you off. College courses and evening classes are totally different - or at least they should be. If in doubt ask to speak to the tutor or to someone who has already been on the course before you sign up.

And even if you don't aspire to learn enough to be able to use your linguistic skills in a job, you could still take conversation classes so you can speak a bit of the language when you go abroad on your holidays. It is amazing what a sense of achievement and self confidence you can get when you manage to communicate the simplest things to a local in their own language: simply ordering a meal or buying stamps for your postcards home.

The best way to improve your language skills is to practice speaking, preferably to a native speaker in their country. But if you don't have the time or the money to go abroad yet, don't worry. There are plenty of places in the UK to learn a wide variety of languages, from Spanish to Somali. We've listed some language institutions below, but also find out what language courses your local college offers, and what evening classes there are locally.

Languages

Alliance Française
1 Dorset Square
London NW1 6PU, UK

Tel: +44 (0) 20 7723 6439
www.alliancefrancaise.org.uk

Alliance Française is a non-profit-making organisation funded by a trust with a network of Alliances in 138 countries. Teaching centres are spread throughout the country, from Jersey to Glasgow, and courses range from intensive to evening classes. For example, a two-week intensive course in London costs £220 and gets you 15 hours' tuition per week (Mon-Fri, 10am-1pm). See also Learning Abroad: Languages: French.

Canning House
2 Belgrave Square
London SW1X 8PJ, UK

Tel: +44 (0) 20 7235 2303
www.canninghouse.com

The Canning House Education and Cultural Department provides information about Latin America, Portugal and Spain. Among various information leaflets (all £4) it publishes a list of universities and language centres offering language courses, with prices and dates. You can use the centre's library, which houses over 60,000 books for research. Library membership costs £20. Membership of Canning House (£40 a year, £30 for students) gets you involved in all sorts of London-based Hispanic/Latin events, such as film, poetry readings and talks.

Goethe Institut

Languages Department, 50 Princes Gate, Exhibition Road, London SW7 2PH, UK

Tel: +44 (0) 20 7596 4004
www.goethe.de/ins/gb/lon

The Goethe Institut is probably the best-known international German language schools network, with 125 centres in 76 countries. It is a non-profit organisation funded by the German government offering a wide variety of courses as well as having a lending library and multimedia centre.

Courses in London cater for all levels and include two-and-a-half-week intensive courses. Typical prices are £345 for the intensive German course (Mon-Fri 9am-1pm), or £245 for the General German Language course (52 lessons: three a week spread over one semester of 17 weeks).

Institut Français

17 Queensberry Place
London SW7 2DT, UK

Tel: +44 (0) 20 7581 2701
www.ambafrance.org.uk/institut

About 6000 students pass through the Institut Français each year - it's the official French government centre of language and culture in London. The institute's courses are mainly in the evening and at weekends, but there is also a two-week intensive French course.

Courses are held at all levels and most cost around £230, with a £30 discount if you book early. As well as conversation and grammar classes, there is a mind-boggling range of cultural courses, including news and current affairs, philosophy, history and politics, and French cartoons!

Instituto Cervantes

326/330 Deansgate, Campfield Avenue Arcade, Manchester M3 4FN, UK

Tel: +44 (0) 161 661 4200
www.cervantes.org.uk

Instituto Cervantes is a Spanish government- funded 'ambassador' for Spanish culture in the UK. Its database provides information about language course locations. The Instituto runs its own Spanish courses throughout the academic year in Leeds and Manchester.

As well as learning the Spanish language, Instituto Cervantes can really immerse you in Spanish culture - there are dance courses (flamenco, tango, salsa), guitar courses and regular 'Spanish evenings' with talks and music. The 10-week flamenco course (2 hours per week) in Manchester costs £95; the 10-week guitar course costs £120. There's also an on-line language course which lasts 3 months (based on you putting in about 3 hours a week). Membership of Instituto Cervantes libraries costs £15 and gets you access to Spanish magazines, videos, CDs and DVDs.

Russian Language Centre

11 Coldbath Square
London EC1R 5HL, UK

Tel: +44 (0) 20 7689 5400
www.russiancentre.co.uk

The Russian Language Centre in London offers a flexible approach to learning Russian, with a range of courses available: standard, accelerated and private. The classes run in the evenings and a term's standard course (one evening a week) costs £287.50.

SOAS (School of Oriental and African Studies)
SOAS Language Centre, University of London,
Thornhaugh Street, Russell Square,   Tel: +44 (0) 20 7898 4888
London WC1H 0XG, UK   www.soas.ac.uk

The SOAS (part of the University of London) runs courses for all levels in Arabic language, culture and civilization. Courses range from year-long full-time to Saturday and evening classes. SOAS students have free access to a huge library and resources room.

SOAS also offers a wide range of other languages including from Africa: Afrikaans, Amharic, Hausa, Shona, Somali, Swahili, Twi, Yoruba and Zulu; Near and Middle East: Arabic, Hebrew, Kurdish, Persian, Turkish; Asia: Bengali, Burmese, Chinese, Gujarati, Hindi, Indonesian, Japanese, Korean, Malay, Nepali, Punjabi, Sanskrit, Tamil, Thai, Urdu, Vietnamese. On one of its other courses you could try your hand at exquisite Chinese calligraphy.

Online learning

Companies offering language courses have cottoned on to the fact that many of us are welded semi-permanently to our computers.

You can now get very comprehensive language courses on CD-ROM which include booklets or pages that can be printed off. The better ones use voice recognition as well, so you can practise your pronunciation. These can also be found in book stores.

The internet itself is also a good source of language material. There are many courses, some with free access, some that need a very healthy credit card. If all you want is a basic start, then take a look at **www.bbc.co.uk/education/languages/** which offers you the choice of beginner's French, German and Spanish complete with vocab lists to download, all for free.

As well as courses, there are translation services, vocab lists and topical forums - just do a web search and see how many sites come up. Lots of them are free.

Practice makes perfect

When you need to practise, find out if there are any native speakers living in your town - you could arrange your own language and cultural evenings. Terrestrial TV stations run some language learning programmes, usually late at night. If you have satellite or cable TV you can also watch foreign shows - though this can be a bit frustrating if you're a beginner.

It's best to video the programmes so you can replay any bits that you didn't understand the first time round. Once you're getting a bit more advanced then you can try tuning your radio in to foreign speech-based shows.

Champs-Elysées   Tel 0800-833 257

If you already have a fair grasp of a language, the best way to prevent rustiness is to continue hearing or speaking it. Champs-Elysées produces monthly or bimonthly tapes (in French, German, Spanish and Italian) that

7

Learning in the UK | Online

279

sound like authentic radio shows from the relevant countries. This is a ood way to keep up to date with current affairs in your chosen country, as well as keeping up your listening and understanding skills. Subjects are wide-ranging, and there's something to interest everyone.

The tapes have been well-received by teachers and reviewers, but are a bit expensive for the average gap year student. It costs extra for the glossy booklet containing a transcript of the programme and help with vocabulary.

Music

Perhaps you always wanted to learn the saxophone, but never quite got 'round to it? Now would be an ideal time to start. If you're interested, your best bet is to find a good private tutor. Word of mouth is the best recommendation, but some teachers advertise in local papers, and you could also try an online search engine like Musicians' Friend (www.musiciansfriend.co.uk).

If you already play an instrument, you could broaden your experience by going on a residential course or summer school. These are available for many different ability levels, although they tend to be quite pricey. There are a number of websites dedicated to music that will list courses (try www.excel-ability.com/Music/). Here are a few of the courses we've heard about.

Music

Instituto Cervantes
326/330 DeansgateCampfield Avenue Arcade,   Tel: +44 (0) 161 661 4200
Manchester M3 4FN, UK   www.cervantes.org.uk

Instituto Cervantes is a Spanish government-funded 'ambassador' for Spanish culture in the UK. Its database provides information about Spanish, guitar, flamenco, salsa and tango courses. Membership of Instituto Cervantes libraries costs £15 and gets you access to Spanish magazines, videos, CDs and DVDs. See Learning UK: Languages for info about Spanish courses.

Lake District Senior Summer School
Stricklandgate House   Tel: +44 (0) 1539 724441
92 Stricklandgate   Fax: +44 (0) 1539 741882
Kendal, Cumbria LA9 4PU, UK   www.ldsm.org.uk

The Lake District Senior Summer School is an ensemble-based course for string players and pianists intending to pursue careers as professional musicians. Coaching is given by top instrumentalists and ensembles. The two-week course runs in early August, costing around £500, which includes tickets to events at the Lake District Summer Music Festival.

London Music School
131 Wapping High Street   Tel: +44 (0) 20 7265-0284
E1W 3NG London, UK   www.londonmusicschool.com

The London Music School offers a Diploma in Music Technology, open to anyone with musical ability aged 17 or over. The six-month course starts in April and costs £2820 plus a £125 registration fee, but if you're strapped for cash they might give you a discount. The course explores professional recording and you get to use a 24-track studio.

North London Piano School

78 Warwick Avenue	Tel: +44 (0) 208 958 5206
Edgeware, Middlesex HA8 8UJ, UK	www.learnmusic.com/nlps

The North London Piano School offers a residential Summer Course at Queenswood, Potters Bar in August, costing from £500 including meals and accommodation.

Oxford Flute Summer School

9 Pinehurst	Tel: +44 (0) 1403 259 463
Horsham	Fax: +44 (0) 1403240610
West Sussex RH12 2DL, UK	www.impulse-music.co.uk/oxford-flutes.htm

The Oxford Flute Summer School runs from mid-August, costing from £430. Tuition is available at different levels to suit your standard.

Photography

There are lots of photography courses available, from landscape photography to studio work. Don't kid yourself that a photography course is going to get you a job and earn you pots of money, but there's nothing to stop you enjoying photography as a hobby or sideline.

photography

Experience Seminars
Unit 6 Hill Farm, Wennington, Huntingdon,
Cambridgeshire PE28 2LU, UK

Tel: +44 (0)1487 772804
Fax: +44 (0)1487 772809

Experience Seminars hosts a range of workshops throughout the UK, which are designed to provide a fast track way of learning photography and digital imaging techniques.

Royal Photographic Society
The Octagon
Milson Street, BA1 1DN Bath, UK

Tel: +44 (0) 1225 462 841
www.rps.org

The Royal Photographic Society holds photography courses, from landscape photography to studio work, throughout the year. The price for a weekend course ranges from £79 for the basic beginners' course to £130 for the more advanced.

Sport

After all that studying maybe all you want to do is get out there and do something. If you're the energetic type and hate the thought of spending your gap year stuck behind a desk, why not get active and do some sport?

There are sports courses for all types at all levels, from scuba diving for beginners to advanced ski instructor qualification courses. Of course if you manage to get an instructor's qualification you may be able to use it to get a job (see Working Abroad)

If you hated sport at school, try giving it another chance during your gap year - you may be surprised how much you like it.

X-rated
If you want a real adrenalin rush, go for one of the extreme sports like, street luge or skyboarding. Skyboarding is basically a combination of skydiving and snowboarding - you throw yourself out of a plane wearing a parachute and perform acrobatic stunts on a board. Or you could try Street Luge - where you hurtle down a street on nothing but a narrow aluminium rail, with no brakes!

Or if you like company when you're battling against the elements, then you could get involved in adventure racing: teams race each other across rugged terrain without using anything with a motor, for example skiing, hiking, sea kayaking. Team members have to stay together throughout the race. Raid Gauloises (five-person teams, two weeks, five stages, half the teams don't finish!) and Eco-Challenge (ten days, 600km, several stages and an environmental project) are the two most well-known adventure race events.

282

The annual X Games feature a wide range of extreme sports and take place during one week in summer (including aggressive in-line skating) and another week in winter (including mountain bike racing on snow). Check out their website http://expn.go.com/ for the full details.

If you want to get wet, then try diving, kayaking, sailing, surfing, water polo, windsurfing, or whitewater rafting.

And if those don't appeal then there's always abseiling, badminton, baseball, basketball, bungee jumping, cavediving, cricket, fencing, football, golf, gymnastics, hang gliding, hockey, horse riding, ice hockey, ice skating, jet skiing, motor racing, mountain biking, mountain boarding, netball, parachuting, polo, rock climbing, rowing, rugby, running, skateboarding, skating, ski jumping, skiing, skydiving, skysurfing, snooker, snow mobiling, snowboarding, squash, stock car racing, tennis or trampolining! If the sport you are interested in isn't listed below then try contacting the relevant national association (eg the LTA for tennis) and asking them for a list of course providers.

Sport

BERSA (British Elastic Rope Sports Association)

33a Canal Street
Oxford
Oxfordshire OX2 6BQ

Tel: +44 (0) 1865 311 179
Fax: +44 (0) 1865 426007
www.bersa.org

Not for people who lie about their weight - if you say you're lighter than you are... splat! Bungee-jumping is still a very scary sport, but regulations set up by BERSA have made it safer, and you need to check that any jump site you consider is certified by BERSA before you take the plunge. The chances are that you will bungee-jump from a crane any height from 150 feet upwards (apparently the biggest crane in England is 325 feet high) and it will cost you around £50. Many sites offer a reduced rate on your second jump. Remember as you leap off that what you are doing is jumping from very high up with a glorified elastic band tied to your feet!

Big Squid Scuba Diving Training and Travel

72 Hubert Grove, Clapham,
London SW9 9PD

Tel: +44 (0) 20 7733 6966

Big Squid offers a variety of dive courses using the PADI and TDI systems of diver education. Beginners can start with Discover Scuba courses (a trial dive in the pool) or go straight on to the Open Water Diver course.

Britannia Sailing Schools

Tel: +44 (0) 1473 787019
www.britanniasailingschool.co.uk

Britannia Sailing is a well-established company on the east coast offering all aspects of sailing instruction and yacht charter. It is approved by the Royal Yachting Association and teaches the full RYA syllabus. Based at Shotley Marina near Ipswich, they are perfectly placed to take full advantage of all that the east coast has to offer the yachtsman - the sheltered and uncrowded waters offer good sailing with many idyllic anchorages.

If you want to travel further afield, the coasts of France, Belgium and The Netherlands are all within a day's sail. They offer first-class facilities; the practical courses take place on spacious and modern yachts and the theory courses are taught in their dedicated classroom within the marina. Instructors are trained to the highest standards and selected for their personality as well as their sailing ability.

British Mountaineering Council

177-179 Burton Road	Tel: +44 (0) 870 010 4878
West Didsbury	Fax: +44 (0) 161 445 4500
M20 2BB Manchester	www.thebmc.co.uk

The British Mountaineering Council is the representative body that exists to protect the freedoms and promote the interests of climbers, hillwalkers and mountaineers, including ski-mountaineers.

British Offshore Sailing School - BOSS

Hamble Point Marinak, School Lane	Tel: +44 (0) 23 8045 7733
Hamble, Hampshire SO31 4NB	Fax: Tel: +44 (0) 23 8045 7733

BOSS offers complete 5-day and weekend RYA shore-based and practical training courses from Hamble Point Marina. If your aim is to get a job in the marine industry, BOSS run a 'Fastrak' course - intensive professional sail-training course which takes you from beginner to Yachtmaster in just 18 weeks.

Bungee Inc

Po Box 647	Tel: +44 (0) 1895 833067
UB9 4LU Uxbridge	Fax: +44 (0) 1895 833067

Bungee Inc is a company of specialist Bungee jumpers and enthusiasts who specialise in mobile bungee and demonstration events throughout the United Kingdom. They operate so that they can share their expertise in bungee with the public and give everyone who wants to try it the opportunity to jump without having to fly to New Zealand! They are happy to train groups or individuals at their sites.

Bungeezone

www.bungeezone.com/orgs

Bungee-jumping associations worldwide.

Commodore Yachting

Commodore House, 63 The Hillway,	
Portchester, Hants PO16 8BP	Tel: +44 (0) 23 9279 3421

Based at Haslar Marina in the Solent, Commodore Yachting offers sailing courses from 'the basic competent crew' to the more experienced 'Yachtmaster Offshore'. Practical course sizes are kept to a maximum of five students on 8-berth yachts, which allows for a good level of individual training.

Devon & West Yacht School

Tel: +44 (0) 1803 883718

RYA approved sail training from Competent Crew to Yachtmaster. Practical courses cost £310 per person; theory courses also available.

Kiteboarding UK

Tel: +44 (0) 1502 512768

Kiteboarding UK offer kiteboarding lessons on their council-approved training area at Kesslingland beach near Lowestoft. Two types of lesson are availiable: Land based (£60) and water based (£90).

Lawn Tennis Association (Coaching Dept.)

The Queen's Club
West Kensington, London W1H 9EG

Tel: +44 (0) 20 7381 7000
www.lta.org.uk

The LTA runs coaching courses with three levels of qualification: Development, Club and Performance, all running for 14 days over five months. Before you start any of these you need to do the two-day Tennis Assistants course (£55). The Development Course takes you to a level where you can get coaching jobs (though some employers will expect you to be a 'Licenced Coach').

After the Development Course the LTA will tell you about employment opportunities, and on the LTA website there's a list of UK tennis clubs you can apply to, or where you can advertise your brilliance as a coach to less brilliant players. ìThe best way to get tennis coaching jobs is to look in the back pages of magazines like Tennis World.î says Emma Ridout, now at Emmanuel College, Cambridge University, ìThat's how I managed to land a five-month coaching contract in Greece.î

London Scuba Diving School

Rabys Barn, New Chapel Road,
Lingfield, Surrey RH7 6LE

Tel: +44 (0) 700 027 2822

Anyone into scuba knows you can book a holiday abroad and take scuba diving lessons when you get there, renting the kit as you learn. (Make sure your instructor is qualified.) But it may be safer to train in the UK first - then you can get the most from your holiday trying out (and improving) your scuba skills.

The London Scuba Diving School walks you underwater on the floors of swimming pools in Battersea and Bayswater. It also arranges one-week diving holidays in the Red Sea where divers can explore the wreck of the merchant ship Dunraven (sunk in 1876). Diving limit 30 metres. Accommodation is in a 13-cabin cruiser where night dives are possible. Prices £600-£700.

Marine Divers (British Sub-Aqua Club School 388) Hong Kong

3E, Block 18, Dynasty View, 11 Ma Wo Road,
Tai Po, New Territories, Hong Kong, China

Tel: +852 2656 9399

Become a BSAC Open Water Instructor. In 6-8 weeks train from beginner to Instructor. Training and fun in Hong Kong (The City of Life), with optional 5-day trip to the Philippines. Various packages. Dive the World once qualified - and get paid! Possible employment opportunities.

285

National Mountaineering Centre

Plas-y-Brenin   Tel: +44 (0) 1690 720 214
Capel Curig, Bettws-y-Coed, Gwynedd LL24 OET, Wales   www.pyb.co.uk

For those hoping to reach dizzy heights, the National Mountaineering Centre offers a vast range of activities and courses. There are 170 courses in Wales, Scotland and the Swiss Alps priced from £99 upwards.

The recommended course for those wanting to gain experience in all outdoor pursuits is the week-long multi-activity course. Priced at £310, it includes indoor climbing, skiing, kayaking, navigation and mountain walking. This price includes accommodation for the week (and there's also a weekend course at £145).

ProAdventure Limited

Registered office 23, Castle Street, Llangollen LL20 8NY, Wales   Tel: +44 (0)1978 861912

Based in Wales, ProAdventure offers different activity courses around the UK, including canoeing, kayaking, rock climbing and mountain biking. Most courses last two or three days at a cost of around £210.

Suffolk Sailing

Unit 75, Claydon Business Park, Gipping Road,   Tel: +44 (0) 1473 833010
Great Blakenham, Ipswich, Suffolk IP6 0NL   Fax: +44 (0) 1473 833020

Although mainly suppliers of sailing safety equipment, Suffolk Sailing does offer a one-day RYA/DOT Basic Sea Survival Course for Small Craft.

The course includes:

- Preparation for sea survival - survival, difficulties and requirements; equipment available; training drills; actions prior to abandonment.
- Practical wet drill - liferaft launching, boarding; survival whilst in water; capsize drill; final abandonment.
- Principles of survival - protection in both hot and cold conditions; location; water rationing and collection; food rationing; survival craft ailments.
- Lifejackets and liferafts - life jacket design, construction,wearing and use; safety harness design and use; liferaft standards, design, launching, equipment; actions taken whilst in liferaft.
- Search and rescue - rescue by helicopter; coastguard, SAR organisation.

Sunsail

The Port House   Tel: +44 (0) 23 9222 2224
Port Solent, Portsmouth, Hampshire PO6 4TH   Fax: +44 (0) 23 9221 9827

Sunsail offers the full range of RYA yacht courses as well as their own teaching programmes; all instructors are RYA qualified. The company has bases in the UK, the Canaries and Thailand.

The Blacup Training Group

Freepost, New Road,   Tel: 01728 727727
Framlingham, Suffolk IP13 9BR   Fax: 01728 724306

This educational group provides training for all things animal. If you want to go into veterinary practice then The Blacup Training Group could very well have something of value to you. From horse management to regular veterinary training, there are a host of different courses on offer.

The Talland School of Equitation

Church Farm
Siddington
Cirencester, Glos GL7 6EZ

Tel: 01285 652318
Fax: 01285 659409
www.talland.net

The Talland School of Equitation is a world-renowned BHS and ABRS approved equestrain centre offering top class training for those wishing to gain professional qualifications. With British Horse Society courses to Fellowship level, gap year students can choose between intensive short courses, which enable you to teach for the remainder of your year out, or longer working courses.

Talland offers the opportunity for complete beginner to advanced rider to train on top-quality horses under highly-qualified instructors (including current international and ex-Olympic riders). You can also watch international horses and riders in training. The British Horse Society qualifications are recognised worldwide and ex-Talland students can be found across the globe.

UKSA (United Kingdom Sailing Academy)

West Cowes, Isle of Wight

Tel: +44 (0) 1983 203014
Fax: +44 (0) 1983 295938

The United Kingdom Sailing Academy (UKSA), based in Cowes, trains watersport instructors, professional skippers and crews for yachts. The Academy has modern facilities, including residential accommodation and a fleet of over 300 craft.

Gappers train with UKSA for six months, in Cowes and Barbados, to become multi-qualified water sport instructors just at the time when major water activity holiday companies are recruiting staff for the summer season (600 companies worldwide recruit directly through the Academy). If you have a yachting background you can complete the Professional Crew and Skipper Training (PCST) course in the first six months, before seeking employment. Qualifications gained last from 2 to 4 years so you can use them to find further employment in the international holiday market in the future.

Wellington Equestrian Education

Heckfield, Hook, Hampshire RG27 OLJ

Wellington Equestrian Education offers training towards BHS exams in exchange for work. Working students spend at least 12 months as part of the Wellington Riding team. Students can work towards the 5 BHS exams throughout their year, becoming qualified as a riding instructor - BHSPI. This course offers a sound grounding for anyone wishing to pursue an equine career as you will have the opportunity to learn all aspects of the industry.

TEFL

Teaching English as a Foreign Language qualifications are always useful for earning money wherever you travel abroad. The important thing to check is that the qualification you will be gaining is recognised by employers. Most courses should also lead on to help with finding employment.

TEFL

Intensive TEFL Courses

ITC, 26 Cockerton Green,
Darlington, County Durham DL3 9EU

Tel: 08456 445464
Fax: +44 (0) 1325 366167
www.tefl.co.uk

ITC are recognised as one of the forerunners of approved intensive weekend TEFL courses in the UK. Established for 12 years, we have trained many students who have since found new careers teaching English in the UK and abroad. Fully qualified and experienced tutors run our weekend courses throughout the UK, enabling our students to attend without the inconvenience of taking time away from their work or study. All of our courses are held in conference venues of major cities throughout the country, which are easily accessible by road or rail. The cost for the weekend course is £210 and provides you with an informative, educational and enlightening experience that will give you an approved 20-hour certificate.

After the weekend you have the option of taking our new distance-learning course, costing £120 which is a direct follow on from the weekend, providing you with a further graded TEFL Certificate. Job opportunities and contacts are available to all our students, but unlike other TEFL providers we do not charge for this facility, but consider it part of the ongoing service that ITC provide. To find out more telephone 08456 44 54 64 for an information pack or visit our web site www.tefl.co.uk

i-to-i

Woodside House
261 Low Lane
Leeds LS18 5NY

Tel: +44 (0) 870 333 2332
Fax: +44 (0) 113 205 4619
www.i-to-i.com

i-to-i, a highly respected gap year organisation, pioneered the weekend and online TEFL courses. The i-to-i TEFL course fully prepares participants to teach English abroad with maximum convenience - both of time and money. Fully qualified TEFL tutors conduct courses all over the UK and Ireland, and, whether you want to travel and teach or simply try something different, the i-to-i TEFL course is open to everyone. Also, with its innovative online course (at www.onlinetefl.com) i-to-i's TEFL training is available anywhere in the world, so you can even earn a certificate whilst travelling. The i-to-i TEFL course is both creative and dynamic, and enables you to plan, prepare and teach your own lessons with confidence. Employment information is also provided. The cost for the live or online course is £195, and will award you a TEFL certificate. i-to-i is an ODLQC-accredited TEFL provider.

Oxford House College
28 Market Place, London W1W 8AW   Tel: +44 (0) 20 7580 9785

Oxford House College provides a CELTA (UCLES examining body) certificate and runs a wide range of courses. The main full-time course running four weeks costs £680 including exam fee.

There's also a part-time course covering the same ground at £750 including the exam fee, which runs for 13 weeks, three evenings a week plus three Saturdays. If you call in at Oxford House they'll show you their 'giant jobs board' where they post notices of TEFL job vacancies worldwide.

Saxoncourt & English Worldwide
124 New Bond Street   Tel: +44 (0) 20 7491 1911
London W15 1DX   Fax: +44 (0) 207 493 3657

Saxoncourt is an EFL recruitment consultancy placing over 600 English instructors with private language schools in up to 20 different countries worldwide each year.

If you don't yet have your TEFL qualification, Saxoncourt also runs full-time four-week courses in London and Oxford, leading to either the Trinity TESOL diploma or the Cambridge CELTA qualification.

Saxoncourt Teacher Training
59 South Molton Street, London W1K 5SN   Tel: +44 (0) 20 7499 8533

This central London school runs ten weeks of one-week Gap Teaching Skills courses a year, preparing about 600-800 gap year students for teaching posts abroad - not just teaching English, but other subjects too.

TTI (Teacher Training International School of English)
148-150 Camden High Street   Tel: +44 (0) 800 174 031
London NW1 ONE   Fax: +44 (0) 800 174 031

TTI runs a TEFL course (three times a week for six weeks: £630) at the end of which you gain its TEFL certificate. The course includes grammar awareness, teaching practice and written assessments. You can make up your mind about the course at a 'taster day', costing £35, once every six weeks.

TEFL Training
Friend's Close   Tel: +44 (0) 1993 891 121
Stonefield, Witney, Oxfordshire OX29 8PH   Fax: +44 (0) 1993 891 686

TEFL Training runs intensive weekend courses all through the year (£210 or £185 with a student card) with an optional follow-through course (£110) which constists of 80 hours of home study. Together they result in a certificate of 100 hours.

290

Chapter 8
Working in the UK

Why work when you can party?

During a time where the world seems to be your oyster working might be the last thing on your mind. Unfortunately, it could well prove necessary or perhaps even desirable. Some industries (especially media, medicine and law) are very competitive and any experience, paid or unpaid, might make all the difference down the line when you have to prove to a potential employer that you really are committed. A gap year is also a great time to get a foot in the door and get recognised; in fact many students go back to the same firms after graduation. If you're not sure what you want to do as a career, then a gap year could be a great time to try out different jobs, to get a feel for what you might want to do in the future.

Going to university is an expensive thing to do. The vast majority of students graduate heavily in debt, which can prove to be a true burden later on in their lives. So earning just a little bit now could really help your bank balance in the future. Or maybe it's just that you need a little extra cash to go travelling with later on in the year. Whatever the reason, start looking earlier, rather than later, to avoid disappointment.

Getting the job

Now this is the tough part. How do you get that first job with no prior experience? What can you possibly offer? The key is creativity. Show the company you're applying to that you can offer them something that nobody else can, and do this by giving them an example. If you're applying to an advertising firm, for instance, then mock up some adverts to show them. Find out about the company and show your knowledge about the industry. Instead of telling them you're willing and keen, show them by being proactive and persevering.

If you are going for a less creative industry, such as medicine or law, then showing that you are more than competent and willing is all that you can really do. Saying this, you have to make sure that you stick out from other applicants, including a photo (that doesn't make you look like a criminal) with your CV is a good start.

Contacts

Over the next few pages we list some companies that specifically employ gap year students or companies that we think are worth contacting. But, take this as a starting point - the tip of the iceberg - there are hundreds of other companies out there waiting to be impressed by you. Research is key. Tailor each application towards that specific company, and never expect to get a job, you have to work at it. The general rule is that nobody will call you back - be the one that gets in contact with them.

293

Job surfing

Some of the major job agencies, and many smaller ones, now have websites. You don't get the personal touch from a website that you do by going into a local branch and getting advice or registering face-to-face, but recruitment websites are really useful if you know what you want to do and you have a 'skills profile' that one of their customers is looking for. Some of them are aimed at graduates and students, others at a general audience, others at specific areas of work (IT, for example). Here are a few to start with:

www.activate.co.uk	www.milkround.co.uk
www.excite.co.uk	www.monster.com
www.fish4jobs.co.uk	www.peoplebank.com
www.ft.com	www.reed.co.uk
www.gradunet.co.uk	www.search.co.uk
www.jobserve.com	www.stepstone.com
www.jobsunlimited.co.uk	www.uk.careers.yahoo.com

If you're interested in working for a particular company, take a look at its website - the bigger firms usually have a recruitment page.

On spec

If contacts, advertisements, agencies or the internet all fail there is always DIY job-hunting. Just walk into shops and restaurants to ask about casual work or use a phone directory (eg Yellow Pages) to phone businesses (art galleries, department stores, zoos...) and ask what is available. Ring up, ask to speak to the personnel manager, and ask if and when they have jobs available and how you should apply. If they ask you to write in, you can do it after the call. If you go in, make sure you look smart.

Opportunities in the big professional firms are not always well-publicised. Temporary jobs (except agency-filled ones) are often filled by personal contact. If you have a burning desire to work for an architects' or lawyers' firm, for example, and you find nothing advertised, you could try phoning through a list to ask if work is available.

Banking: approach your local branches for work experience.

Education: Most educational work experience is tied in with travelling abroad, to places like Africa or Asia, mostly to teach English. However, there are ways of gaining experience back home in England. A very popular way is to see if the school that you have just left would like classroom helpers, or perhaps help teaching a younger sports team. The key with this is to ask around and see what might be available. As well as straight teaching, any experience with children can be very useful, so try looking at camps and sports teams that may need help - there are a few contacts for camps within the Seasonal Work section.

Legal and medical: As everybody knows these two professions are extremely hard to pursue, so any amount of work experience could prove to be very useful. There's plenty of work experience available, but lots of competition for the places so start looking early. Nearly all NHS hospitals look for volunteer staff if you can't find anything worthwhile that you could get paid for, so just contact the HR (Human Resources) Manager at your local hospital.

Media, publishing and advertising: Working on television or the radio is a very competitive career, and it is because of this the media is one of the hardest industries to break into. Work experience is highly recommended. Many companies are very willing to try out gap-year students as trainees, as raw talent is such a limited commodity they want to nurture it a much as possible - plus it's cheap. Many theatres provide work experience for gap year students, so it's definitely worthwhile contacting your nearby production company. This industry recognises creativity and application probably more than any other, so starting out early and fiercely is the only way to do it.

Interviews

So, you've got an interview. How do you going about impressing your potential employers? Confidence and knowledge is probably top of the list for employers, so that that is what you must portray, even if you're a bag of nerves and haven't got a clue. Make sure you are dressed appropriately (cover tattoos, remove nose piercings etc, don't show too much flesh, have clean and brushed hair - all the stuff that your teachers/parents tell you and really annoys you). If you're going for a creative job (advertising, art etc) then you can probably be more casual - when you phone the secretary to confirm your interview time and venue, you can ask whether you'll be expected to dress formally. Stand straight, keep eye contact with the interviewer and smile. Finally, be positive about yourself - don't lie, but focus on your good points rather than your bad ones

Gap year specialists

If you would like to get a work placement from a gap year specialist, a good starting point is The Year Out Group, an association of organisations formed to promote the concept and benefits of well-structured year out programmes and to help people select suitable and worthwhile projects. The Group's member organisations provide a wide range of year out placements in UK and overseas including structured work placements.

Year Out Group members are expected to put potential clients and their parents in contact with those who have recently returned. Year Out Group considers it important that these references are taken up at least by telephone and, where possible, by meeting face to face.

Year Out Group Membership (January 2004): Academic Year in the USA & Europe; Africa & Asia Venture; Africa Conservation Experience; Art History Abroad; BSES Expeditions; BUNAC; CESA Languages Abroad; Changing Worlds; Coral Cay Conservation; Council Exchanges; CSV (Community Service Volunteers); Flying Fish; Frontier Conservation; GAP Activity Projects; Gap Challenge/World Challenge Expeditions; Greenforce; i-to-i International Projects; Madventurer; Outreach International; Project Trust; Quest Overseas; Raleigh International; St James & Lucie Clayton College; Students Partnership Worldwide; Tante Marie; Teaching & Projects Abroad; Travellers Worldwide; Trekforce Expeditions; The International Academy; The Smallpeice Engineering Gap Year; The Year in Industry; VentureCo; Year Out Drama; Wind, Sand & Stars.

The Year Out Group	**Queensfield, 28 King's Road** **Easterton, Wiltshire SN10 4PX** **Tel: 07980 395789** see: www.gap-year.com

Money, money, money

So you got the job, you've put in the hours and you are just waiting for the cash to roll in...

Pay, tax and National Insurance

You can expect to be paid in cash for casual labour, by cheque (weekly or monthly) in a small company and by bank transfer in a large one. Always keep the payslip that goes with your pay, along with your own records of what you earn (including payments for casual labour) during the tax year: from 6 April one year to 5 April the next. You need to ask your employer for a P46 form when you start your first job and a P45 form when you leave (which you take to your next employer).

If you are out of education for a year you are not treated as a normal taxpayer. Personal allowances - that is the amount you can earn before paying tax, are reviewed in the budget each year in April. To find out the current tax-free personal allowance rate call the Inland Revenue helpline or go to **www.inlandrevenue.gov.uk**

Helen joined a Price Waterhouse Cooper gap year and is now studying at Warwick University:

I have always been interested in a career in business and so the PwC Gap Year scheme seemed the perfect answer.

It enabled me to experience working life, earn some money and travel during my gap year, as well as meet other people in the same position as me. I joined one of the PwC London offices for 6 months after completing A-Levels in Maths, History and German. I learnt so much from the placement; and apart from technical skills, I developed confidence, presentation skills, team working and definitely the art of 'small talk'!

These skills have already been invaluable in my university life and as well as in my travels to Thailand, Australia and USA during the last six months of my gap year.

In addition to the benefits I gained in my year out, I returned to PwC during my summer vacation after my first year at university. This placement provided me with further experience of working and really helped me to fine tune my options as a graduate. The programme has definitely opened up doors for me both at university and beyond.

Minimum wages, maximum hours

Since we published our last edition the Government has reviewed the minimum wage rate and introduced a new category.

Workers aged 16-18 now have a minimum wage of £3.50 an hour, 18-21 workers should get £4.10 an hour and 22-plus workers should get £4.85 per hour.

To check on how the National Minimum Wage applies to you, use the TIGER interactive website or phone the National Minimum Wage Helpline on 0845 6000 678. This is also the number to ring if you think you are being underpaid and want to complain. All complaints about underpayment of the National Minimum Wage are treated in the strictest confidence.

There is also a law on working hours which the UK has had to put into force to comply with European Union legislation. This says that (with some exemptions for specific professions) no employee should be expected to work more than 48 hours a week. Good employers do give you time off 'in lieu' if you occasionally have to work more than 48 hours a week. Others take no notice, piling a 60-hour-a-week workload on you. This is against the law and, unless you like working a 12-hour day, they must stop. You are also entitled to four weeks paid leave per year, a day off each week and an in-work rest break if the working day is longer than six hours.

Gap year employers

Over the next few pages we list companies that either have specific gap year employment policies or that we think are worth contacting. We've split them into three groups: arts festivals, seasonal work and general employers. This isn't a comprehensive list, so it's still worth checking the internet and your local companies (in the Yellow Pages, for example).

Arts festivals

Whether musical, literary or dramatic, there are loads of festivals taking place up and down the country every year. You need to apply as early as possible, as there aren't that many placements. Satellite organisations spring up around core festivals, so if you are unsuccessful at first, try to be transferred to another department. The work can be paid or on a voluntary basis. Short-term work, including catering and stewarding, is available mainly during the summer. Recruitment often starts on a local level, so check the local papers and job agencies.

Arts Festivals

Brecon Jazz Festival

Festival Office
The Watton, Brecon, Powys LD3 7EF, Wales

Tel: +44 (0) 1874 611622
Fax: +44 (0) 1874 622583

This sleepy mid-Wales town turns into New Orleans in August every year as jazz bands and singers from all over the world congregate.

Brighton Literary Festival

12A Pavilion Buildings, Castle Square,
Brighton, East Sussex BN1 4EE

A handful of volunteer posts are open during the festival in May, working in the education and press office departments.

Cheltenham Festivals

Cheltenham Town Hall, Imperial Square,
Cheltenham, Gloucestershire GL50 1QA

Tel: +44 (0) 1242 775825

This company runs festivals throughout the year, including jazz, science, music, folk, fringe and literary events. There are usually a number of placements available, although they tend to be unpaid.

Edinburgh International Festival

The Hub
Castlehill, EH1 2NE Edinburgh, Scotland

Tel: +44 (0) 131 473 2099
Fax: +44 (0) 131 473 2002

Big and long-established late summer festival that has managed to stay cutting-edge. Paid employment is available in the centre's press office, front of house, shop and café and banqueting and hub tickets. Applications by post and e-mail.

Facilities Management Catering

Church Road
Wimbledon
London SW19 5AE

Tel: +44 (0) 20 8947 7430
Fax: +44 (0) 20 8944 6362
fmccatering.co.uk

The official caterers to the Wimbledon Tennis Championships, FMC employ keen, hard-working gappers from mid-June to early July. Contact the company for an application pack.

Hay Festival

General Manager Administration
The Drill Hall, 25 Lion Street,
HR3 5AD Hay-on-Wye

Tel: +44 (0) 1497 821217
Fax: +44 (0) 1497 821066

One of the most famous literary festivals in the UK. Most departments take on extra workers for festival fortnight, including stewards, extra staff for the box-office and the bookshop and three interns. Accommodation and food are provided.

Working in the UK | Art festivals

The Gap-Year Guidebook 2005/2006

Seasonal work

A great way to make some quick cash, either to save up for travelling or to spend at home is seasonal work. There are always more jobs going at Christmas in the Post Office sorting office or in local shops. In the summer it can be a lot of fun to fruit pick for example - and also a great way to work on your tan (try www.pickingjobs.com) which links farms world-wide with students looking for holiday work.

Seasonal Work

Acorn Adventure
22 Worcester Road, Stourbridge,
West Midlands DY8 1AN   Tel: +44 (0) 1384 446057

Acorn Adventure runs adventure holiday camps from April until September based in nine centres in France, Italy, Spain and the UK - their main customers are school groups.

Camp Beaumont
The Old Rectory   Tel: +44 (0) 1263 823000
Beeston Regis, Norfolk NR27 9NG   Fax: +44 (0) 1263 823002

Have the Summer of your life working at Camp Beaumont Summer Camps! We need vibrant and energetic people to work as Group Leaders, responsible for the round-the-clock welfare of a group of children.

visit: www.gap-year.com

Facilities Management Catering

Church Road
Wimbledon
London SW19 5AE

Tel: +44 (0) 20 8947 7430
Fax: +44 (0) 20 8944 6362
fmccatering.co.uk

The official caterers to the Wimbledon Tennis Championships, FMC employ keen, hard-working gappers from mid-June to early July. Contact the company for an application pack.

PGL

PGL Recruitment Team, Alton Court,
Penyard Lane, Ross-on-Wye, Herefordshire HR9 5GL

Tel: 0870 401 4411
Fax: 0870 401 4444

PGL runs activity holidays and courses for children. Each year the company employs over 2000 young people to work as instructors, group leaders, catering and support staff at its centres in the UK, France and Spain.

General companies

Abbey National

Check the local press or ask your local branch about short term employment opportunities. Take a look at www.jobsatabbeynational.co.uk for jobs nationally.

Alliance & Leicester

3rd Floor, Building 4, Narborough, Leicester LE9 5XX

A&L can't guarantee work but it will keep your CV on file in case a project comes up that needs extra staff, usually at the Narborough customer services centre.

Arcadia Group plc

For jobs in branches (Burton Menswear, Dorothy Perkins, Evans, Hawkshead, Principles, Racing Green, Topshop/Man), apply directly to your local branch.

Bank of Scotland

Their Vacation Placement scheme is run every year in different divisions of the bank from June to September. To apply, send your CV and a letter by December to one of the following addresses:

Personal Banking: Director of Human Resources, Bank of Scotland, Cherrybank, Perth PH2 0NG

Business Banking: Director of HR, Bank of Scotland, Capital House, Queens Park Road, Chester CH38 7AW

Corporate Banking: Director of HR, Bank of Scotland, The Mound, Edinburgh EH1 1YZ

IT Centre: Director of HR, Bank of Scotland, 2 Bankhead Crossway North, Edinburgh EH11 4EF

BDO Stoy Hayward

8 Baker Street, London W1M 1DA

Tel: +44 (0) 20 7486 5888

A firm of chartered accountants, BDO Stoy Hayward has several gap year vacancies in the London office. Successful applicants will be employed as audit assistants within one of the general business groups. Most placements run for nine

Fun jobs in fundraising !

We're looking for dynamic personalities to join our face-to-face fundraising teams, raising awareness and support for some truly amazing organisations like **Amnesty International, Greenpeace** and **Mencap**. You'll be working away from home, travelling around the UK, meeting some fantastic people *and* earning decent money towards university or travel. We provide the team's accommodation and car, flexible work schedules and full training. We ask for a minimum five week commitment, lots of enthusiasm and heaps of energy.

Do something worthwhile - join us!

Apply at
www.funjobs4u.co.uk
or call our recruitment team on
08454 583 901

DialogueDirect
FUNDRAISING

months from September to May, but shorter placements can also be arranged. Some of the other offices across the UK also take applications for gap year placements. Applicants should contact the office they are interested in directly for more information.

Bierrum International Ltd

Bierrum HouseHigh Street, Houghton Regis,	Tel: +44 (0) 1582 845 745
Nr Dunstable, Bedfordshire LU5 5BJ	Fax: +44 (0) 1582 845 746

A civil engineering firm which takes one gap year student a year through YINI. You can also contact them direct for other short-term work.

Blue Circle Industries
Group Personnel Manager, Blue Circle Industries plc,
84 Eccleston Square, London SW1V 1PX

Possibility of some clerical/WP/DB/DTP work for a few weeks at a time. Send a CV and letter.

Boots
Recruitment of post-GCSE and A level students is done with a view to long-term employment in the company for which full training is given. However, eight-week vacation placements are offered to university students. The best approach is to contact your local store and ask about temporary employment opportunities.

BP Amoco
Recruitment Adviser, BP Amoco PLC,
Britannic House, 1 Finsbury Circus, London EC2M 7BA

Eight-week placements are offered to generalists in their penultimate year and vacation or one-year placements to technologists in their second and third years. For more information contact the above address or, for temporary opportunities, contact your local BP Centre.

Cadbury Schweppes

25 Berkeley Square	Tel: +44 (0) 20 7409 1313
London W1J 6HB	Fax: +44 (0) 20 7830 5200

Cadbury Schweppes places people on work experience in response to specific business needs. Contact the business units direct.

Carlton Communications
Personnel Manager, Carlton Television,
101, St Martin's Lane, London WC2N 4AZ

Holding company for Carlton Television. There are few opportunities and they are inundated with applications, so preference is given to those who specifically want a career in TV. Apply in writing.

Demos

The Mezzanine, Elizabeth House,	
39 York Road, London SE1 7NQ	Tel: +44 (0) 20 7401 5330

Independent research institute, specialising in research into public policy issues. Occasional vacation work available. Send CV and letter.

Working in the UK | General companies

DialogueDirect Ltd

MacMillan House
38 St Aldates
OX1 1BN Oxford, United Kingdom

Tel: +44 (0) 865 297514
Fax: +44 (0) 1865 297529
www.dialoguedirect.co.uk

DialogueDirect is a professional fundraising agency, dedicated to recruiting long-term supporters for charities and the not-for-profit (NPO) sector. It currently represents Greenpeace, Amnesty International, The Children's Society, WaterAid, Mencap, and Plan.

DialogueDirect's street-based, face-to-face fundraising teams travel around the UK, meeting people and raising awareness of leading charities and NPOs. The role of the fundraiser is to inform potential donors about the aims of charitable partners' latest campaigns and encourage them to offer their support through regular monthly donations. Each team has a Team Leader and all 'dialoguers' are trained in the techniques of fundraising, as well as the specific campaigns.

Team transport and accommodation is provided, together with excellent wages, and flexible work schedules. DialogueDirect also provides great opportunities for personal development and good promotional prospects.

EMI Group

4 Tenterden Street, Hanover Square,
London W1A 2AY

Tel: +44 (0) 20 7355 4848

Short term employment is available according to company demand. Contact individual businesses such as EMI Music International (Tel: +44 (0) 20 7467 2000) or EMI Records UK (Tel: +44 (0) 20 7605 5000).

Foreign Office

King Charles St, SW1A 2AH London

As a member of the Diplomatic Service, you could be doing political or economic work in their Embassy in Moscow, helping companies export their products, or you could be doing consular work in Hanoi. See their website for more about careers and opportunities in the Diplomatic Service.

Future Publishing Ltd

Beauford Court, 30 Monmouth Street,
Bath BA1 2BW

Tel: +44 (0) 1225 442244

Future Publishing provides opportunities for gap year students to get a taste of the publishing industry. They publish many magazines including Total Film and PC Format. Placements are only for a short amount of time, but you do gain valuable work experience.

Halifax plc

Trinity Road, Halifax, West Yorkshire HX1 2RG
For temporary vacation work contact regional offices.

HSBC (Midland Bank)

Hong Kong & Shanghai Banking Corporation may have vacancies at regional branches. Check the local press or ask your local branch about short term employment opportunities. Posts generally arise on an ad hoc basis.

IBM UK Ltd

Student Employment Officer, IBM UK Ltd,
Recruitment Department, PO Box 41,
North Harbour, Portsmouth, Hampshire PO5 3AU   Tel: +44 (0) 1705 426 426

IBM aims to take at least 50 gap year students into its UK pre-university employment programme. Most successful candidates have at least two As and a B at A level and many jobs require aptitudes found in those planning to read subjects like computing, engineering and science. The programme opens in September: apply as early as you can in spring 2004 for September 2004 places. Students are asked their preference for locations, and the most strongly technical placements are in Warwick and Hursley, near Winchester. Some students return to IBM in vacations afterwards and on graduation.

IMI plc

PO Box 216, Witton, Birmingham B6 7BA   Tel: +44 (0) 121 356 4848

IMI operates a global graduate development programme and offers vacation work from June to September to penultimate year engineering (mechanical, electrical or manufacturing) students leading to possible sponsorship through the final year at university.

ILA (Independent Living Alternatives)

Trafalgar House   Tel: +44 (0) 20 8906 9265
Grenville Place   Fax: +44 (0) 20 8906 9265
London NW7 3SA   www.I-L-A.fsnet.co.uk

ILA is a charity run by people with direct experience of disability. It provides full-time personal assistants to disabled people who want to live in their own homes, as well as relevant advocacy, counselling and information. ILA needs full-time volunteers with four months to spare to work as personal assistants, providing physical support (helping someone to get out of bed, get dressed, and have a wash) and doing practical things like cooking, shopping and housework. No experience is necessary but personal assistants must be over 18. The work averages four days a week and you get a living allowance (£63.50 a week) for food, travel and leisure, plus free accommodation.

Johnson & Johnson

Manufacturer of hospital products, with a factory in Yorkshire. Worth sending a speculative letter and CV.

Kingswood Study Centres

West Runton   Tel: +44 (0) 1263 579 157
Cromer   Fax: +44 (0) 1263 835192
Norfolk NR27 9NF   www.kingswoodjobs.co.uk

Join Kingswood's Activity Instructor Development Programme and gain training, qualifications and experience within the Tourism Industry, all while having the time of your life! Modern Apprenticeship wage also includes free food and accommodation.

Land Securities
5 Strand, London WC2N 5AF   Tel: +44 (0) 20 7413 9000

Although Land Securities doesn't offer placements to pre-university gappers, graduates who have taken a year out are looked on favourably for recruitment. Enquiries to the Personnel Department.

London Electricity
Templar House, 81-87 High Holborn,
London WC1V 6NV   Tel: +44 (0) 20 7242 9050

Industrial placements are available for undergraduates as part of their course, but only for those budding engineers among you. Apply by post with a CV to the Personnel Division.

Modern Painters
3rd Floor   Tel: +44 (0)20 7407 9246/47
52 Bermondsey Street, London SE1 3UD   Fax: +44 (0)20 7407 9242

Modern Painters magazine has a limited amount of internships in its sales and editorial departments. This could be a very good option if you a particularly artistic. The internships last for three months.

Natives
39-43 Putney High Street   Tel: +44 (0)8700 463377
SW15 1SP London   Fax: +44 (0) 8451 275 048

In summer 2003 opportunities included travel sales, information assistant, sales consultant, chef at a surfing lodge and fitness instructor. Natives features a range of UK based jobs for those seasonnaires looking to return to the UK full time, or for anyone looking for something different.

Nortel Networks
The Resourcing Organisation, Maidenhead Office Park,
Westacott Way, Maidenhead, Berkshire SL6 3QH   Tel: +44 (0) 1628 432000

Operates through the Year in Industry Scheme, but also welcomes speculative applications from gap year students. Send CV and letter.

Norwich Union/HSBC
PO Box 4, Surrey Street,
Norwich, Norfolk NR1 3NG   Tel: +44 (0) 800 092 9561

Contact local branches, or for specific interest areas (eg statistics, human resources, marketing) write to the Resourcing Manager at the above address.

Outdoor Trust
Windy Gyle, Belford, Northumberland NE70 7QE   Tel: +44 (0) 1668 213 289

The Outdoor Trust is a registered charity based in Northumberland that organises outdoor pursuits for schools, individuals, youth groups and management training programmes.

Powergen

Westwood Way, Westwood Business Park,
Coventry, West Midlands CV4 8LG   Tel: +44 (0) 2476 424 723

Powergen offers sandwich placements for undergraduates as well as occasional summer vacancies. For speculative applications contact the personnel department at the above address stating whereabouts in the country you would like to work and they will refer you to the relevant regional manager.

PricewaterhouseCoopers

Southwark Towers   Tel: +44 (0) 808 100 1500
32 London Bridge Street, London SE1 9SY   www.pwc.com/uk/careers

The PwC Gap Year programme is open to high calibre students who are looking for a challenge during their year out. Our seven-month placement provides students with a great opportunity to join one of the world's largest Professional Services organisations, doing real work and making a real contribution. We recruit into many different areas of our firm, so you could find yourself working as part of our clients teams in Assurance & Audit, Tax, Forensic Services or Actuarial Services. Impress us during your placement and your hard work will be rewarded with University Sponsorship worth £1,500 each year and further work experience with us. We are looking for students with 300 UCAS points in any subject (excluding General Studies).

Royal & SunAlliance

Personnel Department, St Mark's Court,
Chart Way, Horsham, West Sussex RH12 1XL   Tel: +44 (0) 1403 232323

Gap year students are taken on according to business needs. Send a CV and letter stating what experience you wish to gain.

Royal Bank of Scotland

PO Box 31, 42 St Andrew's Square,
Edinburgh EH2 2YE, Scotland   Tel: +44 (0) 131 556 8555

Vacation work is available. Contact your local branch for details.

Scottish Courage Brewing

Production Personnel Director, John Courage House,
1 Broadway Park, South Gyle, Edinburgh EH12 9GQ, Scotland

Recruiting is done locally on an ad hoc basis. Write in for work placements specifically in production.

Tesco

There are numerous job opportunities in Tesco stores throughout the UK. Ask in a store near you for more details about the jobs on offer.

The BBC

The BBC advertises heavily about the work experience they offer and it is known to be of the highest standard and therefore very hard to get to do. Work experience is available in many different divisions of the BBC. If you want more than a short work placement then they also offer traineeships in all sorts of areas. The BBC also host many career fairs throughout the year.

307

The National Magazine Company Ltd

National Magazine House   Tel: +44 (0)20 7439 5000
72 Broadwick Street, London W1F 9EP   Fax: +44 (0)20 7439 6886

The National Magazine Company runs many of the UK's leading magazines, including Esquire, Cosmo and Good Housekeeping. There is quite a lot of work experience available and can all be accessed by their website.

The Year Out Group

Queensfield   Tel: +44 (0) 7980 395789
28 King's Road, Easterton, Wiltshire SN10 4PX   www.yearoutgroup.org

The Year Out Group is an association of leading Year Out organisations that was formed in 1998 to promote the concept and benefits of well-structured year out programmes, to promote models of good practice and to help young people and their advisers in selecting suitable and worthwhile projects. In 2001, the then 23 members of the Group accounted for 18,000 structured year out placements. There are now 28 members (listed below) with several applications in the pipeline.

The Group's member organisations provide a wide range of Year Out placements in UK and overseas that cover courses and cultural exchanges, expeditions, volunteering and structured work placements. All members have agreed to adhere to the Group's Code of Practice (published on the website) and are in the process of developing more detailed operational standards for each of the four sectors mentioned above. The Group's website also contains guidelines for students and advisers. These include questions that potential 'gappers' should ask providing organisations as they look for the programme that best suits their needs. Year Out Group monitors information published by its members for accuracy.

Year Out Group members are expected to put potential clients and their parents in contact with those that have recently returned. Year Out Group considers it important that these references are taken up at least by telephone and, where possible, by meeting face to face. From October 2002 Group members have agreed to spell out their complaints procedure in their contracts. Year Out Group can advise on making complaints but is not itself able to deal with complaints. Nor is Year Out Group able to 'police' the 18,000 placements provided by its members but it can take action if any member is shown to be consistently negligent.

There will always be less-than-perfect organisations among members of a trade association and good ones that are not. There are some small specialist organisations with excellent reputations that cannot afford the membership fees. Whether or not an organisation is a member of Year Out Group, the questions in the student guidelines can be used to advantage.

Year Out Group Membership (January 2003): Academic Year in the USA & Europe; Africa & Asia Venture; Africa Conservation Experience; Art History Abroad; BSES Expeditions; BUNAC; CESA Languages Abroad; Coral Cay Conservation; Council Exchanges; CSV (Community Service Volunteers); Flying Fish; Frontier Conservation; GAP Activity Projects; Gap Challenge/World Challenge Expeditions; Greenforce; i to i International Projects; Outreach International; Project Trust; Quest Overseas; Raleigh International; Students Partnership Worldwide; Teaching & Projects Abroad; Travellers; Trekforce Expeditions; The International Academy; The Smallpeice Engineering Gap year; The Year in Industry; Year Out Drama.

Thorn UK
Baird House, Arlington Business Park, Theale, Reading, Berkshire RG7 4SATel: +44 (0) 1734 306030

Possibility of some vacancies, though opportunities are limited. Speculative letters to the Human Resources Department.

Transco
31 Homer Road, Solihull, West Midlands B91 3LT   Tel: +44 (0) 121 626 4431

See Year in Industry listing

Unilever
Unilever has summer placements available for penultimate-year undergraduates. Advice to gap year students is to approach some of the largest subsidiaries: Bird's Eye Walls, Walton-on-Thames, Surrey; Lever UK, Kingston upon Thames, Surrey.

Unipart
Unipart House, Unipart, Cowley, Oxford, Oxfordshire OX4 2PG

Speculative applications for Unipart's Year in Industry project should be sent to DCM Human Resources at the above address.

United Biscuits
Human Resources, Hayes Park, Hayes End Road,
Hayes, Middlesex UB4 8EE   Tel: +44 (0) 20 8234 5000

Although there are no gap year placements, sandwich (degree) students should contact the Graduate Resourcing Department for an updated list of placements.

Virgin Radio
Beccy and Anthony, Work Experience,   Tel: +44 (0) 20 7434 1215
Virgin Radio, 1 Golden Square, London W1F 9DJ   Fax: +44 (0) 20 7434 1197

Virgin Radio offers unpaid work experience for between two and four weeks. These places are hotly sought after and if you have any experience at all it will help a lot. Hospital radio is smiled upon, as is any other type of radio volunteer work.

Whitbread
Whitbread Court, PO Box 777, LU5 5XE Dunstable

Contact restaurants and pubs individually for holiday work.

WPP Group Plc
Programme Co-ordinator, 27 Farm Street, London W1X 6RD   Tel: +44 (0) 20 7408 2204

WPP Group is a leading communications services group. Through its member companies, the group offers clients advertising, media, information and consultancy, public relations and public affairs, promotions, direct marketing and other specialist communications.

WPP runs the WPP Fellowship programme for graduates, to develop high-calibre management and talent with work experience across, and understanding of, a range of marketing disciplines. WPP is looking for gappers who are resourceful, committed to marketing, intellectually curious and will take a rigorous and creative approach to problem solving.

309

Year in Industry

National Office
The University of Southampton
SO17 1BJ Southampton

Tel: +44 (0) 23 8059 7061
Fax: +44 (0) 23 8058 3266
www.yini.org.uk

The Year in Industry is a national organisation, which places bright, motivated gap year students with companies for paid, 12-month, degree relevant work placements. Students are matched with companies on the basis of their chosen degree subject.

Yorkshire Water

PO Box 52, BD3 7YD Bradford

Tel: +44 (0) 1274 692 060

Individual enquiries about work experience should be made to the number above. Most of the 'opportunities' are unpaid, but there can be paid placements, depending on current projects.

Chapter 9
Volunteering UK

At the risk of sounding all 'worthy', if you spend at least some of your gap year doing something for the benefit of others you'll get both a satisfying sense of achievement and an opportunity to learn about other people as well as a lot about yourself.

Don't feel that to do anything really worthwhile you have to go abroad - there are many deserving cases right on your doorstep. You might also find that if you do voluntary work close to home it will make you more involved in your own community.

Although the definition for 'voluntary work' is strictly-speaking work that you're not paid for, voluntary schemes (especially the government-inspired ones) will often pay you some 'pocket money' and may also give you free meals and accommodation. Each scheme varies in what it provides - there are no rules. The point is that these are not 'jobs'; what you will be doing is altruistic: helping someone or a specific cause, usually a charity, whether you're working directly with children with special needs or doing the office filing for a charity.

Volunteering can also be an opportunity to gain relevant work experience. If you know, for example, that you want a career in retail, a stint with Oxfam will teach you a surprising amount. Many charity shops recognise this and offer training. Or perhaps you could find yourself helping develop a charity's website.

Below we list the contact details of a number of charities and organisations that are grateful for volunteers - go to **www.gap-year.com** for a direct link to their websites and e-mails. If you can't find anything that interests you here, then there are a number of organisations which place people with other charities or with a wide national network of their own - an internet search should give you a good list.

The following websites provide useful links and information about volunteering:

www.do-it.org.uk
www.namss.org.uk
www.ncvo-vol.org.uk
www.timebank.org.uk
www.vois.org.uk

Charity CHICK

Janice, 28, from Tyne and Wear, is an Arts graduate, who had spent three years trying to define a career since leaving university, with limited success.

Through the WorldWide Volunteering database she found CHICKs, a Devon based charity, who specialise in providing adventure holidays for children from inner city areas:

I found I was just drifting, unsure of what I really wanted to do, or even what my skills were.

My confidence was suffering as a result.

I decided to look into volunteering as a way of experiencing new things, and increasing my skills and self esteem.

As it was my first placement, I was nervous, but I needn't have worried. The staff really valued the volunteers help and we were instantly made to feel part of the team.

I enjoyed every minute of my week.

It has given me a much improved sense of self confidence and since returning from CHICKS, I've volunteered for two local children's charities and am currently applying for jobs in the charity sector. To anyone thinking of volunteering, give it a go.

You have nothing to lose and so much to gain.

Voluntary organisations

Barnabas Trust
Carroty Wood   Tel: +44 (0) 1732 366 766
Higham Lane   Fax: +44 (0) 1732 366 767
Tonbridge, Kent TN11 9QX   www.barnabas.org.uk

Opportunities are available to assist in the practical running of the Barnabas Trust centres.

Break
Residential Volunteers' Co-ordinator   Tel: +44 (0) 1263 822161
Davison House, 1 Montague Road, Sheringham,   Fax: +44 (0) 1263 822181
Norfolk NR26 8WN   www.break-charity.org

BREAK runs two residential holiday/respite centres in Norfolk, offering children and adults with learning and physical disabilities week-long holiday breaks.

BTCV

Conservation Centre
Balby Rd
DN4 0RH Doncaster

Tel: +44 (0) 1302 57224
Fax: +44 (0) 1302 310167
www.btcv.org

BTCV runs working conservation holidays in England, Wales, Scotland and Northern Ireland, which last from two days to two weeks.

BTCV Scotland

Balallan House
24 Allan Park
FK8 2QG Stirling, Scotland

Tel: +44 (0) 1786 479697
Fax: +44 (0) 1786 465359
www.btcv.org.uk

CONSERVATION, ENVIRONMENT

BTCV Scotland provides all-year-round environmental volunteering opportunities for over 6000 people a year. Depending on the amount of time you have you could go on a conservation working holiday, get involved in running one of their Green Gyms, join a Volunteer Officer programme, assist their renowned 'Action Recycle' projects, help organise and run a National Environmental Skills training programme or become a Biodiversity Action Team member. No skills are required, just an interest in the environment and people. BTCV Scotland provides expenses for all regular volunteers, and accommodation for those working from the Inverness office.

Camphill Communities in the UK

55 Cainscross Road
Stroud, Gloacestershire GL5 4EX

Tel: +44 (0) 1453 753142
Fax: +44 (0) 1453 757469

Camphill is a worldwide network of communities dedicated to work and life with children, adolescents or adults with developmental and other disabilities.

Careforce

35 Elm Road
New Malden
Surrey KT3 3HB

Tel: +44 (0) 20 8942 3331
Fax: +44 (0) 20 8942 3331
www.careforce.co.uk

Each year Careforce recruits Christians aged 18 to 30 and places them at churches and community projects across the UK.

Central Scotland Forest Trust

Hillhouseridge
Shottskirk Road
ML7 4JS Shotts, Scotland

Tel: +44 (0) 1501 822 015
Fax: +44 (0) 1501823919
www.csct.co.uk

COMMUNITY, CONSERVATION, ENVIRONMENT, FARMING

CSCT organises volunteers to help with ecological improvements in Central Scotland. Work includes fence repairing and path building.

Centre for Alternative Technology

Machynlleth, Powys
SY20 9AZ, Wales

Tel: +44 (0) 1654 705 951
Fax: +44 (0) 1654 702782
www.cat.org.uk

COMMUNITY, CONSERVATION, ENVIRONMENT

The Centre for Alternative Technology (CAT) runs one-week 'short term volunteer' programmes throughout the summer, as well as a full-time 'long term volunteer'

(LTV) programme which usually lasts for six months. Anyone can apply to be an LTV but those with specific skills and experience to offer have a head start. At present CAT takes on LTVs in biology, building, engineering, gardening, information, media, publications and site maintenance. There are limited places for LTVs to stay on the CAT site as part of Site Community. All CAT volunteers are entirely self-funding for the duration of their stay: organic, vegetarian staff lunches are provided and travel expenses paid to those living off site.

Children's Country Holidays Fund

Holiday Project Manager	Tel: +44 (0) 20 7928 6522
CCHF	Fax: +44 (0) 20 7401 3961
42-43 Lower Marsh, SE1 7RG London	www.childrensholidays-cchf.org

CHILDREN

The Children's Country Holidays Fund (registered charity number 206958) provides holidays for London children who would otherwise not get one. Volunteers are required to be activity holiday camp supervisors in the summer school holidays. The week-long camps are residential and incorporate a wide range of activities to provide a fun, safe and memorable holiday for 32 children aged 8-12. Supervisors are responsible for the care, welfare and entertainment of four children within a larger group of 32, under an experienced leader and deputy. Training is provided and all travel, board and accommodation costs are met.

Children's Trust

Tadworth Court	Tel: +44 (0) 1737 365000
Tadworth	Fax: +44 (0) 1737 365001
Surrey KT20 5RU	www.thechildrenstrust.org.uk

The Children's Trust run a residential centre for about 80 severely disabled children, and is currently expanding. Volunteers help with the day-to-day needs of the children.

Churchtown Outdoor Adventure Centre

Churchtown	Tel: +44 (0) 1208 872 148
Lanlivery	Fax: +44 (0) 1208 873 377
Bodmin, Cornwall PL30 5BT	www.wft.org.uk

COMMUNITY

The Churchtown Outdoor Adventure Centre is an activity holiday centre for people of all ages, many disabled. Volunteers stay for a minimum of one month, looking after the visitors and helping with activities; you get pocket money and board.

CSV (Community Service Volunteers)

237 Pentonville Road	Tel: +44 (0) 800 374 991
London N1 9NJ	Fax: +44 (0) 20 7837 9318
England	www.csv.org.uk

ALL TYPES

CSV, a registered charity, has matched over 21,000 full-time volunteers to placements over the last decade. Volunteers must be aged 16+ (or 18+ if you are from outside the UK) and able live away from home for between 4 and 12 months. Volunteers receive free accommodation, food and travel plus a weekly allowance of £27. No minimum qualifications or previous experience are needed; just enthusiasm and commitment.

DialogueDirect Ltd

MacMillan House
38 St Aldates
OX1 1BN Oxford, United Kingdom

Tel: +44 (0) 865 297514
Fax: +44 (0) 1865 297529
www.dialoguedirect.co.uk

DialogueDirect is a professional fundraising agency, dedicated to recruiting long-term supporters for charities and the not-for-profit (NPO) sector. It currently represents Greenpeace, Amnesty International, The Children's Society, WaterAid, Mencap, and Plan.

DialogueDirect's street-based, face-to-face fundraising teams travel around the UK, meeting people and raising awareness of leading charities and NPOs. The role of the fundraiser is to inform potential donors about the aims of charitable partners' latest campaigns and encourage them to offer their support through regular monthly donations. Each team has a Team Leader and all 'dialoguers' are trained in the techniques of fundraising, as well as the specific campaigns.

Team transport and accommodation is provided, together with excellent wages, and flexible work schedules. DialogueDirect also provides great opportunities for personal development and good promotional prospects.

Environmental Task Force

Tel: +44 (0) 845 606 2626
www.thesite.org/newdeal

ENVIRONMENT

Part of the Government's New Deal for people aged 18-24, this scheme offers the opportunity to work on an environmental project for six months. While you're on the scheme you are still entitled to the Job Seekers' Allowance, as well as a grant of up to £400 and travel expenses.

Friends of The Earth

26-28 Underwood Street
N1 7JQ London

Tel: +44 (0) 20 7490 1555
Fax: +44 (0) 20 7490 0881
www.foe.co.uk

Friends of The Earth welcomes volunteers at their head office in London, or at any of their regional offices. Work may involve administrative work - from helping with mailouts and press cuttings to research and information gathering. Wherever possible, FOE aim to identify specific roles providing opportunity for the development and acquisition of skills.

HiPACT

PO Box 770
York House
Empire Way, Wembley, Middlesex HA9 0PA

Tel: +44 (0) 208 900 1221
Fax: +44 (0) 208 900 0330
hipact.sentral.co.uk

TEACHING

HiPACT is an association of British Universities which aims to widen participation in higher education. It offers opportunities to volunteer both in the UK and abroad. In the UK you could help at one of the summer schools run each year at various universities throughout the country. The summer schools are attended by students from schools that rarely send their pupils on to higher education. As a current undergraduate or recent graduate, you could help lead workshops on career choice, self-confidence or overcoming difficulties.

317

INDEPENDENT LIVING ALTERNATIVES
LOOKING FOR SOMETHING DIFFERENT?

ILA is looking for volunteer, with four months to spare, to enable disabled people to live independently. No experience is necessary as all training and on-going support is provided; you must be 18+ and have an empathy with the philosophy of ILA. You will work on average 4 days per week and receive £63.50 living expenses and accommodation. A placement with ILA is a chance for you to meet new people and try new things. You will gain a direct insight into disability and work experience which may help you to find employment in the future and you'll have plenty of free time to see London!

Independent Living Alternatives, Trafalgar House, Grenville Place, London, NW7 3SA
tel/fax: 00 44 (0)20 8906 9265
email to: mail@I-L-A.fsnet.co.uk   web: www.I-L-A.fsnet.co.uk

Charity Registration No: 802198

ILA (Independent Living Alternatives)

Trafalgar House	Tel: +44 (0) 20 8906 9265
Grenville Place	Fax: +44 (0) 20 8906 9265
London NW7 3SA	www.ILAnet.co.uk

ILA is a charity run by people with direct experience of disability. It provides full-time personal assistants to disabled people who want to live in their own homes, as well as relevant advocacy, counselling and information. ILA needs full-time volunteers with four months to spare to work as personal assistants, providing physical support (helping someone to get out of bed, get dressed, and have a wash) and doing practical things like cooking, shopping and housework. No experience is necessary but personal assistants must be over 18. The work averages four days a week and you get a living allowance (£63.50 a week) for food, travel and leisure, plus free accommodation.

L'Arche

GY/04	Tel: +44 (0) 800 917 1337
Freepost BD 3209	Fax: +44 (0) 1535 656426
Keighley, West Yorkshire BD20 9BR	www.larche.org.uk

L'Arche (French for 'The Ark') began as a small community in a house in Trosly-Breuil in France more than 30 years ago and is now an international movement with 120 communities in 30 countries. It aims to provide local communities - a cluster of houses, usually within walking distance of each other and with access to a workshop - for adults with learning disabilities. The work could be weaving, for example, or making candles. Volunteer assistants are 'welcome to share life with those who need help to learn' both in communities in the UK and abroad. To

318

volunteer abroad you need to contact communities direct; L'ARCHE can supply you with a list of their communities worldwide.

Millennium Volunteer Connexions Service
The Youth Volunteering Team
Department for Education and Skills,   Tel: +44 (0) 870 000 2288
Room E4C, Moorfoot, S1 4PQ Sheffield   www.mvonline.gov.uk

Launched in 1999 for 16- to 24-year olds the Millennium Volunteer programme is still going strong. The idea is that you volunteer your time to help others, doing something you enjoy.

Monkey Sanctuary
Murrayton   Tel: +44 (0) 1503 262 532
Nr Looe, Cornwall PL13 1NZ   www.monkeysanctuary.org

Monkey Sanctuary provides a home to a colony of Amazonian woolly monkeys and rescued ex-pets. Volunteers help all year round, making monkey food, cleaning enclosures, helping serve the public in the summer and maintenance and other projects in the winter. Volunteers do not work directly with the monkeys.

National Trust for Scotland
Wemyss House   Tel: +44 (0) 131 243 9300
28 Charlotte Square   Fax: +44 (0) 131 243 9301
EH2 4ET Edinburgh, Scotland   www.nts.org.uk

CONSERVATION, ENVIRONMENT

The National Trust for Scotland is a conservation charity that protects and promotes Scotland's natural and cultural heritage for present and future generations to enjoy. Contact them to find out about volunteering opportunities.

New Deal
                                        Tel: 0845 606 2626
                               www.thesite.org.uk/newdeal

As part of its New Deal project, the government runs a Work in the Voluntary Sector scheme which allows you to work for a voluntary organisation whilst still being able to claim Job Seekers' Allowance. There's a similar scheme for working on an environmental project for six months.

NSPCC
42 Curtain Road   Tel: +44 (0) 20 7596 3700
London EC2A 3NH   www.nspcc.org.uk

COMMUNITY, CHILDREN, FUNDRAISING, OFFICE WORK

Volunteers can either do (primarily) fundraising work in their local area (see your local branch for details), or office work at head office in London.

9

Volunteering UK

Outdoor Trust

Windy Gyle
Belford, Northumberland NE70 7QE

Tel: +44 (0) 1668 213 289
www.outdoortrust.co.uk

Based in Northumberland, The Outdoor Trust organises outdoor pursuits for schools, individuals, youth groups and management training programmes.

Oxford Centre for Enablement

Nuffield Orthopaedic Centre NHS Trust
Windmill Road, Headington, Oxford OX3 7LD

Tel: +44 (0) 1865 227600
Fax: +44 (0) 1865 737260

CARING

The Oxford Centre for Enablement cares for both the assessment and management of clients with recent neurological disability as well as those with longer term disability. Volunteers are needed at the centre to help with creative activities, gardening, table games, story groups, computers and cooking as well as outings, and also to help on holidays.

You must be over 19 and fit, healthy and patient. Those who go on the holidays, are away for a week at a time but helpers at the centre will be required on occasional days for an indefinite period. On the holidays, accommodation and travel are paid for by the centre but a small donation towards food costs is appreciated. No accommodation is provided at the centre.

Rainforest Concern

27 Lansdowne Crescent
London W11 2NS

Tel: +44 (0) 20 7229 2093
www.rainforest.org.uk

FUNDRAISING

Rainforest Concern has office work placements in London to help in the fundraising department. Ideally volunteers should be able to work for longer than two months. Rainforest Concern also runs a scheme with Quest Overseas sending volunteers to projects in Ecuador and Costa Rica to help in the construction of rainforest corridors.

Rempart

1 rue des Guillemites
75004, Paris, France

Tel: +33 (0) 1 42 71 96 55
Fax: +33 (0) 1 42 71 73 00
www.rempart.com

CONSERVATION

Rempart organises short voluntary work schemes around the world, including in the UK. The projects are all based around restoration and maintenance of historic sites and buildings, from the glamour of castles in Dumfries to the more practical historic pathways in Wales. You need some previous experience and to be prepared to work hard - usually 30-35 hours per week. Expect to pay about £10 per day to cover food and lodging, depending on where you are placed. Rempart is a French company, so don't expect to be able to book or organise the trip in English.

RSPB (Royal Society for the Protection of Birds)

The Lodge
Sandy
Bedfordshire SG19 2DL

Tel: +44 (0) 1767 680 551
Fax: +44 (0) 1767 683262
www.rspb.org.uk

Operating on 39 reserves around the UK, the RSPB Residential Voluntary Wardening Scheme provides practical experience of the day-to-day management of an RSPB reserve by living and working on the reserve as a volunteer.

SHAD

SHAD Wandsworth
5 Bedford Hill
London SW12 9ET

Tel: +44 (0) 20 8675 6095
Fax: +44 (0) 20 8673 2118
www.shad.org.uk

COMMUNITY, SOCIAL CARE

Volunteers needed in London! Are you aged over 18 years, with 4 months (or more) to spare? Personal Assistants are needed to enable physically disabled adults to live independently in their own homes.

Volunteers get: training; excellent work experience; rent free flat-share, with other volunteers; £60 per week personal allowance; expenses; generous time off.

Shaftesbury Society

Burton Hill School
Malmesbury
Wiltshire SN16 0EG

Tel: +44 (0) 1666 822 685
Fax: +44 (0) 1666 826 022
www.shaftesburysoc.org.uk

COMMUNITY, CARING

The Shaftesbury Society provides care and education services for people with physical and learning disabilities, and support for people who are disadvantaged or on a low income. Contact them direct for volunteering opportunities.

Tent City

Milfields Road
Hackney, London E5 0AR (sae needed)

Tel: +44 (0) 20 8743 5708
www.tentcity.co.uk

OFFICE

Volunteers are needed to work in reception and help to maintain the London Tent City campsite.

The Blackie/Great Georges Community Cultural Project

Great George Street
L1 5EW Liverpool
England

Tel: +44 (0) 151 709 5109
Fax: +44 (0) 151 709 4822
www.theblackie.org.uk

The Blackie, one of Britain's longest-running community cultural projects, invites volunteers for innovative projects - co-operative games, publications, youth arts - home and touring. Accommodation available.

The Simon Community

PO Box 1187
London NW5 4HW
England

Tel: +44 (0) 20 7485 6639
Fax: +44 (0) 20 7482 6305
www.waterloo.com/simon/

COMMUNITY

The Simon Community is a partnership of homeless people and volunteers living and working with London's street homeless. They need full-time residential volunteers all year round. This is a real challenge which offers work experience in many areas, especially if you intend to work professionally with vulnerable people. Volunteers need to be 19+, and to commit for between six months to two years. Pocket money, time off, paid leave and training are provided.

The Year Out Group

Queensfield
28 King's Road, Easterton, Wiltshire SN10 4PX

Tel: +44 (0) 7980 395789
www.yearoutgroup.org

COMMUNITY, CONSERVATION, ENVIRONMENT, TEACHING

The Year Out Group is an association of leading year out organisations that was formed in 1998 to promote the concept and benefits of well-structured year out programmes, to promote models of good practice and to help young people and their advisers in selecting suitable and worthwhile projects. In 2001, the then 23 members of the Group accounted for 18,000 structured year out placements. There are now 28 members (listed below) with several applications in the pipeline.

The Group's member organisations provide a wide range of year out placements in UK and overseas that cover courses and cultural exchanges, expeditions, volunteering and structured work placements. All members have agreed to adhere to the Group's Code of Practice (published on the website) and are in the process of developing more detailed operational standards for each of the four sectors mentioned above. The Group's website also contains guidelines for students and advisers. These include questions that potential 'gappers' should ask providing organisations as they look for the programme that best suits their needs. Year Out Group monitors information published by its members for accuracy.

Year Out Group members are expected to put potential clients and their parents in contact with those that have recently returned. Year Out Group considers it important that these references are taken up at least by telephone and, where possible, by meeting face to face. From October 2002 Group members have agreed to spell out their complaints procedure in their contracts. Year Out Group can advise on making complaints but is not itself able to deal with complaints. Nor is Year Out Group able to 'police' the 18,000 placements provided by its members - but it can take action if any member is shown to be consistently negligent.

There will always be less-than-perfect organisations among members of a trade association and good ones that are not. There are some small specialist organisations with excellent reputations that cannot afford the membership fees. Whether or not an organisation is a member of Year Out Group, the questions in the student guidelines can be used to advantage.

Year Out Group Membership (February 2003): Academic Year in the USA & Europe; Africa & Asia Venture; Africa Conservation Experience; Art History Abroad; BSES Expeditions; BUNAC; CESA Languages Abroad; Coral Cay Conservation; Council Exchanges; CSV (Community Service Volunteers); Flying Fish; Frontier Conservation; GAP Activity Projects; Gap Challenge/World Challenge Expeditions;

Greenforce; i-to-i International Projects; Outreach International; Project Trust; Quest Overseas; Raleigh International; Students Partnership Worldwide; Teaching & Projects Abroad; Travellers Worldwide; Trekforce Expeditions; The International Academy; The Smallpeice Engineering Gap Year; The Year in Industry; Year Out Drama.

Time for God

2 Chester House	Tel: +44 (0) 20 8883 1504
Pages Lane	Fax: +44 (0) 20 8365 2471
Muswell Hill, London N10 1PR	www.timeforgod.org.uk

COMMUNITY, CULTURE, ENVIRONMENT, RELIGIOUS, YOUTH WORK, CARE WORK

Time for God co-ordinates national and international projects, including youth and community work, homeless and rehabilitation projects in the UK, USA, Europe, Australia, Ghana etc. Start dates are January and September. Fees apply.

UNICEF (United Nations Childrens Fund)

| 55 Lincoln's Inn Fields | Tel: +44 (0) 20 7405 5592 |
| WC2A 3NB London | www.unicef.org.uk |

UNICEF campaigns and sets up initiatives to promote better health, education and sanitation for children around the world. It normally has two or three volunteers working in its main office at any one time, and local offices will always need help: apply to them direct.

Volunteer Development England

New Oxford House	Tel: +44 (0) 121 633 4555
16 Waterloo Street	Fax: +44 (0) 121 633 4043
B2 5UG Birmingham	www.vde.org.uk

VDE matches people wanting to volunteer with local and national voluntary or community groups that are looking for help. Contact the address above, your nearest volunteer bureau or take a look at their website. Length of work depends on the individual's interests and commitments, and the requirements of the charities involved. Expenses are paid.

Volunteer Reading Help

| Charity House,14-15 Perseverance Works, | Tel: +44 (0) 870 77 44 300 |
| 38 Kingsland Road, London E2 8DD | www.VRH.org.uk |

VRH is a national charity that helps primary school children who find reading a struggle. Training takes 6 hours and volunteers work with the same children every week, giving at least an hour of their time.

Whizz-Kidz

1 Warwick Row	Tel: +44 (0) 20 7233 6600
London SWIE 5ER	Fax: +44 (0) 20 7233 6611
England	www.whizz-kidz.org.uk

Whizz-Kidz aims to improve the lives of disabled under-18s by providing wheelchairs, trikes, walking aids and so on. Contact them direct to find out about overseas challenge events such as climbing Kilimanjaro or walking the Great Wall of China.

Winged Fellowship Trust
Angel House
20-32 Pentonville Road, London N1 9XD

Tel: +44 (0) 20 7833 2594
www.wft.org.uk

Runs five separate centres around the country, providing holiday and respite opportunities for people with disabilities and their carers. Volunteers are welcomed and needed, and will receive accommodation and board. No experience is necessary. Usual placements are for one or two weeks, but longer placements can be arranged, especially at a new centre offering outdoor pursuits, where specialist training is provided.

Workaway.info
www.workaway.info

ANIMALS, COMMUNITY, CONSERVATION, CULTURE, ENVIRONMENT, FARMING, SAFARI, TEACHING, TRAVEL

Workaway.info holds a database of families, individuals or organizations around the world who are looking for volunteer help in a range of different fields - from painting to planting, building to baby-minding or shopping to shearing. In exchange, volunteers get free food and accommodation and the chance to live in a different culture. Workaway.info introduces working travellers and language learners to like-minded hosts, with no expensive agency fees.

Workaway recommends that travellers arrange an initial trial period (5 days to a week) with the view of extending should both parties wish to (some workers end up staying for up to a year and become life long friends!) This gives both parties an 'opt out clause' in case of unforeseeable circumstances, or if they simply don't get on! Workaway's aim is to promote cultural understanding between different peoples and lands throughout the world and enable people travelling on a limited budget to fully appreciate living and working in a foreign environment.

WorldWide Volunteering for Young People
7 North Street Workshops
Stoke Sub Hamdon
Somerset TA14 6QR

Tel: +44 (0) 1935 825588
Fax: +44 (0) 1935 825775
www.wwv.org.uk

Worldwide Volunteering publishes the UK's most authoritative online and CD-ROM database of volunteering opportunities for 16-25 year olds. The unique software matches volunteers' wishes against the requirements of over 1,000 organisations with over 300,000 annual placements throughout the UK and worldwide.

Young People's Trust for the Environment and Nature Conservation
8 Leapale Road
Guildford, Surrey GU1 4JX

Tel: +44 (0) 1483 539 600
www.yptenc.org.uk

The Young People's Trust for the Environment and Nature Conservation provides free lectures and information to local schools in Surrey, Dorset and the Lake District. Also runs the Young Environmentalist of the Year Awards (YEYA), the Barclaycard Livingland Awards and the Millennium Living for the Future Awards. Contact them direct if you would like to help them with some of your time and energy.

Youth Hostel Association

Trevelyan House
Dimple Road
Matlock, Derbyshire DE4 3YH

Tel: +44 (0) 870 870 8808
Fax: +44 (0) 1629 592627
www.yha.org.uk

The YHA has 230 Youth Hostels around the country and needs volunteers to help with running them and maintaining the local environment and paths, as well as fundraising.

Appendices

Choosing a tutorial college

Standards vary and it's best to check out two or three colleges before you choose. Here are some things to check before you decide:

- Does the college get results? For the last few years The Daily Telegraph has regularly published a table in early September giving the average A level retake grade improvements at tutorial colleges.
- Does the college have a good reputation? Get references from former students – the college should be happy to supply you with contact names.
- Has the college been inspected by the Department for Education and Skills (DfES) or an independent body such as BAC (the British Accreditation Council for Independent Further and Higher Education) or CIFE (the Council for Independent Further Education)?
- Does the college teach the right subjects?
- Does the college teach the same syllabus (eg OCR/French) that you studied at school?
- What time of year are the courses run? (this affects what you can do during the rest of your year out).
- Who will be teaching you? Check their qualifications and how familiar they are with the syllabus.
- Is the place up-to-date? near transport? does it have quiet study rooms and good facilities?
- What does it cost? What are the hourly rates?
- What do get for your money? How many hours of group teaching each week and how many one-to-one tutorials?

Retakes

There are several reasons why you might find yourself considering retakes: maybe because your grades are too low to meet a conditional offer (and the university won't negotiate with you to admit you on lower grades), or because illness interfered with exams, for example.

But beware, getting better grades second time round doesn't guarantee you a university place – often unis will demand even higher grades if it's taken you two bites at the cherry (unless of course you've got a really good excuse, like illness).

Grade appeals

The A level marking scandal in 2002 has left many people wondering just how much we can trust exam results. If you really think you've been done down by a tired exam marker, a misleading or misprinted question or some other factor, you can appeal against your result.

You appeal first to the examination board that set the exam, and if you don't think the adjudication is just, you can go on to appeal to the Examination Appeals Board (EAB). Be warned: this process takes a long time and there's no guarantee the appeal will go your way.

Retake timing

Now that modular A levels are firmly entrenched you may be able to retake the modules you did badly in while you are still at school instead of having to retake them in your year out.

Unfortunately for some gap year students, the rules on AS/A level module retakes are being changed. In the past it was easier to raise A level grades by resitting just one or two modules. That way, you could get the necessary qualifications for university entrance without re-learning an entire two-year syllabus.

Keeping quiet about the first result and retaking a module more than once to upgrade was also possible until the universities began to ask for information about previous results to be declared. So now you need to make sure your chosen university course doesn't set higher entry grades for exams taken at a second sitting. And under the new A level system, retaking a module more than once is no longer allowed.

In some cases you may find that when you retake a certain exam you have to change exam board – this can be a problem in some subjects (eg languages with set texts) and you may therefore have to resit your A levels a whole year after the original exams, which can seriously disrupt your gap year. Check with your exam board as early as you can.

The Gap-Year Guidebook 2005/2006

Tutorial colleges like to keep students working on A levels for a full year. That keeps the college full and tutors paid. But many agree that the best thing is to get resits over before work already done is forgotten. So the best timing, if you are academically confident and want to enjoy your gap year, is to go to a tutorial college in September and resit the whole exam or the relevant modules in January – if sittings are available then.

Languages

If you have only language AS levels, A2 levels or A levels to retake, there are several options:

♦ Take an extra course or stay in the country of the relevant language and return to revise for a summer resit, choosing the same exam board (courses abroad, however, are not usually geared to A level texts).

♦ Check with tutorial colleges how much of your syllabus module or modules (the chosen literature texts are crucial) overlap with those of other exam boards. This may give you the chance to switch exam boards and do a quick retake in January.

♦ Cram for as long as necessary at a specialist language college. Some British tutorial colleges and language course organisers have links with teaching centres in France so it's worth checking this out before signing on.

Retake results

Those who sit A level retakes in January and get the grades needed for a chosen place will not have to wait until August for that place to be confirmed. Examining boards will feed the result directly into UCAS so you will know your place has been clinched. A technicality, but comforting for gap year students who want to go away.

And don't forget that if you have a firm choice conditional offer and you make the grades asked for, the university can't back out. It has an obligation to admit you.

A level examining boards

There are five A level examining boards: AQA (Assessment and Qualifications Alliance), Edexcel, OCR (Oxford, Cambridge & RSA), Northern Ireland (CCEA) and Wales (WJEC). All these boards now provide their exam timetables on the internet about nine months in advance: we've provided their details below, along with those of other exam-related organisations.

AQA (Assessment and Qualifications Alliance)

Stag Hill House
Guildford, Surrey GU2 7XJ

Tel: +44 (0) 1483 506506
www.aqa.org.uk

CCEA (Northern Ireland Council for the Curriculum, Examinations and Assessment)

Clarendon Dock
29 Clarendon Road
Belfast BT1 3BG, N Ireland

Tel: +44 (0) 28 9026 1200
Fax: +44 (0) 28 9026 1234
www.ccea.org.uk

EAB (Examination Appeals Board)

83 Piccadilly
London W1J 8QA

Tel: +44 (0) 20 7509 5995
www.theeab.org.uk

This is the final court of appeal for exam grades. Centres and private candidates only go to the EAB if an appeal to the relevant examination board for an exam paper has failed. The EAB website has a notice board showing when appeals are going to be heard.

EDEXCEL

One90 Highbolborn
32 Russell Square
WC1B 5DN London WC1V 7BH

Tel: +44 (0) 870 240 9800
Fax: +44 (0)20 7758 6960
www.edexcel.org.uk

IBO (International Baccalaureate Organisation)

Route des Morillons 15
CH-1218
Grand-Saconnex, Geneva, Switzerland

Tel: +41 22 791 7740
Fax: +41 22 791 0277
www.ibo.org

Central body for the development, administration and assessment of the International Baccalaureate Diploma Programme.

OCR (Oxford Cambridge & RSA Examinations)

9 Hills Road
Cambridge
CB2 1PB

Tel: +44 (0) 1223 552552
Fax: (0)1223 552553
www.ocr.org.uk

QCA (Qualifications and Curriculum Authority)

83 Piccadilly
London W1J 8QA

Tel: +44 (0) 20 7509 5555
www.qca.org.uk

The QCA is the body that (along with the Qualifications, Curriculum and Assessment Authority for Wales: ACCAC) approves all syllabuses and monitors exams (grading standards, for example).

You can get some basic explanations of the new A level system on its website, though much QCA information is aimed at teachers rather than those who are going to sit the exams.

SQA (Scottish Qualifications Authority)

Hanover House	Tel: +44 (0) 845 279 1000
24 Douglas Street	Fax: +44(0)141 242 2244
Glasgow G2 7NQ, Scotland	www.sqa.org.uk

Central body for the development, administration and assessment of Scottish qualifications, including Standard Grade, Highers, Advanced Highers, HNCs, HNDs and SVQs.

WJEC (Welsh Joint Education Committee)

245 Western Avenue	Tel: +44 (0) 29 2026 5000
CF5 2YX Cardiff, Wales	www.wjec.co.uk

Colleges accredited by BAC and CIFE

The following independent sixth-form and tutorial colleges offering A level tuition (one-year, two-year, complete retakes, modular retakes or intensive coaching) are recognised by the British Accreditation Council (BAC, Tel: 020 7224 5474, www.the-bac.org) and/or the Council for Independent Further Education (CIFE, Tel: 020 8767 8666, www.cife.org.uk). Of course a college can have a good reputation and acheive excellent results without accreditation.

Abacus College (Oxford)	BAC	Tel: +44 (0) 1865 240 111
Abbey College (Malvern)	BAC	Tel: +44 (0) 1684 892 300
Abbey College (Birmingham)	CIFE	Tel: +44 (0) 121 236 7474
Abbey College (Cambridge)	CIFE	Tel: +44 (0) 1223 578 280
Abbey College (London, W2)	CIFE	Tel: +44 (0) 20 7229 5928
Abbey College (Manchester)	CIFE	Tel: +44 (0) 161 236 6836
Albany College (London, NW4)	CIFE	Tel: +44 (0) 20 8202 5965
Ashbourne Independent Sixth Form College (London, W8)	CIFE	Tel: +44 (0) 20 7937 3858
Bales College (London, W10)	CIFE	Tel: +44 (0) 20 8960 5899
Basil Paterson Tutorial College (Edinburgh)	BAC	Tel: +44 (0) 131 556 7698
Bath Academy (Bath)	BAC	Tel: +44 (0) 1225 334 577
Bellerbys College (Hove)	CIFE	Tel: +44 (0) 1273 323 374
Bosworth Independent College (Northampton)	CIFE	Tel: +44 (0) 1604 239 995

Brooke House College (Market Harborough)	CIFE	Tel: +44 (0) 1858 462 452
Cambridge Arts and Sciences (Cambridge)	BAC	Tel: +44 (0) 1223 314 431
Cambridge Centre for Sixth Form Studies (Cambridge)	BAC/CIFE	Tel: +44 (0) 1223 716 890
Cambridge Seminars (Cambridge)	BAC	Tel: +44 (0) 1223 313 464
Cambridge Tutors College (Croydon)	CIFE	Tel: +44 (0) 20 8688 5284
Centre for International Education (Oxford)	BAC	Tel: +44 (0) 1865 202 238
Cherwell College (Oxford)	CIFE	Tel: +44 (0) 1865 242 670
Collingham (London, SW5)	CIFE	Tel: +44 (0) 20 7244 7414
Concord College (Shrewsbury)	CIFE	Tel: +44 (0) 1694 731 631
David Game College (London, W11)	BAC	Tel: +44 (0) 20 7221 6665
Davies, Laing & Dick (London, W2)	CIFE	Tel: +44 (0) 20 7727 2797
Dean College (London, N7)	BAC	Tel: +44 (0) 20 7281 4461
Dorton College of Further Education (Nr Sevenoaks)	BAC	Tel: +44 (0) 1732 764 123
Duff-Miller Sixth Form College (London, SW7)	CIFE	Tel: +44 (0) 20 7225 0577
Exeter Tutorial College (Exeter)	CIFE	Tel: +44 (0) 1392 278 101
Fine Arts College (London, NW3)	BAC/CIFE	Tel: +44 (0) 20 7586 0312
Harrogate Tutorial College (Harrogate)	CIFE	Tel: +44 (0) 1423 501 041
Irwin College (Leicester)	CIFE	Tel: +44 (0) 1162 552 648
King's School (Oxford)	BAC	Tel: +44 (0) 1865 711 829
Lansdowne College (London, W8)	CIFE	Tel: +44 (0) 20 7616 4400
Lyceum Centres (London, E6)	BAC	Tel: +44 (0) 20 8552 5429
Mander Portman Woodward (Birmingham)	CIFE	Tel: +44 (0) 121 454 9637

Mander Portman Woodward (London, SW7)	CIFE	Tel: +44 (0) 20 7584 8555
Mander Portman Woodward (Cambridge)	CIFE	Tel: +44 (0) 1223 350 158
Modes Study Centre (Oxford)	CIFE	Tel: +44 (0) 1865 249 349
New College (Cardiff)	BAC	Tel: +44 (0) 29 20463 355
Oxford Business College (Oxford)	BAC	Tel: +44 (0) 1865 791 908
Oxford Tutorial College (Oxford)	CIFE	Tel: +44 (0) 1865 793 333
Padworth College (Nr Reading)	CIFE	Tel: +44 (0) 118 983 2645
Rochester Independent College (Rochester)	BAC	Tel: +44 (0) 1634 828 115
St Andrew's (Cambridge)	BAC	Tel: +44 (0) 1223 360 040
St Clare's (Oxford)	CIFE	Tel: +44 (0) 1865 552 031
Stafford House College (Canterbury)	BAC	Tel: +44 (0) 1227 866 540
Surrey College (Guildford)	CIFE	Tel: +44 (0) 1483 565887
The Tuition Centre (London, NW4)	CIFE	Tel: +44 (0) 20 8203 5025
Wentworth Tutorial College (London, NW11)	CIFE	Tel: +44 (0) 20 8458 8524

visit: www.gap-year.com

1b Applying to University

The number of students who took up university and college places in Autumn 2003 was the highest ever. According to provisional UCAS figures (at 30 June 2004), the number of applicants increased by 2.9% from 437,615 in 2003 to 450,147 in 2004, and the number of accepted applicants (at 15 September 2004) increased by 2.1% from 350,724 to 358,229.

You may make the decision to take a year off well in advance. Many students have already chosen to defer university entrance because there are things they would like to use the time to do. For 2003 entry, 40,406 applicants made at least one application for deferred entry. Some students choose not to apply at all until after they get their A level grades.

Other students find themselves taking a gap year on shorter notice. For example, they may take a year off because their A level grades are not what they had expected – either too low to win the university place they accepted, or high enough to win them a place at a better university than the ones they applied to. Whatever the reason, the result is a gap year.

Application Process

UCAS (the Universities and Colleges Admissions Service) handles applications to all UK universities (except the Open University) as well as to most other institutions that offer full-time undergraduate higher education courses. This includes applications for Oxford, Cambridge and for degrees in medicine, dentistry and veterinary science/medicine, although they have to be in earlier than for other universities and colleges and for other subjects.

UCAS

Rosehill,
New Barn Lane,
Cheltenham GL52 3LZ

Tel: 0870 1122211
Minicom: 01242-544942
E-mail: enquiries@ucas.ac.uk
Website: www.ucas.com

UCAS offers a distribution service to companies who wish to send promotional material to students. UCAS handles the distribution itself and does not pass on your personal details, which remain confidential. If you prefer not to receive this kind of material however, you can opt out when filling in your UCAS application.

You can apply for six different courses at any UCAS institution, except for medical courses A100, A101, A103, A104, A106, dentistry courses: A200, A203, A204, A205, A206 and veterinary science courses: D100, D101 for which you can make just four choices. If you are using the 'two-track' application procedure for art and design courses you can use up to three of your choices in Route B. If you are applying for art and design through Route B, you can still only apply to a maximum of six choices overall. The different combinations that you can use are listed on the

UCAS website. You can hold on to two of the offers you get: one 'firm (first) choice' and one 'insurance (second choice) place'. So you may have to be cautious about the courses you pitch for.

Online and Offline Applications

UCAS has a secure, web-based application system called ucasapply. Each school, college, careers agency or British Council Office that has registered with UCAS to use ucasapply appoints a co-ordinator who manages the way it is used. For students, registering to the new system takes a few minutes and costs nothing. Once a student has registered, they are given a username and are asked to choose a password that they will need to use each time they want to access their application forms. Applicants can use this new system anywhere that has access to the web. The new service works in tandem with the ucascourse (an online course search service).Check out the UCAS website for more information at **www.ucas.com**.

UCAS says that this method of applying is much easier to use because the software automatically checks the data and alerts you to possible errors. Common mistakes such as incorrect course codes are quickly discovered. UCAS says that processing times are much shorter too that in the near future all applications will be made this way.

There is also an offline application system that allows applicants to fill in their application forms on a PC at their school, college, local careers service, or even at home. You can't use it to apply on an individual basis – applications must be submitted to UCAS through a teacher or careers adviser, either via the internet, e-mail or by floppy disk.

A level results

A level results come out in mid-August. Depending on your grades one of the following will happen:

♦ Firm (first) choice uni writes to confirm offer of a place
♦ Insurance (second choice) uni writes to confirm offer of a place
♦ Clearing
♦ Retakes

Before you make any decisions make sure you know all the angles: retakes may be the only way for you to get to university, but most universities will demand even higher results the second time around, an expectation confirmed by Glasgow university: "We expect slightly higher requirements if you don't get good enough grades in one A level attempt".

The UCAS Tariffs

The UCAS Tariff was first used for those applying to enter HE in 2002. Since its introduction it has expanded to cover additional qualifications. It is a points-based system, which establishes agreed equivalences between different types of qualifications. It provides admissions tutors with a way of comparing applicants with different types and volumes of achievement.

UCAS is keen to encourage all universities and colleges to use the Tariff to make the application system more uniform across the country. Three quarters of universities and colleges now use the Tariff, but some admissions tutors are sticking to what they know and understand: good A level grades.

More information and a copy of the latest Tariff is available at http://www.ucas.com/candq/tariff/index.html

There is also a tariff calculator online to help you work out the value of your qualifications.

QUALIFICATION	GRADE	POINT SCORE
A2, Scottish Advanced Higher	A	120
and Vocational A level*	B	100
	C	80
	D	60
	E	40
AS Level and	A	60
Vocational AS level	B	50
	C	40
	D	30
	E	20
Scottish Higher	A	72
	B	60
	C	48

Key dates

In 1999 and 2000, UCAS met with universities and colleges to agree a number of changes to the UCAS application system. The last two, UCAS Extra and Invisibility of Choices, were put in place for 2003 entry. This is what will happen if you apply for a university course starting in autumn 2003 or 2004, so if you are thinking of taking a gap year you'll need to know that:

♦ The main deadline for applications for all universities (except Oxford, Cambridge, Medicine, Dentistry, Veterinary Medicine or Veterinary Science courses and Route B Art and Design programmes) is now 15 January.

♦ There's to be a new 'commitment to clear, transparent admissions policies'. Universities are putting 'Entry Profiles' on their websites to tell students about entry requirements, including skills, personal qualities, or experience not necessarily connected with academic qualifications.

♦ UCAS Extra has been designed for applicants who have been considered at all six of their choices, but who do not have a place. Extra allows them to make additional choices through UCAS, one at a time. The service runs from mid-March to the end of June, so you won't have to wait until Clearing to find a place. If you are eligible for Extra, UCAS will automatically send you an Extra Passport and information about what you need to do next.

♦ 'Invisibility of choices' means that universities and colleges cannot see which other universities or colleges a student has applied to until that applicant has replied to an offer or goes into UCAS Extra.

The autumn term is when Year 13 students usually begin to apply for university and college places through the UCAS system (though some super-organised schools and students start preparations in the summer of Year 12).

The information you need for applying to university or college is online at www.ucas.com or comes from the UCAS Directory, which lists all courses and institutions. The Directory is available free to schools, or you can order a copy from UCAS for £6. Bear in mind that courses can be added or deleted after the Directory is published, an up-to-date list of courses is always available on the UCAS website. Information about applying for university or college places appears in the UCAS guide How to Apply, which is also online or is sent to you automatically when you send for an application form. Here are some key dates:

◆ University open days organised from spring each year.

◆ UCAS Directory is published annually in May for the following year's courses. For example, the edition for 2006 entry will be published in May 2005.

◆ Applications for 2006 entry which include any Oxford or Cambridge choices or any Medicine courses: A100, A101, A102, A103, A104, A106, Dentistry courses: A200, A203, A204, A205, A206 or Veterinary Science courses: D100, D101 should be returned to UCAS by 15 October 2005.

◆ Other applications for 2006 entry (except Route B applications for art and design courses: see How to Apply) should be returned to UCAS between 1 September 2005 and 15 January 2006.

◆ When your form is received UCAS sends you a letter stating your choices and application number. If there seems to be a mistake, call UCAS immediately, quoting your application number.

Universities and colleges start to notify UCAS of their decisions for 2006 entry after October 2005. Applicants receive decisions via UCAS (interview, unconditional offer, conditional offer or unsuccessful application).

◆ You should reply to offers as soon as you receive all your university decisions from UCAS.

◆ UCAS has two main deadlines. 15 January is the initial closing date. Applications received after 15 January are marked 'late'. After 15 January the university or college you have applied to does not guarantee that it will consider your application. 30 June is the final closing date. Applications received after this date go straight into Clearing.

◆ A level results will be published on Thursday, 18 August 2005.

◆ Note that UCAS advises that applicants should confirm their acceptance of an offer of a university place as quickly as possible.

◆ After the A level results are released, UCAS will automatically send out Clearing Entry forms (CEFs) to applicants who have missed their grades, who have not received offers earlier in the year, who have declined all offers made to them, who have applied after the final closing date 'late' (see above), or who haven't found a place using ucasextra.

◆ A list of vacancies for degrees, HNDs and other undergraduate courses is published on the UCAS website at **www.ucas.com** as soon as results are released. This on-line vacancy service is updated several times a day. Vacancy listings are also published by some of the national daily newspapers from A level results day.

Clearing closes at the end of September.

Languages

If you have only language AS levels, A2 levels or A levels to retake, there are several options:

♦ Take an extra course or stay in the country of the relevant language and return to revise for a summer resit, choosing the same exam board (courses abroad, however, are not usually geared to A level texts).

♦ Check with tutorial colleges how much of your syllabus module or modules (the chosen literature texts are crucial) overlap with those of other exam boards. This may give you the chance to switch exam boards and do a quick retake in January.

♦ Cram for as long as necessary at a specialist language college. Some British tutorial colleges and language course organisers have links with teaching centres in France so it's worth checking this out before signing on.

Retake results

Those who sit A level retakes in January and get the grades needed for a chosen place will not have to wait until August for that place to be confirmed. Examining boards will feed the result directly into UCAS so you will know your place has been clinched. A technicality, but comforting for gap year students who want to go away.

And don't forget that if you have a firm choice conditional offer and you make the grades asked for, the university can't back out. It has an obligation to admit you.

A level examining boards

There are five A level examining boards: AQA (Assessment and Qualifications Alliance), Edexcel, OCR (Oxford, Cambridge & RSA), Northern Ireland (CCEA) and Wales (WJEC). All these boards now provide their exam timetables on the internet about nine months in advance: we've provided their details below, along with those of other exam-related organisations.

Deferred entry, rescheduled entry, or post A level application?

There are three ways to handle university entrance if you want to take a gap year. The safest is usually to apply for deferred entry, but not all courses accept deferred entry candidates. At Bristol University the admissions office is reluctant to make deferred entry offers for the History degree course, and if it does, it demands higher grades. The reason: demand for the course was too high in 2000 and increased again in 2001. By 15 January 2002, over 1600 applications have already been received for the 72 places on this course. A set number of these places are allocated for those taking a gap year, but these are even more limited so competition is even higher! Our advice is to talk to the admissions office before making a decision about taking a gap year.

If you're applying to uni for 2005-06 but hoping to defer your place until 2006 watch out for the new rules on fees.

For more information visit **www.dfes.gov.uk/studentsupport**, or contact your LEA.

1 Deferred entry

♦ Check first with the appropriate department of the university you want to go to that they are happy to take students after a gap year. If it's a popular course, preference may go to the current year applications.

♦ On your UCAS application form there is a specific 'Defer entry' column in the key 'Courses' section. Click in the 'Defer entry' box for all (or some) of the courses you apply for, having checked that they will still be available a year later. Talk to your teachers first and follow instructions in How to Apply.

♦ If you are planning to take a gap year, you will need to explain why in your Personal Statement on the UCAS application. You need to convince the university that a year off will make you a better applicant, so give an outline of what you plan to do and why.

♦ Send your completed application to UCAS, like any other student applying for entry without taking a gap year. Those who do so well before the 15 January deadline, however, may be among the first to start receiving replies (via UCAS). You will get a call for selection interview(s), a rejection or an offer which is conditional on getting specific A level grades or total point score.

♦ From the 15 January deadline to 30 June, UCAS will forward 'late' applications to universities 'for consideration at their discretion'. Applications received after 30 June go straight into Clearing.

♦ **NOTE:** Some academics are not happy with deferred entry because it means it might be nearly two years before you reach higher education. During that time a course may have changed, or you may have changed. So your application may be looked on unfavourably without you knowing why. Most departments at many universities are in favour of a gap year but they are not all in favour of deferred entry. If they interview you in November 2004 for a place in October 2006 it will be 23 months before they see you again. Check it out with the university department first.

Rescheduled entry

This is when you apply for a place for the coming university year, not the one after. Then, after A level results, if you have won a place at the university of your choice, you can negotiate directly with that university as an individual about deferring your entry for another year. If they say yes, you will receive a 'changed entry date confirmation letter'. You must reply to UCAS within seven days to accept the place, using the form that is attached to the letter. If the university says no, you have the options of either taking your insurance place, if they agree to you deferring your entry, or starting the application process all over again the following year.

NOTE: Some admissions tutors say that to give up a place on a popular course is risky, because the university will not be happy after you have messed them about. Others say that if a course has over-recruited, your deferral will be welcome. Tread carefully.

Post A level applications

If you take A levels in June 2005, you can still apply through UCAS after the results come out in August. You will go straight into Clearing. If you do not send in a UCAS application before the end of the 2005 entry cycle, (30 September 2005) you should apply – between 1 September 2005 and 15 January 2006 - for entry in the following year.

Universities cannot accept who don't apply through UCAS, and who then ring up at the last minute to try to get a place on a course. It can play havoc with the targets they set to fund the places they offer. Universities lose financially if they 'undershoot' or 'overshoot' the predicted number of students on a specific course.

Faculty check: all subjects

If you want to take a gap year, remember (before you apply) to contact the appropriate department or faculty at the university you would like to go to, and find out if they approve of a gap year or not. Prepare a good case for it before you phone. It is advisable to do this even if you are an absolutely outstanding candidate, because on some courses a year off is considered a definite disadvantage. This is usually the case where a degree course is very long or requires a large amount of remembered technical knowledge at the start.

Art and design

Applying through UCAS to your chosen college of Art and Design might involve applying by two different routes (Route A and Route B). You must make your Route A application by 15 January and your Route B application between 1 January and 24 March. You can apply to only three Route B choices. When you send off your UCAS form with your Route A choices, remember to indicate that you intend to apply through Route B as well, so that UCAS will send you further documentation.

Medicine, dentistry and veterinary science/medicine

If you hope to pursue a career in medicine, dentistry or veterinary science/medicine, you can use no more than four (of your possible six) choices in any one of those three subject areas. The courses involved are:

Medical courses: A100, A101, A102, A103, A104, A106

Dentistry courses: A200, A203, A204, A205, A206

Veterinary Scienc/Medicine courses: D100, D101

Don't forget that UCAS must receive ALL applications for these courses by 15 October.

Foundation degrees

The Foundation Degree (not to be confused with a foundation year), started in autumn 2001. It is a two-year 'vocational' degree – in other words, a degree in work-related subjects like computing or business studies rather than purely academic subjects. Students (of any age) do work experience as part of the course, and the degree will be convertible to an honours degree by adding further study afterwards. This makes getting a degree more flexible, and adds another opportunity to take a gap year – you could take a Foundation Degree, then have a gap year, then restart studies later to convert your Foundation Degree into a full Honours Degree.

Financing Your Studies

Most Students apply to the Students Loans Company **www.slc.co.uk** for a loan and the amount received depends on their family's income.

Loans don't have to be paid back until your income reaches a certain level (from April 2005 the level will be raised from £10,000 a year to £15,000 a year before tax). Repayments are linked to salary.

From 2005-2006 a new Higher Education Grant of up to £1,000 a year will be available to new students from lower-income families and some grant assistance will also be available to those whose families earn up to £20,000.

Applications are made through your local education authority (LEA) and should be made early (certainly before July). Your LEA will assess how much you get depending on your family's income.

Useful Reading

You can get booklets on student loans and on Financial Support for Higher Education Students from your Lea, or **www.dfes.gov.uk/studentsupport**, or by calling 0800 731 9133

Bursaries, scholarships and sponsorship

Although the number of fully-sponsored degrees on offer from the public or private sector declined in the 1990s, many organisations still offer sponsorship to students to study for a degree. Nowadays this is sometimes on condition that they join the sponsoring company or institution for a period when they graduate. The Army is one example from the public sector (Tel: 01980 618 181).

If you're looking for sponsorship, The Year in Industry improves your chances and removes the need to write endless letters (Tel: 0161 275 4396), or you may be interested in the offer from the Smallpeice Trust (Tel: 01926 333200).

University of Aberdeen	Tel: +44 (0) 1224 272 000 www.abdn.ac.uk
University of Abertay Dundee	Tel: +44 (0) 1382 308 000 www.abertay.ac.uk
Anglia Polytechnic University	Tel: +44 (0) 1245 493 131 www.anglia.ac.uk
Aston University	Tel: +44 (0) 121 204 3000 www.aston.ac.uk
University of Bath	Tel: +44 (0) 1225 388 388 www.bath.ac.uk
University of Birmingham	Tel: +44 (0) 121 414 3344 www.bham.ac.uk
Bolton Institute	Tel: +44 (0) 1204 900 600 www.bolton.ac.uk
Bournemouth University	Tel: +44 (0) 1202 524 111 www.bournemouth.ac.uk
University of Bradford	Tel: +44 (0) 1274 733 466 www.brad.ac.uk
University of Brighton	Tel: +44 (0) 1273 600 900 www.brighton.ac.uk
University of Bristol	Tel: +44 (0) 117 928 9000 www.bristol.ac.uk
Brunel University, West London	Tel: +44 (0) 1895 274 000 www.brunel.ac.uk
University of Buckingham	Tel: +44 (0) 1280 814 080 www.buckingham.ac.uk
Buckingham Chilterns University College	Tel: +44 (0) 1494 522 511 www.bcuc.ac.uk
University of Cambridge	Tel: +44 (0) 1223 337 733 www.cam.ac.uk

343

University of Central England in Birmingham	Tel: +44 (0) 121 331 5000 www.uce.ac.uk
University of Central Lancashire	Tel: +44 (0) 1772 201 201 www.uclan.ac.uk
City University	Tel: +44 (0) 20 7040 5060 www.city.ac.uk
Coventry University	Tel: +44 (0) 2476 887 688 www.coventry.ac.uk
Cranfield University	Tel: +44 (0) 1234 750 111 www.cranfield.ac.uk
De Montfort University	Tel: +44 (0) 1162 551 551 www.dmu.ac.uk
De Montfort University - Bedford	Tel: +44 (0) 1234 351 966 www.dmu.ac.uk
De Montfort University - Leicester	Tel: +44 (0) 1162 551 551 www.dmu.ac.uk
De Montfort University - Milton Keynes	Tel: +44 (0) 1908 695 511 www.dmu.ac.uk
University of Derby	Tel: +44 (0) 1332 590 500 www.derby.ac.uk
University of Dundee	Tel: +44 (0) 1382 223 181 www.dundee.ac.uk
University of Durham	Tel: +44 (0) 191 374 2000 www.dur.ac.uk
University of East Anglia	Tel: +44 (0) 1603 456 161 www.uea.ac.uk
University of East Anglia - University College Suffolk	Tel: +44 (0) 1473 255 885 www.suffolk.ac.uk
University of East London	Tel: +44 (0) 20 8590 7722 www.uel.ac.uk
University of Edinburgh	Tel: +44 (0) 131 650 1000 www.ed.ac.uk
University of Essex	Tel: +44 (0) 1206 873 333 www.essex.ac.uk

European Business School - London   Tel: +44 (0) 20 7487 7505
                                       www.ebs.london.ac.uk

University of Exeter   Tel: +44 (0) 1392 263 263
                                       www.exeter.ac.uk

University of Glamorgan   Tel: +44 (0) 800 716 925
                                       www.glam.ac.uk

University of Glasgow   Tel: +44 (0) 141 339 8855
                                       www.gla.ac.uk

Glasgow Caledonian University   Tel: +44 (0) 141 331 3000
                                       www.gcal.ac.uk

University of Gloucestershire   Tel: +44 (0) 1242 532 700
                                       www.chelt.ac.uk

University of Greenwich   Tel: +44 (0) 20 8331 8000
                                       www.gre.ac.uk

Heriot-Watt University   Tel: +44 (0) 131 449 5111
                                       www.hw.ac.uk

University of Hertfordshire   Tel: +44 (0) 1707 284 000
                                       www.herts.ac.uk

University of Huddersfield   Tel: +44 (0) 1484 422 288
                                       www.hud.ac.uk

University of Hull   Tel: +44 (0) 1482 346 311
                                       www.hull.ac.uk

Keele University   Tel: +44 (0) 1782 621 111
                                       www.keele.ac.uk

University of Kent at Canterbury   Tel: +44 (0) 1227 764 000
                                       www.ukc.ac.uk

Kingston University   Tel: +44 (0) 20 8547 2000
                                       www.kingston.ac.uk

Lancaster University   Tel: +44 (0) 1524 65201
                                       www.lancs.ac.uk

University of Leeds   Tel: +44 (0) 113 243 1751
                                       www.leeds.ac.uk

Leeds Metropolitan University   Tel: +44 (0) 113 283 2600
                                       www.lmu.ac.uk

University of Leicester   Tel: +44 (0) 116 252 2522
                                       www.le.ac.uk

1C

Appendix | 1C

345

| University of Lincoln | Tel: +44 (0) 1482 440 550 |
| | www.lincoln.ac.uk |

| University of Liverpool | Tel: +44 (0) 151 794 2000 |
| | www.liv.ac.uk |

| Liverpool Hope University College | Tel: +44 (0) 151 291 3000 |
| | www.livhope.ac.uk |

| Liverpool Institute for Performing Arts | Tel: +44 (0) 151 330 3000 |
| | www.lipa.ac.uk |

| Liverpool John Moores University | Tel: +44 (0) 151 231 2121 |
| | www.cwis.livjm.ac.uk |

University of London   Tel: +44 (0) 20 7862 8004
(contact colleges directly)   www.lon.ac.uk
◆ Birkbeck College   Tel: +44 (0) 20 7631 6000
                                                                www.bbk.ac.uk

◆ British Institute in Paris   Tel: +33 1 44 11 73 73
                                                             www.bip.lon.ac.uk

◆ Courtauld Institute of Art   Tel: +44 (0) 20 77848 2777
                                                           www.courtauld.ac.uk

◆ Goldsmith's College   Tel: +44 (0) 20 7919 7171
                                                          www.goldsmiths.ac.uk

◆ The Guy's, King's   Tel: +44 (0) 20 7848 6971
    and St Thomas' School of Medicine   www.kcl.ac.uk/depsta/medicine
◆ Heythrop College   Tel: +44 (0) 20 7795 6600
                                                            www.heythrop.ac.uk

◆ Imperial College at Wye   Tel: +44 (0) 20 758 95111
                                                               www.wye.ac.uk

◆ Imperial College of Medicine   Tel: +44 (0) 20 7589 5111
                                                             www.med.ic.ac.uk

◆ Imperial College of Science, Technology and Medicine Tel: +44 (0) 20 7589 5111
                                                                 www.ic.ac.uk

◆   Institute of Education   Tel: +44 (0) 20 7612 6000
                                                               www.ioe.ac.uk

◆ King's College London   Tel: +44 (0) 20 7836 5454
                                                               www.kcl.ac.uk

◆ London Business School   Tel: +44 (0) 20 7262 5050
                                                               www.lbs.ac.uk

◆ London School of Economics and Political Science Tel: +44 (0) 20 7405 7686
                                                               www.lse.ac.uk

◆ London School of Hygiene and Tropical Medicine Tel: +44 (0) 20 7636 8636
                                                              www.lshtm.ac.uk

◆ London School of Jewish Studies   Tel: +44 (0) 20 8203 6427
                                                               www.lsjs.ac.uk

◆ Queen Mary, University of London   Tel: +44 (0) 20 7882 7882
                                                               www.qmw.ac.uk

◆ Royal Academy of Music	Tel: +44 (0) 20 7873 7373 www.ram.ac.uk
◆ Royal Free and University College Medical School	Tel: +44 (0) 20 7679 2000 www.rfc.ucl.ac.uk
◆ Royal Holloway, University of London	Tel: +44 (0) 1784 434 455 www.rhul.ac.uk
◆ The Royal	Tel: +44 (0) 20 7468 5000 www.rvc.ac.uk
◆ School of Oriental and African Studies	Tel: +44 (0) 20 7637 2388 www.soas.ac.uk
◆ School of Pharmacy	Tel: +44 (0) 20 7753 5800 www.ulsop.ac.uk
◆ School of Slavonic and East European Studies	Tel: +44 (0) 20 7636 8000 www.ssees.ac.uk
◆ St Bartholomew's and The Royal School of Medicine and Dentistry	Tel: +44 (0) 20 7377 7747 www.mds.qmw.ac.uk
◆ St George's Hospital Medical School	Tel: +44 (0) 20 8672 9944 www.sghms.ac.uk
◆ University College London	Tel: +44 (0) 20 7387 7050 www.ucl.ac.uk
◆ London Guildhall University	Tel: +44 (0) 20 7320 1000 www.lgu.ac.uk

1C

Appendix | 1C

Loughborough University Tel: +44 (0) 1509 263 171
www.lboro.ac.uk

University of Luton Tel: +44 (0) 1582 734 111
www.luton.ac.uk

University of Manchester Tel: +44 (0) 161 275 2000
www.man.ac.uk

University of Manchester Institute of Science and Technology (UMIST) Tel: +44 (0) 161 236 3311
www.umist.ac.uk

Manchester Metropolitan University Tel: +44 (0) 161 247 2000
www.mmu.ac.uk

Middlesex University Tel: +44 (0) 20 8362 5000
www.mdx.ac.uk

Napier University Tel: +44 (0) 131 444 2266
www.napier.ac.uk

University of Newcastle Tel: +44 (0) 191 222 6000
www.ncl.ac.uk

University of North London Tel: +44 (0) 20 7607 2789
www.unl.ac.uk

University of Northumbria at Newcastle Tel: +44 (0) 191 232 6002
www.unn.ac.uk

University of Nottingham	Tel: +44 (0) 115 951 5151
	www.nott.ac.uk
Nottingham Trent University	Tel: +44 (0) 115 941 8418
	www.ntu.ac.uk
Open University	Tel: +44 (0) 1908 274 066
	www.open.ac.uk
University of Oxford	Tel: +44 (0) 1865 270 000
	www.ox.ac.uk
Oxford Brookes University	Tel: +44 (0) 1865 741 111
	www.brookes.ac.uk
University of Paisley	Tel: +44 (0) 141 848 3000
	www.paisley.ac.uk
University of Plymouth	Tel: +44 (0) 1752 600 600
	www.plymouth.ac.uk
University of Portsmouth	Tel: +44 (0) 2392 876 543
	www.port.ac.uk
Queen Margaret University College	Tel: +44 (0) 131 317 3000
	www.qmuc.ac.uk
Queen's University of Belfast	Tel: +44 (0) 28 9024 5133
	www.qub.ac.uk
University of Reading	Tel: +44 (0) 1189 875 123
	www.rdg.ac.uk
Robert Gordon University	Tel: +44 (0) 1224 262 000
	www.rgu.ac.uk
Royal College of Art	Tel: +44 (0) 20 7590 4444
	www.rca.ac.uk
Royal College of Music	Tel: +44 (0) 20 7589 3643
	www.rcm.ac.uk
University of Salford	Tel: +44 (0) 161 295 5000
	www.salford.ac.uk
University of Sheffield	Tel: +44 (0) 114 222 2000
	www.shef.ac.uk
Sheffield Hallam University	Tel: +44 (0) 114 225 5555
	www.shu.ac.uk

visit: www.gap-year.com

South Bank University	Tel: +44 (0) 20 7928 8989 www.sbu.ac.uk
University of Southampton	Tel: +44 (0) 23 8059 5000 www.soton.ac.uk
University of St Andrews	Tel: +44 (0) 1334 476 161 www.st-andrews.ac.uk
Staffordshire University	Tel: +44 (0) 1782 294 000 www.staffs.ac.uk
University of Stirling	Tel: +44 (0) 1786 473 171 www.stir.ac.uk
University of Strathclyde	Tel: +44 (0) 141 552 4400 www.strath.ac.uk
University of Sunderland	Tel: +44 (0) 191 515 2000 www.sunderland.ac.uk
University of Surrey	Tel: +44 (0) 1483 300 800 www.surrey.ac.uk
University of Surrey Roehampton	Tel: +44 (0) 20 8392 3000 www.roehampton.ac.uk
University of Sussex	Tel: +44 (0) 1273 606 755 www.sussex.ac.uk
University of Teesside	Tel: +44 (0) 1642 218 121 www.tees.ac.uk
Thames Valley University	Tel: +44 (0) 20 8579 5000 www.tvu.ac.uk
Trinity College of Music	Tel: +44 (0) 20 8305 3888 www.tcm.ac.uk
University of Ulster	Tel: +44 (0) 8 700 400 700 www.ulst.ac.uk
University of Wales (contact colleges directly)	Tel: +44 (0) 29 2038 2656 www.wales.ac.uk
◆ The University of Wales, Aberystwyth	Tel: +44 (0) 1970 623 111 www.aber.ac.uk
◆ University of Wales, Bangor	Tel: +44 (0) 1248 351 151 www.bangor.ac.uk
◆ University of Wales - Cardiff University	Tel: Tel: +44 (0) 29 2087 4000 www.cardiff.ac.uk
◆ University of Wales Institute, Cardiff	Tel: +44 (0) 29 2050 6070 www.uwic.ac.uk

Appendix | 1C

1C

349

- ◆ University of Wales, Lampeter   Tel: +44 (0) 1570 422 351
  www.lamp.ac.uk

- ◆ University of Wales College of Medicine   Tel: +44 (0) 29 2074 7747
  www.uwcm.ac.uk

- ◆ University of Wales College, Newport   Tel: +44 (0) 1633 430 088
  www.newport.ac.uk

- ◆ University of Wales, Swansea   Tel: +44 (0) 1792 205 678
  www.swansea.ac.uk

University of Warwick   Tel: +44 (0) 2476 523 523
www.warwick.ac.uk

University of the West of England, Bristol   Tel: +44 (0) 117 965 6261
www.uwe.ac.uk

University of Westminster   Tel: +44 (0) 20 7911 5000
www.wmin.ac.uk

University of Wolverhampton   Tel: +44 (0) 1902 321 000
www.wlv.ac.uk

University of York   Tel: +44 (0) 1904 430 000
www.york.ac.uk

Country Info

Once you have chosen where you want to go, whether one country or a dozen, do some research. It would be a shame to travel to the other side of the world and then miss what it has to offer. There are loads of websites giving interesting and useful factual advice (weather, geographical, political, economic) as well as those that are more touristy.

Foreign Office warnings

It's worth bearing in mind that economic and political situations can change rapidly in countries, so check with the Foreign and Commonwealth Office that the country is still safe to travel to before you go. There's a link to their website on www.gap-year.com. It's important to look at the lists of specific areas which travellers should avoid. It's also worth noting the phone numbers of all British embassies and consulates in areas where you may be travelling in case you need to contact them for help.

Telephone or e-mail home regularly to save your family a lot of worry and British embassies a lot of wasted time. Just to give you a taste, the following pages contain data for individual countries: the FCO warnings given here were correct at time of going to press in January 2004, make sure you check with the FCO for up-to-date information.

Afghanistan
- Population: estimated to be 28.7 million (UN) with an estimated total of 2 million refugees in Pakistan and 800,000 in Iran (UN September 2004
- Location: Southern Asia ◆ Capital: Kabul
- Currency: Afghani ◆ Religion: Sunni Muslim, Shi'a Muslim
- Languages: Afghan Persian (Dari), Pashtu, Turkic languages (primarily Uzbek and Turkmen), 30 minor languages (primarily Balochi and Pashai), much bilingualism
- British Embassy, Kabul: +93 70 221 212

Albania
- Population: 32 million ◆ Location: South-east Europe ◆ Capital: Tirana
- Currency: Lek (ALL) ◆ Religion: Muslim, Albanian Orthodox, Roman Catholic
- Languages: Albanian (Tosk is the official dialect), Greek
- British Embassy, Tirana: +355 4 2 34973/4/5

Algeria
- Population: 14 million (2003 est) ◆ Location: Northern Africa ◆ Capital: Algiers
- Currency: Algerian Dinar (DZD) ◆ Religion: Sunni Muslim 99%, Christian, Jewish
- Language: Arabic (official language), French and Berber dialects.
- British Embassy, Algiers: +213 21 230068

Andorra

- Population: 68,000 ♦ Location: South-west Europe ♦ Capital: Andorra la Vella
- Currency: euro ♦ Religion: Roman Catholic
- Language: Catalan (official), French, Castilian, Portuguese
- British Consulate-General, Barcelona: +34 933 666 200

Angola

- Population: 14 million (2003 est) ♦ Location: Southern Africa
- Capital: Luanda ♦ Currency: Kwanza
- Religion: Indigenous beliefs, Roman Catholic, Protestant
- Language: Portuguese (official), Bunta and other African language
- British Embassy, Luanda: +244 2 334582/3

Antigua and Barbuda

- Antigua and Barbuda - Population: 75,000 (Census 2001 Estimates) including about 1,200 Montserratians living in Antigua. Barbuda's population of 1,400 live mostly in or near the town of Codrington. Population growth rate: 0.74% (2001 estimate).
- Location: Caribbean ♦ Capital: Saint John's
- Currency: East Caribbean dollar (XCD) ♦ Religion: Christian
- Language: English (official), local dialects
- British High Commission: +268 462 0008/9; +268 463 0010

Argentina

- Population:37.8 million ♦ Location: Southern South America
- Capital: Buenos Aires ♦ Currency: Argentine Peso (ars)
- Religion: Christian (predominantly Roman Catholic), Jewish
- Language: Spanish (official), English, Italian, German, French
- British Embassy, Beunos Aires: +54 11 4808 2200

Armenia

- Population: 3.3 million ♦ Location: South-western Asia
- Capital: Yerevan ♦ Currency: Dram (AMD)
- Religion: American apostolic, other Christian, Yezidi (Zoroastrian/animist)
- Language: Armenian 96%, Russian 2%, other 2%
- British Embassy, Yerevan: +374 1 264 301

Australia

- Population: 20.2 million ♦ Location: Australasia ♦ Capital: Canberra
- Currency: Australian dollar (AUD) ♦ Religion: Anglican, Roman Catholic
- Language: English, native languages
- British High Commission, Canberra: +61 2 6270 6666

Austria

- Population: 8.2 million ♦ Location: Central Europe
- Capital: Vienna♦ Currency: euro (EUR); Austrian schilling (ATS)
- Religion: Christian (predominantly Roman Catholic), Muslim
- Language: German ♦ British Embassy, Vienna Tel: +43 1 716130

Azerbaijan

- Population: 8.3 million ♦ Location: South-western Asia
- Capital: Baku (Baki) ♦ Currency: Azerbaijani manat (AZM)
- Religion: Muslim, Russian Orthodox, Armenian Orthodox,

♦ Language: Azerbaijani (Azeri), Russian, Armenian, other
♦ British Embassy, Baku: +99 412 975188/89/90

Bahamas

♦ Population: 300,500 ♦ Location: Caribbean, chain of islands in the North Atlantic Ocean
♦ Capital: Nassau ♦ Currency: Bahamian dollar (BSD)
♦ Religion: Baptist, Anglican, Roman Catholic, Methodist, Church of God
♦ Language: English, Creole (among Haitian immigrants)
♦ British High Commission: +1 242 325 7471

Bahrain

♦ Population: 656,400 ♦ Location: Middle East, archipelago in the Persian Gulf
♦ Capital: Manama ♦ Currency: Bahraini dinar (BHD)
♦ Religion: Shi'a Muslim, Sunni Muslim ♦ Language: Arabic, English, Farsi, Urdu
♦ British Embassy, Manama: +973 574 100; +973 574 167
(Information Hot-Line); +973 960 0274 (Emergency Number)

Bangladesh

♦ Population: 133.4 million ♦ Location: Southern Asia ♦ Capital: Dhaka
♦ Currency: taka (BDT) ♦ Language: Bangla, English
♦ Religion: Muslim, Hindu ♦ British High Commission, Dhaka: +880 2 882 2705

Barbados

♦ Population: 275,000 ♦ Location: Caribbean
♦ Capital: Bridgetown ♦ Currency: Barbados Dollar
♦ Religion: Anglican, Methodist, Pentecostal, Roman Catholic
♦ Language: English
♦ British High Commission, Bridgetown: +1 246 430 7800

Belarus

♦ Population:10.3 million ♦ Location: Eastern Europe
♦ Capital: Minsk ♦Currency: Belorussian Ruble
♦ Religion: Eastern Orthodox Christian ♦ Language: Belorussian
♦ British Embassy, Minsk: +375 172 105920/1

Belgium

♦ Population: 10.2 million
♦ Location: Western Europe ♦ Capital: Brussels ♦ Currency: Euro
♦ Religion: Roman Catholic ♦ Language: Flemish and French
♦ British Embassy, Brussels: +32 2 287 6211

Belize

♦ Population: 256,000 ♦ Location: Middle America ♦ Capital: Belmopan
♦ Currency: Belize Dollar ♦ Religion: Roman Catholic ♦ Language: English, Creole, Spanish
♦ British High Commission, Belmopan: +501 822 2146

Benin

♦ Population: 6.5 million ♦ Location: Western Africa
♦ Capital: Porto-Novo (official), Contonou (de facto)
♦ Currency: Franc CFA (Communaute financiere africaine)
♦ Religion: Indigenous beliefs, Christian, Muslim ♦ Language: French
Fon Yoruba
♦ Community Liaison Officer (consular emergencies only): +229 30 32 65;
British Deputy High Commissioner, Lagos, Nigeria: +234 1 2625 930/7
(Visa enquiries)

Country Information | 2

353

Bhutan

- ◆ Population: 2 million ◆ Location: Southern Asia
- ◆ Capital: Thimphu ◆ Currency: Ngultrum
- ◆ Religion: Buddhist, Hindu ◆ Language: Dzongkha
- ◆ UK has no diplomatic representative in Bhutan. Contact British Deputy High Commission, Kolkata (Calcutta), India: +91 33 2288 5172/73/74/75/76

Bolivia

- ◆ Population: 8.3 million ◆ Location: Central South America
- ◆ Capital: La Paz ◆ Currency: Boliviano ◆ Religion: Roman Catholic
- ◆ Language: Spanish, Quechua ◆ British Embassy, La Paz: +591 2 2433424

Bosnia and Herzegovina

- ◆ Population: 3.9 million ◆ Location: South-eastern Europe ◆ Capital: Sarajevo
- ◆ Currency: Dinar ◆ Religion: Muslim, Orthodox, Catholic, Protestant
- ◆ Language: Serbian, Croatian, Bosnian
- ◆ British Embassy, Sarajevo Tel: +387 33 204 781/2/3

Botswana

- ◆ Population: 1.5 million ◆ Location: Southern Africa ◆ Capital: Gaborone
- ◆ Currency: Pula ◆ Religion: Christian, indigenous beliefs
- ◆ Language: Setswana, English
- ◆ British High Commission, Gaborone: +267 395 2481

Brazil

- ◆ Population: 176.3 million ◆ Location: Eastern South America ◆ Capital: Brasilia
- ◆ Currency: Real ◆ Religion: Roman Catholic ◆ Language: Portuguese
- ◆ British Embassy, Brasilia: +55 61 329 2300

Brunei Darussalam

- ◆ Population: 351,000 ◆ Location: South-eastern Asia
- ◆ Capital: Bandar Seri Begawan ◆ Currency: Brunei dollar
- ◆ Religion: Muslim, Buddhist, Christian
- ◆ Language: Malay, English, Chinese
- ◆ British High Commission, Bandar Seri Begawan: +673 2 226001

Bulgaria

- ◆ Population: 8 million ◆ Location: South-eastern Europe ◆ Capital: Sofia
- ◆ Currency: Lev ◆ Religion: Bulgarian Orthodox, Muslim, Roman Catholic, Jewish
- ◆ Language: Bulgarian ◆ British Embassy, Sofia: +359 2 933 9222

Burkina Faso

- ◆ Population: 13 million (UN estimate 2003) ◆ Location: Western Africa
- ◆ Capital: Ouagadougou
- ◆ Currency: Franc CFA ◆ Religion: Muslim, Christian, indigenous beliefs
- ◆ Language: French, tribal languages
- ◆ British Honorary Consul, Ouagadougou: +226 30 73 23 (consular emergencies); British Embassy, Abidjan, Côte d'Ivoire: +225 20 300 803 (visas)

Burma - *see Myanmar*

Burundi

- ◆ Population: 6.85 million ◆ Location: Central Africa ◆ Capital: Bujumbura
- ◆ Currency: Burundi franc ◆ Religion: Roman Catholic, Protestant, indigenous beliefs
- ◆ Language: Kirundi, French, Swahili
- ◆ British Embassy, Liaison Office, Bujumbura: +257 827 602

Cambodia

- Population: 12 million ◆ Location: South-eastern Asia
- Capital: Phnom Penh ◆ Currency: Riel ◆ Religion: Buddhist
- Language: Khmer, French, English
- British Embassy, Phnom Penh : +855 23 427124; +855 23 428295

Cameroon

- Population: 15.8 million ◆ Location: Western Africa ◆ Capital: Yaounde
- Currency: Franc CFA ◆ Religion: indigenous beliefs, Christian, Muslim
- Language: Fench, English
- British High Commission, Yaounde: +237 222 05 45; +237 222 07 96

Canada

- Population: 31.49 million ◆ Location: Northern North America
- Capital: Ottawa ◆ Currency: Canadian Dollar
- Religion: Roman Catholic, United Church ◆ Language: English, French
- British High Commission, Ottawa: +1 613 237 1530

Cape Verde

- Population: 405,000 ◆ Location: Western Africa ◆ Capital: Praia
- Currency: Cape Verdean Escudo ◆ Religion: Roman Catholic
- Language: Portuguese, Creole
- Honorary British Consulate (emergencies only): +238 32 66 25/26/27; refer to British Embassy, Dakar, Senegal: +221 823 7392/9971

Central African Republic

- Population: 3.8 million ◆ Location: Central Africa
- Capital: Bangui ◆ Currency: Franc CFA
- Religion: indigenous beliefs, Protestant, Roman Catholic, Muslim
- Language: French, Sangho, Arabic
- refer to British High Commission, Yaounde: +237 222 05 45; +237 222 07 96

Chad

- Population: 8.7million ◆ Location: Central Africa ◆ Capital: N'djamena
- Currency: Franc CFA ◆ Religion: Muslim, Christian, traditional beliefs
- Language: French, Arabic, Tribal languages
- British Consulate, Ndjamena : +235 841 1102

Chile

- Population: 15.82 million ◆ Location: Southern South America ◆ Capital: Santiago de Chile
- Currency: Peso ◆ Religion: Roman Catholic, Evangelical, Jewish, Muslim
- Language: Spanish, Mapuche, Aymara, Quechua
- British Embassy, Santiago: +56 2 335 5988

China

- Population: 1.29 Billion ◆ Location: Eastern Asia ◆ Capital: Beijing ◆ Currency: Yuan
- Religion: Officially atheist. Daoist (Taoist), Buddhist, Muslim, Christian
- Language: Putonghua, Cantonese ◆ British Embassy, Beijing: +86 10 6532 1961

Colombia

- Population: 44 million ◆ Location: Northern South America ◆ Capital: Bogota
- Currency: Colombian Peso ◆ Religion: Roman Catholic ◆ Language: Spanish
- British Embassy, Bogotá: +57 1 317 6690; +57 1 317 6310/21

2

Country Information | 2

355

Comoros

- ◆ Population: 600,000
- ◆ Location: Southern Africa, group of islands in the Mozambique Channel
- ◆ Capital: Moroni ◆ Currency: Franc CFA
- ◆ Religion: Sunni Muslim, Roman Catholic ◆Language: French, Arabic
- ◆ British Consulate, Moroni: +269 733182 (staff resident in Madagascar)

Congo

- ◆ Population: 2.9 million ◆ Location: Western Africa, ◆ Capital: Kinshasa
- ◆ Currency: Congolese franc ◆ Religion: Christian, animist, Muslim
- ◆ Language: French (official), Lingala and Monokutuba (trade languages), plus many local languages and dialects
- ◆ British Honorary Consulate (limited service only): +242 88 44904; refer to Bristish Embassy, Kinshasa, Democratic Republic of Congo: +243 98 169 100/200, +243 98337007(emergencies only)

Congo, Democratic Republic of the

- ◆ Population: 58.78 million Location: Central Africa
- ◆ Capital: Brazzaville ◆ Currency: CFA franc
- ◆ Religion: Roman Catholic, Protestant, Kimbanguist, Muslim, indigenous beliefs
- ◆ Language: French (official), Lingala (trade language), Kingwana, Kikongo, Tshiluba
- ◆ British Embassy, Kinshasa: +243 98 169 100/200, +243 98337007(emergencies only)

Costa Rica

- ◆ Population: 4.2 million ◆ Location: Central America
- ◆ Capital: San Jose ◆ Currency: Costa Rican colon CRC
- ◆ Religion: Roman Catholic, Evangelical, Protestant
- ◆ Language: Spanish (official), English spoken around Puerto Limo
- ◆ British Embassy, San Jose: +506 258 2025

Côte d'Ivoire

- ◆ Population: 16.8 million ◆ Location: Western Africa
- ◆ Capital: Yamoussoukro ◆ Currency: CFA franc
- ◆ Religion: Christian, Muslim, indigenous. Most foreigners (migratory workers) are Muslim
- ◆ Language: French (official), Dioula plus up to 60 other native dialects
- ◆ British Embassy, Abidjan: +225 20 300 800; +225 20 300 803 (Visa/consular)

Croatia

- ◆ Population: 4.3 million ◆ Location: South-eastern Europe
- ◆ Capital: Zagreb ◆ Currency: Kuna
- ◆ Religion: Christian (mostly Roman Catholic), Orthodox, Muslim
- ◆ Language: Croatian 96%, other 4% (incl Italian, Hungarian, Czech, Slovak, & German)
- ◆ British Embassy, Zagreb: +385 1 6009 100; +385 1 6009 122 (Visa and Consular)

Cuba

- ◆ Population: 11.2 million ◆ Location: Caribbean ◆ Capital: Havana
- ◆ Currency: Cuban peso
- ◆ Religion: Roman Catholic, Santeria (Afro-Cuban), Protestant
- ◆ Language: Spanish
- ◆ British Embassy, Havana: +53 7 204 1771

Cyprus

- Population: 754,100 ◆ Location: Eastern Mediterranean
- Capital: Nicosia ◆ Currency: Cyprus pound
- Religion: Greek Orthodox, Muslim, Maronite, Armenian Apostolic
- Language: Greek, Turkish, English
- British High Commission, Nicosia: ++357 22 861125 (information); +357 22 861200 (Consular)

Czech Republic

- Population: 10.2 million ◆ Location: Central Europe ◆ Capital: Prague
- Currency: Czech koruna ◆ Religion: Atheist, Roman Catholic, Protestant, Orthodox
- Language: Czech ◆ British Embassy, Prague: +420 2 5740 2111

Denmark

- Population: 5.3 million ◆ Location: Northern Europe
- Capital: Copenhagen ◆ Currency: Danish krone
- Religion: Evangelical Lutheran, Protestant, Roman Catholic, Muslim
- Language: Danish, Faroese, Greenlandic (an Inuit dialect), German (small minority)
- British Embassy, Copenhagen: +45 35 44 52 00

Djibouti

- Population: 740,000 ◆ Location: Eastern Africa ◆ Capital: Djibouti
- Currency: Djiboutian franc ◆ Religion: Muslim, Christian
- Language: French (official), Arabic (official), Somali, Afar
- British Consulate, Djibouti: +253 3 85007 (staff resident in Addis Ababa)

Dominica, Commonwealth of

- Population: 70,000 ◆ Location: Caribbean
- Capital: Roseau ◆ Currency: East Caribbean dollar
- Religion: Roman Catholic, Protestant
- Language: English (official), French patois
- British High Commission, Roseau: +246 430 7800

Dominican Republic

- Population: 8.7 million ◆ Location: Caribbean ◆ Capital: Santo Domingo
- Currency: Dominican peso ◆ Religion: Roman Catholic ◆ Language: Spanish
- British Embassy, Santo Domingo: +1 809 472 7111; +1 809 399 7599 (out of hours emergencies)

East Timor - *see Timor-Leste*

Ecuador

- Population: 12.65 million ◆ Location: Western South America
- Capital: Quito ◆ Currency: US dollar ◆ Religion: Roman Catholic
- Language: Spanish (official), Amerindian languages (especially Quechua)
- British Embassy, Quito: +593 2 2970 800/1

Egypt

- Population: 70.7 million ◆ Location: Northern Africa
- Capital: Cairo ◆ Currency: Egyptian pound
- Religion: Muslim (mostly Sunni), Coptic Christian
- Language: Arabic (official), English and French understood by the educated
- British Embassy, Cairo: +20 2 794 08 50/52/58

Country Information | 2

357

El Salvador

- Population: 6.4 million ◆ Location: Middle America ◆ Capital: San Salvador
- Currency: US dollar ◆ Religion: Roman Catholic
- Language: Spanish, Nahua (among some Amerindians)
- British Embassy, San Salvador closed in July 2003; refer to Bristish Embassy, Guatemala City, Guatemala: +502 367 54 25/26/27/28/29

Equatorial Guinea

- Population: 498,000 ◆ Location: Western Africa ◆ Capital: Malabo
- Currency: CFA franc
- Religion: Christian (predominantly Roman Catholic), indigenous religions
- Language: Spanish (official), French (official), pidgin English, Fang, Bubi, Ibo
- Refer to British High Commission, Yaounde: +237 222 05 45; +237 222 07 96

Eritrea

- Population: 3.3 million ◆ Location: Eastern Africa ◆ Capital: Asmara
- Currency: Nafka ◆ Religion: Christian (mostly in the central highlands), Muslim (mostly outside the highlands)
- Language: Tigrinya, Tigre Arabic, English
- British Embassy, Asmara: +291 1 12 01 45

Estonia

- Population: 1.4 million ◆ Location: Eastern Europe ◆ Capital: Tallinn
- Currency: Estonian kroon ◆ Religion: Evangelical Lutheran, Orthodox Christian
- Language: Estonian (official), Russian, Ukrainian, Finnish, other
- British Embassy, Tallinn: +372 667 4700

Ethiopia

- Population: 70.7 million ◆ Location: Eastern Africa ◆ Capital: Addis Ababa
- Currency: birr ◆ Religion: Muslim, Orthodox Christian, animist
- Language: Amharic, Tigrinya, Oromigna, Guaragigna, Somali, Arabic, other local languages, English (major foreign language taught in schools)
- British Embassy, Addis Ababa: +251 1 612354

Fiji

- Population: 856,000 ◆ Location: Oceania ◆ Capital: Suva
- Currency: Fijian dollar ◆ Religion: Christian, Hindu, Muslim
- Language: English (official), Fijian, Hindustani
- British High Commission, Suva: +679 3229 100

Finland

- Population: 5.2 million ◆ Location: Northern Europe ◆ Capital: Helsinki
- Currency: euro ◆ Religion: Evangelical Lutheran, Russian Orthodox
- Language: Finnish 93% (official), Swedish 6% (official), small Sami- and Russian-speaking minorities ◆ British Embassy, Helsinki: +358 09 2286 5100

France

- Population: 61.2 million ◆ Location: Western Europe ◆ Capital: Paris
- Currency: euro ◆ Religion: Christian (predominantly Roman Catholic), Muslim, Jewish
- Language: French ◆ British Embassy, Paris: +33 1 44 51 31 00

Gabon

- ◆ Population: 1.2 million ◆ Location: Western Africa ◆ Capital: Libreville
- ◆ Currency: CFA franc ◆ Religion: Christian, animist, Muslim
- ◆ Language: French (official), Fang, Myene, Nzebi, Bapounou/Eschira, Bandjabi
- ◆ British Consulate, Libreville: +241 762200 (all staff resident at Yaounde, Cameroon)

Gambia

- ◆ Population: 1.4 million ◆ Location: Western Africa ◆ Capital: Banjul
- ◆ Currency: dalasi ◆ Religion: Muslim, Christian, indigenous beliefs
- ◆ Language: English (official), Mandinka, Wolof, Fula, indigenous vernaculars
- ◆ British High Commission, Banjul: +220 495133/4; +220 497590 (Visa)

Georgia

- ◆ Population: 4.4 million ◆ Location: South-western Asia
- ◆ Capital: Tbilisi ◆ Currency: lari
- ◆ Religion: Georgian Orthodox, Muslim, Russian Orthodox, Armenian Apostolic
- ◆ Language: Georgian 71% (official), Russian 9%, Armenian 7%, Azeri 6%
- ◆ British Embassy, Tbilisi: +995 32 955 497; +995 32 998 447

Germany

- ◆ Population: 83.2 million ◆ Location: Central Europe
- ◆ Capital: Berlin ◆ Currency: euro
- ◆ Religion: Protestant, Roman Catholic, Muslim,
- ◆ Language: German ◆ British Embassy, Berlin: +49 30 20457 0

Ghana

- ◆ Population: 20.2 million ◆ Location: Western Africa ◆ Capital: Accra
- ◆ Currency: cedi ◆ Religion: Christian, Muslim, indigenous beliefs
- ◆ Language: English (official), African languages (incl Akan, Moshi-Dagomba, Ewe, and Ga)
- ◆ British High Commission, Accra: +233 21 221 665; +233 21 7010 721 (Visa)

Greece

- ◆ Population: 10.6 million ◆ Location: Southern Europe
- ◆ Capital: Athens ◆ Currency: euro
- ◆ Religion: Greek Orthodox, Muslim
- ◆ Language: Greek 99% (official), English, French
- ◆ British Embassy, Athens: +30 210 727 2600

Grenada

- ◆ Population: 89,000 ◆ Location: Caribbean ◆ Capital: St George's
- ◆ Currency: East Caribbean dollar ◆ Religion: Roman Catholic, Protestant
- ◆ Language: English (official), French patois
- ◆ British High Commission, St George's: +1 473 440 3222/3536

Guatemala

- ◆ Population: 11.23 million ◆ Location: Central America
- ◆ Capital: Guatemala ◆ Currency: quetzal
- ◆ Religion: Roman Catholic, Protestant, indigenous Mayan beliefs
- ◆ Language: Spanish 60%, Amerindian languages 40% (23 officially recognized including Quiche, Cakchiquel, Kekchi, Mam, Garifuna, and Xinca)
- ◆ British Embassy, Guatemala City: +502 367 54 25/26/27/28/29

Country Information | 2

2

359

Guinea

- Population: 8.5 million ◆ Location: Western Africa
- Capital: Conakry ◆ Currency: Guinean franc
- Religion: Muslim, Christian, indigenous beliefs
- Language: French (official), each ethnic group has its own language
- British Embassy, Conakry: +224 45 58 07; +224 46 16 80

Guinea-Bissau

- Population: 1.3 million ◆ Location: Western Africa
- Capital: Bissau ◆ Currency: CFA franc
- Religion: indigenous beliefs, Muslim, Christian
- Language: Portuguese (official), Crioulo, African languages
- Honorary British Consulate (limited emergency service): +245 20 12 24/16; refer to British Embassy, Dakar, Senegal: +221 823 7392/9971

Guyana

- Population: 749,000 ◆ Location: Northern South America ◆ Capital: Georgetown
- Currency: Guyanese dollar ◆ Religion: Christian, Hindu, Muslim
- Language: English, Amerindian dialects, Creole, Hindi, Urdu
- British High Commission, Georgetown: +592 226 58 81/82/83/84

Haiti

- Population: 8.3 million ◆ Location: Caribbean, ◆ Capital: Port-au-Prince
- Currency: gourde ◆ Religion: Roman Catholic, Protestant
- Language: French (official), Creole (official)
- British Consulate, Port-au-Prince: +509 257 3969 (staff resident in Kingston)

Honduras

- Population: 6.9 million ◆ Location: Middle America ◆ Capital: Tegucigalpa
- Currency: lempira ◆ Religion: Christian (predominantly Roman Catholic)
- Language: Spanish, Amerindian dialects
- British Embassy, Tegucigalpa closed November 2003; refer to British Embassy, Guatemala City: +502 367 54 25/26/27/28/29
  Hong Kong (The Hong Kong Special Administration of China)
- Population: 6.8 million ◆ Location: Eastern Asia
- Currency: Hong Kong dollar ◆ Religion: Buddhism, Taoism, Christianity, Islam, Hindu, Sikh, Jewish ◆ Language: Chinese (Cantonese), English
- British Consulate General, Hong Kong: ++852 2901 3000

Hungary

- Population: 10 million ◆ Location: Central Europe ◆ Capital: Budapest
- Currency: forint ◆ Religion: Roman Catholic, Calvinist, Lutheran
- Language: Hungarian ◆ British Embassy, Budapest: +36 1 266 2888

Iceland

- Population: 279,000 ◆ Location: Northern Europe
- Capital: Reykjavik ◆ Currency: Icelandic krona
- Religion: Evangelical Lutheran, Protestant, Roman Catholic
- Language: Icelandic, English, Nordic languages, German widely spoken
- British Embassy, Reykjavik: +354 550 5100

India

- Population: 1,049.7 million ◆ Location: Southern Asia ◆ Capital: New Delhi
- Currency: Indian rupee ◆ Religion: Hindu, Muslim, Christian, Sikh, Buddhist, Jain, Parsi
- Language: Hindi (written in Devanagari script; national language), 18 main and regional official state languages (incl Bengali, Marathi, Urdu, Gujarati, Bihari, Oriya, Telegu, Tamil & Punjabi), plus 24 languages, 720 dialects and 23 tribal languags (according to FCO), English (officially an associate language, used particularly for political, and commercial communication)
- British High Commission, New Delhi: +91 11 2687 2161

Indonesia

- Population: 214 million estimate ◆ Location: South-eastern Asia
- Capital: Jakarta ◆ Currency: Indonesian rupiah
- Religion: Muslim, Protestant, Roman Catholic, Hindu, Buddhist
- Language: Bahasa Indonesia (official, modified form of Malay), English, Dutch, local dialects (mostly Javanese)
- British Embassy, Jakarta: +62 21 315 6264; +62 811 802435 (Out of hours emergencies)

Iran

- Population: 70 million ◆ Location: Middle East
- Capital: Tehran ◆ Currency: Iranian rial
- Religion: Shi'a Muslim, Sunni Muslim, Zoroastrian, Jewish, Christian, and Baha'i
- Language: Persian (Farsi), Azeri (northwest around Tabriz), Kurdish (west), Arabic, Luri, Baluchi
- British Embassy, Tehran: +98 21 67050 11/19

Iraq

- Population: 24 million ◆ Location: Middle East
- Capital: Baghdad ◆ Currency: Iraqi dinar
- Religion: Muslim (Shi'a 60%-65%, Sunni 32%-37%), Christian
- Language: Arabic, Kurdish (official in Kurdish regions), Assyrian, Armenian

Ireland

- Population: 3.9 million ◆ Location: Western Europe
- Capital: Dublin ◆ Currency: euro ◆ Religion: Roman Catholic, Church of Ireland, Presbyterian, Methodist, Jewish
- Language: Irish (Gaelic), English ◆ British Embassy, Dublin: ++353 205 3700

Israel

- Population: 6.7 million ◆ Location: Middle East
- Capital: Jerusalem ◆ Currency: new Israeli shekel
- Religion: Jewish, Muslim (mostly Sunni Muslim), Christian
- Language: Hebrew (official), Arabic used officially for Arab minority, English
- British Embassy, Tel Aviv: +972 3 725 1222
  British Consulate-General, Jerusalem: +2 541 4100

Italy

- Population: 57.7 million ◆ Location: Southern Europe
- Capital: Rome ◆ Currency: euro
- Religion: Christian (predominantly Roman Catholic), Jewish, Muslim

Country Information | 2

361

- Language: Italian (official), German (predominant in Trentino-Alto Adige region), French (minority language in Valle d'Aosta region), Slovene (minority language in Trieste-Gorizia area)
- British Embassy, Rome: +39 06 4220 0001; +39 06 4220 2603 (out of hours)

Ivory Coast - *see Côte d'Ivoire*

Jamaica

- Population: 2.7 million ♦ Location: Caribbean ♦ Capital: Kingston
- Currency: Jamaican dollar ♦ Religion: Protestant, Roman Catholic, spiritual cults
- Language: English, patois English
- British High Commission, Kingston: +1 876 510 0700

Japan

- Population: 127 million ♦ Location: Eastern Asia ♦ Capital: Tokyo
- Currency: yen ♦ Religion: Shinto, Buddhist, Christian
- Language: Japanese ♦ British Embassy, Tokyo: +81 3 5211 1100

Jordan

- Population: 5.2 million ♦ Location: Middle East ♦ Capital: Amman
- Currency: Jordanian dinar ♦ Religion: Sunni Muslim, Christian
- Language: Arabic (official), English ♦ British Embassy, Amman: +962 6 592 3100

Kazakhstan

- Population: 16.7 million ♦ Location: Central Asia ♦ Capital: Astana
- Currency: tenge ♦ Religion: Muslim, Russian Orthodox, Protestant
- Language: Kazakh (Qazaq, state language), Russian (official, used in everyday business, designated the 'language of interethnic communication')
- British Embassy, Almaty: +7 573 150 2200 ; +7 3272 508280 (Visa / Consular)

Kenya

- Population: 31 million ♦ Location: Eastern Africa
- Capital: Nairobi ♦ Currency: Kenyan shilling
- Religion: Protestant, Roman Catholic, indigenous beliefs, Muslim
- Language: English (official), Kiswahili, numerous indigenous languages
- British High Commission, Nairobi: +254 20 284 4000

Kiribati

- Population: 96,000 ♦ Location: Oceania
- Capital: Tarawa ♦ Currency: Australian dollar
- ♦ Religion: Roman Catholic, Protestant (Congregational), Seventh-Day Adventist, Muslim, Baha'i, Latter-day Saints, Church of God
- Language: I-Kiribati, English (official) ♦ British High Commission, Tarawa: +686 22501

Korea, DPR (North Korea)

- Population: 22.2 million ♦ Location: Eastern Asia
- Capital: Pyongyang ♦ Currency: North Korean won
- Religion: Buddhist and Confucianist, Christian, Chondogyo ♦ Language: Korean
- British Embassy, Pyongyang: +850 2 381 7980/4 (International); 02 382 7980/2 (Local dialling); +850 2 381 7993 (Out of hours emergency)

Korea, Republic of (South Korea)

- Population: 48.3 million ◆ Location: Eastern Asia
- Capital: Seoul ◆ Currency: South Korean won
- Religion: Christian, Buddhist, Confucianist, Shamanist, Chondogyo
- Language: Korean, English ◆ British Embassy, Seoul: +82 2 3210 5500

Kuwait

- Population: 2.1 million ◆ Location: Middle East ◆ Capital: Kuwait
- Currency: Kuwaiti dinar ◆ Religion: Muslim (Sunni 70%, Shi'a 30%), Christian, Hindu, Parsi
- Language: Arabic (official), English widely spoken
- British Embassy, Kuwait: +965 240 3334/5/6

Kyrgyzstan

- Population: 4.8 million ◆ Location: Central Asia ◆ Capital: Bishkek
- Currency: Kyrgyzstani som ◆ Religion: Muslim, Russian Orthodox
- Language: Kyrgyz – official language, Russian – official language
- British Consulate, Bishkek: +996 312 680 815

Laos

- Population: 5.5 million ◆ Location: Southeastern Asia ◆ Capital: Vientiane
- Currency: kip ◆ Religion: Buddhist, animist, Christian
- Language: Lao (official), French, English, and various ethnic languages
- British Embassy, Vientiane: +856 21 413606

Latvia

- Population: 2.4 million ◆ Location: Eastern Europe ◆ Capital: Riga
- Currency: Latvian lat ◆ Religion: Lutheran, Roman Catholic, Russian Orthodox
- Language: Latvian, Lithuanian, Russian ◆ British Embassy, Riga: +371 777 4700

Lebanon

- Population: 3.7 million ◆ Location: Middle East ◆ Capital: Beirut
- Currency: Lebanese pound ◆ Religion: Muslim (Shi'a, Sunni, Druze, Isma'ilite, Alawite or Nusayri), Christian (Orthodox Christian, Catholic, Protestant), Jewish
- Language: Arabic (official), French, English, Armenian
- British Embassy, Beirut: +961 1 990 400; +961 4 417 007 (24 hours)

Lesotho

- Population: 1.9 million ◆ Location: Southern Africa ◆ Capital: Maseru
- Currency: loti ◆ Religion: Christian, indigenous beliefs
- Language: Sesotho (southern Sotho), English (official), Zulu, Xhosa
- British High Commission, Maseru: +266 22313961

Liberia

- Population: 3.36 million estimate ◆ Location: Western Africa ◆ Capital: Monrovia
- Currency: Liberian dollar ◆ Religion: indigenous beliefs, Christian, Muslim
- Language: English (official), plus 16 indigenous languages
- British Honorary Consulate, Monrovia: +231 226 056; +37747 651 6973 (mobile)

Libya

- Population: 5.4 million ◆ Location: Northern Africa ◆ Capital: Tripoli
- Currency: Libyan dinar ◆ Religion: Sunni Muslim
- Language: Arabic, (Italian and English understood in major cities)
- British Embassy, Tripoli: +218 21 335 1084

Country Information | 2

363

Liechtenstein

- Population: 34,000 ◆ Location: Central Europe ◆ Capital: Vaduz
- Currency: Swiss franc ◆ Religion: Christian (predominantly Roman Catholic)
- Language: German (official), Alemannic dialect ◆ British Embassy, Vaduz (staff reside in Berne, Switzerland): +41 31 359 7700

Lithuania

- Population: 3.6 million ◆ Location: Eastern Europe ◆ Capital: Vilnius
- Currency: litasl ◆ Religion: Roman Catholic (primarily), Lutheran, Russian Orthodox, Protestant, Evangelical Christian Baptist, Muslim, Jewish
- Language: Lithuanian (official), Polish, Russian
- British Embassy, Vilnius: +370 5 246 29 00

Luxembourg

- Population: 451,000 ◆ Location: Central Europe ◆ Capital: Luxembourg
- Currency: euro ◆ Religion: Roman Catholic, Protestant, Jewish, Muslim
- Language: Luxembourgish, German, French
- British Embassy, Luxembourg: + 22 98 64; +021 186 653 (out of hours duty officer)

Macedonia

- Population: 2 million ◆ Location: Eastern Europe ◆ Capital: Skopje
- Currency: Macedonian denar ◆ Religion: Orthodox, Muslim
- Language: Macedonian, Albanian, Turkish, Serbian
- British Embassy, Skopje: + 389 2 3299 299

Madagascar

- Population: 17 million ◆ Location: Southern Africa ◆ Capital: Antananarivo
- Currency: Malagasy franc ◆ Religion: indigenous beliefs, Christian, Muslim
- Language: French (official), Malagasy (official)
- British Embassy, Antananarivo: +261 20 2249 378/379/380

Malawi

- Population: 11.65 million ◆ Location: Southern Africa ◆ Capital: Lilongwe
- Currency: Malawian kwacha ◆ Religion: Protestant, Roman Catholic, Muslim, indigenous beliefs ◆ Language: English (official), Chichewa (official)
- British High Commission, liongwe: +265 1 772 400; +265 1 772 550

Malaysia

- Population: 25.7 million ◆ Location: South-eastern Asia
- Capital: Kuala Lumpur ◆ Currency: ringgit
- Religion: Muslim, Buddhist, Daoist, Hindu, Christian, Sikh; Shamanism (East Malaysia)
- Language: Bahasa Melayu (official), English, Chinese dialects (Cantonese, Mandarin, Hokkien, Hakka, Hainan, Foochow), Tamil, Telugu, Malayalam, Panjabi, Thai, plus several indigenous languages spoken in East Malaysia, (incl Iban & Kadazan)
- British High Commission, Kuala Lumpur: +60 3 2170 2200

Maldives

- Population: 320,200 ◆ Location: Southern Asia ◆ Capital: Male ◆Currency: rufiyaa ◆ Religion: Sunni Muslim ◆ Language: Maldivian Dhivehi, English
- British High Commission, Malé (staff reside in Colombo, Sri Lanka): +94 11 2437336

Mali

- Population: 11.3 million ◆ Location: Western Africa ◆ Capital: Bamako
- Currency: CFA franc ◆ Religion: Muslim, indigenous beliefs, Christian
- Language: French (official), Bambara, numerous African languages
- British Embassy Liaison Office, Bamako: +223 277 46 37

Malta

- Population: 400,000 ◆ Location: Southern Europe ◆ Capital: Valletta
- Currency: Maltese lira ◆ Religion: Roman Catholic
- Language: Maltese (official), English (official)
- British High Commission, Valletta: +356 2323 0000

Marshall Islands

- Population: 70,800 ◆ Location: Oceania, atolls and reefs in the North Pacific Ocean
- Capital: Majuro ◆ Currency: US dollar ◆ Religion: Christian (mostly Protestant)
- Language: English, 2 major Marshallese dialects, Japanese
- British Embassy, Majuro (staff resident in Suva, Fiji): +679 322 9100

Mauritania

- Population: 2.8 million ◆ Location: Northern Africa
- Capital: Nouakchott ◆ Currency: euro
- Religion: Hassaniya Arabic (official), Pulaar, Soninke, Wolof (official), French
- Language: Muslim 100% ◆ British Honorary Consul, Nouakchott: +222 525 83 31

Mauritius

- Population: 1.2 million ◆ Location: Southern Africa ◆ Capital: Port Louis
- Currency: ouguiya ◆ Religion: Hinduism, Christian, Muslim
- Language: English (official), Creole, French (official), Hindi, Urdu, Hakka, Bhojpuri
- British High Commission, Port Louis: +230 202 9400;
  +230 252 8006 (Duty Officer)

Mexico

- Population: 103.4 million ◆ Location: Central America
- Capital: Mexico (Distrito Federal) ◆ Currency: Mexican peso
- Religion: Christian (predominantly Roman Catholic)
- Language: Spanish, various Mayan, Nahuatl, and other regional indigenous languages
- British Embassy, Mexico City: +52 55 5242 8500

Moldova

- Population: 4.4 million ◆ Location: Eastern Europe ◆ Capital: Chisinau
- Currency: Moldovan leu ◆ Religion: Eastern Orthodox, Jewish, Baptist
- Language: Moldovan (very similar to Romanian), Russian (official), Gagauz
  (a Turkish dialect) Ukranian
- British Embassy, Chisnau (emergency services only): +373 22 38 991

Monaco

- Population: 32,000 ◆ Location: Western Europe ◆ Capital: Monaco ◆ Currency: euro
- Religion: Roman Catholic ◆ Language: French (official), English, Italian, Monegasque
- British Consulate, Monaco: +377 93 50 99 66

Country Information | 2

365

Mongolia

- Population: 2.7 million ◆ Location: Northern Asia
- Capital: Ulaanbaatar◆ Currency: togrog/tugrik
- Religion: Tibetan Buddhist Lamaism, Muslim, Shamanism, and Christian
- Language: Khalkha Mongol 90%, Turkic, Russian (1999)
- British Embassy, Ulaanbaatar: +976 11 458 133

Morocco

- Population: 31.2 million ◆ Location: Northern Africa ◆ Capital: Rabat
- Currency: Moroccan dirham ◆ Religion: Roman Catholic
- Language: Arabic (official), Berber dialects, French (commerce and government)
- British Embassy, Rabat: +212 0 37 72 9696

Mozambique

- Population: 18.4 million ◆ Location: Southern Africa ◆ Capital: Maputo
- Currency: metical ◆ Religion: indigenous beliefs, Christian, Muslim
- Language: Portuguese (official), indigenous dialects
- British High Commission, Maputo: +258 1 320 111/2/5/6/7

Myanmar (formerly Burma)

- Population: 50 million ◆ Location: Northern Africa ◆ Capital: Rangoon
- Currency: Kyat ◆ Religion: Buddhism (offical), Christianity, Islam, Animist
- Language: Burmese ◆ British Embassy, Rangoon: +95 1 370866/7

Namibia

- Population: 1.8 million ◆ Location: Southern Africa ◆ Capital: Windhoek
- Currency: Namibian dollar ◆ Religion: Christian
- Language: English (official), Afrikaans, German
- British Embassy, Windhoek: +264 61 274800

Nauru

- Population: 12,300 ◆ Location: Oceania
- Capital: Yaren District no official capital ◆ Currency: Australian dollar
- Religion: Christian (two-thirds Protestant, one-third Roman Catholic)
- Language: Nauruan (official), English (commerce and government, widely understood)
- British Embassy, Nauru (staff resident in Suva, Fiji): +679 322 9100

Nepal

- Population: 25.9 million ◆ Location: Southern Asia ◆ Capital: Kathmandu
- Currency: Nepalese rupee ◆ Religion: Hinduism, Buddhism, Islam
- Language: Nepali (official), Newari (mainly in Kathmandu), Tibetan languages (mainly hill areas), Indian languages (mainly Terai areas)
- British Embassy, Kathmandu: +977 1 4410583; +977 1 4411281

The Netherlands

- Population: 16.2 million ◆ Location: Europe ◆ Capital: Amsterdam
- Currency: euro ◆ Religion: Roman Catholic, Protestant, Muslim
- Language: Dutch ◆ British Embassy, The Hague: +31 (0) 70 4270 427

New Zealand

- Population: 3.9 million ◆ Location: Oceania ◆ Capital: Wellington
- Currency: New Zealand dollar ◆ Religion: Anglican, Presbyterian, Roman Catholic, Methodist, Baptist

visit: www.gap-year.com

- Language: English (official), Maori (official)
- British High Commission, Wellington: +64 4 924 2888

Nicaragua

- Population: 5 million ◆ Location: Central America ◆ Capital: Managua
- Currency: gold cordoba ◆ Religion: Roman Catholic, Protestant
- Language: Spanish (official) ◆ British Embassy, Managua: +505 2 780 014

Niger

- Population: 11.3 million ◆ Location: Western Africa ◆ Capital: Niamey
- Currency: CFA franc ◆ Religion: Muslim, indigenous beliefs, Christian
- Language: French (official), Hausa, Djerma
- British Consulate, Niamey: +227 725 046

Nigeria

- Population: 129.9 million ◆ Location: Western Africa ◆ Capital: Abuja
- Currency: naira ◆ Religion: Muslim, Christian, indigenous beliefs
- Language: English (official), Hausa, Yoruba, Igbo (Ibo), Fulani
- British High Commission, Abuja: +234 9 413 2010/2011

Norway

- Population: 4.5 million ◆ Location: Northern Europe
- Capital: Oslo ◆ Currency: Norwegian krone
- Religion: Evangelical Lutheran (state church), Protestant, Roman Catholic
- Language: Norwegian (official) ◆ British Embassy, Oslo: +47 23 13 27 00

Oman

- Population: 2.7 million ◆ Location: Northern Europe
- Capital: Muscat ◆ Currency: Omani rial
- Religion: Ibadhi Muslim, Sunni Muslim, Shi'a Muslim, Hindu
- Language: Arabic (official), English, Baluchi, Urdu, Indian dialects
- British Embassy, Muscat: +968 609000; +968 9200865 (out of hours emergencies)

Pakistan

- Population: 147.7 million ◆ Location: Southern Asia ◆ Capital: Islamabad
- Currency: Pakistani rupee ◆ Religion: Muslim (Sunni, Shi'a), Christian, Hindu
- Language: Punjabi, Sindhi, Pashtun, Urdu, Balochi, English (official)
- British High Commission, Islamabad: +92 51 220 6071/5; +92 51 2822 131/5

Palestine (Palestinian National Authority)

- Population: 3.5 million ◆ Location: Middle East
- Currency: New Israeli Shekel, Jordanian Dinar (West Bank Only)
- Religion: Muslim, Christian ◆ Language: Arabic, English
- British-Consulate General: +972 (02) 541 4100 (24-hour switchboard)

Panama

- Population: 2.9 million ◆ Location: Central America ◆ Capital: Panama
- Currency: balboa ◆ Religion: Roman Catholic, Protestant
- Language: Spanish (official), English ◆ British Embassy, Panama City: +507 269 0866

Papua New Guinea

- Population: 5,7 million ◆ Location: South-eastern Asia,
- Capital: Port Moresby ◆ Currency: kina

Country Information | 2

367

- Religion: Christian according to its constitution, Roman Catholic, Lutheran, Presbyterian, Methodist, London Missionary Society, Anglican, Evangelical Alliance, Seventh-Day Adventist
- Language: English, Pidgin English, Hiri Motu
- British High Commission, Port Moresby: +675 325 1677; +675 683 1627 (mobile - emergencies only)

Paraguay

- Population: 5.9 million ◆ Location: Central South America
- Capital: Asuncion ◆ Currency: guarani ◆ Religion: Roman Catholic, Mennonite
- Language: Spanish (official), Guarani (official)
- British Embassy, Asunción: +595 21 612 611

Peru

- Population: 27.14 million ◆ Location: Western South America
- Capital: Lima ◆ Currency: nuevo sol ◆ Religion: Roman Catholic
- Language: Spanish (official), Quechua (official), Aymara
- British Embassy, Lima: +51 1 617 3000

Philippines

- Population: 84.5 million ◆ Location: South-eastern Asia ◆ Capital: Manila
- Currency: Philippine peso ◆ Religion: Roman Catholic, Protestant, Muslim, Buddhist
- Language: Filipino (official), English (official), plus eight major dialects
- British Embassy, Manila: +63 2 816 7116

Poland

- Population: 38.6 million ◆ Location: Central Europe ◆ Capital: Warsaw
- Currency: zloty ◆ Religion: Roman Catholic, Eastern Orthodox, Protestant
- Language: Polish ◆ British Embassy, Warsaw: +48 22 625 3030

Portugal

- Population: 10.1 million ◆ Location: South-western Europe ◆ Capital: Lisbon
- Currency: euro ◆ Religion: Roman Catholic, Protestant
- Language: Portuguese ◆ British Embassy, Lisbon: +351 21 392 4000

Qatar

- Population: 793,000 ◆ Location: Middle East ◆ Capital: Doha
- Currency: Qatari riall ◆ Religion: Muslim ◆ Language: Arabic (official), English
- British Embassy, Doha: +974 442 1991

Romania

- Population: 22.3 million ◆ Location: Southeastern Europe ◆ Capital: Bucharest
- Currency: leu ◆ Religion: Eastern Orthodox, Protestant, Catholic, Muslim
- Language: Romanian (official), Hungarian, German
- British Embassy, Bucharest: +40 21 201 7200

Russia

- Population: 144.9 million ◆ Location: Northern Asia ◆ Capital: Moscow
- Currency: Russian ruble ◆ Religion: Russian Orthodox, Muslim
- Language: Russian ◆ British Embassy, Moscow: +7 095 956 7200

Rwanda

- Population: 7.4 million ◆ Location: Central Africa
- Capital: Kigali ◆ Currency: Rwandan franc
- Religion: Roman Catholic, Protestant, Adventist, Muslim, indigenous beliefs

- Language: Kinyarwanda (official; universal Bantu vernacular), French (official), English (official), Kiswahili (Swahili; used in commercial centres)
- British Embassy, Kigali: +250 84098; +250 85771

Saint Lucia

- Population: 160,000 ◆ Location: Caribbean ◆ Capital: Castries
- Currency: East Caribbean dollar ◆ Religion: Roman Catholic, Anglican, Protestant
- Language: English (official), French patois
- British High Commission, Castries: +1 758 45 22484/5

Saint Vincent and the Grenadines

- Population: 116,400
- Location: Caribbean, islands between Caribbean Sea and North Atlantic Ocean
- Capital: Kingstown ◆ Currency: East Caribbean dollar
- Religion: Anglican, Methodist, Roman Catholic, Seventh Day Adventist, Hindu
- Language: English ◆ British Embassy, Kingstown: +784 457 1701

Samoa

- Population: 175,000 ◆ Location: Oceania, islands in the South Pacific Ocean
- Capital: Apia ◆ Currency: Tala ◆ Religion: Roman Catholic, Methodist, Mormon
- Language: Samoan, English ◆ British High Commission, Apia: +64 4 924 2888

São Tomé & Príncipe

- Population: 176,000 ◆ Location: Western Africa ◆ Capital: Sao Tomé
- Currency: dobra ◆ Religion: Christian
- Language: Portuguese, Lungwa Santomé, regional dialects
- British Consulate, Sao Tomé: +239 12 21026/7

Saudi Arabia

- Population: 24.3 million ◆ Location: Middle East ◆ Capital: Riyadh
- Currency: Saudi Riyal ◆ Religion: Muslim (Sunni, Shia). The public practice of any other religion is forbidden
- Language: Arabic, English ◆ British Embassy, Riyadh: +966 (0) 1 488 0077

Senegal

- Population: 10.6 million ◆ Location: Western Africa
- Capital: Dakar ◆ Currency: CFA franc
- Religion: Muslim, indigenous beliefs, Christian (mostly Roman Catholic)
- Language: French (official), Wolof, Pulaar, Jola, Mandinka
- British Embassy, Dakar: +221 823 7392

Serbia & Montenegro (formerly Federal Republic of Yugoslavia)

- Population: 10 million ◆ Location: South-eastern Europe
- Capital: Belgrade (Serbia), Podgorica (Montenegro)
- Currency: dinar (Serbia), euro (Montenegro)
- Religion: Serbian Orthodox, Islam, Roman Catholic
- Language: Serbian, Albanian, Hungarian
- British Embassy, Belgrade: +381 11 2645 055

Seychelles

- Population: 80,400 ◆ Location: Eastern Africa, group of islands in the Indian Ocean
- Capital: Victoria ◆Currency: Seychelles rupee
- Religion: Christian (predominantly Roman Catholic)
- Language: English, French, Creole ◆ British High Commission: +248 283 666

Country Information | 2

369

Sierra Leone

- Population: 4.6 million ◆ Location: Western Africa ◆ Capital: Freetown
- Currency: leone ◆ Religion: Muslim, indigenous beliefs, Christian
- Language: English (official), Mende (principal vernacular in the south), Temne (principal vernacular in the north), Krio (English-based Creole)
- British High Commission, Freetown: +232 22 232 961

Singapore

- Population: 4.2 million ◆ Location: Southeastern Asia ◆ Capital: Singapore
- Currency: Singapore dollar
- Religion: Buddhist (Chinese), Muslim (Malays), Christian, Hindu, Sikh, Taoist, Confucianist ◆ Language: Chinese, Malay, Tamil, English
- British High Commission, Singapore: +65 6424 4200

The Slovak Republic

- Population: 5.4 million ◆ Location: Central Europe
- Capital: Bratislava ◆ Currency: Slovak koruna
- Religion: Roman Catholic, Protestant, Orthodox
- Language: Slovak (official), Hungarian
- British Embassy, Bratislava: +421 2 5998 2000

Slovenia

- Population: 1.9 million ◆ Location: Central Europe ◆ Capital: Ljubljana
- Currency: tolar ◆ Religion: Roman Catholic, Lutheran, Muslim
- Language: Slovene, Italian, Hungarian
- British Embassy, Ljubljana: +386 1 200 3910

Solomon Islands

- Population: 450,000 ◆ Location: Oceania, group of islands in the South Pacific Ocean
- Capital: Honiara ◆ Currency: Solomon Islands dollar ◆ Religion: Christian
- Language: English, Pidgin, 92 indigenous languages
- British Embassy, Honiara: +677 21705/6

Somalia

- Population: 10.4 million ◆ Location: Eastern Africa ◆ Capital: Mogadishu
- Currency: Somali shilling ◆ Religion: Sunni Muslim
- Language: Somali (official), Arabic, Italian, English
- British Embassy, Mogadishu: +252 1 20288/9; NB embassy was temporarily closed.

South Africa

- Population: 44.8 million ◆ Location: Southern Africa ◆ Capital: Pretoria
- Currency: rand ◆ Religion: Christian, Muslim, Hindu, indigenous beliefs, animist
- Language: 11 official languages: English, Afrikaans, Zulu, Xhosa, Sepedi, Setswana, Sesotho, Zitsonga, Siswati, Tschibenda, Ndebele
- British High Commission, Pretoria: +27 12 421 7733

Spain

- Population: 42.88 million ◆ Location: South-western Europe ◆ Capital: Madrid
- Currency: euro ◆ Religion: Roman Catholic, Protestant
- Language: Castilian Spanish (official), Catalan, Galician, Basque
- British Embassy, Madrid: +34 91 700 8200

visit: www.gap-year.com

Sri Lanka

- Population: 20.5 million estimate ◆ Location: Southern Asia ◆ Capital: Colombo
- Currency: Sri Lankan rupee ◆ Religion: Buddhist, Hindu, Christian, Muslim
- Language: Sinhalese, Tamil, English
- British High Commission, Colombo: +94 11 2437336

Sudan

- Population: 35.1 million ◆ Location: Northern Africa ◆ Capital: Khartoum
- Currency: Sudanese dinar ◆ Religion: Sunni Muslim (in north), animist, Christian (mostly in south and Khartoum)
- Language: Arabic (official), Nubian, Ta Bedawie, diverse dialects of Nilotic, Nilo-Hamitic, Sudanic languages, English ◆ British Embassy, Khartoum: +249 11 777105

Suriname

- Population: 436,500 ◆ Location: Northern South America
- Capital: Paramaribo ◆ Currency: Suriname guilder
- Religion: Hindu, Muslim, Roman Catholic, Dutch Reformed, Moravian, Jewish, Baha'i
- Language: Dutch (official), English, Sranan Tongo (Creole), Hindustani, Javanese
- British Consulate: +597 402558; +597 403824

Swaziland

- Population: 1 million ◆ Location: Southern Africa ◆ Capital: Mbabane
- Currency: lilangeni ◆ Religion: Christian, indigenous beliefs
- Language: English, siSwati ◆ British High Commission, Mbabane: +268 404 2581

Sweden

- Population: 8.9 million ◆ Location: Northern Europe ◆ Capital: Stockholm
- Currency: Swedish krona ◆ Religion: Lutheran, Roman Catholic, Orthodox, Baptist, Muslim, Jewish, Buddhist ◆ Language: Swedish
- British Embassy, Stockholm: +46 8 671 3000

Switzerland

- Population: 7.3 million ◆ Location: Central Europe ◆ Capital: Berne
- Currency: Swedish franc ◆ Religion: Roman Catholic, Protestant
- Language: Swiss German (official), French, Italian, Rhaeto-Rumantsch
- British Embassy, Berne: +41 31 359 7700

Syria (The Syrian Arab Republic)

- Population: 18 million ◆ Location: Middle East ◆ Capital: Damascus
- Currency: Syrian pound (also called lira) ◆ Religion: Sunni Muslim, Alawite, Druze, Muslim sects, Christian, Jewish ◆ Language: Arabic; Kurdish, Armenian, Aramaic, Circassian, French, English◆ British Embassy, Damascus: +963 11 373 9241/2/3/7

Taiwan

- Population: 23 million ◆ Location: Eastern Asia ◆ Capital: Taipei
- Currency: new Taiwan dollar ◆ Religion: Buddhist, Taoist, Christian
- Language: Mandarin Chinese (official), Taiwanese, Hakka
- British Embassy: see China

Tajikistan

- Population: 6.7 million ◆ Location: Central Asia ◆ Capital: Dushanbe
- Currency: somoni ◆ Religion: Sunni Muslim, Shi'a Muslim
- Language: Tajik, Russian ◆ British Embassy, Dushanbe: +992 372 24 22 21

Country Information | 2

2

The Gap-Year Guidebook 2005/2006

Tanzania

- Population: 36 million ◆ Location: Eastern Africa ◆ Capital: Dar es Salaam
- Currency: Tanzania shilling ◆ Religion: Christian, Muslim, indigenous beliefs
- Language: Kiswahili, English ◆ British High Commission, Dar es salaam: +255 22 211 0101; 255 (0) 744 242 242 (emergencies only)

Thailand

- Population: 63.1 million estimate ◆ Location: South-eastern Asia ◆ Capital: Bangkok
- Currency: baht ◆ Religion: Buddhism, Muslim, Christian, Hindu
- Language: Thai ◆ British Embassy, Bangkok: +66 2 305 8333

Timor-Leste

- Population: 925,000 ◆ Location: South-eastern Asia ◆ Capital: Dili
- Currency: US dollar ◆ Religion: Roman Catholic, Protestant, Muslim, Hindu, Buddhism
- Language: Tetum (officail), Portuguese (official), BahasaIndonesian, English
- British Embassy, Dili: +670 332 2838; +670 723 1606 (out of hours emergency only)

Togo

- Population: 4.7 million ◆ Location: Western Africa ◆ Capital: Lome
- Currency: CFA franc ◆ Religion: indigenous beliefs, Christian, Muslim
- Language: French, Kabiye, Ewe ◆ British Consulate, Lomé: currently no service contact British High Commission, Accra, Ghana +233 21 221 665

Tonga

- Population: 100,200 ◆ Location: Oceania, archipelago in the South Pacific Ocean
- Capital: Nuku'alofa ◆ Currency: Pa'anga
- Religion: Christian ◆ Language: Tongan, English
- British High Commission, Nuku'alofa: +676 24285/24395

Trinidad and Tobago

- Population: 1.2 million ◆ Location: Caribbean
- Capital: Port-of-Spain ◆ Currency: Trinidad and Tobago dollar
- Religion: Roman Catholic, Hindu, Anglican, Muslim, Presbyterian
- Language: English (official), Hindi, French, Spanish, Chinese
- British High Commission, Port of Spain: +1 868 622 2748

Tunisia

- Population: 9.9 million ◆ Location: Northern Africa ◆ Capital: Tunis
- Currency: Tunisian dinar ◆ Religion: Muslim Christian ◆ Language: Arabic, French
- British Embassy, Tunis: +216 71 846 184

Turkey

- Population: 67.8 million ◆ Location: southeastern Europe/southwestern Asia
- Capital: Ankara ◆ Currency: Turkish lira ◆ Religion: Muslim
- Language: Turkish, Kurdish ◆ British Embassy, Ankara: +90 312 455 3344

Turkmenistan

- Population: 5.2 million ◆ Location: Central Asia ◆ Capital: Ashgabat
- Currency: Tenge ◆ Religion: Sunni Muslim
- Language: Turkmen, Russian ◆ British Embassy, Ashgabat: +993 12 363 462/63/64

Tuvalu

- Population: 10,200 ◆ Capital: Funafuti
- Currency: Australian dollar, Tuvaluan dollar
- Religion: Church of Tuvalu, Seventh-Day Adventist, Baha'i

- Language: Tuvaluan, English
- British High Commission, Funafuti (staff resident in Suva, Fiji): +679 322 9100

Uganda

- Population: 24.6 million ◆ Location: Eastern Africa
- Capital: Kampala ◆ Currency: Uganda shilling
- Religion: Roman Catholic, Protestant, Muslim, indigenous beliefs
- Language: English (official national language), Luganda Luo, Ateso, Runyankole, Rukiga, Rutoro, Runyoro ◆ Religion: Christian, Muslim
- British High Commission, Kampala: +256 78 312000

Ukraine

- Population: 48.4 million ◆ Location: Eastern Europe ◆ Capital: Kiev
- Currency: hryvnia ◆ Religion: Ukrainian Orthodox (Moscow Patriarchate, Kiev Patriarchate), Ukrainian Catholic (Uniate), Ukrainian Autocephalous Orthodox, Jewish
- Language: Ukrainian, Russian, Romanian, Polish, Hungarian
- British Embassy, Kiev: +380 44 490 3660

United Arab Emirates

- Population: 3.4 million ◆ Location: Middle East ◆ Capital: Abu Dhabi
- Currency: Emirati dirham ◆ Religion: Muslim (Shi'a), Hindu
- Language: Arabic (official) ◆British Embassy, Abu Dhabi: +971 2 6101 100

United States of America

- Population: 294 million ◆ Location: North America ◆ Capital: Washington, DC
- Currency: US dollar ◆ Religion: Protestant, Roman Catholic, Jewish
- Language: English, Spanish ◆ British Embassy, Washington D.C.: +1 202 588 6500

Uruguay

- Population: 3.4 million ◆ Location: Southern South America
- Capital: Montevideo ◆ Currency: Uruguayan peso
- Religion: Roman Catholic, Protestant, Jewish
- Language: Spanish ◆ British Embassy, Montevideo: +598 2 622 36 30/50

Uzbekistan

- Population: 25.6 million ◆ Location: Central Asia ◆ Capital: Tashkent
- Currency: sum ◆ Religion: Sunni Muslim ◆ Language: Uzbek , Russian, Tajik
- British Embassy, Tashkent: +99871 120 78 52/53/54

Vanuatu

- Population: 200,000 ◆ Location: Oceania, group of islands in the South Pacific Ocean
- Capital: Port Vila ◆Religion: Presbyterian, Anglican, Roman Catholic
- Language: Bislama (offical), English (official), French (official), plus over 130 vernacular languages ◆ British High Commission, Port Vila: +678 23100

Venezuela

- Population: 24.3 million ◆ Location: Northern South America
- Capital: Caracas ◆ Currency: bolivar ◆ Religion: Roman Catholic
- Language: Spanish ◆ British Embassy, Caracas: +58 212 263 8411

Vietnam

- Population: 80 million ◆ Location: Southeastern Asia ◆ Capital: Hanoi
- Currency: Vietnamese dong (US dollar widely accepted)
- Religion: Buddhist, Cao Dai, Christian (predominantly Roman Catholic, some Protestant), indigenous beliefs ◆ Language: Vietnamese
- British Embassy, Hanoi: +84 4 936 0500; +84 90340 4919 (Duty Officer's mobile for emergencies only)

Yemen

- Population: 20 million ◆ Location: Middle East ◆ Capital: Sana'a
- Currency: Yemeni rial ◆ Religion: Muslim
- Language: Arabic ◆ British Embassy, Sana'a: +967 1 2640 81/82/83/84

Yugoslavia - see Serbia & Montenegro

Zambia

- Population: 10.7 million ◆ Location: Southern Africa ◆ Capital: Lusaka
- Currency: Zambian kwacha ◆ Religion: Christian, Muslim, Hindu, indigenous beliefs
- Language: English (official language of government), plus over 80 languages
- British High Commission, Lusaka: +260 1 251133

Zimbabwe

- Population: 11.6 million ◆ Location: Southern Africa
- Capital: Harare ◆ Currency: Zimbabwean dollar
- Religion: Christian, indigenous beliefs, Hindu, Muslim, Jewish
- Language: English (official), Shona, Ndebele
- British Embassy, Harare: +263 4 772990; +263 4 774700

TRAVEL WITH CARE
Information provided by Homeway

When you go on your gap-year travels you want to know for sure that you're going to be healthy, comfortable and safe - that's where Homeway comes in. Homeway has been providing quality products and advice that you can trust to gappers since 1989. They have all the latest gadgets as well as the essentials. Homeway is a family company, they're always happy to talk to you and answer your questions. What's more - they operate a fast, efficient mail order service and guaranteed next working day delivery for telephone orders.

Potable Aqua

Take a look over the next few pages to get an idea of what Homeway can offer you. All of the products you see here are available from the Gap-Year Shop by mail order - phone 0870 748 9565 or you can order direct from www.gap-yearshop.com which has the complete up-to-date range.

WATER AND WATER PURIFICATION

One of the main ways gap travellers get ill is by drinking contaminated water - it can ruin your gap experience and the health problems can last long after you've come home.

It's usually best not to drink the local water in Africa, India, the Far East, Central and South America. Don't use it to brush your teeth or to wash food either. If you don't have the facilities to wash food with safe water, the best rule is: don't eat it unless you can peel it!

There are different ways to get 'safe water':

- ❐ Bottled, as long as checked for secure cap and no discolouration (fizzy water is safest)
- ◎ Boiled water – minimum boiling time 5 minutes. Not always 100% effective
- ❐ Iodine – short term use, not recommended for more than 28 days. Not effective on some cysts
- ◎ Chlorine (Puritabs) + filter – satisfactory and can be used long term
- ❐ Purifier – ideal: easy to use and TOTALLY SAFE.

SUN PROTECTION

Just because you're not lying around on a beach sunbathing doesn't mean you can't get sunburned. Remember to protect all exposed skin at all times in sunny climates and at high altitudes. If you allow your skin to burn it increases your chances of getting skin cancer later. You need to use products that protect you from UVA and UVB rays - the creams and lotions that bind to your skin are the easiest because they don't wash off so you only have to apply it once a day. After a while, say 3 to 4 weeks, your skin will acclimatise so you won't need to use so much.

Ultrasun range

Tel: 0870 748 9565   www.gap-yearshop.com

Homeway

PROTECTION AGAINST INSECTS

DEET Repellents
Repel Range

Insect bites are not only irritating but can be life threatening as they can transmit diseases including Malaria. They can be a problem wherever you go in the world, but if you travel to Africa, India, the Far East and Central & South America you will almost certainly need insect protection: skin repellents, a room vapouriser/coil and a net. Make sure you take the right level of insect protection for where you are travelling. You must also talk to your doctor before you go to any malarial areas, as prophylaxis will also be needed.

Insect repellents for the skin

DEET (Diethyltoluamide) repellents, which have been around for nearly 50 years, are regarded by most experts to be the most effective repellents available. Independent safety tests have shown there are no dangerous side effects on people or the environment if DEET is used correctly. DEET is designed for use on your skin. It can also be applied to natural fabrics but will destroy synthetic fabrics and plastics. Remember to take your watch off before using DEET-based repellents.

100% DEET: 5-6 hours protection. Use when re-application is impractical. Short-term use. Not suitable for sensitive or sunburnt skin.

55% DEET: 4-5 hours protection. Considered safe for everyday use.

25% DEET: 2-3 hours protection. Ideal for sensitive skins and faces.

Non-DEET Repellents
EcoGuard

Non-DEET repellents come in many formulations, mostly made using natural ingredients. Generally regarded as a good alternative, but DEET is the No1 choice for malarial areas.

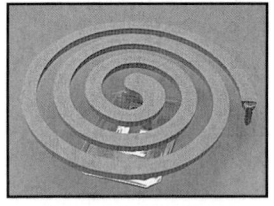

Mosquito Coil

Insect repellents for fabrics and clothing:

DEET-free sprays, formulated for fabrics. Use on collars, cuffs, hat brims *etc*. Used with skin repellents, they provide a real armour against insect bites.

Insect repellents for the room:

Room Spray: to kill flying and crawling insects.

Room Vapouriser: ideal if you know you will have electricity. Vapourisers plug into electric sockets and can be switched on and off.

Coils: useful for the outdoors.

Homeway

Tel: 0870 748 9565 www.gap-yearshop.com

Nets

Bed Nets: Insects are most active at night. Using a bed net impregnated with the insecticide perme-thrin will ensure protection from bites and in many countries is essential to protect you against Malaria. If you are using your net for more than 6 months then it will need re-impregnating. Nets come in various styles and you need to choose what will suit your trip best. Gap-Year Shop has a wide range of nets and are always happy to advise you on your choice, but these are the general guidelines for choosing your net:

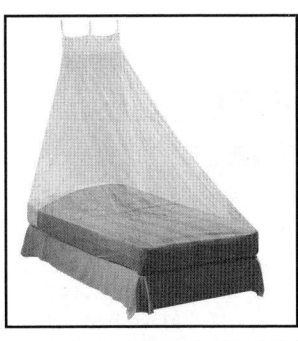

Wedge Net

◎ Hostels and outdoor use: *wedge net* or *pop up net*

❏ Long term static use with periods of travel: *wedge* and *bell nets*

◎ Long term use where there is a frame facility: *box net.*

Head Nets: Useful for keeping biting insects away from the face and neck.

Mattress covers: mattresses can harbour all sorts of creepy crawlies. A light-weight impregnated mattress cover will make sure you sleep undisturbed.

HEALTH

First Aid kit

You won't be able to just walk into a chemist so it is sensible to carry the basics with you.

A good First Aid Kit should definitely have:

Homeway International
First Aid Kit

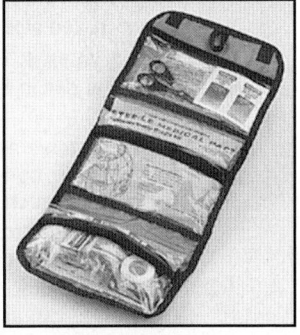

◎ Plasters ❏ Scissors ◎ Bandages ❏ Non-stick dressings ◎ Skin closure strips (steristrips) ❏ Micropore tape ◎ Safety pins ❏ Antiseptic wipes and cleanser ◎ Painkiller tablets such as paracetamol ❏ Anti diarrhoea tablets.

For international travel you should also consider:

Re-hydration sachets (in case you get diarrhoea) ◎ sting relief ❏ anti-biotics (*see your doctor*) ◎ sterile medical/needle kit ❏ DVT anti-embolism socks ◎ insect repellents ❏ net ◎ water purification kit.

Dental check-up

Go to see your dentist before you travel - toothache will ruin your trip and you might find it difficult to get treatment abroad. If you have crowns or fillings then it is sensible to carry a *Dental First Aid Kit* – see the Gap-Year Shop at www.gap-year.com

DVT - Deep Vein Thrombosis

DVT is a clot of blood formed in the deep vein of your lower leg. To start with you might feel intense pain in the calf of your leg. Chest pain and breathlessness may follow. You are particularly at risk during long flights and journeys if you :

◎ Are taking the contraceptive pill
❑ Are over 6 foot or under 5 foot
◎ Are overweight
❑ Have a history of heart problems, varicose veins or family history of blood clots
◎ Have had recent surgery

If you are at all worried, then go to see your doctor. Avoid alcohol, tea and coffee and drink lots of water and soft drinks on flights. Take regular exercise. Wear medically approved flight socks, fitted by calf and leg measurement and not by shoe size. See www.gap-yearshop.com for fitting advice.

HIV/AIDS

AIDS (Acquired Immune Deficiency Syndrome) is caused by the HIV (Human Immuno-Deficiency) virus. HIV infection is incurable and there is no vaccine. HIV/AIDS can be caught through:

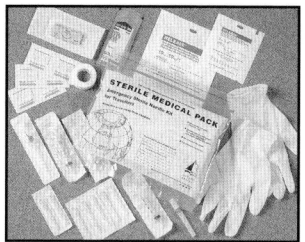

Homeway Sterile Medical Pack

◎ an infected needle or syringe during medical and dental treatment, skin piercing, tattooing or drug use.
❑ blood transfusions of HIV-infected blood.
◎ unprotected sex with an infected person.

To protect yourself when travelling (you are particularly at risk in Asia, Africa, India, Central and South America) we suggest you:

◎ Carry a *Sterile Medical Pack*. For use by medical personnel, this is a heat sealed pack containing sterile needles, syringes *etc.* Remember, simple procedures such as a blood test require a needle.
❑ Don't have tattoos, body piercing or acupuncture unless you are sure that sterilised needles are being used.
◎ Ensure that blood is screened if you need a blood transfusion. The British Consulate can assist.
❑ Use condoms every time.

SAFETY

Remember that every country has people who are happy to steal or hurt you. You are especially vulnerable as a traveller because you won't know the surrounding area and can easily be spotted.

Photocopy all important documents and details like your passport numbers, traveller's cheques, card details, insurance documents, tickets, itinerary *etc*

Homeway

Tel: 0870 748 9565 www.gap-yearshop.com

and leave one set at home with someone you can contact easily in case they are stolen. It is also a good idea to keep a set of copies somewhere in your luggage when travelling.

Here are a few tips for your safety:

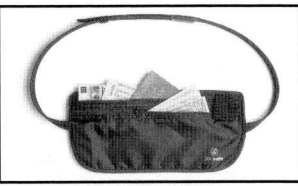

- ◎ Don't carry large sums of money around.
- ❏ Don't wear expensive jewellery.
- ◎ Try not to draw attention to yourself.
- ❏ Treat locals respectfully.
- ◎ Keep valuables/money/tickets/passports safely hidden in a money belt or waist wallet etc
- ❏ Carry a personal attack alarm

Pacsafe Waist Wallet

Locks

It is worth investing in some locks and padlocks to keep you and your gear safe and deter thieves. Gap-Year Shop has a wide range of locks and padlocks including:

- ◎ *Combination padlocks* which are great as there's no key to lose - as long as you can remember the number!
- ❏ *Rucksack locks:* these fit on the rucksack straps which can be a deterrent to opportunist thieves.
- ◎ *Cable locks:* secure your luggage to an immovable object.
- ❏ *Door Locks:* easily fitted to inward opening doors (at hostels for example) to stop intruders coming into your room.
- ◎ *Pacsafe:* a mesh cage which fits over your rucksack and can be secured to an immovable object. Prevents anyone slashing your rucksack. Good for overland truck expeditions.

Pacsafe combination lock

Torches

A good torch is essential. Electricity supplies in many countries are erratic and generators are usually turned off at night. A head or ear torch is really useful for night reading and hands free jobs.

TRAVEL ACCESSORIES

Rucksacks, suitcases and backpacks

A 65 litre bag is a good general size, especially for women. Higher capacity may seem a good idea when you're trying to pack every thing in - but remember you're going to have to carry it. *Rucksacks:* Look for padded adjustable back system, internal support bars, padded shoulder straps and hip belt. Side pockets and a double accessed main compartment are

Aztec Tacuba 65 +10 litre

useful too. *Convertible bags:* give great versatility. You might also want to consider a rucksack travel bag – a large lockable bag for protecting a rucksack when travelling by air or coach. Also doubles as an extra storage bag.

Sleeping bags
Sold as 2, 3 or 4-season bags (light, medium and warm). A mid-range priced bag (£50-£80) will give years of wear and unless you're going somewhere very cold, a 2/3 season bag should be fine. Look on our shop website for useful information on 'How to choose a Sleeping Bag'.

Aztec Hobo Convertible Suitcase/Backpack

Elite Micro 2 - 3 Season before 50% compression

Sleeping bag liners: Cotton or silk sheets sewn up to fit in a sleeping bag. Highly recommended as they save washing the sleeping bag, add another layer and are needed in certain hostels where sleeping bags aren't allowed. Look out for ones with a 'NoBug' treatment.

Practical stuff
Washing: it's a good idea to take ◉ liquid bio-degradable soap for washing in all types of water and temperatures ◻ travel bath & sink plug (it's impossible to improvise if one is missing!) ◉ travel wash for clothing ◻ pegless washing line Antibacterial Hand Cleaner.

Nobac Travel towel

Penknife or multi-purpose tool: Lots of types depending on your budget. Remember: you are not allowed to carry these in your hand luggage on a plane.

Keeping dry: A *rain cape* can double up as a ground sheet and fits over you and your rucksack.

Waterproof pouches are available in a range of shapes and sizes to fit pretty much anything you own. The *AquaPac Range* is suitable for watersports, diving and underwater photography.

Useful extras:
◉ Sewing Kit ◻ Cutlery set with Can/Bottle Opener ◉ Waterproof matches ◻ Whistle/compass ◉ 10 Band World Radio ◻ Alarm clock ◉ Duck/Gaffer tape ◻ Travel Towel ◉ Pillow

'Cyclone' Windproof and waterproof matches